Aesthetics of Music

Volume 6

Books by David Whitwell

Philosophic Foundations of Education
Foundations of Music Education
Music Education of the Future
The Sousa Oral History Project
The Art of Musical *Conducting*
The Longy Club: 1900–1917
A Concise History of the Wind Band
Wagner on Bands
Berlioz on Bands
Chopin: A Self-Portrait
Liszt: A Self-Portrait
Schumann: A Self-Portrait In His Own Words
Mendelssohn: A Self-Portrait In His Own Words
La Téléphonie and the Universal Musical Language
Extraordinary Women

Aesthetics of Music Series

Aesthetics of Music in Ancient Civilizations
Aesthetics of Music in the Middle Ages
Aesthetics of Music in the Early Renaissance
Aesthetics of Music in Sixteenth-Century Italy, France and Spain
Aesthetics of Music in Sixteenth-Century Germany, the Low Countries and England
Aesthetics of Baroque Music in Italy, Spain, the German-Speaking Countries and the Low Countries

The History and Literature of the Wind Band and Wind Ensemble Series

Volume 1 The Wind Band and Wind Ensemble Before 1500
Volume 2 The Renaissance Wind Band and Wind Ensemble
Volume 3 The Baroque Wind Band and Wind Ensemble
Volume 4 The Classical Period Wind Band and Wind Ensemble
Volume 5 The Nineteenth-Century Wind Band and Wind Ensemble
Volume 6 A Catalog of Multi-Part Repertoire for Wind Instruments or for Undesignated Instrumentation before 1600
Volume 7 Baroque Wind Band and Wind Ensemble Repertoire
Volume 8 Classic Period Wind Band and Wind Ensemble Repertoire
Volume 9 Nineteenth-Century Wind Band and Wind Ensemble Repertoire
Volume 10 A Supplementary Catalog of Wind Band and Wind Ensemble Repertoire
Volume 11 A Catalog of Wind Repertoire before the Twentieth Century for One to Five Players
Volume 12 A Second Supplementary Catalog of Early Wind Band and Wind Ensemble Repertoire
Volume 13 Name Index, Volumes 1–12, The History and Literature of the Wind Band and Wind Ensemble

www.whitwellbooks.com

David Whitwell

Aesthetics of Music

Volume 6
Aesthetics of Baroque Music in Italy, Spain, the German-Speaking Countries and the Low Countries

Edited by Craig Dabelstein

Whitwell Publishing • Austin, Texas, USA

Whitwell Publishing, Austin 78701
www.whitwellbooks.com

 First edition 1997.
Second edition 2013

Printed in the United States of America

Paperback
ISBN-13: 978-1-936512-62-1
ISBN-10: 1936512629

Composed in Minion Pro

CONTENTS

FOREWORD

We define Music to be that form of music performed live before listeners. We define Aesthetics in Music to be a study of the nature of the perception of music by the listener.

We believe the performance of music in actual practice falls naturally into four classes. These are Art Music, Educational Music, Functional Music and Entertainment Music.

I. Art Music

Art Music we believe is defined by four conditions, *all* of which *must always be present.* These are:

1. *Art music is inspired.* Art music is music in which it seems evident that the composer has made an honest attempt to communicate genuine feelings. Feelings, which may range from lofty and noble to superficial and vulgar, must be presumed to be generally recognizable in music, as they are in any other art form, including painting, sculpture, dance, and architecture. In Art Music, lofty and noble feelings are paramount.

   Due to the common genetically understood nature of emotions, it must also be understood that in music emotions or feelings cannot be 'faked.' They will always be recognized as such by any contemplative listener.

2. *Art Music has no purpose other than the communication of its own aesthetic content.* Art Music is free of any purpose or function, save the spiritual communication of pure beauty.

3. *Art Music is that which enjoys a performance faithful to the intent of the composer.*

4. *Art Music must have a listener capable of contemplation.*

If any of these conditions are missing, the performance must result in a lesser aesthetic experience. For example, the *Ninth Symphony* of Beethoven played in a stadium, during the half-time of a professional football game, would fail for the lack of the presence of Condition Number Four. The same Symphony heard in a concert hall, but in a poor performance, not faithful to the intent of the composer, would fail for the lack of the presence of Condition Number Three.

II. Educational Music

Educational Music may or may not have the same conditions as Art Music, excepting Condition Number Two; it may or may not occur within an educational institution. Educational Music is didactic music, music which has the specific and *additional* aim to educate. In the strictest sense, if the *primary purpose* of Music is to educate, it cannot be Art Music—for Art Music has no purpose.

III. Functional Music

Functional Music is music put at the service of something else. We include here, for example, all kinds of religious music, music for weddings, music for the military, and occupational music. Functional Music may share the same conditions as Art Music, excepting Condition Number Two.

One may ask, How can a Mozart Mass be called Functional Music, and not Art Music? If the observer were not contemplatively listening to the music, but were rather contemplating religious thoughts, then the Mozart Mass becomes merely a very high level of Functional Music. If, on the other hand, the observer is a contemplative listener of music, forgetting about religion, then the Mozart Mass is Art Music, but has failed in its purpose as church music.

Military and wedding music are examples of music in which the contemplative listener is missing entirely. How about airport, supermarket and elevator music where there is no listener at all? According to the definition we have given above, recorded music without listeners is not to be considered music at all.

IV. Entertainment Music

Entertainment Music is music with no object other than to please. It will always be missing Condition Four, the contemplative listener. For this reason, Entertainment Music may be inspired music, but the composer is unlikely to be inspired by lofty and noble emotions, knowing there will be no contemplative listener. Entertainment Music and Art Music can never be the same thing because of Condition Number Two: Art Music has no purpose other than the communication of its own aesthetic content. It is inconsistent with the nature of great art to have any extrinsic purpose, including the purpose to entertain.

The first philosopher to address the impact which Art has on an observer was Aristotle, in his *Poetics*, as part of a discussion of Tragedy, which like music has both a material, written form and a live performance form. In this treatise, Aristotle first considers the nature and contribution of each of the specific components of the written form of the Tragedy in his typically methodical style. His great contribution, however, comes when he has completed this discussion, for he then goes beyond the material form of the play itself to discuss the observer. He makes it clear that not only is the end purpose of the elements of the play to produce a specific experience in the observer, but that the nature of this experience is what distinguishes Tragedy from other dramatic forms, such as Spectacle. It was in this moment that he created a new branch of Philosophy which we call 'Aesthetics.'

Our purpose is to provide a source book of representative descriptions of actual performances, observations by philosophers, poets and other commentators which contribute insights to our understanding of what music meant to listeners during the early Renaissance. It is for this reason that when discussing contemporary treatises on music that we concentrate on those passages which offer insights relative to the aesthetics of music and musical performance rather than the usual technical subjects such as scales, modes and counterpoint which fill most books on Renaissance music.

Since traditional musicology has focused almost exclusively on sacred and secular vocal music of the Renaissance, we have also included numerous references which we hope will reveal a much wider world of music during this period.

We are also interested in contemporary views on the physiology of knowing, especially with regard to the relationship of the senses and Reason, and related psychological ideas, such as Pleasure and Pain and the Emotions, which might offer a frame of reference for their perspective on the perception of music.

This is the sixth volume in a series of eight, ranging from the music of the ancient civilizations through the Baroque Period.

David Whitwell
Austin, Texas

ACKNOWLEDGMENTS

This new edition would not have been possible without the encouragement and help of Craig Dabelstein of Brisbane, Australia. His experience as a musician and educator himself has contributed greatly to his expertise as editor of this volume.

David Whitwell
Austin, 2013

1 THE MUSICAL SCENE IN ITALY

Italy was still not Italy.[1] One of Europe's oldest civilizations remained, since the fall of the Roman Empire, a series of individual kingdoms, principalities, duchies, city-republics and the land controlled by the pope. Spain, Austria, France, and the popes kept the peninsula in a continual life of conflict. That out of this had come the Renaissance in the fifteenth and sixteenth centuries is a tribute to the power of art.

One is tempted to suppose that, after the extraordinary leadership of Italy in the arts during the Renaissance, she needed a period of rest. A more objective view might see the influence of a colder intellectual climate caused by the Church after the Council of Trent.[2] This is most apparent in painting, where nudes were no longer allowed and only the fervent pleas of a group of artists prevented the Pope Clement VIII from having Michelangelo's *Last Judgment* completely painted over. In music, the noble patrons turned to entertainment and great numbers of distinguished musicians left for other countries, making Italian music important everywhere except in Italy.

MUSIC OF THE COURT

Those musicians who remained in Italy found themselves domestic servants to an aristocracy (including the nobles of the Church) which preferred to be entertained to being moved. Even Monteverdi, a genius who clearly saw the future of music, spent much of his life working for nobles incapable of appreciating his ability. In one letter he complains that due to the pressure of composing music for a court wedding,

> I have had a frightful pain in my head and so terrible and violent an itching around my waist, that neither by cauteries which I have had applied to myself, nor by purges taken orally, nor by blood-letting and other potent remedies has it so far been possible to get even partly better. My father attributes the cause of the headache to mental strain.

1 Our purpose here is not an attempt to summarize the development of Baroque music itself in Italy, and its composers, but rather to present a brief overview of the environment in which the music was performed and its general aesthetic nature. At the same time, we take the opportunity to include important material not found in general music history texts.

2 The Inquisition remained a fearful part of the conservative Church climate. Monteverdi, in his letters, writes of having to go to great lengths to have his son (a doctor of medicine!) released from prison for having read a book which he did not realize was on the prohibited list.

Further, he complains, that after suffering from cold, lack of clothing, servitude, and very nearly lack of food, at the wedding His Highness failed to compliment his work before the noble guests. Nevertheless, he concludes the letter 'I bow and kiss your hands.'[3]

Pressed to compose music for a court allegorical pageant, he wearily wrote a Mantuan court official, 'how can I, by such means, move the passions?'[4]

In such an environment, the composer takes his joy where he can find it. Monteverdi wrote the music for an allegorical tournament celebrating the marriage of Duke Odoardo Farnese of Parma and Margherita de' Medici of Florence in 1628 and even he must have been pleased with a moment described by one eyewitness.

> As soon as Signora Settimia, representing Aurora, began to sing, all conversation among the spectators ceased … All ears were so consoled by the sweetness of the voice and the divine quality of the song, that among the 10,000 people seated in the theater, there was no one … who did not grow tender at the trills, sigh at the sighs, become ecstatic at the ornaments, and who was not stupefied and transfixed by the miraculous beauty and song of an heavenly siren.[5]

During the first part of the seventeenth century many court entertainments were of the allegorical type we associate with the sixteenth century, which only reminds us that, except for opera, most musical traditions passed into the seventeenth century unmindful that the Baroque Period at arrived. Such an entertainment, a large-scale allegorical ballet, was given by the 'Most Serene Infantas of Savoy, in honor of Madame of France,' at the court in Turin in 1620.[6] An eyewitness reports that the evening began with a lavish banquet with music.

> These gastronomic pleasures were further enhanced by the sweetness of the music, which gave nourishment to the ears and filled the souls of those present with contentment.

This banquet concluded at midnight! Following a trumpet fanfare,

> The entire cloth was seen to disappear in a flash behind the clouds, revealing all at once such a quantity of wonderful and admirable things that many of those present were lost in amazement. In the first place, the scene depicted a parched Alpine mountain, with crags vegetated by nothing but a few nettles and briars among the cracks and stiff, unyielding and discolored grass. At the top of this mountain, the Temple of Glory shone out with brightest rays; this was made in crystal with columns of gold. In the middle, the Most Serene Infantas Maria and Caterina could be seen with twelve of their ladies dressed as queens. At the foot, in the middle, Toil wielded his bludgeon, striking down lions, serpents, wild boars and sundry other beasts; at the base of

3 Letter to Annibale Chieppio (December 2, 1608), quoted in Claudio Monteverdi, *The Letters of Claudio Monteverdi*, trans. Denis Stevens (Cambridge: Cambridge University Press, 1980), 57ff.

4 Ibid., 115ff.

5 Quoted in Tim Carter, 'The North Italian Courts,' in *The Early Baroque Era* (Englewood Cliffs: Prentice Hall, 1994), 39.

6 This description is found in Lorenzo Bianconi, *Music in the Seventeenth Century*, trans. David Bryant (Cambridge: Cambridge University Press, 1987), 271ff.

> the mountain, Love, Indolence, Oblivion, Sloth, Slumber, Gluttony, Sin and Pleasure sleepily and lazily kept watch.

Now, Toil sang a madrigal.

> He who treads the flowery path
> Of tyrant pleasure
> Finally will wretched fall,
> Deceived, in the bottomless pit of everlasting loss …

Following this song, the Sins began a ballet.

> The cornetts and trombones took up a broken melody with artfully contrived retardations, to which rhythm the Sins recommenced their ballet … in perfect measure and in such perfect time as to leave an indelible impression on the minds of those present.

Now Heroic Virtue sang a song, followed with another song by Apollo. Next the Muses 'added their full chorus of voices' prior to an appearance of the Poets and another ballet.

> To the sound of a grave and dramatic harmony they formed a most graceful ballet with unsurpassable elegance and design.

Following the ballet and a song by Glory, the temple of Glory was slowly exposed from inside the mountain. Suddenly an arch rose, upon which were seated Victory, Fame and Honor. Now, holding her scepter, Glory sang again,

> Go forth, ye who earned,
> On the path of toil,
> The laurels of Glory …

After an hour, the ballet concluded with 'a most beautiful ballet of forty figures,' to the music of violins, followed by all the singers and instrumentalists joining together for 'a melody of extraordinary sweetness.' The ballet was over, but not the dancing. The violins remained to play branles 'and other favorite dances for the pleasure of the ladies and gentlemen present.'

Among the entertainments popular among the aristocracy in seventeenth-century Italy were the horse ballets, which also spread to Germany as 'Ross Ballet' and to France as 'Carrousel.' These entertainments evolved as a replacement for the earlier tournaments, which had become too dangerous after the invention of firearms. Typically these horse ballets were given in the central plaza of the city, with great tiers of benches forming a stadium of sorts. There was usually a central allegorical theme (such as the early 'War of Love' in 1615 in Florence), large constructed floats and military troops arranged in symmetrical formations.

For one of these events in 1628, Monteverdi had to set a thousand lines of text to music. He confesses in a letter than when he could no longer find 'emotional variety, I tried to change the instrumentation.'[7] The music most often consisted of the aristocratic trumpet and timpani corps, but since their repertoire was memorized little has survived.

There was also a curious military relationship with these horse ballets, for in the previous centuries the problem of the organization and movement of large movements of troops had evolved into theories of complicated geometric patterns as the basis of attack and defense. Consequently Baroque military treatises often chart their formations on the basis of choreographic principles rather than from purely strategic logic. An example is Möller's *Trilekunst zu Fuss* (Lübeck, 1672) which recommends for the defense of Lübeck the placing of the troops in a configuration resembling the coat-of-arms of the city![8]

In Venice, instead of the horse ballets the public saw great water pageants sponsored by the aristocracy. In 1685, for example, a great naval 'battle' was given in honor of the visiting Duke of Brunswick. This 'battle' was fought between Venetian and Turkish galleys, with the former achieving a glorious victory. The musicians are described as 24 trumpets, oboes, drums and 36 singers.[9] The visiting Englishman, John Evelyn, observed the annual water procession on Ascension Day in 1645 and recalls,

> innumerable Gallys, Gundolas, & boates filled with Spectators, some dressed in Masqurade, Trumpets, musique & Canons, filling the whole aire with din.[10]

Monteverdi in a letter of 1627 mentions such a procession to celebrate a naval victory during which 'solemn music' was sung.[11]

Continuing the Renaissance custom, many nobles continued to maintain high quality musical establishments. An extant letter of Monteverdi reveals that he had been instructed by the court at Mantua to lure away a five-member wind band currently employed by the Spanish governor of Milan. Monteverdi describes their abilities, indicating they do equally well in functional and concert music, and makes recommendations regarding their salary.[12] We get a glimpse of the range of duties for such a wind band in a letter several years later, when Monteverdi is again commissioned to find a player. Monteverdi, in reporting on his conversation with a prospective player, says he told him,

> If His Highness the Prince were pleased to take you on, this gentleman very much likes not only to hear a variety of wind instruments, he also likes to have the said musicians play in private,

7 Letter to Alessandro Striggio (February 4, 1628), quoted in Monteverdi, *The Letters*, 390.

8 Paul Nettl, 'Equestrian Ballets of the Baroque Period,' *The Musical Quarterly* 19, no. 1 (Jan, 1933): 74, http://www.jstor.org/stable/738825. One can see examples of these figures in Machiavelli's *The Art of War*.

9 Pompeo Molmenti, *Venice* (London, 1908), I, iii, 198.

10 John Evelyn, *The Diary of John Evelyn* (Oxford, 1955), II, 432.

11 Letter to Enzo Bentivoglio (September 25, 1627), quoted in Monteverdi, *The Letters*, 370.

12 Letter to Alessandro Striggio (August 24, 1609), Ibid., 64.

> in church, in procession, and atop city walls; now madrigals, now French songs, now airs, and now dance songs.[13]

In a letter of 1623 he reports that while good wind players are in abundance, he cannot find suitable soprani or continuo players and only a moderate theorbo player.[14] In numerous other letters Monteverdi reports back on prospective singers, discussing in detail their artistic and vocal qualities.

The private trumpet and timpani corps belonging to the individual Italian nobles must have represented their patrons in all important personal appearances. Typical extant accounts record twelve trombetti dressed in crimson velvet performing for the wedding of Ereditario in Florence in 1661[15] and to welcome the return of Vittorio Amedeo II of Torino with his new bride, Anna d'Orléans, niece to Louis XIV, after their wedding in Paris.[16] Some of these aristocratic trumpeters are still known to us by name, among them two in Florence, the German player known as Simone di Lionardo and the famous Girolamo Fantini.[17]

The popes also had trumpet corps, called 'concerto de' 4 trombetti dell'Inclito Popolo Romano.' Their statutes of 1717 reveal they also had alternate members called *coadiutori* and *sopranumerari* (the timpani position is not recorded until 1734). Their pay included additional funds for the persons who cared for their horses, their clothes and their barbers. The statutes specify payment of six *giulli* per day when they were asked to appear in university or diplomatic ceremonies and if they complained about their fees they were subject to a fine. The statutes of 1734 addresses problems of discipline, such as abusiveness and fighting among themselves.[18] Joining these ceremonial players was an ensemble of fourteen musicians called the 'Tamburini del Popolo Romano.' Their leader, called *Capo tamburo*, carried the pope's personal flag.

From the eighteenth century there are extant documents relative to the pope's wind band, which went under the names *musici del concerto di Campidoglio* and *Concerto de tromboni e cornetti del Senato et inclito Popolo Romano* (1702) and *Concerto Capitolino* (1705). They were housed in the Castel Sant'Angelo and their Constitution of 1705 refers to a leader, called *Priore*, who was elected each month by the other members and who was responsible for the selection of their repertoire. The members are cautioned against blasphemy and are urged to show the necessary respect toward their colleagues. One record identifies the ensemble as six trombones and two cornetti, performing for papal and civic ceremonies as well for the meals of the Sig. Conservatori.[19]

13 Letter to Prince Francesco Gonzaga (March 26, 1611), Ibid., 81.

14 Ibid., 266.

15 Gaetano Imbert, *La vita fiorentina nel Seicento* (Firenze: Bemporad, 1906), 75ff.

16 Luisa Saredo, 'Il Matrimonio di Vittorio Emanuele II su documenti inediti,' in *Nuova Antologia* (1885), XLI, fasc. ix.

17 Alessandro Vessella, *La Banda* (Milan: Instituto editoriale nazionale, 1935), 94.

18 Ibid., 115ff.

19 Ibid., 103ff, 110ff.

In addition the popes, dukes and lesser nobles were active in sponsoring concerts during seventeenth-century Italy. Sometimes these consisted of opera, given in private palace theaters or as in Venice concerts sponsored by aristocratic 'academies.' In Rome the cardinals and other Church princes were especially involved in the support of music, sometimes taking a personal role. Benedetto Pamphili (1653–1730), grand nephew to pope Innocent X, wrote the libretto for *Il trionfo del Tempo e del Disinganno*, the first oratorio of Handel. In a letter of 1620, Monteverdi mentions his *Lament of Apollo* being performed during a regular series of one-hour concerts held in the home of a 'certain gentleman of the Bembo family, where the most important ladies and gentlemen come to listen.'[20]

In speaking of the aristocratic patronage of music in Italy, one cannot pass by Christina of Sweden (1626–1689) who arrived in Rome in 1656 and became the center of intellectual and musical life there for the next thirty-three years. In Christina we come to one of the most remarkable women in history. She might well carry off the prize for best mind, among all past European rulers, male or female.

Her father was the highly educated, courteous, generous and handsome Gustavus Adolphus of Sweden. He loved Christina dearly, but the mother, Maria Eleanora of Brandenburg, could not hide her disappointment that the child was a girl, and not a boy, heir. It seems clear that Christina was therefore driven to be both. She played the masculine role in dress, language, riding and hunting. A Spanish envoy reported, 'She cannot bear the idea of marriage, because she was born free and will die free.' She probably also knew she was unlikely to find a husband her equal, indeed one wonders who, save another Leonardo da Vinci, he might have been.

Christina became queen at age eighteen in a burst of energy and display of self-discipline that must have caused astonishment in all who knew her. The above-mentioned envoy reported,

> She spends only three or four hours in sleep. When she wakes she spends five hours in reading ... She never drinks anything but water; never has she been heard to speak of her food, whether it was well or ill cooked ... Ambassadors speak only with her, without ever being passed on to a secretary or minister.

It is difficult to guess what she was reading those five hours, so extraordinary was the diversity of her interests. By age eighteen she spoke German, French, Italian, Spanish and Latin, later adding Greek, Hebrew and Arabic. She loved poetry and assembled a great library, which included rare manuscripts she collected. She brought, or attracted, scholars and thinkers of every field of science, philosophy and theology. She founded seven colleges and urged Swedish scholars to write in Swedish, in order that all her people might benefit. Who could disagree with Pascal, who said she was queen of the realm of mind, as well as of government, or with Milton who thought she should govern the entire world.

20 Letter to Alessandro Striggio (February 1, 1620), quoted in Monteverdi, *The Letters*, 167.

This great education brought her inevitably to philosophy, and so she brought to Stockholm the greatest philosopher of her age, René Descartes. Poor Descartes, who like all good philosophers preferred to sleep late, thought he might not survive her demand that their conversations began the day at 5:00 AM. In fact, making these early morning walks in the snow, he caught pneumonia and died. How rare it might have been to listen in on these conversations, listening as Christina questioned Descartes on Plato! Once when he contended that all animals are but mechanisms, she responded that she had never seen her watch give birth to baby watches! She left a manuscript containing her personal maxims, and we would like to think the first of these was in answer to Descartes' famous one, 'I think, therefore I am.'

> One is, in proportion as one can love.
> To undeceive men is to offend them.
> Extraordinary merit is a crime never forgiven.
> More courage is required for marriage than for war.
> Philosophy neither changes men nor corrects men.

She began to become interested in Catholicism and in 1652 requested that several Jesuits come, in disguise, to discuss Catholic theology with her. In Sweden it was at this time impossible for her to become a Catholic and retain her crown, for her father had died to protect Protestantism. After much soul searching and negotiation she abdicated in 1654. She left Stockholm that night, dressed as a man, to begin a long trip to Italy.

In her passage through Italy she was welcomed in town after town like some modern victorious Caesar. She entered Rome riding on a white horse, through the triumphal arch and the Porta del Popolo, passing great crowds of soldiers and the public, to be welcomed by Alexander VII in the Vatican.

Christina began her new life with the joy of visiting museums, libraries and academies, astonishing all with her knowledge of Italian history, and being entertained by the great families of Rome. Here also she founded the leading salon of Rome, bringing together prelates, scholars and composers. Among the latter she received Corelli, who dedicated his first publication of sonatas to her, and Scarlatti, whose operas she produced in her private theater. She collected art and books, which later became treasures of the Vatican Library, and led a movement to inspire Italian writers to return to the purity of language and expression found under the Medici.

Christina lived in one of the great palaces of Rome and remained at heart a queen. When she died in 1689 at age sixty-three and was buried in St. Peter's, an Italian poet, Filicïa, reflected that her kingdom consisted of 'all those who thought, all those who acted, and all those who were endowed with intelligence.'

Another foreign queen in Rome was Maria Casimira (1641–1716), widow of Jan III of Poland. Like Christina she established her local reputation by her support of the arts and as Christina had hired Alessandro Scarlatti as her *maestro di cappella*, Maria hired his son, Domenico Scarlatti.

The salons hosted by these aristocratic ladies had an important counterpart in the male gatherings called Academies. These were meetings of noble and upper class persons interested in intellectual discussion. A contemporary treatise, in fact, defines an academy as,

> an assembly of free and virtuous intellects, ready to look for knowledge with honest and friendly emulation; who under prescribed laws and statutes exert themselves in different honorable studies, now learning, now teaching, in order to become each day more virtuous and more wise.[21]

One of the more notable of these, the *Accademia Filarmonica* of Bologna, had a division for composers. To become a member, a composer submitted an *a cappella* composition of at least four voices, which was first examined by a special committee to determine if it were worthy. Next it was circulated among the composers who were already members and this was followed by an interview with the candidate during which questions about the composition could be asked. Finally, the question of admittance was voted on by the entire academy and if the candidate obtained a two thirds majority vote, he was admitted.[22]

Some of the private male academies made important musical contributions. One sponsored by the prince Ruspoli in Rome heard more than fifty cantatas by Handel and another hosted by cardinal Ottoboni frequently heard the trio sonatas by Corelli. A German visitor, J. F. A. von Uffenbach recorded his impressions of an oratorio performance in Ruspoli's palace in 1715, which is enlightening in its mix of aesthetic insight and aristocratic protocol.

> They performed a magnificent concert, or so-called oratorio, which so enraptured me that I was convinced that I had never heard anything of the kind so perfectly done before in my life … Everyone listened so attentively to the excellent singers that not even a fly stirred except when a cardinal or a lady entered [while the music continued!], whereupon everyone stood, but afterwards sat down again in their former places … About halfway through the performance there was an interval during which large quantities of drinks, ices, cakes and coffee were brought in and offered to everyone. Then the second half of the work was given, and that altogether the performance lasted some four hours.[23]

One of the movements which the intellectual discussions of the academies resulted in at the beginning of the eighteenth century was a renewed fascination with the lives of the ancient Greeks, Romans and the period of the medieval crusades. Another was an interest in works dealing with Nature, of which the *Four Seasons* of Vivaldi is the most familiar today. Perhaps another manifestation of this interest were outdoor performances on noble estates, sometimes called 'Serenatas,' which were sometimes organized like elaborate Renaissance allegorical pageants, although on a smaller scale.

---

21 Scipione Bargagli, *Della lodi dell' accademie …* (Florence, 1569), 13.

22 Ursula Brett, *Music and Ideas in Seventeenth Century Italy* (New York: Garland Publishing, 1989), 55.

23 Quoted in Malcolm Boyd, 'Rome: the Power of Patronage,' in *The Late Baroque Era* (Englewood Cliffs: Prentice Hall, 1994), 59.

The most important musical contribution by Italy to the Baroque was opera and it too was a child of an aristocracy group of nobles, known as the Camerata.[24] We may well assume, by their fierce competition for credit, that the composers present at the birth of real opera were aware that an important new form had been born.[25] Caccini insisted on replacing some of the music of Peri's *Euridice* with his own compositions under the argument that the singers who were his students could sing only music written by their master, and then tried to claim ownership of the work itself. And when Rinuccini printed his libretto for *Euridice* still another composer, Cavalieri, writes in a letter of November 1600, 'Rinuccini acts … as if he had been the inventor of this way of representing [action] in music; but this was invented by me, and everyone knows this.'

During the course of the seventeenth century opera replaced the older Renaissance allegorical pageants and horse shows as the entertainment of preference. It is no surprise that much of the old pageantry remained, as we can see in a description of a performance of the opera *Berenice* (1680), by Giovanni Freschi, which included a procession of a chorus of one hundred virgins, several hundred soldiers, two elephants, six trumpeters on horse, six drummers, six trombones, six 'great' flutes, six minstrels with Turkish instruments, six with 'octave' flutes and six 'cymbalists.'[26] And like the earlier allegorical pageants, the seventeenth-century operas did not fail to underwrite the themes of power and privilege which kept the nobles comfortable and the lower class at bay.

Venice alone had seven different theaters for opera by the end of the seventeenth century and between 1662 and 1680 nearly one hundred different operas were heard there.[27] There is an interesting contemporary account of opera in Venice, written by a canon of St. Mark's, Cristoforo Ivanovich, in 1681.[28] He begins by describing the various entertainments to be enjoyed in Venice, season by season. It is under Winter, that he turns to opera.

> This brings the Carnival season, for which outsiders flock to the city, and which sees the citizens themselves in continuous activity, after the year's employment in political or domestic affairs. The opera houses are first to begin; this they do with incredible magnificence and splendor, by no means inferior to that practiced in various places by the magnificence of princes, with the sole difference that the latter procure the enjoyment of all through their own generosity, while opera in Venice is business and thus lacks that decorum with which marriages and births are frequently celebrated by princes with a view to the greater display of their magnificence and power. The performance of these *drammi*, as also of comedies, continues without interruption until the final day of Carnival; in this way, each evening brings a variety of entertainments of several hours' length, held in a number of different theaters (each of which traditionally offers two different productions per season as a means of drawing the crowds).

24 The aesthetic views of this group are discussed in the following chapter.

25 The following is discussed in Nino Pirrotta and Elena Povoledo, *Music and Theatre from Poliziano to Monteverdi* (Cambridge: Cambridge University Press, 1982), 238ff.

26 John Sainsbury, *Dictionary of Musicians* (London, 1825).

27 A comprehensive description of opera in Venice is given in Bianconi, *Music in the Seventeenth Century*, 180ff.

28 Quoted in Ibid., 303ff.

Ivanovich compares the construction of modern theaters with those of ancient Rome, pointing out that in stead of tiers there are now private boxes. In the middle section, however, 'benches are rented out on a day-to-day basis without social distinction.' Whereas the entertainments of ancient Rome were famously brutal, today, he observes,

> musical theater exists more as relief for the soul and as virtuous recreation. The appearance of ingenious machines, as suggested by the drama, combines with the costumes and scenic display in a way which proves extremely attractive and which fully satisfies the universal curiosity aroused. In this way, lifelike elephants and real-life camels have been seen to walk the stage, as also grandiose chariots drawn by horses or other wild beasts; other sights include flying horses, dancing horses, the most magnificent machines represented by air, earth and sea with fantastic contrivances and laudable invention, to the point at which royal apartments, illuminated as for night, have been seen to descend from the air with the entire company of actors and instrumentalists, and then to return whence they came, with the great admiration of all.

The canon discusses various arrangements by which one can pay for the private boxes, but in general he is alarmed at the great cost of opera.

> A theater, before enjoying any profit whatever, has many expenses to sustain, all of which regard the performance of the dramas. The first and greatest of these expenses concerns the remuneration of the singers, the pretensions of these men and women having reached excessive levels (where earlier they were happy to perform irrespective of gain, or at most for honest recognition). It is also necessary to pay the composer of the *dramma per musica*. There follow the expenses for the costumes, *mutazioni di scena* and construction of the machines; an agreement must be reached with the *maestro de' balli*, and the various instrumentalists and theatrical hands must be paid on a nightly basis ... Sufficient, at the beginning, were two delightful voices with a few arias to bring pleasure and a limited number of *mutazioni di scena* to satisfy the curiosity; today, more attention is paid to a voice that does not live up to expectations than to many of the greatest singers in Europe ... These are the reasons for which expenses increase year by year, though prices at the door have actually fallen. The very continuation of opera could well be placed in jeopardy if this current state of affairs is not regulated more carefully.

He concludes with a summary of the kinds of profit which opera brings to a town, including financial profit. More important than this, he finds,

> No pleasure can be greater than that which is born from the harmonies taught by the very motion of the spheres: these qualities, together with the other particular circumstances of theatrical entertainments, render the latter enjoyable thrice over: pomp and display for the eye, music for the ear, poetry for the intellect.

Ivanovich, being a prince of the Church, and thus associated with the noble class, he has one more worry.

> The low price charged at the entrance reduces the means available to meet the considerable cost of the pomp and display, facilitates access on the part of the ignorant and tumultuous masses and lowers the dignity of that very virtue which exists no less for delight than for profit.

One visiting diplomat was amazed to find performances of opera continuing in Venice even in times of war.[29] The Englishman, John Evelyn, documents well-established opera in Venice already when he visited in 1645.

> This night, having with my Lord Bruce taken our places before, we went to the Opera, where comedies and other plays are represented in recitative music, by the most excellent musicians, vocal and instrumental, with variety of scenes painted and contrived with no less art of perspective, and machines for flying in the air, and other wonderful nations; taken together, it is one of the most magnificent and expensive diversions the wit of man can invent. The history was, Hercules in Lydia; the scenes changed thirteen times. The famous voices, Anna Rencia, a Roman, and reputed the best treble of women; but there was a eunuch who, in my opinion, surpassed her.[30]

By the end of the century, a French visitor in Venice was relatively unimpressed.

> It is undeniable matter of fact, that the ornaments of those here fall extremely short of [Parisian operas]: the habits are poor, no dances, and commonly no machines, nor any illuminations, only some candles here and there, which deserve not to be mentioned. It is dangerous not to magnify the Italian music, or to say, at least, anything against it.[31]

Joseph Addison, visiting in 1701, was more impressed with opera in Venice, although he found it somewhat ridiculous 'to hear one of the rough old Romans squeaking through the mouth of a eunuch.'[32]

But this was also public opera and some of the eyewitness accounts of the behavior of the public are quite remarkable. The visiting German, Uffenbach, refers to an opera performance in 1715 which Vivaldi conducted.

> For fear of being maltreated and covered with spit as on the previous occasion, we took a box, not very expensive, and we had our revenge in behaving in relation to the people below as people had to us, a thing which previously would have seemed impossible to me ... The singers were incomparable.[33]

---

29 He is quoted in Ellen Rosand, 'Venice, 1580–1680,' *The Early Baroque Era* (Englewood Cliffs: Prentice Hall, 1994), 90.

30 John Evelyn, *Diary* (London, 1907), I, 202.

31 François Maximilien Misson, *A New Voyage to Italy* (London, 1695), I, 191ff.

32 Joseph Addison, *Remarks on Several Parts of Italy in 1701* (London, 1705), 96ff.

33 Quoted in Alan Kendall, *Vivaldi* (London: Granada Publishing, 1979), 97.

Curiously, similar behavior is mentioned five years later by a visiting Englishman.

> There are no open galleries, as in London, but the whole from bottom to top is all divided into boxes, which one with another will contain about six persons each. They have a scandalous custom [in Venice] of spitting out of the upper boxes, as well as throwing parings of apples or oranges, upon the company in the pit, which they do at random, without any regard where it falls; though it sometimes happens upon some of the best quality; who, though they have boxes of their own, will often come into the pit, either for the better seeing of the company, or sometimes to be nearer the stage, for the better hearing of some favorite songs.[34]

This same visitor also mentions that some listeners bring their own copies of the libretti, which they read with the help of 'wax candles in their hands.' The candles, unfortunately, 'are frequently put out by the [spit] from above.'

Although the noble aspirations of the Camerata had long since given way to the demands of entertainment, Italian opera, as it spread across Europe, was a source of pride to Italians, as we can see in this rather smug observation by Pier Jacopo Martello.

> Music alone ... contains the all important secrets of the separation of the soul from all human concerns, at least for that period of time in which the soul is held enthralled by the notes in their artful handling of the consonance of voices and instruments ... This art has been developed to the utmost perfection in Italy; it is thus only correct that Italy should adopt it as its favorite and most magnificent type of theatrical entertainment, one indeed which raises a smile even in the most severe of judges; likewise, it is only correct that foreign nations should consent to the importation of a model of entertainment so justly found pleasing in Italy.[35]

Italian opera, as it spread throughout Europe, carried with it the first celebrity singers, who became the daily topic of discussion in newspapers and by the public. We will allow sketches of two sopranos from Venice represent this large body of colorful singers.

Francesca Cuzzoni (1700–1770) made her debut in Venice in 1718 and her success was followed by performances throughout Italy. She was known for her perfect intonation, creativity in improvisation and by a unique ability to crescendo and diminuendo by minute degrees.

She made her first of many trips to London in 1722 where she was engaged by Handel, who greeted her by announcing, 'Madame, I well know that you are a veritable female devil; but I myself, I will have you know, am Bellzebub, chief of the devils.' In a rehearsal for her appearance in his *Ottone*, she declared that she disliked the aria, 'Falsa immagine,' and refused to sing it. She quickly changed her mind when Handel threatened to throw her out a window and thereafter this aria became the one that made her career in London. She is well remembered for her musical duels with another Italian soprano in London, Bordoni.

---

34 Ibid., 110.

35 Pier Jacopo Martelli, *Storia e ragione d'ogni poesia* (1744), quoted in Bianconi, *Music in the Seventeenth Century*, 167.

Faustina Bordoni (1700–1781) was born to a noble Italian family, one which previously governed the Venetian Republic. Famous for what Charles Burney called 'a new kind of singing, by running improvisation with a neatness and velocity which astonished all who heard her,' she was heard by Handel, who took her to London for a production of his *Alessandro* in 1726.

The London audience, however, quickly took sides, some becoming supporters of Bordoni and some of Cuzzoni, and began to compete in the applause and boos they awarded their favorite. During a performance of Bononcini's *Astianatte*, in 1727, when Bordoni tried to sing the supporters of Cuzzoni rose up in a chorus of hisses, boos, and roars. A fight broke out in the pit and soon, on the stage itself, the two sopranos began to fight and tear each other's hair while the spectators smashed the scenery! This great competition was satirized by Gay in his *The Beggar's Opera* of 1728.[36]

The great popularity of the prima donna with the general audience cannot be entirely separated from the fact that opera itself was by the end of the Baroque becoming more and more of an entertainment form. The great librettist, Metastasio, expresses his concern for the direction of Italian opera in a letter of 1750.

> In Italy, at present, there is a taste for nothing but extravagance, and vocal symphonies; in which we sometimes hear an excellent violin, flute or oboe; but never the singing of a human creature. So that music is now to excite no other emotion than that of surprise. Things are carried to such excess, that if not soon reformed, we shall justly become the buffoons of all other nations. Composers and performers being only ambitious of tickling the ear, without ever thinking of the hearts of the audience, are generally condemned in all theaters, to the disgraceful office of degrading the acts of an opera, into *intermezzi* for the dances, which occupy the attention of the people, and chief part of the spectators.[37]

Metastasio was all the more sensitive to this decay in the aesthetic aim of the theater for he had been witness to an earlier period in which the audience wept in response to the singing on the stage.[38]

36 Bordini married the famous German composer Johann Adolf Hasse and followed him to Dresden where they lived in happiness for thirty years, before retiring to Venice. Cuzzoni, passing through the Netherlands after she had lost her voice, was thrown into prison for her debts. By giving performances for the governor of the prison, she gradually repaid her debt and made her way to Bologna. There, in extreme poverty and squalor, she supported herself by making buttons.

37 Letter to Farinelli, August 1, 1750, in Charles Burney, *Memoirs of the Life and Writings of the Abate Metastasio* (New York: Da Capo Press, 1971), I, 375ff.

38 Letter of 1731, in Ibid., 75.

CIVIC MUSIC

While opera had begun as a private entertainment of the aristocratic class, by the middle of the seventeenth century opera was beginning to transform itself into a medium for public amusement, and at the same time a commercial business. Venice led the way in making such music available to the middle class in productions touring throughout Italy. There was still aristocratic support and money involved, however, and for the canon Cristoforo Ivanovich it brought recollections of the use of mass entertainment for political control by the ancient Roman emperors.

> Abundance and display are the tools of delicate political operation, on which can depend the good fortunes of the government itself; through these, if used in honest measure, a prince can acquire the love of his people, by whom the yoke is never more easily forgotten than when they are sated or constrained by the pleasures. The common people, when they have nothing better to gnaw, turn to gnawing the reputation of princes; deprived of entertainment their idleness can easily degenerate, with the most dreadful of consequences …
>
> Public performances, since their introduction in Venice, have continued to take place every year during Carnival, thus setting an example which has come to be followed in many other parts of Europe.[39]

An important by-product of this transformation was the introduction of the repertoire principle. Purely private opera, like most music making throughout the eighteenth century, consisted of a work written for only one performance. Once opera had become a commercial affair, the idea of sharing repertoire quickly occurred and by the end of the Baroque the same operas were being heard throughout Italy.

In Rome the concept of public opera had a more difficult path due to opposition from the Church, which since its very beginning had attacked the theater for promoting sin. Now the Church was also bothered by its secular content and apparently by the idea of the public spending its money for such entertainment.[40] The Jesuit priest, Giovan Ottonelli, in a publication of 1652,[41] discussed some of the Church's concern, including the idea of an artistic medium devoted to profit and the use of female singers. Pope Innocent XII (1691–1700) even had an opera house in Rome torn down!

Nevertheless opera continued in Rome and where there is opera there must be opera teachers. A famous castrato, Giovanni Bontempi, has left a fascinating account of vocal study in Rome during the 1640s.

> The schools of Rome obliged their pupils to dedicate a total of one hour per day to the singing of difficult things; this served for the acquisition of experience. One hour on the trill, another

39 Quoted in Bianconi, *Music in the Seventeenth Century*, 304.

40 Boyd, 'Rome: The Power of Patronage,' 55.

41 *Cristiana moderazione del teatro* (1652).

> on *passaggi*, a third on the study of letters, a fourth on training and other exercises—in the presence of the master and/or in front of the mirror—with the purpose of eliminating all unseemly movement of body, face, brows and mouth. These were the morning activities.
>
> After noon, pupils underwent half an hour of theoretical training, half an hour of counterpoint above a cantus firmus, an hour of instruction and practice in counterpoint in open score and a further hour in the study of letters; the remainder of the day was spent at the harpsichord or in the composition of some psalm, motet, canzonetta or other form of song, in accordance with individual flair and ability. These were the normal exercises for days on which pupils remained indoors.
>
> Outdoor exercises consisted of frequent trips to sing and listen to the echo outside Porta Angelica, with the aim of increasing self-criticism of the scholar's tone of voice; participation in almost all the music of the various churches of Rome; observation of the manners of performance of the many illustrious singers who flourished under Urban VIII; later, at home, practice in these manners of singing and description thereof of the maestro: who himself, in his efforts to impress them more firmly upon the minds of the pupils, added all necessary warnings and other remarks. These exercises and general training in the art of music are those given us in Rome by Virgilio Mazzocchi, illustrious professor and maestro di capella of St. Peter's.[42]

In Venice and Naples forms of comic opera emerged as a popular medium attended by large crowds of paying citizens. It was for the Naples stage that the famous Pietro Metastasio (1698–1782) began his career. The Frenchman, Charles de Brosses, traveling in Italy in 1739, has left an account of hearing an opera in Naples which emphasizes the strong role of the public.

> This was the first grand opera that we had seen. The work by Sarri, a clever musician, but dry and sad, was not very good, but as a reward, was very well played. The famous Senesino played the main role; I was enchanted with the tastefulness of his singing and his bearing on the stage. But I felt with astonishment that the natives were not at all satisfied. They complained that he sang in a *stile antico*. I must tell you that musical taste changes here at least every ten years; all the applause was reserved for the Baratti woman, a new actress, pretty and easygoing, who was playing a man's part, a touching circumstance which perhaps contributed not a little to her getting such support …
>
> An opera would not please at all if there were not, among other things, a pretended battle; one hundred rascals on both sides perform it, but they are careful to put in the first rows a certain number of swashbucklers who know how to handle weapons.[43]

Very little research has been done on the subject of civic wind band in this period of Italian history, but the names of such groups turn up in passing in various accounts. One reads of the *Cappella e del Concerto della Signoria* of Siena, whose leader, Alberto Gregori, was considered

42 From *Historia musica* (Perugia, 1695), quoted in Bianconi, *Music in the Seventeenth Century*, 61.

43 Charles de Brosses, 'Lettres familières écrites en Italie en 1739,' quoted in Carol MacClintock, *Readings in the History of Music in Performance* (Bloomington: Indiana University Press, 1979), 362ff.

the first trombonist of Italy.[44] In Palermo a civic document of 1619 speaks of the trumpets and shawms [*pifari*] of the *musica di città*.[45] A manuscript in Berlin, composed ca. 1700 for the *Sonatori di fiato* by Francesco Magini, a professor at the conservatory of Rome, and the extant sonatas of Gussaghi (1608) dedicated to the 'Excellent Virtuosi' of Venice, specifically the cornettist, Lodovico Cornale, also are testimonials to the presence of these civic bands.

The civic musicians for whom we have frequently quoted references are those from Bologna. One document pictures the civic trumpeters and the civic wind band escorting the city fathers.

> When they appear in public, these *Signori* are dressed in rich robes of silk, and during the winter they are muffled up with very precious furs as well. They are accompanied by a very respectable household of eight trumpeters, with a drummer, or player of the nakers, who with these trumpets play certain Moorish drums. To both the arms of liberty; also eight excellent musicians with trombones and cornetts …[46]

Another report speaks of the trombone and cornett ensemble performing concerts for the public from a balcony of the city hall as well as at the church of St. Petronio.[47]

By the seventeenth century the range of concert venues was beginning to expand. The jurist, Grazioso Uberti, in a book of 1630, mentions that concerts could be heard in 'schools, private houses where concerts are given, palaces of princes, churches, oratories, open-air settings and the homes of composers.'[48] We can assume there must have been much musical activity among the more prosperous merchant class in the major Italian cities, but virtually no research has concentrated on this facet of Baroque music. We have one insight relative to the German composer, Johann David Heinichen (1683–1729) who visited Venice in 1670 to study the Italian opera style. He became acquainted with the wealthy merchant, Bianchi, whose wife, Angioletta, was an active singer. There is one account of a performance which this family organized which included a work written by Heinichen. An eyewitness reported that this music,

> was performed from the water before the home of the merchant, which stood … on the Grand Canal. Crowds of people gathered on the bridge and along the canal. As the first aria was sung, however, the clocks of the city began to strike, preventing the people from hearing. They began to indicate their vexation over this by stirring up such a loud noise that one could no longer hear the music. Madame Angioletta immediately asked them politely to be quiet to permit the music to continue. All became quiet again, though a repetition of the first aria was asked for, after

44 Vessella, *La Banda*, 96.

45 G. Di Marzo, *Diario della città di Palermo* (1871), II, 94.

46 Vizani (1602), quoted in Don Smithers, *The Music and History of the Baroque Trumpet* (London: Dent, 1973), 77ff.

47 Ibid.

48 *Contrasto musico*, quoted in Bianconi, *Music in the Seventeenth Century*, 71.

> which a tremendous cry of approval arose from the crowd; and the remainder of the serenade was received with no less approval.[49]

A final manifestation of the growing public participation in music can be seen in an expanding market of publications of self-tutors for learning to play the violin and other instruments.

CHURCH MUSIC

The greatest activity in Church related music occurred, of course, in the many churches of Rome, where also the Church sponsored educational institutions and the lay religious fraternities both sponsored a great deal of performance. The actual music for the service was retarded in development by the conscientious efforts of the popes to observe the dictates of the Council of Trent, which kept polyphony as the model, outlawed secular melodies and discouraged instrumental accompaniment and improvisation.

Things became temporarily more progressive under Pope Urban VIII (1623–1644), who loved music. He devoted more funds to music, including enlarging his choir, and appears to have been more tolerant of instrumental music, judging by some extant prints. Among these are the *Sacri armonici concentus* (1640) by Gregorius Urbanus, which contains independent instrumental works; the collection of Masses (1634) by Chinelli for voices and trombones; the *Messe à cinque* by Polidori, for five-part chorus, cornetti, trombones and organ; the *Pange lingua* by Bigaglia, for SATB chorus and three trombones and the eight *Cantate* for solo voice, oboe and *Flageoletto* by Torri. One chaplain, Nicolo Rubini, was also a famous cornettist, known as 'Il Cavaliere del Cornetto,' but his life was cut short by a murderer.

During this period, especially for special Church festival days, more modern forms such as concerti began to appear. André Maugars, a violist and secretary attached to Cardinal Richelieu, was sent to Rome in 1639 on a diplomatic mission and reported back, 'I have listened carefully to the most celebrated concerts in Rome.' He has recorded one of the most interesting eyewitness accounts of the performance of church concerti in the manner of those described extensively in theory in Praetorius, *Syntagma Musicum*, III.

> To enable you to understand this distribution better, I will give you an example by describing to you the most celebrated and most excellent concert, which I heard at Rome the eve and the day of Saint Dominic at the church of the Minerva. This church is rather long and wide and there are two large elevated organs, one on each side of the main altar, where they had also placed two choirs. Along the nave there were eight other choirs, four on one side and four on the other, raised on platforms eight or nine feet high, an equal distance from one another and all facing one another. With each choir there was a portative organ, as is the custom. You must not be astonished, because one can find more than two hundred organs in Rome, while in Paris one could scarcely find two of the same tuning. The leading conductor beat the measure for the

49 J. A. Hiller, *Lebensbeschreibungen berümter Musikgelehrten und Tonkünstler* (Leipzig, 1784), 137.

main choir, accompanied by the best voices. With each of the others there was a [sub-conductor] who did nothing but keep his eyes on the leading conductor, to conform his own beat to the leader's; in this way all the chorus sang in the same time, without dragging. The counterpoint was decorated, full of fine chants, and many agreeable recitatives. Sometimes a high voice [*dessus*] in the first choir did a *récit*, then one of the 3rd, 4th, or 10th answered. Sometimes two, three or four voices from the different choirs sang together, sometimes the parts of all the choirs recited, each in turn, in emulation of each other. Sometimes two choirs contended with each other, then two others answered. Another time three, four and five solo voices sang together, and at the *Gloria Patri* all the choirs joined together. I must admit that I have never been so delighted; but especially in the Hymn and in the Prose, where ordinarily the conductor tries to do better, I heard singing that was perfectly beautiful: very elegant variety, very excellent inventions, and delightful different movements. In the Anthems they had also very lovely instrumental performances, with one, two, or three violins with the organ, and with archlutes playing certain dance tunes and answering each other.

Let us place our hands, Sir, on our consciences and let us judge sincerely if we have similar performances; and even if we should have them, it seems to me that we do not at present have the voices; they would need a long period of performing together, whereas the Italian musicians never practice but sing all their parts at sight. And what I find more admirable is, that they never miss, though the music is very difficult, and that a voice in one choir often sings with the voice of another choir, which perhaps has never been seen or heard. What I beg you to notice is that they never sing the same Motets twice, though scarcely a day passes that there is not a festival in some church where some good music is played, so that one is assured every day of some new composition.[50]

Urban VIII also allowed secular elements associated with opera to become accepted in the form of large theater works focusing on the lives of the saints. These must have been tedious for one of them, *Il palazzo incantato*, by Luigi Rossi, lasted eight hours in performance! One eyewitness to the changing style of Church music during the reign of Urban VIII was the nobleman, Vicenzo Giustiniani. The reader will especially notice his reference to the addition of improvisation in the old style [sixteenth century] polyphony.

In the present course of our age music is not much in use, not being practiced in Rome by gentlemen, nor do they sing together with several voices as in past years, notwithstanding that it would provide the greatest possible opportunity to unify and sustain evening parties. Indeed, music is reduced to an unusual and almost new perfection, being practiced by a great number of good musicians who … bring the greatest pleasure to whomever hears them by their artistic and sweet song. For having left the old style, which was somewhat unpolished, and also the excessive [improvisation] with which they embellished it, they now devote their attention for the most part to a recitative style, gracefully embellished with ornaments appropriate to the thought; and from time to time they execute passages with judgment and distinctness and with

50 André Maugars, 'Response faite à un curieux sur le Sentiment de la Musique d'Italie, Ecrite à Rome le premier Octobre 1639,' quoted in Carol MacClintock, *Readings in the History of Music in Performance* (Bloomington: Indiana University Press, 1979), 118ff.

appropriate and varied consonances to mark the end of each period, in which the composers of today are wont to produce boredom with excessive and too frequent cadenzas [cadences]. Above all, they make the words clear, using one note for each syllable; now piano, now forte, now slow, now fast—by the expression of their faces and by their gestures giving meaning to what they are singing, but with moderation and not in excess …

This style has even been introduced for the singing of Latin verses and hymns and odes of piety and devotion, sung with sweetness and great decorum, and so as to make the words and ideas clear and distinctly heard.

Today in compositions to be sung in church not so much value is given as formerly to the solidity and artistry of the counterpoint as to the great variety and diversity of the embellishments, and to the use of several choirs at solemn feasts with the accompaniment of orchestras of various instruments; even the recitative style is introduced. This music demands great practical knowledge and liveliness of invention and effort to write rather than great maturity and knowledge of refined counterpoint.[51]

We have another eyewitness report of one of these 'recitative style' performances in Rome, by André Maugars a few years later.

There is still another kind of music which is not performed in France and which for this reason deserves my telling you about it separately. It is called *Stile recitativo*. The best that I have heard was in the Saint Marcel Chapel, where there is a congregation of the Brothers of the Holy Crucifix, composed of the greatest nobles of Rome, who as a consequence have the power to bring together every rarest thing in Italy; and, indeed, the most excellent composers seek the honor of having their compositions heard there, and try to present what is best in their studios.

This admirable and ravishing music is heard only on Fridays during Lent, from three to six o'clock. The church is not nearly as big as the Sainte Chapelle in Paris. At the end is a specious … screen with a medium-sized organ, very sweet and very suitable for voices. At the two sides of the church there are two small galleries where were located the best musical instruments. The voices began with a Psalm in the form of a Motet and then the instruments played a very good Sinfonia. The voices after this sang a story from the Old Testament in the form of a *comédie spirituelle*, like that of Susanna, of Judith and Holofernes, of David and Goliath. Each singer represented a personage of the story and perfectly expressed the energy of the words. Then one of its most celebrated preachers recited the Exhortation. When this was finished, the music recited the Evangel of the day, like the story of the Good Samaritan, the feast at Canaan, the story of Lazarus, of Mary Magdalen, of Our Lord's Passion, the singers imitating to perfection the personages the Evangelist writes about. I cannot praise the Recitative Music enough; one must hear it to judge of its merit.[52]

51 Vicenzo Giustiniani, *Discorso sopra la Musica* (ca. 1628), trans. Carol MacClintock (Rome: American Institute of Musicology, 1962), 77.

52 André Maugars, 'Response faite à un curieux sur le Sentiment de la Musique d'Italie, Ecrite à Rome le premier Octobre 1639,' 118ff.

Maugars has also left an interesting account of improvisation in Roman church music, which is particularly valuable for being a rare eyewitness report of the playing of the great Frescobaldi.

> As to the instrumental music, it was composed of an organ, a large clavecin, two or three violins, and two or three archlutes. At times a single violin sounded with the organ, and then another answered; another time all three played different parts together; and then all the instruments repeated together. Sometimes an archlute performed a thousand variations on ten or twelve notes, each note five or six measures long; then another played the same passage differently, I remember one violin played purely chromatically, and though at first it seemed to me very hard on the ears, nevertheless I gradually grew accustomed to this manner and took great pleasure in it. But specially the great Frescobaldo brought out a thousand kinds of inventions on his clavier, the organ always holding firm.
>
> It is not without reason that this famous organist has acquired such a reputation in Europe; because his printed works render sufficient evidence of his skill, to judge his profound knowledge adequately you must hear him as he improvises toccatas full of refinement and admirable inventions. That is why he deserves that you hold him up as a unique player to all our organists, to make them want to come to hear him in Rome.[53]

The dogma and practice of Roman Church music had temporarily survived the humanists, but it found a more difficult challenge in the popularity of opera and the growing participation of the public in secular music in general during the sixteenth century. Subsequently, a series of papal edicts, in 1657, 1662, 1678 and 1692 were issued in an attempt to prevent secular influences from entering the service. In the 'Edict on Music' of 1665, the pope demands that no words but the Latin in the Roman Missal be used and that the music be 'grave, ecclesiastical and devout' in character.[54] The rather dark character of this attack can be seen in the following provisions.

> Eighth, that within a period of twenty days from the publication of the present edict by the Fathers Superior and others whose duty it is, that shutters or narrow grilles be placed in the choirs, be the latter temporary or permanent, and that the said shutters be of such a height as the singers will not be seen, under pain of privation of office and other penalties at the discretion of the Holy Visitation.
>
> Ninth, that no maestro di cappella or other person entrusted with ordering the music or giving the beat contravene the aforesaid prescriptions under pain of privation of office and perpetual disqualification from the exercise of this office and the right to make music; and, moreover, that he be punished with a fine of 100 scudi, of which one quarter be given the denouncer (whose name will be held secret), three quarters to the holy places at the discretion of the Holy Visitation, and with other penalties—including corporal punishment—at the discretion of the said Holy Visitation.

53 Ibid., 119ff.

54 The full text is quoted in Bianconi, *Music in the Seventeenth Century*, 108ff.

During the early part of the seventeenth century, the most progressive Church music was heard in Venice at St. Mark's, where the great tradition of instrumental music begun at the end of the sixteenth century continued to develop. An Englishman, Thomas Coryat, visiting in 1608, has left an account of hearing both the older trombones and cornetts and one of the new strings.

> At that time I heard much good Musicke in Saint Markes Church, but especially that of a treble violl which was so excellent, that I thinke no man could surpasse it. Also there were sagbuts and cornets as at St. Laurence feast which yeeled passing good musicke.[55]

Since Venice, and some Northern courts, had managed to preserve limited independence from the pope, some progress toward carrying the new ideas of the Baroque into church music occurred. Already in 1614 we can see in Alessandro Grandi, then working in Ferrara but soon to become *vicemaestro* to Monteverdi at St. Mark's, a desire to introduce the principles, if not the style, of the Camerata into his motets. In the preface to this publication, Grandi makes both a subtle attack on the old, but official, polyphonic style and a subtle argument for something new.

> Here, the clarity of the words is not impaired by the fugues of the composer, nor [are the words] rendered any less excellent through the art of song; on the contrary, the latter is elevated and humbled, runs, rests and cries with the former words; in whatever way the former is arranged, the latter gives rise to a more effective portrayal of the affections therein.[56]

Monteverdi refers to the tradition of winds supporting the voices in a letter of 1616 when he recommends this for a theatrical work as well.

> There are two more choruses ..., but it seems to me that these ought to be doubled by wind instruments, for if they were performed in this way, what pleasure—I ask Your Lordship—would they not bring to the senses![57]

A very large number of instrumental works, especially canzoni, were published at this time in Venice and records at the cathedral prove this music was performed during the service. In particular, between 1600 and 1620 many canzoni were published by such composers as Canale, Quagliati, Bonelli, Troilo, Bona, Merula, among many others, in addition to collections of such works. Among the latter is the collection published by Rauerij (Venice, 1608), which includes some Gabrieli works found nowhere else and the canzona for four instrumental choirs by Massaino.[58] This cathedral was also a great center for organ playing and

55 Quoted in Egon Kenton, *Life and Works of Giovanni Gabrieli* (Rome: American Institute of Musicology, 1967), 37.

56 Quoted in Bianconi, *Music in the Seventeenth Century*, 118.

57 Letter to Alessandro Striggio (December 29, 1616), quoted in Monteverdi, *The Letters*, 120.

58 This collection is available in a modern score from Leland Bartholomew, Music Department, Fort Hays State College, Fort Hays, Kansas.

the organists there were especially known for their improvisation. But even in Venice one could be too progressive. The officials of the cathedral in 1639 issued an edict warning that,

> in musical solemnities, the use of instruments other than those normally used in the church is not allowed; in particular, refrain from the use of warlike instruments such as trumpets, drums and the like, more suitable for armies than for the house of God ... and that all the musicians, secular and ecclesiastical alike, while serving their musical functions, must come dressed in surplices; and, finally, that the transposition of words or the singing of newly-invented words not contained in the holy books [are not] permitted except at Offertory, Elevation and after the Agnus Dei.

The lay religious fraternities in Venice were especially known for their private support of Church music. The French ambassador to the Republic of Venice in 1607–1609, Jean-Baptiste Duval, recorded seeing 'six oboe players dressed in long robes with wide sleeves of dark blue or of rosy silk' representing the fraternity of St. Theodore in the annual Corpus Christi procession.[59]

These lay organizations also sponsored concerts of their own, the most documented of which were given at the Scuole San Rocco. Thomas Coryat, describes a performance there on 16 August 1608, which included among its participants none other than Giovanni Gabrieli. Of particular interest is the description of a countertenor, whom the writer could hardly believe was not a castrato.

> This feast consisted principally of Musicke, which was both vocall and instrumental, so good, and delectable, so rare, so admirable, so super-excellent, that it did even ravish and stupifie all those strangers that never heard the like. But how others were affected with it I know not; for mine own part I can say this, that I was for the time even rapt up with Saint Paul into the third heaven. Sometimes there sung sixteen or twenty men together, having their master or moderator to keepe them in order; and when they sang, the instrumentall musitians played also. Sometimes sixeteene played together upon their instruments, ten Sagbuts, foure Cornetts, and two Viol-de-gambaes of a extraordinary greatness; sometimes tenne, six Sagbuts and foure Cornets; sometimes two, a Cornet and a treble violl. Of these treble viols I heard three severall there, whereof each was so good, especially one that I observed above the rest, that I never heard the like before. Those that played upon the treble viols, sung and played together, and sometimes two singular fellowes yeelded admirable sweet musicke, but so still that they could scarce be heard but by those that were very neare them. These two Theorbists concluded that nights musicke, which continued three whole hours at the least. For they beganne about five of the clocke, and ended not before eight. Also it continued as long in the morning: at every time that every severall musicke played, the Organs, whereof there are seven faire paire in that room, standing all in a rowe together, plaied with them. Of the singers there were three or foure so excellent that I think few or none in Christendome do excell them, especially one, who had such a peerless and (as I may in a manner say) such a supernaturall voice for such a privilege for the sweetness of his voice as sweetness, that I think there was never a better singer in all the world,

59 Ibid., 35ff.

> insomuch that he did not onely give the most pleasant contentment that could be imagined, to all the hearers, but also did as it were astonish and amaze them. I alwaies thought that he was a Eunuch, which if he had beene, it had taken away some part of my admiration, because they do most commonly sing passing well; but he was not, therefore it was much the more admirable. Againe it was the more worthy of admiration, because he was a middle-aged man, as about forty yeares old. For nature doth more commonly bestowe such singularitie of voice upon boyes and striplings, than upon men of such yeares. Besides it was farre the more excellent, because it was nothing forced, strained or affected, but came from him with the greatest facilitie that ever I heard. Truely, I thinke that had a Nightingale beene in the same roome, and contended with him for the superioritie, something perhaps he might excell him, because God hath granted that little birdie such a privilege for the sweetness of his voice, as to none other: but I thinke he could not much. To conclude, I attribute so much to this rare fellow for his singing, that I thinke the country where he was borne, may be proude for breeding so singular a person as Smyrna was of her Homer, Verona of her Catullus, or Mantua of Virgil. But exceeding happy may the Citie or towne, or person bee that possesseth this miracle of nature.[60]

Unfortunately this great tradition declined throughout the seventeenth century.

During the latter part of the seventeenth century the popes felt the need to make the rules of church music even more conservative. Thus in Rome now a 'grave and devout' style was required, sung only by male voices out of sight of the congregation. The organ was accepted, but other instruments were still discouraged except for special festivals. In Venice the brilliant instrumental forces heard in St. Mark's early in the century became the subdued music of string trios by the end of the century.

During the second half of the seventeenth century instrumental music began to flourish in both monasteries and convents, as well as in the *ospedali*, charitable institutions and schools for orphans, which in the case of those in Naples and Venice began to develop into early conservatories. We are fortunate to have eyewitness accounts of several of the individual *ospedali*. In 1698 the Russian, Petr Tolstago, wrote from Venice regarding the *Incurabili*:

> In Venice there are convents where the women play the organ and other instruments and sing so wonderfully that nowhere else in the world could one find such sweet and harmonious song. Therefore people come to Venice from all parts with the wish to refresh themselves with these angelic songs, above all those of the Convent of the Incurables.[61]

A rather extraordinary account of another of these *ospedali*, that of the *Mendicanti*, is found in the *Confessions* of Jean-Jacques Rousseau, dating from two years after the death of Vivaldi.

> A kind of music to my mind far superior to that of the operas, and which has not its like in Italy is that of the *scuole* ... Every Sunday at the Church of each of these schools one has during Vespers motets for full choir and orchestra composed and directed by the greatest masters in

60 Quoted in Denis Arnold, 'Music at the Scuola di San Rocco,' *Music and Letters* 40, no. 3 (July, 1959): 236ff, http://www.jstor.org/stable/729389.

61 Quoted in W. Kolneder, *Antonio Vivaldi, his life and work* (London, 1756), 10ff.

> Italy, performed in balconies with grilles, entirely by girls of whom the oldest is not twenty. I can imagine nothing so voluptuous, so touching as this music ... The church [the *Mendicanti*] was always full of those who liked this sort of music; even the actors from the Opera would come and conform themselves to the true taste in singing on these excellent models. What grieved me were those accursed grilles, which only allowed the sound to pass, and hid from me the angels of beauty of which the sound was worthy. I only talked of that. One day when I was talking about it to Monsieur le Blond:
>
> 'If you are so curious,' he said to me, 'to see these little girls, it is easy to satisfy you. I am one of the administrators of the house; I want to give you tea there with them.'
>
> I did not let him rest until he had kept his word to me. As we entered the salon which enclosed these such coveted beauties, I felt a shiver of love that I had never felt before. Monsieur le Blond introduced one after another to me of these famous singers whose voices and names were all known to me. 'Come, Sophia ...' she was horrible. 'Come, Cattina ...' she was blind in one eye. 'Come, Bettina ...' smallpox had disfigured her. There was hardly one that did not have some notable defect. The executioner laughed at my cruel surprise ... I was grieved.[62]

Naturally we are most interested today in the *Seminario musicale dell' Ospitale della Pietà*, for it was there that the great Vivaldi was employed between 1704 and 1740. An account from early in Vivaldi's tenure records a visit by Frederick IV, King of Denmark and Norway.

> His Majesty made an appearance at the Pietà at eleven o'clock in the morning after hearing the embassy from the lords of Savoy, and the girls sang with the instruments of the maestro [Vivaldi] who occupies the podium in the absence of Gasparini. Great was the applause for the *Credo* and *Agnus Dei* that were performed with the instruments, and then there was a concerto in great taste, as was appropriate.[63]

There is a curious reference to this *Ospitale*, and its musical activities, by a traveling Englishman in 1720. We can only speculate that it was for the benefit of the English reader back home that he characterizes Vivaldi as an eunuch and the general environment more like a Turkish harem!

> There are in Venice four of these female hospitals ... the Incurabili, the Pietà, Ospitaletto and the Mendicanti ...
>
> Every Sunday and holiday there is a performance of music in the chapels of these hospitals, vocal and instrumental, performed by the young women of the place; who are set in a gallery above and are hid from any distinct view of those below by a lattice of iron-work. The organ parts, as well as those of the other instruments, are all performed by the young women. They have a eunuch for their master and he composes their music. Their performance is surprisingly good; and many excellent voices are among them.[64]

---

62 J. J. Rousseau, *Confessions*, II, vii.

63 Quoted in Remo Giazotto, *Antonio Vivaldi* (Turin, 1973), 105.

64 Quoted in Marc Pincherle, 'Vivaldi and the *Ospitali* of Venice,' *The Musical Quarterly* 24, no. 3 (July, 1938): 301, doi:10.1093/mq/XXIV.3.300.

Another interesting account, because it hints at the amorous activities for which the Italian Catholic institutions were known, is by K. L. von Poellnitz, who visited in 1729.

> I am in some doubt whether I should reckon the music of the Venetian churches in the number of its pleasures; but on the whole, I think I should, because certainly their churches are frequented more to please the ear, than for real devotion. The church of La Pietà which belongs to the nuns who know no other father but love, is most frequented. These nuns are entered very young, and are taught music, and to play on all sorts of instruments, in which some of them are excellent performers. Apollonia actually passes for the finest singer, and Anna-Maria for the first violin in Italy. The concourse of people to this church on Sundays and holidays is extraordinary. It is the rendezvous of all the coquettes in Venice, and such as are fond of intrigues have here both their hands and hearts full. Not many days after my arrival in this city I was at this very church, where was a vast audience, and the finest of music.[65]

In 1739, just before Vivaldi retired from this service, another visitor recalled,

> The most transcendent music here is that provided by the Ospitali. There are four of these, all of them for girls—illegitimate, orphans, or those whose relatives are not able to care for them. They are being brought up at the expense of the state and are being trained most especially to excel in music. In addition they sing like angels, they play the violin, the flute, the organ, the clarinet, the violoncello, and the bassoon. In short, there is no instrument so large as to give them pause … They are the sole performers at each concert, and some forty of them take part. I swear there is nothing more pleasing to be seen than one of these pretty young sisters in her white dress with a cluster of pomegranate blossoms over one ear, conducting an orchestra and beating time with all the grace and precision imaginable.[66]

In this same year Charles de Brosses also mentions the quality of the orchestral performances.

> The one of the four *ospedali* I visit most often, and where I enjoy myself most, is the Ospedale della Pietà; it is also the first for the perfection of the symphonies. What strictness of execution! It is only there that one hears the first attack of the bow, so falsely vaunted at the Paris Opéra.[67]

It is generally understood that a great deal of Vivaldi's music, in particular the concerti, was composed for these students. Pincherle finds proof of this in the 'extreme rapidity of composition, as evidenced by the autographs.'[68] This facility in composition is evidenced by Vivaldi himself, as recalled by Charles de Brosses in 1739.

65 K. L. von Poellnitz, *Memoirs* (London, 1737), I, 414.

66 Quoted in Arnold, 'Music at the Scuola di San Rocco,' 301ff.

67 Charles de Brosses, *Lettres familières sur l'Italie* (Paris, 1931), I, 238ff.

68 Arnold, 'Music at the Scuola di San Rocco,' 310.

> Vivaldi has become one of my intimate friends, so as to sell me some very expensive concertos. He has in part succeeded, and I too in that which I desired, namely to hear him and have frequent good musical recreation: he is a *vecchio* with a prodigious fury for composition. I have heard him boast that he has composed a concerto, with all its parts, faster than a copyist could write it out.[69]

Another extraordinary testimonial to the speed with which Vivaldi composed is found in the diary of J. F. von Uffenbach. On 6 March 1715, he writes,

> After the meal, Vivaldi, the famous composer and violinist came to my lodging, since I had sent to his house several times to invite him. I spoke to him of some concerti grossi that I would have liked to have from him, and ordered them from him. Since he belonged to the circle of the Cantores I had some bottles of wine brought, and he played some very difficult improvisations for me on the violin, quite inimitable. Close to I admired his art even more, and I realized from the evidence that he played extraordinarily difficult and varied things, but in a manner that was neither pleasant nor cantabile.[70]

Then, only three days later, we find this entry:

> In the afternoon Vivaldi came to my lodging and brought, as I had ordered from him, ten concerti grossi which he said he had composed specially for me.

Ten concerti grosso in three days?! In any case, the assumption that many of the concerti were written for his students is clearly suggested in the duties outlined in his contract of 1735.

> The same maestro will have to provide for our girls concertos and other compositions for all sorts of instruments, and he will have to come with the assiduousness necessary for instructing the girls and making them well able to perform them.[71]

We might add that we find evidence of both the speed of composition and the educational purpose in such musical shorthand as 'Alberti-bass' figures in upper melodic voices.

69 Charles de Brosses, *Lettres familières sur l'Italie*, I, 237ff.

70 Quoted in Kendall, *Vivaldi*, 100.

71 Archivio di Stato, Venice, Ospitali, busta 692, Notatorio Q, fol. 113r.

MILITARY MUSIC

During most of the seventeenth century, military music in Italy seems to have consisted only of trumpets and timpani, belonging to units of civic militia as well as those attached to nobles.[72]

The first Hautboisten military band appears to have been brought to Italy from Paris by Vittorio Amadeo II when he married the niece to Louis XIV in 1684. At this time the name of his court wind band changes from *banda di tromboni* to *banda di hautbois*.[73] The first 'oboe bands' appear in Rome in 1708 as *piccoli concerti*, consisting of oboes, bassoons and timpani, but appear to have been organized privately, independent of the civic government.[74]

At the end of the seventeenth century German influence begins to be seen in the Italian military bands, due to the presence of Austrian and German troops associated with the War of the Spanish Succession. In some cases the Italian bands appear to have had German leaders, as in the case of Giorgio Cristoforo Albmeyer, who led the *Hautbois* of the Reggimento Rhebinder in around 1720.[75]

---

72 Vessella, *La Banda*, 123ff.

73 Ibid., 130ff.

74 Ibid., 123ff.

75 Ibid., 168.

2 ON THE CAMERATA AS A HARBINGER FOR THE BAROQUE

MUSICOLOGY AS A MODERN UNIVERSITY FIELD OF STUDY began in the nineteenth century in Germany. The men who first dedicated themselves to the academic study of early music began with a very understandable decision to focus on actual surviving music. But this meant that their studies would be centered on church music for the church was the only institution known to them which had preserved earlier music. Their decision to limit their studies in this way had two very detrimental consequences for decades of following music students.

First, by failing to include in their early music studies a broader historical and sociological perspective the early musicologists were generally unaware of the vast contributions to aesthetic music history by civic music, court music and military music. This in turn resulted in their failure to find the substantial collections of early music which represented these areas. As a result, until fairly recently 'Music of the Renaissance Period' meant to most university students primarily Roman Church music. Not only did this give modern students a very narrow, even negligent, view of the actual practice of music in society between 1300 and 1600, but for the men who actually lived in the Renaissance Church music was the most insignificant part of the music they heard in their daily lives. The composer Machaut, on whom musicological studies focus for the study of early 14th century music, would have been astounded if he could have been told that history would only remember him for his church music.

Second, by limiting their focus to church music the early musicologists gave following students an incorrect understanding of the societal value of the music they were studying. Nothing symbolizes this problem so much as the study of the polyphonic church music of the sixteenth century. Musicology has focused on this period of contrapuntal music with extensive books and treatises dealing with the theoretical art of writing this kind of music. But it can be widely documented that for the persons who actually lived in the sixteenth century this kind of music had little interest for they considered it already old-fashioned and Scholastic.

It follows that the early musicologists failed to understand the currents of musical thought which resulted in and became Baroque music. What the music of the Renaissance really represented was the end of a one thousand year period when the Church opposed all recognition of emotion and insisted that music be thought of instead as part of the field of mathematics, one direct result being our music notational system. One can say that during the Renaissance society was rediscovering what music really is, a language of feeling.

What the Baroque Period was really all about was an enthusiastic focus by scholars and composers on trying to discover how music communicated feeling, becoming in Germany a separate field of study called the Doctrine of the Affections. This had been the particular focus of the distinguished and educated men known as the Camerata who following a decade or so of discussion founded modern opera. Their goal was to leave mathematics behind and to recreate stage productions in which music expressed the strong emotions which they found documented in ancient Greek literature. The Camerata then, together with the first generations of opera, can be taken as a symbol for a new kind of music, music whose purpose is to communicate emotions to the listener.

The early musicologists, focused as they were on Church music which had deliberately excluded emotions in music, misinterpreted the statements made by members of the Camerata and its associated composers such as Monteverdi. For example, Manfred Bukofzer, in his famous book, *Music in the Baroque Era*, quotes Berardi's *Miscellanea Musicale* (1689) as saying that in Baroque music, '*the word is the master of harmony*.'[1] Bukofzer follows this by saying that this 'neat antithesis merely paraphrases Monteverdi' ['*the word is mistress of the music*']. Later, on his own, Bukofzer says of opera, 'The baroque artist saw in music a heteronomous art, *subordinated to words*.'[2]

Julius Portnoy, in discussing 'The Aesthetics of Music in the Baroque Era,' writes of this same period of the origin of opera, 'The recitative … was created so that the *music could be subordinated to the words*.'[3] Portnoy goes on to paraphrase two of the most important composers of original opera: Caccini as saying '*that music was primarily speech* and rhythm and lastly melody,' and Peri as saying '*the composer should emulate the speaking person* in song.'[4] Portnoy summarizes by saying the Camerata produced 'a *word-dominated art form* in which the music only supported the spoken word.'[5]

If the reader is given the impression in the above statements, which are shared by many other books, that in the view of the Camerata and the earliest opera which followed the words were more important than the music, he will have been significantly misinformed.

The fact is that the views quoted above are representative of an apparent critical misunderstanding by the early musicologists of a line by Plato. They found this line among the papers of the members of the Camerata who had been debating the values of their understanding of ancient Greek music, known only through comments by the ancient philosophers, and 'modern' music, their music of the seventeenth century. In his *Republic* Plato had written,

1 Manfred F. Bukofzer, *Music in the Baroque Era* (New York: Norton, 1947), 4. All italics in the first two paragraphs are ours.

2 Ibid., 8.

3 Julius Portnoy, *The Philosopher and Music* (New York: The Humanities Press, 1954), 128.

4 Ibid., 129. Both Caccini and Peri are incorrectly quoted.

5 Ibid., 130.

> Song is composed of three things, the words, the tune and the rhythm … Music and the rhythm must follow the speech.'[6]

We know that Monteverdi had read this same passage in the Latin translation by Marsilio Ficino and he quotes it as follows in the Foreword to his fifth book of madrigals,

> Of this Plato speaks as follows: 'the Song is composed of three things: the words, the harmony and the rhythm' and a little further on, 'And the rhythm and the harmony follow the words, and not the words these.'

The very next sentence by Monteverdi is an important key to what the members of the Camerata were thinking:

> Do not the manner of expression and the words follow and conform to the disposition of the soul?

The reference here to the 'soul' reflects a long usage by medieval Church philosophers as a place to locate the emotions, a subject greatly resisted by the Church. Monteverdi's point is that it is not words which are the mistress of the music, but the *emotions* of the words which are the mistress of the music. In other words, the emotions of the words (the melody) dictates the use of the rest of the harmony and rhythm. There is no question what Monteverdi's intent was here for it was in this volume of madrigals that he made his famous break with the old mathematical–contrapuntal Church style and introduced what he called a new practice, 'On the Perfection of Modern Music.' The new music was highly emotional and included the widely known 'Cruda Amarilli.'

This is exactly what the first opera was all about, finding a stage vehicle in which expressing the feeling of the words would result in stronger drama than mere speech. And of course that has remained the definition of opera forever after: Opera is about communicating emotions through music. No one goes to an opera to follow the plot.

Nineteenth-century opera alone should have alerted the early musicologists that they had it all wrong. But they missed the point and they seemed to have also missed the abundant testimony by various writers during the Renaissance and the Baroque that music must supply the emotion for the words. Here is a sampling:

Vincenzo Calmeta (d. 1508), a secretary to the Duchess Beatrice d'Este of Milan

> We must praise the good judgment of those, who in singing put all their effort into expressing the words well … and have them accompanied by the music in the manner of masters accompanied

6 Plato, *Republic*, III, 398d, trans. Paul Shorey (Cambridge, Harvard University Press, 1969. Curiously, Oliver Strunk, in *Source Readings in Music History* (New York: Norton, 1950) quotes the very same Shorey translation but with no explanation changes the first word to read, 'Melody is composed of three things, the words, the harmony and the rhythm.'

by their servants ... not making the thoughts and emotions subservient to the music, but the music to the emotions and thoughts.[7]

Franchino Gaffurio, music theorist, 1451–1518

Let the composer of music strive to adapt the melody in its sweetness to the words of the song, so that when the words concern love or a longing for death or some lamentation, he will articulate and arrange doleful sounds so far as he can, as the Venetians are wont to do.[8]

Paolo Cortese, papal secretary, 1465–1510

It can be rightly said that the motions of the souls are usually appeased and excited with more vehemence by the poems produced in this genre; for, when the rhythms of the words and sentences are combined with the sweetness of the melodic modes, nothing can prevent [the listener] from being exceedingly moved because of the power of the ear and of its similarity to the soul.[9]

Vincenzo Galilei, 1520–1591, musician, theorist, composer and father of the famous astronomer

Using few notes is natural both in speaking and singing, since the purpose of one and the other is solely the expression of the thoughts of the soul by means of words, which, when well expressed and understood by the listeners, generate in them whatever emotions the musician cares to treat through this medium.[10]

In referring to the sixteenth-century polyphonic Church composers he writes,

And in truth the last thing the [contrapuntal] moderns think of is the expression of the words with the passion that these require ... And if it were permitted me, I should like to show you, with several examples of authority, that among the most famous contrapuntists of this century there are some who do not even know how to read, let alone understand. Their ignorance and lack of consideration is one of the most potent reasons why the [contrapuntal] music of today does not cause in the listeners any of those virtuous and wonderful effects that ancient music caused.[11]

7 Quoted in Pirrotta and Povoledo, *Music and Theatre from Poliziano to Monteverdi*, 28.

8 Ibid., 161.

9 Paolo Cortese, 'De cardinalatu libri tres,' quoted in Nino Pirrotta, *Music and Culture in Italy from the Middle Ages to the Baroque* (Cambridge: Harvard University Press, 1984), 105.

10 'Dubbi intorno a quanto io ho detto dell'uso dell'enharmonio,' quoted in Claude V. Palisca, *Humanism in Italian Renaissance Musical Thought* (New Haven: Yale University Press, 1985), 393.

11 Vincenzo Galilei, 'Dialogo della musica antica e della moderna,' in Strunk, *Source Readings*, 313.

Gioseffo Zarlino, 1517–1590, important Italian theorist

If poets are not permitted to write a comedy in tragic verse, it is not permissible for a musician to combine harmony and words in an unsuitable manner. Thus, it will not be appropriate for him to use sad harmony and grave rhythms for cheerful subjects, and he is not permitted to use cheerful harmony and light or fast rhythms, call it what we may, where funereal matters are treated. On the contrary, he should use cheerful harmonies and fast rhythms for cheerful subjects and sad harmonies and grave rhythms for sad subjects, so that everything may be done with proportion …

He should take care to accompany each word in such a manner that, when the word denotes harshness, hardness, cruelty, bitterness, and other things of this sort, the harmony will be similar to these qualities, namely, somewhat hard and harsh, but not to the degree that it would offend. Similarly, when any of the words express complaint, sorrow, grief, sighs, tears, and other things of this sort, the harmony should be full of sadness.[12]

In another place he writes,

Even in our times we see that music induces in us various passions in the way that it did in antiquity. For occasionally, it is observed, when some beautiful, learned, and elegant poem is sung by someone to the sound of some instrument, the listeners are greatly stirred and moved to do different things, such as to laugh, weep, or to similar actions.[13]

Girolamo Cardano, 1501–1576, Italian philosopher and mathematician

A song is related to music.[14]

Pierre de Ronsard, 1524–1585, leading poet of the original French Pléiade

And, if I am able, I will reinstitute the use of the lyre, which in our day has been revived in Italy: which lyre alone should, and has the power to infuse soulful expression into verse and can give it the right weight of grave earnestness.[15]

Pontus de Tyard, 1521–1605, French philosopher and member of the Pléiade

Music's purpose seems to be that of setting the word in such a fashion that anyone listening to it will become impassioned and carried away by the mood of the poet. The musician who knows how to deploy the solo voice to this end best attains his goal, in my opinion. Contrapuntal music most often brings to the ears only a lot of noise, from which you feel no vivid effect.[16]

---

12 Gioseffo Zarlino, *On the Modes*, trans. Vered Cohen (New Haven: Yale University Press, 1983)., 94ff. Later, in Ibid., 98, Zarlino gives specific rules for preventing 'barbarism' in assigning note values to words.

13 'Istitutioni,' II, 9, p. 75, quoted in Palisca, *Humanism*, 37ff.

14 Clement Miller, *Hieronymus Cardanus, Writings on Music* (American Institute of Musicology, 1973), 108.

15 François Lesure, *Musicians and Poets of the French Renaissance*, trans. Elio Gianturco (New York: Merlin Press, 1955), 56,

16 *Les Discours philosophiques* (Paris, 1587) quoted by Daniel Heartz, 'The Chanson in the Humanist Era,' in *Current Thought in Musicology* (Austin: University of Texas Press, 1976), 227.

These last two quotations by poets remind us that poetry was sung in performance, not spoken, from the time of ancient Greece through the Renaissance. This fact alone should have been known to the early musicologists and it should have alerted them in quoting Plato that if Plato spoke of 'words' or the 'song' it was simultaneously a melody. Therefore any reference to the words being the mistress of the harmony and rhythm, or that the harmony and rhythm must follow the words, makes sense in any period if one takes the meaning to be 'melody is the mistress of harmony and rhythm' or 'the harmony and rhythm must follow the melody.' Knowledge of centuries of performance practice in the field of poetry should have made that clear to the early musicologists.

Even if the early musicologists were unfamiliar with the fact that 'words' meant 'song' in the history of poetry, it remains curious that they interpreted 'word' literally to mean language alone—in view of the literature of the seventeenth century which they surely must have known. It seems clear that the original members of the Camerata understood Plato correctly. Giovanni Doni (1594–1647), writing of the meetings of the Camerata, recalls Giovanni Bardi's analysis of this very passage from Book III of Plato's *Republic*. It is very clear that Bardi, the Godfather of the Camerata, understood Plato to have been thinking of song, and not speech.

> Music is nothing else than the art and fashion of giving to words their proper time-value; since they should be *sung* either fast or slow, accordingly as they are short or long; and practical music is an arrangement of the words (which have been set by the poet into verses of various measure, according to their long or short syllables) such that the words, *sung by the human voice*, shall move, now fast, now slow, now in high tones, now in low, the *song* being either entrusted to *the voice* alone, or accompanied by instruments. *This is Plato's definition*, with which Aristotle and other learned men agree.[17]

This is corroborated by a letter of 1587 by Bardi himself to Caccini. Speaking of the same passage in Plato, Bardi says the sum of the elements mentioned here, which Bardi gives as speech, harmony and rhythm, is 'words well *sung*' [*parole ben cantate*].[18] If this is not clear, Bardi later makes a distinction between earlier polyphony and the goals of the Camerata in an expression very similar to Monteverdi's later 'First' and 'Second Practice.' Bardi writes,

> I say, then, that music as practiced today is divided into two parts. One is that called *counterpoint*; the other we shall call *the art of good singing*.[19]

We believe the correct aesthetic aim of this group of composers is unambiguously given in the Foreword of Monteverdi's *Il quinto libro de' madrigali* (1607), in words attributed to his brother. First, he quotes the passage in Plato we have been discussing.

---

17 Quoted in Donald N. Ferguson, *A History of Musical Thought* (New York: Appleton-Century-Crofts, 1948), 243.

18 Quoted in Claude Palisca, *The Florentine Camerata* (New Haven: Yale University Press, 1989), 92ff.

19 Ibid., 111.

> The *song* is composed of three things: the words, the harmony, and the rhythm.

We believe Monteverdi did not use the word 'melody' in place of 'words' here simply because, like Plato, he is considering the melody as synonymous with the words—it is *sung* poetry. That this had to be his intent is made clear in a letter of 1633 in which he proposes to write a book on the Second Practice. Here he constructs virtually the same sentence, but actually uses the word 'melody' instead of 'song.'

> I am dividing the book into three parts corresponding to the three aspects of *Melody*. In the first I discuss word-setting, in the second, harmony, and in the third, the rhythmic part.[20]

Returning to the Foreword of *Il quinto libro*, in the lines which come next it seems to us that Monteverdi makes this point perfectly clear: *Melody* is the most important element and it is to melody (with words) that harmony is the servant.

> This my brother will make apparent, knowing for certain that in a kind of composition such as this of his, *music turns on the perfection of the melody*, considered *from which point of view* the harmony, from being the mistress [as it was in polyphony], becomes the servant of the words, and the words the mistress of the harmony, to which way of thinking the Second Practice, or modern usage, tends.[21]

In case this is not clear enough, Monteverdi is even more explicit in the passage which follows.

> By First Practice [sixteenth-century polyphony] he understands the [Practice] that considers the harmony not commanded, but commanding, not the servant, but the mistress of the words …
>
> By Second Practice … he understands the [Practice] *that turns on the perfection of the melody*, that is, the one that considers harmony not commanding, but commanded, and makes the words [including melody] the mistress of the harmony.

Monteverdi concludes this passage by quoting Plato once again as saying, 'Does not music also turn on the perfection of the melody?'[22]

20 Letter to Giovanni Doni (October 22, 1633), quoted in Monteverdi, *The Letters*, 410. In the Monteverdi discussion here all italics are ours.

21 Strunk, *Source Readings*, 407ff.

22 Plato, *Gorgias*, 449D.

We read Monteverdi as saying here that it is the *melody with words* which is the mistress and, exactly as he says, the remaining elements of harmony and rhythm are the servant to these. He does *not* say music is the servant of the words.[23]

Finally, and most conclusive of all in our view, is evidence relative to the above mentioned book which Monteverdi said he was going to write on the subject of the Second Practice. The title which he says he will use is *Melody, or the Second Musical Practice.* Nothing could more clearly indicate that the emphasis was melody and not words.

It seems to us that the true meaning of Monteverdi's 'mistress' phrase is exactly the reverse of the meaning heretofore attributed to it by earlier musicologists. We read, as mentioned above, that it is the *melody with words* which is the mistress and, exactly as he says, the remaining elements of harmony and rhythm are the servant to these. And yet, Bukofzer read this very same passage in Monteverdi and concluded,

> Like the *Camerata,* [Monteverdi] laid down the axiom of the dominance of the *words* over the harmony.[24]

There is one portion of the Camerata discussions which may have been responsible for the early musicologists taking the 'words' of the Plato sentence literally and this was their occasional use of the word 'speaking.' Bukofzer, for example, introduces this topic as follows.

> The composers of the *Camerata* repeatedly insisted on the oratorical nature of the recitative—for example, Caccini, who called it 'speaking in music,' and Peri, who admitted that he tried 'to imitate a speaking person in song.'[25]

But it is clear that Caccini and Peri were using 'speaking' as a metaphor for 'communication,' as even today we have an expression, oxymoron though it is, 'Let the music speak for itself.'

The root need for such metaphors and oxymorons lies in a fact made clear by modern clinical brain research. The fact is that words by themselves carry no emotion. The emotional coloring is added, when we speak, by the right hemisphere—even though the right hemisphere itself is mute.[26] Metastasio, in a letter of 1749, makes this same observation.

---

23 In an interesting passage by Roger North, from later in the Baroque when the aria-recitative model had become standard, he preferred the original opera created by the Camerata in which everything was melody (which he calls 'air').

> Therefore I should choose to quit the *recitativo,* or at least the manner of it [today], and conduct the whole opera through a continued current of *ayre,* as in the elder Italian operas … and recitativos … were used. [Quoted in John Wilson, *Roger North on Music* (London: Novello, 1959), 264]

24 Bukofzer, *Music in the Baroque Era,* 33.

25 Ibid., 7.

26 While the early musicologists lacked the modern clinical brain research knowledge, many of their contemporary German understood the bicameral nature of man from personal observation. Wagner, for example, regularly used 'feeling' and 'understanding' exactly as I would say Right Hemisphere and Left Hemisphere.

> For as you know, as well as I, that the same words and sentiments may be uttered, according to the diversity of situation, in such a manner as to express either joy, sorrow, anger, or pity.[27]

This was so apparent to Galilei the he advised a singer to go to the theater, not for amusement, but to observe,

> when one quiet gentleman speaks with another, in what manner he speaks, how high or low his voice is pitched, with what volume of sound, with what sort of accents and gestures, and with what rapidity or slowness his words are uttered. Mark what difference obtains in all these things when one of them speaks with one of his servants, or one of these with another; observe the prince when he chances to be conversing with one of his subjects and vassals; when the petitioner who is entreating his favor; how the man infuriated or excited speaks; the married woman, the girl, the mere child, the clever harlot, the lover speaking to his mistress as he seeks to persuade her to grant his wishes, the man who laments, the one who cries out, the timid man, the man exultant with joy …
>
> When the ancient musician sang any poem whatever, he first considered very diligently the character of the person speaking: his age, his sex, with whom he was speaking, and the effect he sought to produce by this means; and these conceptions, previously clothed by the poet in chosen words suited to such a need, the musician then expressed in the tone [*tono*] and with the accents and gestures, the quantity and quality of sound, and the rhythm appropriate to that action and to such a person.[28]

The reader will notice, at the beginning of the second paragraph, that Galilei, refers to the Greek sung poetry tradition which was what the Camerata hoped to recreate. Once again we see that the goal is not speech, but song.

One might find some explanation for the early musicologists taking the 'words' in Plato as literal speech in the literature of the early Church upon which early musicology was centered. The Church had long held that in Church music it was the words which were important and not the music. It is interesting that Northbrook, after reviewing this early Church literature, adds his sixteenth-century Puritan advice that in singing church music one,

> when he sang he should but little alter his voice, so that he should be like rather unto one that readeth, than unto one that singeth.[29]

To return to Bukofzer's reference to Caccini and Peri and their use of the word 'speaking,' it is important to offer some amplification. Here, again, is Bukofzer's text:

27 Quoted in Burney, *Memoirs of the Life and Writings of the Abate Metastasio*, I, 326.

28 Quoted in Ibid., 318ff. See fn 20, 21 for Zarlino's shocked reaction to this suggestion.

29 John Northbrooke, *A Treatise Against Dicing, Dancing, Plays and Interludes* (1577) (London: The Shakespeare Society, 1843), 108ff.

> The composers of the *Camerata* repeatedly insisted on the oratorical nature of the recitative—for example, Caccini, who called it 'speaking in music,' and Peri, who admitted that he tried 'to imitate a speaking person in song.'

The Caccini phrase comes in context with a criticism of polyphony, which he says only offers delight but does not move the emotions of the listener. It is in reference to the strict rhythmic beat of the mathematics-based polyphony in which any rhythmic rubato was not allowed. But this is not the case with ordinary speech, in which we vary the pace of our speech according to the emotional intent. It was from this perspective that Caccini says he wishes to create a song which proceeds with a certain negligence, by which one 'could *almost* speak in tones.' Caccini's use of this phrase in no way alters the fact that he clearly says he is talking about music and song. Here is what Caccini actually wrote,

> Having thus seen that [polyphony] offered no pleasure beyond that which pleasant sounds could give—solely to the sense of hearing, since they could not move the mind without the words being understood—it occurred to me to introduce a kind of *music* in which one could almost speak in tones, employing in it (as I have said elsewhere) a certain noble negligence of *song*.[30]

Caccini makes a similar statement in his dedication to *Euridice* (1600).

> In this manner of *singing* I have used a certain neglect which I deem to have an element of nobility, believing that with it I have approached that much nearer to ordinary speech.[31]

This search for a new sense of freedom from the chains of the old arithmetic-based notational system must be seen as part of the new search for emotional expression which characterized the Baroque. A similar passage from England is found in a comment by John Playford in 1647.

> I call that the noble manner of singing, which is used without tying a man's self to the ordinary measure of time, making many times the value of the notes less by half, and sometimes more according to the conceit of the words; whence proceeds that excellent kind of singing with a graceful neglect.[32]

We might add, parenthetically, that we still have a long way to go with respect to the tyranny of the old medieval notational system. We recently heard an artist observe that she had spent the first half of her life learning how to sing in time and the second half of her life learning how to sing out of time.

In any case, Caccini calls it *singing*, not speech. It is clear he has in mind something relating to the style of speech, but in neither passage does he suggest his goal is that of Bukofzer's paraphrase, 'speaking in music.'

30 Giiulio Caccini, *Le Nuove Musiche*, ed. H. Wiley Hitchcock (Madison: A-R Editions, 1970), 44.

31 Strunk, *Source Readings*, 371.

32 John Playford, *An Introduction to the Skill of Music* [1674] (Ridgewood: Gregg Press, 1966), 46, 52.

The Peri phrase is found in the Foreword to the publication of *Euridice* (1601), the earliest surviving dramatic work set entirely to music. He is explaining to the reader of the score that since this was a theatrical work, 'it was therefore necessary to imitate speech in *song*.'[33] The important point here is that he is still calling the final result song, and not speech. To 'imitate speech in song,' is, of course, what opera has done ever since.

It is our view, then, that Bukofzer in particular misrepresented the actual views of the members of the Camerata. Indeed, Bukofzer seems rather sensitive about the Camerata (whom he calls 'a noisy group of literati') and their desire to turn music away from mathematics and toward feelings. Of their comments on emotions, Bukofzer writes,

> When the baroque composer spoke about affections, he referred to the extreme and violent ones.

Violent? Bukofzer uses this word several times, as in another place:

> The primary impulse came from the baroque desire to represent affections of violence.

It is our opinion that the word 'violence' was used during the seventeenth century only as a synonym for 'strong.' In Mersenne, for example, in a discussion of the conical bore of the bassoon he finds the conical bore 'renders their tones more violent' than those [instruments which have cylindrical bores].[34] No early writer describes bassoons, shawms and cornetts as 'violent' in the modern sense of the word, hence the word here would appear to refer only to a stronger sound, as compared to flutes, etc.

When Bukofzer says, 'The modern psychology of dynamic emotions did not yet exist in the baroque era,'[35] we have no idea what he was talking about. Modern science has established the fact that emotions are both genetic in origin and universal, which suggests they are very ancient to the species. Given the long period of development of man, it is very doubtful that seventeenth-century man measurably differed from modern man in emotional development.

In any case, it is very clear that the composers of the first opera of the seventeenth century wanted to make music communicate strong feelings to the audience, something which the combination of melody and words in polyphonic music did not do. Passionate (Italian!) speech, they had observed, did communicate feelings and so they used 'speech' as a metaphor to express the function they wished their music to serve. We believe this is exactly what they accomplished and that Robert Donnington was perfectly correct when he defined monody as, 'one actor's cry from the heart.'[36] Christoph Bernhard, in his singing treatise of 1649, supplies a remarkable range of feelings appropriate to this very style of singing.

---

33 Ibid., 373ff.

34 *Harmonie universelle* (Paris, 1636–7), Treatise Five, V, 32.

35 Bukofzer, *Music in the Baroque Era*, 5ff.

36 Robert Donnington, *The Interpretation of Early Music* (New York: Faber, 1964), 168. This scholar adds,

> Renaissance methods of [vocal improvisation] were carried into the early baroque music with very little change ... The effect of the [improvisation] remained essentially melodic.

> In the recitative style, one should take care that the voice is raised in moments of anger, and to the contrary dropped in moments of grief. Pain makes it pause; impatience hastens it. Happiness enlivens it. Desire emboldens it. Love renders it alert. Bashfulness holds it back. Hope strengthens it. Despair diminishes it. Fear keeps it down. Danger is fled with screams. If, however, a person faces up to danger, then his voice must reflect his daring and bravery.[37]

Bernhard is describing singing, not the words. On the evidence of the music they left, we doubt that their intention was ever anything other than expressing feelings through music.[38]

Accounts of performances in which it was not the words but the expressive and emotional power of the performance of the *music* which moved the listeners also form an important part of the background from with the Camerata developed. The first composers of opera were performers themselves. Judging by a description of Peri's singing, by the contemporary, Severo Bonini, their desire to create music which communicated stronger feelings to the listeners must have also been a logical extension of their own performance experience.

> A much learned singer and composer was Signor Jacopo Peri, who would have moved and brought to tears the hardest heart by singing his works.[39]

When it became their goal to reproduce the musical experience of the ancient Greeks, it is clear the Camerata wanted to make music convey stronger emotions than was possible in the polyphony they knew. This emphasis on the emotions was, for Palisca, the very hallmark of Baroque music.

> If we want to ascertain whether we have crossed the boundary into the baroque or out of it, there is no better test than to ask whether the expression of the affections is the dominant goal in fashioning a piece of music.[40]

The members of the Camerata numbered among their criticism of polyphony, both secular polyphony and Church music, that it merely sufficed to 'delight' the ear. By 1581 Galilei was clearly expressing the goals of the new style. 'True music,' he writes, has a primary purpose 'to express the passions' and, secondarily, 'to communicate these with equal force to the minds of mortals for their benefit and advantage.' The older polyphonic composers, with their 'inviolable laws,' he says, are 'directly opposed to the perfection of the true and

37 Quoted in Ellen Harris, 'Voices,' in *Performance Practice: Music after 1600* (New York: Norton, 1989), 110.

38 Charles Butler, *The Principles of Musik in Singing and Setting* [1636] (New York: Da Capo Press, 1970), 95, seems to allow the words to be altered to fit the melody.

> The numerous verses or Rhyme applied to the notes, the philosopher equalizes to the *Melody* itself, for resembling and moving manners and affections.

39 Quoted in Pirrotta and Povoledo, *Music and Theatre from Poliziano to Monteverdi*, 246.

40 Palisca, *Baroque Music*, 5.

best harmonies and melodies.'[41] Later he says the rules of polyphony were never intended to 'express the conceptions of the mind.'[42] Finally, he clearly states the goal of the Camerata.

> For [polyphony's] sole aim is to delight the ear, while that of ancient music is to induce in another the same passion that one feels oneself.[43]

In short order, the various composers were making similar statements of purpose. Cavalieri, in the preface to his *La rappresentatione di Anima* (1600) says his goal is to 'move listeners to different emotions, such as pity and joy, tears and laughter.'[44] Caccini, in his *Le Nuove Musiche*, writes that the goal of his solo songs was 'to move the affect of the soul.'[45] Later, he says the singer's duty is to understand the poet's conception and 'imitating them through affective music and expressing them through affective singing.'[46]

But, how did they arrive at a method to do this? It seems clear that the initial direction the Camerata took in quest of the ancient Greek experience was to attempt to create an imitation of what they knew of the Rhapsodist. This is explained by Jacopo Peri, in the Foreword to *Euridice* (1601). It was the Rhapsodist, in ancient Greece, who sang the 'heroic verses' which Peri mentions and his attempts to describe a style between speech and singing is identical to the descriptions of the Rhapsodists.

> Seeing that dramatic poetry was concerned and that it was therefore necessary to imitate speech in song (and surely no one ever spoke in song), I judged that the ancient Greeks and Romans (who, in the opinion of many, sang their tragedies throughout in representing them upon the stage) had used a harmony surpassing that of ordinary speech but falling so far below the melody of song as to take an intermediate form. And this is why we find their poems admitting the iambic verse, a form less elevated than the hexameter but said to be advanced beyond the confines of familiar conversation. For this reason, discarding every other manner of singing hitherto heard [today], I devoted myself wholly to seeking out the kind of imitation that the ancients assigned to singing and that they called 'diastematica' (that is, sustained or suspended) could in part be hastened and made to take an intermediate course, lying between the slow and suspended movements of song and the swift and rapid movements of speech, and that it could be adapted to my purpose (as they adapted it in reading poems and heroic verses).[47]

Peri is undoubtedly taking credit here for a consensus arrived at over long discussions by the entire group. Unfortunately he does not explain in more detail how the desire to imitate

41 Strunk, *Source Readings*, 306–7.

42 Ibid., 312.

43 Vincenzo Galilei, *Dialogo della musica antica e della moderna* (1581), quoted in Ibid., 317.

44 Quoted in Pirrotta and Povoledo, *Music and Theatre*, 241.

45 Caccini, *Le Nuove Musiche*, 45.

46 Ibid., 47.

47 Strunk, *Source Readings*, 374.

the Rhapsodist evolved into the melodic style of the first operas. He does describe the basis of this style, however, as follows:

> I knew likewise that in our speech some words are so intoned that harmony can be based upon them and that in the course of speaking it passes through many others that are not so intoned until it returns to another that will bear a progression to a fresh consonance.

The style which Peri describes here, and which was originally called *recitar cantando*,[48] appears to the eye as long note values appearing on the stressed syllables of important words, followed by connecting notes in smaller note values. This 'stop and go' appearance causes some to consider this as not being melody at all, but they are wrong. They are judging by the appearance to the eye, and not taking into account the performance in which the singer completed the melody by 'filling in' the long notes. It is apparent that the composers were leaving the long note values on important words for three reasons. First, to mark the important words visually; second, as places for the singers to add, by ornamentation or improvisation, the necessary additional emotional expressivity, and finally because it was felt this improvised expressivity could not be notated. Peri himself describes such a performance that he admired.

> This lady, who has always made my compositions seem worthy of her singing, adorns them not only with those groups and those long windings of the voice, simple and double, which the liveliness of her talent can invent at any moment (more to comply with the usage of our times than because she considers the beauty and force of our singing to lie in them), but also with those elegances and graces that cannot be written or, if written, cannot be learned from writing.[49]

Caccini, in the Foreword of his *Le Nuove Musiche*, begins by explaining that the purpose of his commentary is to address the style of ornamentation and improvisation appropriate to his songs. His chief concern is that he has found some singers using ornaments more suited to instrumental music and others using vocal ornaments indiscriminately. Nevertheless, Caccini is quick to add,

> That we realize how necessary for the musicians a certain judgment is, which sometimes must prevail over [rules of] art ...[50]

and, further,

> Indeed, there are many things used in good singing style that are written in one way but, to be more graceful, are effected in quite another.[51]

48 Nino Pirrotta, 'Temperaments and Tendencies in the Florentine Camerata,' *The Musical Quarterly* 40, no. 2 (April, 1954): 187, http://www.jstor.org/stable/739669.

49 Strunk, *Source Readings*, 375.

50 Caccini, *Le Nuove Musiche*, 50.

51 Ibid.

Caccini provides numerous examples of the kind of improvisation or ornamentation he considers appropriate to this style. Several times he specifies that this must be done for the purpose of moving the emotions of the listener. In one such case, he also endorses rubato. The examples he has given, he says,

> may serve as models from which may be recognized similar places in the pieces where [ornamentation/improvisation] will be the most necessary according to the affects of the words. Whence may appear that noble manner which, not submitting to strict time but often halving the value of the notes according to the ideas of the text, give rise to that kind of singing with so-called 'negligence.'[52]

The term Caccini uses for rubato, 'negligence' [*sprezzatura*], had been introduced to express the quality of nonchalance which a noble should possess by Castiglione in his famous sixteenth century *Book of the Courtier*.

> But having thought many times already about how this grace is acquired (leaving aside those who have it from the stars), I have found quite a universal rule ... and that is to avoid affectation in every way possible ... and [to pronounce a new word perhaps] to practice in all things a certain *sprezzatura*, so as to conceal all art and make whatever is done or said appear to be without effort and almost without any thought about it.[53]

A similar reference to such customary rubato is found in Severo Bonini, *Affetti spirituali a dua voci* (Venice, 1615).

> When the singer sometimes sings alone ... he will be able to beat time by himself, so that he can, according to the needs of the words, sing quickly or slowly, now sustaining, now quickening the beat, for thus demands the Florentine style.[54]

Monteverdi similarly, in his *Madrigali guerrieri et amorosi* (Venice, 1638) speaks of the voice following 'her lament, which is sung to the time of the heart's feeling [*affetto del animo*], and not to that of the hand.'

Finally, Caccini uses this term again in a publication of 1614 as part of some observations he offers singers. Here he says *sprezzatura* relieves a song of 'a certain restricted narrowness and dryness and makes it pleasant, free, and airy.'[55] More interesting here are the recommendations for improvisation related to 'moving the emotions of the listener.'

---

52 Ibid., 55. Curiously, Curt Sachs, in *Our Musical Heritage* (Englewood Cliffs: Prentice-Hall, 1947), 172, gives this an incorrect and negative translation, 'a noble disdain of melody.'

53 Baldassare Castiglione, *The Book of the Courtier*, trans. Charles Singleton (New York: Norton, 1959), 43.

54 Quoted in Donnington, *The Interpretation of Early Music*, 641.

55 Giulio Caccini, *Nuove Musiche e Nuova Maniera di Scriverle*, ed. H. Wiley Hitchcock (Madison: A-R Editions, 1978).

> It is advisable for him who professes to sing alone well, with expression, to know three things. There are: emotion, variety of emotions, and *sprezzatura.*
>
> Emotion, in a singer, is simply that by the power of certain notes and varied stresses, together with modification of the dynamics, and expression of the words and the meaning [*concetto*], projected through song, acts to move the emotions of him who is listening.
>
> Variety of emotions is that transition from one emotion to another, by the same means, the singer being guided by the words and meaning from one moment to another. These must be carefully observed so that, so to speak, the bridegroom and the widower are not clothed alike.

From these quotations it should be apparent to the reader how dependent this music was on the improvised additions by the singer. Nothing is more unfair to these composers than to judge this music as it appears to the eye.

On the other hand, we should not be surprised to find so much improvisation in view of our knowledge of the extensive improvisation which remained a part of opera well into the nineteenth century. Nino Pirrotta speaks of the frottola being 'refreshed, perhaps, by renewed contact with popular music,' and adds,

> In Rome and Naples—and indeed to a certain extent throughout Italy—singers themselves began to decorate this music with elaborate embellishments; this technique of improvisation even began to invade performances of madrigals and sacred music.[56]

Palisca adds that both 'opera and chamber arias of the early seventeenth century are descendants of this improvised singing of poetry.'[57]

Neither should we be surprised at the extent of improvisation in Roman church music throughout the Middle Ages and Renaissance, even though musicology seems to regard this as a closely held secret. After all it was only in the late Middle Ages that instrumentalists even began to *read* music.

The composers associated with the Camerata set out to recreate the specific musical practice of the ancient Greek Rhapsodists and lyric poets. We still don't know enough about the original Greek music to know if they succeeded, but we can clearly see that they achieved something much more important. It was these composers more than any others who brought down the curtain on a one-thousand-year period during which music was thought to be a branch of mathematics. In returning music to it real purpose, the expression of feelings, the Camerata composers did recreate an important aspect of the ancient Greek philosophy of aesthetics in music.

56 Pirrotta, 'Temperaments and Tendencies in the Florentine Camerata,' 174.

57 Palisca, *Baroque Music*, 22.

3 AESTHETIC VIEWS OF ITALIAN MUSICIANS

ON THE AESTHETICS OF MUSIC

To Italy goes the credit for the birth of the Baroque, the central feature of which was a movement to return music to its natural purpose, to express feeling, and draw to an end the long period influenced by the old medieval Scholastic dogma that made music a branch of mathematics. It is somewhat ironic, therefore, that one finds in Italy, not only much progressive thinking, but among composers of the Church many who refused to let go of the Renaissance.

We can see how strong these conservative feelings were in a little squabble in Bologna in the middle of the seventeenth century. This incident began with the hiring of Don Mauritio Cazzati as *maestro di cappella* at the cathedral, S. Petronio in 1657,[1] and his institution of a series of reforms.[2] This effort at reform was met, by the faithful members of the capella under the leadership of the deputy organist, Arresti, with resistance, resignations and remonstrations. Among the latter is a *Dialogo*, a document circulated for the purpose of personally attacking Cazzati. Among the criticisms, some are especially enlightening regarding contemporary practice and values.

> He writes sophisticated introductions to the 'Gloria,' 'Credo,' and 'Laudate Pueri,' which are not used in most chapels;
>
> He uses vocal soloists when he has 80 singers there;
>
> He teaches neither singing nor playing nor counterpoint, and never goes to the school, as is his duty, so that my son finds a way of life and a moral code which is totally unacceptable in this city;
>
> He does not know how to place or order the choirs;
>
> He does not know how to produce the voice and is afraid to sing without the organ, violone and trombone;
>
> He likes to take the credit for other people's compositions and distribute them as his own, even in printed editions; as he did ... when he distributed books around the place which said 'Music by Mauritio Cazzati,' when most of the compositions had been written by Don Lorenzo Perti;
>
> He does not know how to teach the sopranos, who are necessary for the service of the church—which it is his duty to do—and concerning this, he has never crossed the threshold of the school to go and teach them;

1 This 'polemic' is discussed thoroughly in Brett, *Music and Ideas in Seventeenth Century Italy*.

2 Most of these dwelt with the dress and discipline of the singers and are quoted in Ibid., 58ff.

> Finally, he uses Bergamasks, Chaconnes and Ruggieri [as opposed to instrumental canzoni], and calls them Ritornelli.

What followed was a series of publications of tracts by both Cazzati defending himself and others attacking him. The attacks centered on criticism of Cazzati's own compositions for the church, which were made the object of a detailed search for examples where Cazzati did not follow the rules of sixteenth-century church polyphony. Nowhere is this more clearly stated, than in one attack which summarized,

> That the whole cantilena is composed without mode, without reason, with little grace, less elegance, and is bereft of the laws and precepts of the respected Masters, from which one should not depart if one aims to follow the good rules of this mathematical science.

Not to 'follow the rules' was considered by such conservatives to be an indication that the composer was 'lacking in moral and intellectual virtue.' But there was a fundamental aesthetic question raised as well. One measure in Cazzati's composition was attacked for having a sixth above the bass.

> What melodious delight can a miserable sixth, devoid of counterpoint so that I find myself hissing, ever bring to the ear of the listener? Is it enough that music, in order to be beautiful, merely delights the sense of him who listens to it?

The implication here is that the intellectual satisfaction found in hearing the rules followed takes precedence to mere delight of the senses. The opinion was further strengthened by the suggestion that 'the rules' were of divine inspiration, if not divine origin. To these claims, Cazzati answered,

> However, you know, O reader, that the rules of music are not divine precepts, but human opinions and diverse, as may be seen from the printed books: and many virtuosi with printed works to their credit, have claimed to be not in error for the reason that it is necessary to see whether a composition is pleasing. The one which is pleasing, then, can be said to be composed according to the rules; and the one which is not pleasing, even if it be composed in accordance with all the rules, is not good since it displeases—because music is made in order to please and not to displease.[3]

Among the writings of the Italian musicians of the Baroque one also finds comments which reflect the great changes taking place in the practice of music. We have seen, in a previous volume, Italian humanists already in the sixteenth century condemning the old Church polyphonic style. Nevertheless, it is somewhat surprising to find Agostino Agazzari implying as early as 1607 that this style is 'no longer in use,' for as we know it would in fact continue to be used in church music until well into the eighteenth century.

---

3 Ibid., 107.

> That kind of music is no longer in use, both because of the confusion and babel of the words, arising from the long and intricate imitations, and because it has no grace, for, with all the voices singing, one hears neither period nor sense, these being interfered with and covered up by imitations; indeed, at every moment, each voice has different words, a thing displeasing to men of competence and judgment ... Such compositions are good according to the rules of counterpoint, but they are at the same time faulty according to the rules of music that is true and good.[4]

In this same work a comment by Agazzari reflects the growing preference for string instruments. This change in taste, which brought to an end centuries of domination by winds in art music, was due in part to the advance in the quality of the Italian manufacture of string instruments during the seventeenth century and in part because of the interest of the humanists in the ancient Greek accounts of singing accompanied by strings. Of the wind instruments,

> I shall say nothing, because they are not used in good and pleasing consorts, because of their insufficient union with the stringed instruments and because of the variation produced in them by the human breath, although they are introduced in great and noisy consorts.[5]

At the same time, during the second half of the seventeenth century the winds were going through a dramatic transformation, with the retirement of nearly all the Renaissance instruments and their replacement by the modern instruments. Clearly a long period ensued during which makers struggled with improvements and players struggled with having to learn entirely new instruments, resulting in complaints about such things as intonation. A typical example is found in Charles Burney, who maintains he heard Alessandro Scarlatti say, 'My son, you know I hate wind instruments, they are never in tune.'[6]

Another change one finds in the highest levels of society during the Baroque concerns the role of the noble. In the Renaissance the ability to perform was considered a mark of culture, but during the Baroque the noble generally became only the employer of musicians. Gasparini takes it for granted that the noble no longer has time for music. He makes this observation while reflecting that most experts consider three things necessary for the making of a musician: resolve, application and a good teacher. But even more important than these, he says, is a natural disposition. This, he says, is a gift of God and nature and cannot be otherwise obtained at any price.[7]

---

4 Agostino Agazzari, *On Playing upon a Bass in ... Consort*, quoted in Strunk, *Source Readings*, 430. As is our custom in these volumes, with regard to theoretical treatises we quote only passages which reflect on aesthetics and lack space to include discussions which are purely technical in scope.

5 Ibid., 425.

6 Quoted in Donnington, *The Interpretation of Early Music*, 548.

7 Francesco Gasparini, *The Practical Harmonist at the Harpsichord* [1708], ed. Franks S. Stillings (New Haven: Yale School of Music, 1963), 9.

> There are an infinite number of nobles, gentlemen, ladies, and princes, who feel an inclination toward music, but should they start in, it is certain that, because of their customary preoccupation with studies of literature or other gentlemanly exercises, a generation, so to speak, would not suffice them to arrive at the playing of four notes.[8]

Following the aesthetic revolution which returned music to its natural purpose of expressing feeling, and which ushered in the period we call the Baroque, a consensus seemed to emerge in which music was classified according to the categories of church, theater and chamber. This classification served as a means of discussing the aesthetic role of the various elements of music. An example can be seen in Tosi, who argues for entirely separate aesthetic values according to whether the performance takes place in a church, the theater or in the chamber. His most detailed discussion of these distinctions occurs when he discusses the recitative.

> The recitative is of three kinds and ought to be taught in three different manners.
>
> The first, being used in churches, should be sung as becomes the sanctity of the place, which does not admit those wanton graces of a lighter style; but requires some *Messa di Voce*, appoggiaturas and a noble majesty throughout …
>
> The second style is the theatrical, which … cannot be beautiful, if not expressed with that decorum with which princes speak, or those who know how to speak to princes.
>
> The third, which according to the opinion of the most judicious, touches the heart more than the other two, is called *Recitativo di Camera*. This requires a more peculiar skill, by reason of the words, which being, for the most part, adapted to move the strongest passions of the soul, require the teacher to give the student such a lively impression of them, that he may seem to be affected with them himself.[9]

The enormous popularity of the new opera form during the Baroque created an entirely new social phenomenon, the prima donna. Benedetto Marcello gives us a humorous view of the social status of the prima donna in his satirical account of *Theater in the Modern Style*, of 1720. He observes that the composer must not object to the great fees paid the singers and must be content if he himself is paid no more than the trained bear. Also on the street he must walk a step behind the singers, especially the *castrati*. All this, because 'his own reputation, credit, and interests are in their hands.'[10]

In another passage, which reflects the new style of upper and lower line dominance, his recommendation that an impresario can economize on double basses is intended to be a humorous jab at the numerous contemporary theorists who stressed the importance of the bass line. Curiously, he adds, the double basses must be used for tuning.[11]

8 Ibid., 10.

9 P. F. Tosi, *Observations on the Florid Song* (London: Wilcox, 1743), V.

10 Benedetto Marcello, *Il treatro alla moda*, quoted in Strunk, *Source Readings*, 527ff. Marcello (b. 1686) was one of the most gifted composers of the Italian Baroque.

11 Ibid., 530.

Finally, Marcello makes a subtle reference to the eighteenth century tendency for a court to expect its musicians to also work in other non-musical jobs (even Haydn had non-musical duties). Marcello recommends that in the program of an opera, the acknowledgment of the composer should read,

> The music is by the ever most celebrated Signor N. N., conductor of the orchestra, of concerts, of chamber concerts, dancing master, fencing master, etc., etc., etc., etc.[12]

The courts, nevertheless, were where the money was and Tosi offered singers the advice that they take advantage of visiting the many courts of Europe. Visit, he warns, but don't stay,

> for chains, though of gold, are still chains; and they are not all made of that precious metal. Besides, the several inconveniences of disgrace, mortifications, uncertainty and, above all, hindrance of study [are associated with serving a court].[13]

One reason to travel, known to every century, was the hope that the 'grass was greener on the other side of the fence.' Thus, Alessandro Scarlatti, in a letter of 1705 regarding his son, Domenico, announced,

> I am sending him away from Rome, because Rome offers no roof to Music, which lives here like a beggar.[14]

And, of course, the grass was not always greener, as Geminiani observed of London.

> When I first came to London, which was thirty-four years ago, I found music in so thriving a state, that I had all the reason imaginable to suppose the growth would be suitable to the excellency of the soil.
>
> But I have lived to be most miserably disappointed; for though it cannot be said that there was any want of encouragement, that encouragement was ill bestowed.
>
> The hand was more considered than the head; the performance than the composition; and hence it followed, that instead of laboring to cultivate a taste, which seemed to be all that was wanting, the public was content to nourish insipidity.[15]

---

12 Ibid., 531.

13 Tosi, *Observations*, VIII, xii.

14 Alessandro Scarlatti, letter to prince Ferdinand de' Medici, May 30, 1705, quoted in Piero Weiss, *Letters of Composers Through Six Centuries* (Philadelphia: Chilton, 1967), 58.

15 Francesco Geminiani, *A Treatise of Good Taste in the Art of Musick* [1749] (New York: Da Capo Press, 1969), 4.

ON THE PURPOSE OF MUSIC

The far-reaching accomplishment by the late sixteenth-century Italian humanists was the re-establishment of music's most natural purpose, the expression of feeling. They effected this through their philosophical criticism of the old mathematics-based polyphony and by creating modern opera as a demonstration of their aims. This purpose is clearly expressed, in 1600, by Emilio de' Cavalieri in the preface to his *Rappresentazione di Anima, et di Corpo*, where he states that his purpose is to 'move the listener to different emotions, as pity, joy, tears, and laughter, and other similar emotions.'[16] To help make this possible, by way of aiding the listener's hearing the singer, he recommends placing the orchestra behind a curtain and requests they perform without improvisation. It is particularly interesting that he recommends the orchestra members changing instruments, according to the *affetti*, a practice which would explain the very large list of instruments associated with Monteverdi's *Orfeo*.

Also with respect to hearing the singer, Cavalieri recommends performance in a hall seating no more than one thousand! Otherwise,

> If it is presented in very large halls it is not possible to hear all the words; and the singer would have to force his voice, which lessens the emotional effect; also, so much music with the words not being audible becomes tiresome.[17]

With regard to Cavalieri's preference to hide the orchestra behind a curtain, we should mention that Marco da Gagliano, in the preface to his *Dafne* of 1608, takes a different view.

> Make sure that the instruments that are to accompany the solo voices are located so that they can see the faces of the performers, on order that by hearing each other better they may perform together.[18]

Monteverdi, in 1638, makes an interesting general comment about the communication of emotions in present and past music.

> I consider the principal passions or emotions of the soul to be three, namely, anger, serenity, and humility. The best philosophers affirm this; the very nature of our voice, with its high, low and middle ranges, shows it; and the art of music clearly manifests it in these three terms: agitated, soft and moderate. I have not been able to find an example of the agitated style in the works of past composers, but I have discovered many of the soft and moderate types.[19]

---

16 Emilio de' Cavalieri, *Rappresentazione di Anima, et di Corpo*, Preface, quoted in Carol MacClintock, *Readings in the History of Music in Performance* (Bloomington: Indiana University Press, 1979), 183.

17 Ibid., 184.

18 Quoted in Carol MacClintock, *Readings*, 190.

19 Monteverdi, *Madrigali guerrieri ed amorosi* (1638), preface, quoted in Sam Morgenstern, *Composers on Music* (New York: Pantheon, 1956), 22.

Angelo Berardi probably said it best, when he observed in 1681, 'Music is the ruler of the passions of the soul.'[20]

For the goals of the humanists to be manifested, of course, the first responsibility rested with the composer. Thus, Marcello writes of a letter of 1711 that he has tried in his music to lend 'more expression to the words' and refers to the earlier polyphonic style as having a 'natural sterility.'[21] Alessandro Scarlatti (1660–1725) expressed the same concern in a letter to his patron, prince Ferdinand de' Medici. Speaking of his *Il Gran Tamerlano* (1706), Scarlatti relates that he tried to achieve, 'naturalness and beauty, together with the expression of the passion with which the characters speak.'[22] The latter, he said, 'is the very most principal consideration and circumstance for moving and leading the mind of the listener to the diversity of sentiments that the various incidents of the plot of the drama unfold.'

Agazzari, in his treatise on concerti, stresses that the instruments of the accompaniment must also share the responsibility of expressing feelings. 'When there are words,' he says, 'they must be clothed with that suitable harmony which arouses or conveys some passion.'[23]

The great opera librettist, Metastasio, had begun to worry, in a letter of 1747, about the effectiveness of rapidly changing emotions in opera.

> The audience cannot interest themselves, as you would wish, in the agitations of your personages, because there is not sufficient time allowed to render them either hateful or amiable. If the mind of a spectator is removed from its usual temperament and tranquility, the interest does not continue long enough to be remembered in the next scene: so that it becomes torpid and unwilling to be pleased, even to that degree of nausea which soon comes on for those very beauties, which, otherwise, might successfully have solicited and seduced.[24]

In a letter of 1749 to Adolfo Hasse, concerning the opera *Attilio Regolo*, Metastasio reflects the fact that composers were beginning to write out symbols of feelings formerly left to the singers.

> I should hope from such hands as yours, that a recitative always accompanied by instruments, would not be such a tiresome thing as it usually is, from others ... You likewise so well know how to perfect the art, by the judicious and alternate use of *pianos* and *fortes*, by *rinforzandos*, by *staccatos*, *slurs*, accelerating and retarding the measure, *arpeggios*, shakes, *sostenutos* ...[25]

In the same year, Francesco Geminiani also complains that the soul of the expression should lie in the composition itself, not in the additions of the singer.

20 Angelo Berardi, *Ragionamenti Musicali* (Bologna, 1681), 87.

21 Benedetto Marcello, letter to Jacopo Perti, October 4, 1711, quoted in Weiss, *Letters of Composers*, 62.

22 Quoted in Palisca, *Baroque Music*, 236ff.

23 Agostino Agazzari, *On Playing Upon a Bass*, 426.

24 Letter to Abate Pasquini, in Burney, *Memoirs of the Life and Writings of the Abate Metastasio*, I, 191.

25 Letter to Adolfo Hasse, 1749, in Ibid., I, 326.

> What is commonly called good taste in singing and playing, has been thought for some years past to destroy the true melody, and the intention of their composers. It is supposed by many that a real good taste cannot possibly be acquired by any rules of art; it being a peculiar gift of nature, indulged only to those who have naturally a good ear: And as most flatter themselves to have this perfection, hence it happens that he who sings or plays, thinks of nothing so much as to make continually some favorite Passages or Graces, believing that by this means he shall be thought to be a good performer, not perceiving that playing in good taste doth not consist of frequent Passages, but in expressing with strength and delicacy the intention of the composer. This expression is what every one should endeavor to acquire and it may be easily obtained by any person, who is not too fond of his own opinion.[26]

Regarding the music itself, Tosi, in his treatise on singing, stresses in several places that the singer should only sing the *best* music. The best music, he observes, has the capacity to 'instruct the student, perfect the skillful, and delight the listener.'[27] Tosi had a distinct preference for the slower expressive music of the earlier Baroque opera and thus advises singers to tell composers that they want to sing, not dance.[28]

Tosi's comment that singers should sing and not dance, is a reflection of the fact that Italian opera, particularly in Venice, had become as much an entertainment form as an art form, or as a visitor in 1729 gave its purpose, 'to tickle the ears.'

> Care has been taken that none of these famous singers should be disfigured with a beard; however, their smooth faces with their shrill and effeminate voice seem to be something out of character, when they make their appearance on the stage like warlike heroes, animating their troops to second their bravery. But we must observe that operas are not calculated to please the judgment, but to tickle the ear; so that propriety of characters is as little to be expected in these pieces, as sublime and poetical language.[29]

Perhaps only because opera had become an entertainment instead of an art, can one understand a comment in a letter of Abate Conti to Madame de Caylus, in 1727, that 'Vivaldi has produced three operas in less than three months.'[30] Whatever is the truth of that contention, it is clear that Vivaldi had become responsive to the relationship of his operas and the public. In a letter of 1737 he expresses his concern that poor ticket sales would constitute a risk to his reputation.[31]

Ultimately, much of the responsibility for the communication of emotions in music falls to the performer. If there is still a reader somewhere who is under the impression that Baroque

26 Geminiani, *A Treatise of Good Taste in the Art of Musick*, 2.

27 Tosi, *Observations*, VII, xxiv.

28 Ibid., VII, xxxiv.

29 J. G. Keysler, *Travels* (London, 1756), III, 262.

30 Kendall, *Vivaldi*, 129.

31 A. Cavicchi, 'Inediti nell' episolario Vivaldi-Bentivoglio,' in *Nuova Rivista Musicale Italiana*, I (May/June, 1967), 55ff. In another letter [Ibid., 77], Vivaldi adds, 'whoever takes away my honor may take away my life.'

music was mechanical and boring, perhaps this eyewitness description of Corelli will make him wonder if he has been misinformed.

> I never met with any man that suffered his passions to hurry him away so much whilst he was playing on the violin as the famous Arcangelo Corelli, whose eyes will sometimes turn as red as fire; his countenance will be distorted, his eyeballs roll as in an agony, and he gives in so much to what he is doing that he doth not look like the same man.[32]

Just as this description seems very modern to us, so does the prescription for achieving this level of communication offered by the great Baroque violinist, Francesco Geminiani.

> These extraordinary emotions are indeed most easily excited when accompanied with words; and I would besides advise, as well the composer as the performer, who is ambitions to inspire his audience to be first inspired himself, which he cannot fail to be if he chooses a work of genius, if he makes himself thoroughly acquainted with all its beauties; and if while his imagination is warm and glowing he pours the same exalted spirit into his own performance.[33]

The great organist, Girolamo Frescobaldi, reminds the student that the source of the emotions is found in the music itself.

> Since it also seems that many may have neglected the practice of studying the score, I wished to point out that in these things, which do not seem to be governed by the rules of counterpoint, one must first of all seek the feeling of the passage and the aim of the author concerning the effect on the ear, and the way in which one should try to play them.[34]

Frescobaldi mentions the importance of studying the score again in his *Fiori musicali*, where he suggests this practice separates the 'true gold of the *virtuosi* from the actions of the ignorant.'[35]

Marco da Gagliano, in the preface to his *Dafne* (1608), observes that the singer finds these feelings in the words, not in the instructions by the composer.

> The scene of Apollo's lament should be sung with the greatest possible emotion; at the same time the singer should take care to make a crescendo when the words demand it.[36]

Giovanni Bonachelli, in 1642, adds the interesting suggestion that even the tempo is adjusted according to the emotions of the words.

32 Oliver Strunk, 'François Raguenet, Comparison between the French and Italian Music (1702),' *The Musical Quarterly* 32, no. 3 (1946): 419fn., doi:10.1093/mq/XXXII.3.411

33 Geminiani, *Treatise of Good Taste*, 4.

34 Girolamo Frescobaldi, 'Capricci fatti sopra diversi soggetti,' quoted in MacClintock, *Readings*, 135.

35 Quoted in Ibid., 136.

36 Quoted in Ibid., 192ff.

> First they must be concerted together, and the feeling [*affetti*] of the words and the speed must be observed, and especially in the reciting styles, or representative, as others say, and in accordance with the feeling one must guide the beat, sensing it now fast, now slow, according to the occasion, now liveliness, and now languor, as indeed anyone will easily know immediately who possesses the fine manner of singing.[37]

Tosi, although writing a treatise on vocal technique, was never so passionate as when he spoke of 'heart.'

> Oh! how great a master is the heart! Confess it, my beloved singers, and gratefully admit, that you would not have arrived at the highest rank of the profession if you had not been its scholars; admit, that in a few lessons from it, you learned the most beautiful expressions, the most refined taste, the most noble action, and the most exquisite graces: Admit (though it be hardly credible) that the heart corrects the defects of nature, since it softens a voice that's harsh, betters an indifferent one, and perfects a good one: Admit, when the heart sings you cannot dissemble, nor has truth a greater power of persuading. And, lastly, do you convince the world that from the heart alone you have learned that *Je ne sçai quoy*, that pleasing charm, that so subtly passes from vein to vein, and makes its way to the very soul.[38]

One composer who was particularly sensitive to the listener, with respect to the new emphasis on the expression of emotions, was Monteverdi. In a letter of 1617, he recommends, for a court theatrical production, first of all a sinfonia to prepare the minds of the audience.[39] In another letter regarding a court theatrical work, he proposes that a character speak in a soft voice, which 'will give me a chance to introduce to the senses a new kind of music, different from what has gone before.'[40]

ON PERFORMANCE PRACTICE

The new emphasis on feeling in performance at the beginning of the seventeenth century may have helped bring a new respect for the purpose of rehearsal. In a letter of 1607, Monteverdi explains that he is sending the music to a singer in advance,

> so that he can rehearse it and get a firm grasp of the melody together with the other gentlemen singers, because it is very difficult for a singer to perform a part which he has not first practiced, and greatly damaging to the composition itself, as it is not completely understood on being sung for the first time.[41]

37 Giovanni Bonachelli, *Corona di sacri gigli a una, due, tre, quattro, e cinque voci* (Venice, 1642), preface.

38 Tosi, *Observations*, IX, xliv.

39 Letter to Alessandro Striggio (January 6, 1617), quoted in Monteverdi, *The Letters*, 126.

40 Letter to Alessandro Striggio (May 22, 1627), quoted in Ibid., 318.

41 Letter to Annibale Iberti (July 28, 1607), quoted in Ibid., 51.

A letter of 1620 gives some indication of what he meant by sufficient rehearsal.

> Now consider, Your Lordship: what do you think can be done when more than four hundred lines, which have to be set to music are still lacking? I can envisage no other result than bad singing of the poetry, bad playing of the instruments, and bad musical ensemble. These are not things to be done hastily, as it were; and you know from *Arianna* that after it was finished and learned by heart, [then!] five months of strenuous rehearsal took place.[42]

If for no other reason, the context of the rehearsal must have changed dramatically due to the new sense of freedom in time, something which followed naturally from the emphasis on feeling and something impossible under the rigid proportional time system of the old polyphonic style. Already in 1615, in a letter of Monteverdi, we find a new criteria for tempo. In sending the music for a court ballet, he cautions that the works must be conducted 'with a beat suitable to the character of the melodies.'[43] In the same year, Frescobaldi was even more explicit in associating both tempo and rubato with the expression of the text.

> I well know how performers like to indulge in impressive ornaments and many passages. Therefore I take the liberty of adding the following observations to these, my modest products, which I herewith publish …
>
> These pieces should not be played to a strict beat any more than modern madrigals which, though difficult, are made easier by taking the beat now slower, now faster, and by even pausing altogether in accordance with the expression and meaning of the text.[44]

By the end of the Baroque, Tosi was becoming alarmed on hearing singers alter the tempo solely for the reason of engaging in virtuoso improvisation.

> Even among the professors of the first rank there are few, but what are almost insensibly deceived into an irregularity, or hastening of time, and often of both …
>
> I do not advise a student to imitate several of the Moderns in their manner of singing arias, it is from their neglect of keeping time, which ought to be inviolable, and not sacrificed to their beloved [ornamentation].[45]

One of Tosi's chief objections to the singer delaying time to improvise was that at that moment, since the accompaniment stops, there is suddenly an absense of harmony.

On the other hand, lesser disruptions of tempo, which we call today rubato, were not only permitted by Tosi, but were considered as a characteristic of good taste.

---

42 Letter to Alessandro Striggio (January 9, 1620), quoted in Ibid., 160.

43 Letter to Annibale Iberti (November 21, 1615), quoted in Ibid., 108.

44 Girolamo Frescobaldi (1583–1643), *Toccatas and Partitas*, Book I (1615), quoted in Morgenstern, *Composers on Music*, 24.

45 Tosi, *Observations*, VII, xviiff.

> Whoever does not know how to steal time in singing ... is destitute of the best taste and greatest knowledge.
>
> The stealing of time, in the [adagio] is an honorable theft in one that sings better than others, provided he makes a restitution with ingenuity.[46]
>
> ......
>
> [A singer] wants that which teaches to anticipate the time, knowing where to lose it again; and, which is still more charming, to know how to lose it, in order to recover it again.[47]

We also see in a comment by Tosi a reflection of an earlier use of the Italian terms to reflect style, rather than just tempo as familiar to us today. He recommends one should imitate the *Cantabile* of the [early Baroque singers] and the *Allegro* of the Moderns.[48]

While it is our belief that dynamic variety has always existed in performance, the appearance of the music to the eye notwithstanding, one nevertheless senses a new enthusiasm in the discussion of this topic. Scipione Maffei, for example, observed in 1711,

> It is common knowledge among lovers of music that one of the chief methods by which the expert in that art contrive the secret of bringing particular delight to their listeners, is the piano and forte in subject and answer, or the gradual diminishing of the sound little by little, and the sudden return to the full volume of the instrument; which recourse is used frequently and with wonderful effect, in the great concerts of Rome.[49]

Fantini, in 1638, mentions one of the dynamic effects most common to the period.

> It must be pointed out that wherever notes of one, two, or of four beats' length are found, they should be held in a singing fashion, by starting softly, making a crescendo until the middle of the note, and making a diminuendo on the second half until the end of the beat, so that it may hardly be heard.[50]

On the Manners of Singers

It must have been difficult for a singer to please Tosi, even with respect to stage appearance. In general his concern seemed to be that the singer not distract the listener's attention from the music. First, he clearly objected to a cold demeanor on stage.

---

46 Ibid., IX, xliff.

47 Ibid., IX, lxiii.

48 Ibid., VI, xxi.

49 Scipione Maffei, 'Nuova Invenzione d'un Gravecembalo,' in *Giornale dei Letterati d'Italia* (Venice, 1711), V, 144.

50 Quoted in Alan Lumsden, 'Woodwind and Brass,' in *Performance Practice: Music after 1600* (New York: Norton, 1989), 83.

> From the cold indifference perceived in many singers, one would believe that the science of music implored their favor, to be received by them as their most humble servant.[51]

But, on the other hand, too much emphasis on stage appearance was also a source of objection.

> Singers who have nothing but outward appearance, pay a debt to the eyes which it owes to the ears.[52]

Tosi was attentive to the demeaner of his students in every respect, including their personal associations.

> Let the singer shun low and disreputable company, but, above all, such as abandon themselves to scandalous liberties. [Avoid teachers, who] though excellent in this art, whose behavior is vulgar.[53]

No doubt every teacher coached his students on the fine points of court etiquette. An interesting passage in Tosi concerns the problem of dealing with a request to sing for free.

> A discreet person will never use such affected expressions as 'I cannot sing today—I have a cold.' I admit, on certain conjunctures, the pretext is not only suitable, but even necessary; for, to speak the truth, the indiscreet parsimony of some, who would hear music for thanks only, goes so far, that they think a master is immediately obliged to obey them *gratis*, and that the refusal is an offense that deserves resentment and revenge. But if it is a law human and divine, that everybody should live by their honest labor, what barbarous custom obliges a musician to serve without a recompense? A cursed over-bearing; O sordid avarice!
>
> A singer, who knows the world, distinguishes between the different manners of commanding; he knows how to refuse without disobliging, and how to obey with a good grace; not being ignorant, that one, who has his interest most at heart, sometimes finds his account in serving without a gratification.[54]

Included in the broad range of advice which Tosi offered the singer were some more personal admonitions. For one, he reminds the singer of the basis for his status.

> If the words are not heard so as to be understood, there will be no great difference between a human voice and an oboe. This defect, although one of the greatest, is today more than common, to the greatest disgrace of the teachers and the profession; and yet they ought to know, that it is only the words which give preference to a singer above an instrumental performer, assuming they were equal in judgment and knowledge.[55]

51 Tosi, *Observations*, IX, ii.

52 Ibid., IX, lviii.

53 Ibid., IX, viiiff.

54 Ibid., IX, xivff.

55 Ibid., IV, xx.

Tosi also offered the singer this timeless advice:

> Whoever does not aspire to the first rank, begins already to give up the second, and little by little will be content with the lowest.[56]

We are confident that Tosi is thinking here of artistic heights, and not heights of popularity. He once observed, 'a student must not hope for applause, if he has not an utter abhorrence of ignorance.'[57] In similar comments he states,

> It is a folly in a singer to grow vain at the first applause, without reflecting whether they are given by chance, or out of flattery; and if he thinks he deserves them, there is the end of him.[58]
>
> ……
>
> Ignorance hates all that is excellent.[59]

Finally, Tosi makes a nice reflection on critics.

> Great advantage may be gained from the ill-natured critics; for, the more intent they are to discover defects, the greater benefit may be received from them without any obligation.[60]

On Improvisation

Modern writers distinguish between 'ornaments,' which refer to the addition by the performer of single, specific ornaments, and 'ornamentation,' which is really improvisation. The most obvious conclusion that is obtained from Baroque treatises is that improvisation was not only permitted, but expected. Tosi, for example, says a singer may have great knowledge, be able to read at sight the most difficult works and have a well-trained voice which he uses artistically, but if he cannot improvise he cannot be considered distinguished.[61] He adds the important observation that this is a special characteristic of music, for in no other art, such as painting or sculpture, is the artist required to improvise in public. Another way of looking at this responsibility, he points out, is the fact that,

---

56 Ibid., VI, xxiv.

57 Ibid., VI, xxiii.

58 Ibid., IX, xxii.

59 Ibid., VII, 122.

60 Ibid., IX, xxvi.

61 Ibid., Introduction, vi. When Vivaldi was writing out the figured bass for his violin concerto, RV 340, he got bored and wrote '*per i coglioni*,' 'for the dimwits.' See Kendall, *Vivaldi*, 101.

> Poets, painters, sculptors, and even composers, before they expose their works to the public, have all the time needed to correct and polish them; but the singer that commits an error has no remedy; for the fault is committed, and past correction.[62]

For Tosi, the obligation to improvise was nowhere more expected, even required, than in the da capo aria. In one of his most famous lines, after explaining the basic form of the aria, Tosi observes that 'in repeating the Aria, he that does not vary it for the better, is no great Master.'[63] He adds that a moderate singer with good improvisation gets more esteem than a better singer who does not employ it. Indeed, the reason for varied improvisation on the da capo, in Tosi's view, had much to do with judging singers.

> Without varying the Aria, the knowledge of the singers could never be discovered; but from the nature and quality of the variations, it will be easily discerned in two of the greatest singers which is the best.

This famous teacher saw that the singer's success was a matter of experience and taste, not conceptual study alone.

> A singer is under the greatest obligation to the study of the arias; for by them he gains or loses his reputation. To the acquiring this valuable art a few verbal lessons cannot suffice; nor would it be of any great profit to the student, to have a great number of arias, in which a thousand of the most exquisite passages of different sorts were written down: For they would not serve for all purposes, and there would always be wanting that spirit which accompanies extempore performances, and is preferable to all servile imitations.[64]

In general, even taste and skill are of small advantage, he observes, 'if one is not ready at extempore embellishments.' He only warns that 'a superfluity of them should prejudice the composition and confound the ear.' But, so much was ornamentation considered part of the performer's art, that Tosi could observe that if the student learns well to use appoggiaturas he will be able to,

> laugh at those composers who write them in the music, with the intention either to show they are modern or to show that they understand the art of singing better than the singers.[65]

Improvisation was also anticipated by members of an accompanying ensemble. For Agazzari, writing on the art of the continuo bass in 1607, the principle concern centered only on not covering the solo voice.

---

62 Ibid., Introduction, vii.

63 Ibid., VII, ivff.

64 Ibid., VII, iii.

65 Ibid., II, xvi.

> As far as possible try to keep off the same note which the Soprano sings, and avoid making florid divisions on it, so as not to reduplicate the voice part and cover the quality of that voice or the florid divisions which a good singer is making up there.[66]

Later he also cautions the players of the orchestra to take turn in their ornamentation, for,

> each must regard the other, giving it room and not conflicting with it; if there are many, they must each await their turn and not, chirping all at once like sparrows, try to shout one another down.[67]

Particularly interesting insights into ensemble ornamentation is found in a passage written by Pietro della Valle. It is rather amazing to consider this ensemble skill of 1640 when compared to the ensemble experience today. It is especially important for the reader to remember that stylistically everything discussed here was completely absent from the page itself.

> Playing in the company of other instruments does not require the artifices of counterpoint so much as the graces of art; for if the player is good, he does not have to insist so much upon making a display of his own art as upon accommodating himself to all the others … Those who sing and play well have to give time to one another in company, and they have to sport with gracefulness of imitations rather than with too subtle artifices of counterpoints. They will show their art in knowing how to repeat well and promptly what another player has done before; and in then giving room to the others and fit opportunity for them to repeat what they have done; and in this way, with a varied and no less artful manner, though neither so difficult nor such deep knowledge, they will make known to the others their own worth. This is done nowadays not only by the most excellent, but also by the ordinary players, and they know how to do it so well that I do not know how it could have been done better by those of the past, whom I have not heard. When one plays in the company of voices, the same thing I said about playing with instruments must take place, and much more so: because instruments when serving voices as it were the leaders in music, must have no other aim than to accompany them well.[68]

Other writers make an exception to the expectation of improvisation in church music. Viadana, in the preface to his *Church Concerti* of 1602, seems to want to restrict ornamentation to those which he has written out. His suggestion that such improvisation is no longer in style in 1602 must be taken as one of a number of similar clues that sixteenth-century polyphony included much more improvisation than the impression given by most historians today.

> I have not failed to introduce, where appropriate, certain figures and cadences, and other convenient opportunities for ornaments and passagework and for giving other proofs of the aptitude and elegant style of the singers, although, for the most part, to facilitate matters, the stock passages have been used, such as nature itself provides, but more florid …

66 A. Agazzari, *Del sonare sopra' l basso* (Siena, 1607), quoted in Donnington, *The Interpretation of Early Music*, 171.

67 Agostino Agazzari, quoted in Strunk, *Source Readings*, 429.

68 Pietro della Valle, 'Della musica dell'età' (1640), quoted in Donnington, *The Interpretation of Early Music*, 607.

> Concerti of this kind must be sung with refinement, discretion, and elegance, using accents with reason and embellishments with moderation and in their proper place: above all, not adding anything beyond what is printed in them, inasmuch as there are sometimes certain singers, who, because they are favored by nature with a certain agility of the throat, never sing the songs as they are written, not realizing that nowadays their like are not acceptable, but are, on the contrary, held in very low esteem indeed, particularly in Rome, where the true school of good singing flourishes.[69]

This was perhaps the exception which Tosi also had in mind, with respect to ensemble improvisation.

> All compositions for more than one voice ought to be sung strictly as they are written; they require no other art than a noble simplicity.[70]

With this background, we move on to the more interesting question: What can we deduce regarding the actual style and aesthetic goals in Baroque improvisation?

Giovanni Doni writing in 1635 found that more florid improvisation was being done in the theater, before an audience where 'the ignorant always are in greater number than the intelligent.' In contrast,

> In chambers, where somewhat delicate music is accustomed to be sung, and in gatherings of people who understand music, the [improvisation] is not required to be used abundantly, but more sparingly.[71]

Even while observing that improvisation is perhaps more appropriate to the theater, where the audience is 'ignorant,' Doni still emphasizes the importance of emotional expression in improvisation.

> It is indeed true that that improvisation which unfold its passage work [*spasseggiano*] little by little, and uses quicker notes, are more graceful than uniform ones; but perhaps they are not so well suited to sad and languid matters as those which, on the contrary, start quickly, and very gently relax their pace; because they express better a certain languor, and lack of strength. But those which go like waves, that is, now they slacken and now they move on, yet not by jerks and at one blow, but gracefully, are the most beautiful and versatile.[72]

On the other hand, as another writer confirms, there must have been many singers who gave little thought to the musicality of their ornamentation.

---

69 Lodovico Grossi da Viadana, *Cento concerti ecclesiastici*, Preface, quoted in Strunk, *Source Readings*, 420. Viadana (1564–1627) worked as choirmaster in several major cities in Italy and was highly regarded by Praetorius as an authority of the church concerti style.

70 Tosi, *Observations*, IX, xxv.

71 Giovanni Battista Doni, *Trattati di musica* (1635) quoted in Donnington, *The Interpretation of Early Music*, 180.

72 Giovanni Battisti Doni, *Trattati di musica* (1635), ed., A. F. Gori (Florence, 1763), II, 69ff.

> Many persons are deceived, for they wear themselves out making *gruppi*, *trilli*, *passaggi*, and *exclamazioni* with no regard for their purpose or whether or not they are apropos. I certainly do not intend to deprive myself of these adornments, but I want them to be used in the right time and place ... But where the sense does not demand it, leave aside every ornament, so as not to act like that painter who knew how to paint cypress trees and therefore painted them everywhere.[73]

How, then, does one go about learning this art? Less experienced players, as a treatise of 1608 suggests, wrote out their ornamentation at home ['at his ease']. The expectation was no doubt the same as one often hears regarding the cadenzas, that it is all right to write them out—so long as they don't sound written out.

> The good and perfect player of the cornett must have a good knowledge of the art of counterpoint, so that he can make up varied passages at his ease, still more extemporaneously.[74]

Judging by comments by Tosi, one expectation was that all ornamentation should be original and not copied from others.

> A singer should not copy ... to copy is the part of a scholar, that of a master [performer] is to invent.[75]
>
> ......
>
> The most admired graces of a professor ought only to be imitated and not copied; on condition also, that it does not bear even so much as a shadow of resemblance of the original; otherwise, instead of a beautiful imitation, it will become a despicable copy.[76]

The most difficult thing, Tosi says, is to seek inventions which are easy and natural, as well as beautiful.[77] A few of his views on the beautiful in ornamentation include:

> [Ornamentation] must be produced by singular and beautiful invention, remote from all that is vulgar and common ...[78]
>
> [Ornamentation] must be easy in appearance, thereby to give universal delight. That in effect they be difficult that thereby the art of the inventor be the more admired ...
>
> That they be properly introduced, for in the wrong place, they disgust ...
>
> That they should proceed rather from the heart than from the voice, in order to make their way to the heart more easily ...
>
> That they be stolen on the time, to captivate the soul.

73 Marco da Gagliano, *Dafne*, 1608, preface, quoted in MacClintock, *Readings*, 188. Gagliano (1575–1642) was a prolific composer and writer on music.

74 Scipione Cerreto, *Dell'arbore musicale* (Naples, 1608), 41, quoted in Donnington, *The Interpretation of Early Music*, 172.

75 Tosi, *Observations*, IX, xxxii.

76 Ibid., IX, xxxviii.

77 Ibid., VII, xiii.

78 Ibid., X, vff.

In general, he finds,

> A deficiency of ornaments displeases as much as the too great abundance of them; that a singer makes one languid and dull with too little, and cloys one with too much ...[79]

There is one comment by Tosi which leaves us wanting much more detail. What kind of expressive music did he consider was sacred from all ornamentation?

> Where passion speaks, all trills, divisions and graces ought to be silent, leaving it to the sole force of a beautiful expression to persuade.[80]

One finds the spirit of many of these views given in a humorous vein by Marcello in his satire on opera, *Theater in the Modern Style*, of 1720. Here, he first recommends that in coaching the singer, the conductor should,

> teach her to enunciate badly, and with this object to teach her a great number of divisions and graces, so that not a single word will be understood, and by this means the music will stand out better and be appreciated.[81]

If a second singer objects to their status, Marcello recommends writing out ornamentation to the extent that her part has an equal number of notes as the prima donna.

The freedom of singers to augment the communication of emotions through improvisation over long notes of the melody, which corresponded with the key emotional words of the text, quickly led to excesses and later opera became a vehicle for the virtuoso singer. This too becomes a subject for Marcello's humor.

> If nouns such as 'father,' 'empire,' 'love,' 'arena,' 'kingdom,' 'beauty,' 'courage,' 'heart,' appear in the aria, the modern composer should write long coloraturas over them. This applies also to 'no,' 'without,' 'already,' and other adverbs. This serves to introudce a little change from the old custom of using coloratura passages only over words expressing motion or emotion, for instance 'torment,' 'sorrow,' 'song,' 'fly,' 'fall.'[82]

For the modern reader, perhaps the most surprising general information regarding improvisation are indications of an apparent indifference to form itself. Frescobaldi, in 1635, recommends that the organist 'in the canzoni and ricercari may finish at any cadence, should the pieces seem too long.'[83] In two other publications he makes similar comments.

79 Ibid., IX, lii.

80 Ibid., V, iv.

81 Benedetto Marcello, in Weiss, *Letters of Composers*, 528.

82 Ibid., 49.

83 Frescobaldi, *Fiori musicali* (1635), quoted in Morgenstern, *Composers on Music*, 26. Frescobaldi (1583–1643) was one of the best known organists of Italy in the seventeenth century. Called to St. Peter's in Rome as organist in 1608, it was said his first performance drew 30,000 listeners.

> In the Toccatas I have attempted to offer not only a variety of passagework and expressive ornaments but also to make the various sections such that they can be played independently, so that the performer may stop wherever he wishes and not have to play the entire toccata …
>
> In the cadences, even though written in notes of small values, one must sustain them. As the performer approaches the end of a *passaggio* or cadence, the tempo must become more *adagio*.
>
> It is left to the good taste and fine judgment of the performer to decide the tempo that best suits the spirit and perfection of the manner and style of interpretation.[84]
>
> ……
>
> If the work should appear too fatiguing to play from beginning to end, one might begin a passage wherever he most pleases and end with a passage that finishes in the same mode.
>
> The beginning should be played slowly to give greater spirit and beauty to the following passages.[85]

On Ornaments

As we have indicated above, we will not include here the extensive technical comments on the performance of specific ornaments found in Baroque treatises. We are interested, however, in comments which offer hints on the perception of the aesthetic use of these ornaments. The great Italian violin virtuoso, Geminiani, seemed particularly concerned with the aesthetic nature of ornaments. Of the appoggiatura, for example, he observes,

> The superior appoggiatura is supposed to express Love, Affection, Pleasure, etc. It should be made pretty long, giving it more than half the length or time of the note it belongs to … If it be made short, it will lose much of the aforesaid qualities.[86]

He discusses the mordent from the same perspective of the communication of feeling in performance.

> If it be performed with strength, and continued long, it expresses Fury, Anger, Resolution, etc. If it be played less strong and shorter, it expresses Mirth, Satisfaction, etc. But if you play it quite soft and swell the note, it may then denote Horror, Fear, Grief, Lamentation, etc. By making it short and swelling the note gently, it may express Affection and Pleasure.[87]

Geminiani also suggests the style of vibrato could convey either Majesty and Dignity or Affliction and Fear.[88]

84 Frescobaldi, 'Toccate e partite d'intavolatura,' quoted in MacClintock, *Readings*, 133ff.

85 Frescobaldi, 'Capricci fatti sopra diversi soggetti,' quoted in Ibid., 135.

86 Geminiani, *A Treatise of Good Taste in the Art of Musick*, 2.

87 Ibid., 3.

88 Ibid.

It is interesting that Geminiani still considered the basic dynamic markings of *piano* and *forte* to be, like ornaments, subject to the will of the performer.

> They are both extremely necessary to express the intention of the melody; and as all good music should be composed in imitation of a discourse, these two ornaments are designed to produce the same effects that an orator does by raising and falling his voice.[89]

Tosi also offers a few clues regarding the aesthetic quality of ornaments. The use of crescendo and diminuendo on a single pitch, which Tosi calls *Messa di Voce*, never fails to have 'an exquisite effect' when used on an open vowel.[90] The *divisions*, contends Tosi,

> do not have the power to touch the soul, but the most they can do is to raise our admiration of the singer for the happy flexibility of his voice.[91]

Divisions are only beautiful, he says, if they are in tune, accented, equal, distinct and fast. Like trills, if they are used too often they become 'tedious, if not odious.'[92]

A rarely discussed ornament mentioned by Tosi is the 'drag.' In this ornament, the singer begins on a high note and slowly 'drags' the pitch down to a low note, making a diminuendo at the same time from forte to piano and stopping on some notes in the middle on the way down. 'Every good musician takes it for granted,' says Tosi, that no other ornament is 'more apt to touch the heart.'[93]

Tosi was particularly sensitive to ornaments and improvisation at cadences. He objected to trills,

> It grows abominable, when the singer persists with his tiresome warbling, nauseating the judicious, who suffer the more, because they know that the composers leave generally in every final cadence some note, sufficient to make a discreet embellishment ...,[94]

and even a simple anticipation at a cadence, for 'it hurts the ears and is against the rules.'[95]

His greatest artistic objection was to the cadenza, which as the word reminds us was an extended cadence during the Baroque. For Tosi, extended solo improvisation at the cadence, especially in the da capo aria form, was inconsistent with high art.

> Every aria has (at least) three cadences that are final. Generally speaking, the study of the singers of the present times consist in terminating the cadence of the first part with an overflowing

89 Ibid.

90 Tosi, *Observations*, I, xxix.

91 Ibid., IV, i.

92 Ibid., IV, xixff.

93 Ibid., X, xxviii.

94 Ibid., VIII, xiv.

95 Ibid., VIII, xii.

> of passages and divisions at pleasure, and the orchestra waits; in that of the second the dose is increased, and the orchestra grows tired; but on the last cadence, the throat is set a going like a weather-cock in a whirlwind, and the orchestra yawns. But why must the world be thus continually deafened with so many divisions?[96]

Answering his own question, Tosi suggests it is merely 'begging for applause from the blind ignorant.' But, he warns, singers in so doing damage the profession by such practices which are unworthy of the talent given them.

EDUCATIONAL MUSIC

Tosi gives the impression that most vocal teachers he knew were more interested in money than in producing fine artists. Very few teachers will refuse a student, he observes, so long as they are paid and 'little do they care if their greediness ruins the profession.'[97] Beware, Tosi warns the teacher, you will be held responsible for any omissions in your teaching and for any errors you did not correct.[98] Regarding the teacher's demeanor in making such corrections, Tosi offers the following observation.

> Let him be moderately severe, making himself feared, but not hated. I know it is not easy to find the mean between severity and mildness, but I know also that both extremes are bad: too great severity creates stubbornness, and too great mildness creates contempt.

Tosi also has much sound advice for the student, beginning with a comment on a question much discussed in earlier centuries, but rarely mentioned today—Can we expect the quality of the music to be unaffected by the quality of the *character* of the musician?

> After a strict care of his morals, he should give the rest of his attention to the study of singing in perfection, that by this means he may be so happy as to join the most noble qualities of the soul to the excellencies of his art.[99]

Beyond this, since music is an experiential art, in the end one must teach oneself. 'Till a singer pleases himself,' writes Tosi, 'it is certain he cannot please others.'[100]

> Let the student hear as much as he can the most celebrated singers, and likewise the most excellent instrumental performers; because, from the attention in hearing them, one reaps more advantage than from any instruction whatsoever.

96 Ibid., VIII, vff.

97 Ibid., I, iv.

98 Ibid., I, viiiff.

99 Ibid., VI, ii.

100 Ibid., VI, xvii.

Let him endeavor to copy from both, that he may insensibly by the study of others, get a good taste.[101]

Here he means copy the style, not copy the actual material.

> Whoever accustoms himself to have things put in his mouth, will have no invention, and becomes a slave to his memory.[102]

Finally, the student must learn from his mistakes.

> Abhor the example of those who hate correction; for like lighting to those who walk in the dark, though it frightens them, it gives them light.
>
> Learn from the errors of others: O great Lesson! it costs little and instructs much. Of everyone something is to be learned, and the most ignorant is sometimes the greatest master.[103]

FUNCTIONAL MUSIC

Agostino Agazzari, in 1606, was far ahead of his time in beginning to think of the subjective qualities of instruments used in church music.

> The lute in a concerto should be played with pleasing inventiveness and diversity, at times with firm strokes and with soft repercussions, at other times with broad passage work … and with groppi, trills, and accents to make it very attractive …
>
> The viols should be played with full bowing, clear and sonorous …
>
> The violin demands clear and lengthy runs, with scherzi, echoes, and responses, fughette, repetitions in different keys … with groppi and varied trills …
>
> Let it suffice for me to say to you that what is said here should be applied with prudence, warning the organists, the singers, and the ensemble to give each other room, not being offended by the multitude, but with ear and judgment waiting for the time and the place, and not act as though the passage at any one time belongs to the one who shouts the loudest.[104]

While the old polyphonic style continued in church practice in many places, one nonetheless finds clear evidence of the intrusion of more modern influences. In the writings of Banchieri the influence of opera on church music is quite evident.

101 Ibid., VI, xiiiff.

102 Ibid., VI, xxv.

103 Ibid., X, xxxviff.

104 Agostino Agazzari, Letter of 1606, quoted in MacClintock, *Readings*, 131ff.

> The Masses, Psalms, Canticles, Motets and Concerti to be performed with the organ must be in the *affettuoso*, devout, attractive, and *recitativo* styles, imitating the words and employing gravity in concerting them.[105]

He particularly recommends in this regard the works of Viadana, in which 'one, two and three voices sing in *stile recitativo*.' One reference to theater style also reminds us that Italian terms such as 'allegro' had earlier conveyed a style as well as a tempo.

> The *stile allegro* should not always be used, only at certain times; and also at the Elevation of the Holy Sacrament some serious sonata that moves one to devotion should be used.[106]

Whatever was the line between the influence of theatrical styles and the inclusion of actual secular music in the service, it was a line which seems to have been repeatedly crossed. A visitor to Venice in 1709 reported,

> I do not know whether it is to cheer the Satans' days up even more and for the special satisfaction of those who only go to church as they go the the theaters, that they do scarcely ever fail in this noisy music to mingle the same that one has heard at the operas, and which have pleased more, and that with no scandal to the favor of the words which one changes and which, instead of expressing, for example, the loves of Pyramus and Thisbe, say something of the life of the saint whose feast day it is.[107]

Tosi was one who was particularly concerned with what he was hearing in the church.

> Since poor counterpoint has been condemned, in this corrupted age, to beg for a piece of bread in churches, while the ignorance of many exults on the stage, the most part of the composers have been prompted from avarice, or indigence, to abandon in such manner the true study, that one may foresee (in not succored by those few, that still gloriously sustain its dearest precepts) music, after having lost the name of science, and a companion of philosophy, will run the risk of being reputed unworthy to enter into the sacred temples, from the scandal given there, by their Jiggs, Minuets, and Furlanas; and, in fact, where the taste is so depraved, what would make the difference between the church music and the theatrical, if money were received at the church doors?[108]

……

105 Adriano Banchieri, 'Conclusioni nel suono dell' organo,' quoted in Ibid., 129ff. Banchieri (1567–1634) was a priest at the monestery S. Michele near Bologna, as well as a composer and organist.

106 Ibid., 127.

107 Casimir Freschot, *Nouvelle relation de Venise* (Utrecht, 1709), 318.

108 Tosi, *Observations*, VII, xxv.

> [We must condemn] the presumption of a singer who gets the words of the most wanton airs of the theater rendered into Latin, in order to sing them with applause in the Church; as if there were no manner of difference between the style of one and the other; and, as if the scraps of the stage were fit to offer to the Deity.[109]

Marcello, in his satire, *Theater in the Modern Style* [1720] also mentions hearing disguised secular music in the church.

> The composer will have little facility in reading and still less in writing, and therefore will not understand Latin, even though he must compose church music, into which he will introduce sarabands, gigues, courantes, etc., calling them fugues, canons, double counterpoints, etc.[110]

109 Ibid., IX, lxiv.

110 Marcello, *Il treatro alla moda*, quoted in Strunk, *Source Readings*, 525.

4 ITALIAN LITERATURE

Will Durant calls this period of Italian literature, 'The Fallow South.'[1] While music is an important exception to his characterization, his metaphor of a farmer letting his fields rest for a season to represent this period of Italian literature is basically a valid one. In hindsight it is easy to point to such factors as the continuing Inquisition, the Counter Reformation and the political interference by Spain as contributory causes to the relatively weak body of literature extant from this period. Many general studies of this period seem to follow the conclusion of Buckner Trawick, 'Italian literature of the seventeenth century hardly deserves to be mentioned.'[2]

We would not go so far. To ignore this period would be to lose sight of an extraordinary philosopher Athanasius Kircher and a truly exceptional poet, Giambattista Marino, whose verses were set to music by Rossi, Vecchi, Massaino, Frescobaldi and Schütz, among many others.

ON THE PHYSIOLOGY OF AESTHETICS

Marino, in his great pastoral poem, *Adonis*, makes a brief reference to the respective roles of Reason and the senses. His view understandably reflects the ancient Church position that trusting the senses leads man to sin and that their only purpose is to supply information to be acted on by Reason.

> Then penitent at last, with sighs and groans,
> thou shalt perceive with tardy sense how much
> he errs that, following a faithless guide,
> repulsing reason, worships sense alone.[3]

......

1 Will Durant, *The Age of Louis XIV* (New York: Simon and Schuster, 1963), 428.

2 Buckner Trawick, *World Literature* (New York: Barnes & Noble, 1955), II, 33.

3 Giambattista Marino, *L'Adone* (1623), trans. Harold Priest (Ithaca: Cornell University Press, 1967), II, 169. Marino (1569–1625) was a genuine court poet, working for a cardinal, a duke, a queen regent and a king of France. As a young man in Naples, Marino abandoned his studies in law to sow a few wild oats. He was jailed several times, for forgery and for the death, during an abortion, of a young girl he had seduced. Escaping from jail in 1600, his life began to have some stability after he moved to Rome.

But since he's born to speculate, 'tis meet
that every living species shine in him,
that he conduct the fantasies of sense
to intellect, with which he is endowed …
to first make senses capable, then mind,
of grasping what they feel and apprehend.[4]

Marino, in this same poem, describes a 'Garden of Pleasure' based on the five senses. He takes the position of nearly all early philosophers in declaring sight to be the most important of the senses.

Eminent it sits, of senses chief,
and surely the Creator planned it so …[5]

He assigns hearing a near equal position, adding the important observation that the ear is the only door to the soul. He is clearly thinking of music, when he reflects that what enters the ear is sometimes for profit and sometimes for delight.

Nature so formed this sense that it might be
to sweet enticements ready minister,
and yet it is ordained through that same path
each decent influence must enter man,
since all my art and all my discipline
no other passage has unto the soul;
there is one cause but varied the effect,
the one for profit aimed, one for delight.

Because the voice will ever upward mount,
therefore the ear was placed on high also,
and on each side, as if in rivalry,
stands even with the level of the eyes.[6]

4 Ibid., VI, 16.

5 Ibid., VI, 26.

6 Ibid., VII, 11–12.

ON THE PSYCHOLOGY OF AESTHETICS

All poets since antiquity pointed to the irony that the experience of Love contained both pleasure and pain. Marino mentions this in two charming lines, following a musical competition between the unhappy lover and the nightingale, in a section of poetry subtitled, 'The Origin of Music.'[7] Marino concludes it was Love who first taught man music, but,

> What strange, what sweet and bitter harmonies
> the wounded heart must learn at Cupid's school![8]

ON THE PHILOSOPHY OF AESTHETICS

Marino's *Adonis* is set in the form of the Pastoral Romance which had inspired poets since the lyric poets of ancient Greece. In every century this form offered an escape from the grim realities of town and court to seek the simple truths of Nature. The rustic musical instruments one finds here are the same ones mentioned in virtually every poet's treatment of this form. In this case, Adonis finds his natural paradise when he lands on the Island of Cyprus.

> Adonis ventures forth, and everywhere
> hears Procne's warbled notes or Philomel's;
> the forest rings with sounds of shrill bagpipe,
> the swineherd's raucous horn; the fields resound
> with rustic sordine and with flageolet,
> with woodland pipes and shepherds' oaten reeds.[9]

In a 'Palace of Love,' we find more rustic instruments.

> A group of virginal bacchantes here
> stomp and sway about to right and left,
> and there a boisterous throng of Corybantes
> in foolish frenzy wildly run and leap.
> The clashing cymbals, horns, and trumpets hoarse
> now seem to cause the nearby hills to quake.
> This splendid work is of such wondrous art
> that in mute metal it expresses sound.[10]

---

7 Ibid., VII, 57ff.

8 Ibid., VII, 57.

9 Ibid., I, 132.

10 Ibid., II, 32.

And again, near the end of the poem, peasant instruments accompany a Hymn to Bacchus.

Along the margins of the fragrant fields
the zither, organ and the castanet,
the tambourin and flageolet let join
with shepherd's cymbal, whistle, and shrill fife.[11]

One of the most memorable passages in Marino's *Adonis* is a musical contest, a feature nearly always present in these pastoral poems. If this musical contest differs from the model of those of the ancient poets in the absence of the official judges, it surpasses all earlier examples in its poignant description and ultimate tragedy. Here we find an unhappy lover is singing in the forest, 'in piteous sounds that gave vent unto his grief.'[12] A nightingale hears him and begins to imitate his music, which leads to a contest in performance. Marino now gives us an unusually detailed picture of the passionate performance by the unhappy lover.

The skilled musician, viewing scornfully
the competition of this challenger,
and angry that a creature so minute
not only matches but surpasses him,
begins to search out on the lute the tones
most difficult played on the highest frets;
the eloquent, loquacious little tongue
persistent follows, always copies him.

The master reddens with disgust and shame
to have been vanquished by a thing so mean.
He turns the keys, sweeps up and down the strings,
sounds chords in series mounting to the rose.
Defiantly the warbler never stops,
but renders each response more vigorously;
and as the youth diminishes or soars,
he deftly weaves the vocal labyrinth.

Astonished now, the lad became like ice
and irate said: 'I've suffered thee awhile.
Now either thou wilt fail what I perform,
or I'll confess defeat and break my lute.'
He grasped the hollow case tight in his arms,
and as to make a final proof of skill,
with tremolo and syncopy and fugue,
he sought all manner of variety.

11 Ibid., VII, 119.

12 Ibid., VII, 40ff.

Without a pause he strikes, releases, strikes
upon the neck from base to topmost fret,
and as his mood directs he murmurs low,
then swells the tone and plays in style sublime.
Sometimes he vibrates on the treble string,
while pressing with his thumb the major chord;
at other times with gravity profound
he plunges to the bordon's lowest depths.

His hand flies over the strings, now low, now high,
more nimble than the bird itself the hand;
first up, then down, with unexpected leaps
the speeding fingers move in lively dance.
Inimitably he imitates the stress
of fiery conflict and confused assault,
and equals with the sound of his sweet songs
the bellicose uproar and clash of arms.

Trumpets and timpani, such instruments
As Mars employs when marshaling the troops,
with whirlwind roar accelerating fierce,
his art expresses in skilled melody,
and all the while he plays he multiplies
the tempest of roulades in every part;
and while he thus compounds the harmonies,
his small competitor makes no response.

This musical duel continues for many hours until 'the poor bird, exhausted finally, languished, fainted, weakened, and then died.' The youth was much moved by the death of his competitor and, used his lute as a sepulcher to bury the bird,

Then with the feathers of the bird itself
he wrote the history of the event.

Finally, Marino includes some reflections on the ancient association of music and poetry in general. Particularly interesting here are the kinds of aesthetic purposes he gives, as well as the reference to the 'music of the spheres.'

Music and Poesy are sisters twain,
restorers of afflicted human kind,
with power through happy rhymes to make serene
the turbid tempests of our guilty thoughts.
There are no arts more beautiful than these
or more salubrious for troubled minds;
wild Scythia holds no barbarous heart, except
the tiger's, that sweet singing does not charm.

And yet sometimes a wanton kind of verse
can render far less lovely those same charms,
can turn to damage honest pleasantness,
and serve as evil magic for false gods.

……

Whoever harkens as the graceful hand
strikes on the strings of the expressive lyre,
wedding that music's charming melody
with brilliant voices in a sweet accord,
and does not sometimes feel the mighty power
of those same numbers penetrate his heart,
must have a spirit dissonant, that for
the music of the spheres is out of tune.[13]

ON THE AESTHETICS OF MUSIC

Marino presents a passage on the birth of music in his *Adonis*. He mixes Greek mythology of the gods with historical mythology, as in this passage in which the 'clever infant' of the Cyclops discovers the lower part of the overtone series, modeled after an impossible accomplishment attributed to Pythagoras.

Observing that the rhythmic hammer blows
resounding as the anvils were struck home,
whose pounding thunder, beaten out in time,
made it appear a concert in effect,
he started then to reason on the rules
of measure, until then not understood,
and to the great amazement of his sire
he solved the secret of the intervals.[14]

In 1602 Tommaso Campanella wrote a poetical dialogue called 'The City of the Sun,' which describes his view of a fictional, utopian society. Among the officials who watched over this society were those who held offices called 'Magnanimity, Chastity, Fortitude, Zeal, Truth,

13 Ibid., VII, 1–2, 10.

14 Ibid., VII, 59. Marino had a fascination for these kinds of incorporation of material from different sources. Another example is his 'La Musica,' the second of his *Dicerie sacre*, in which he treats the Seven Last Words of Christ on the Cross with the seven reeds of the syrinx of Pan. [See Bianconi, *Music in the Seventeenth Century*, 53]

Beneficence, Gratitude and Mercy.'[15] These were positions elected from candidates who had demonstrated these various qualities.

Education for both sexes began at age three, with language. At age seven they are exposed to the workshops of the various crafts, needle-workers, goldsmiths and painters. The purpose of this was to create respect for honest work, and the Genoese sailor who narrates this tale (having visited this mythical land) observes,

> Thus they laugh at us because we consider craftsmen ignoble and assign nobility to those who are ignorant of every craft and live in idleness.[16]

At the age of seven, also, study of the natural sciences begin and at age ten, mathematics, medicine and the other sciences. Regarding study of the arts, Campanella observes,

> If a woman has skill in painting, she is not forbidden to pursue it. Music, except for the playing of trumpets and drums, is reserved to women and children since they give most pleasure by it.[17]

The uses of music include a brief reference to music therapy, for the cure of 'burning fevers.' Music is also used to praise God, as well as for 'both pastime and pleasure' after dinner. This music consisted of the praise of heroes of every nation and 'hymns in praise of love, wisdom and every virtue.' Music is also used for civic celebrations, for festivals of the zodiac, the anniversary of the state and for the anniversaries of their victories. These,

> they celebrate with music; the women sing, drums and bugles are played, the artillery is fired in salute, and the poets sing the praises of their most virtuous citizens.[18]

Campanella's description of his utopia concludes with a detailed discussion of astrology. The influence of the stars, he finds, is directed more to the senses than to Reason.

> Because the stars gently induce transformations in the senses, those who adhere to the senses more than to reason are subject to the stars …
>
> Heresy is a sensual act, as St. Paul says,[19] and the stars influence sensualists in that direction; rationalists they incline toward the true, holy law of the First Reason, every to be praised. Amen.

---

15 Tommaso Campanella, *La Città del Sole*, trans. Daniel Donno (Berkeley: University of California Press, 1981), 41. Campanella (1568–1626) became a member of the Dominican order at age fourteen. His intellectual curiosity brought him into constant conflict with the Inquisition, resulting in years of imprisonment and unspeakable torture.

16 Ibid., 43.

17 Ibid., 49.

18 Ibid., 105.

19 Galatians 5:19. Modern translations no longer include 'heresy' in this passage.

> Now the works of the flesh are plain: immorality, impurity, licentiousness, idolatry, sorcery, enmity, strife, jealousy, anger, selfishness, dissension, party spirit, envy, drunkenness, carousing, and the like.

Although Campanella clearly confirms here the importance of Reason over the senses, in another place he raises a curious question about intellectuals. In Campanella's utopian state, all aspects of intercourse and procreation are controlled by the state. In this regard, intellectuals are not allowed to procreate 'without first submitting to numerous conditions and restrictions stretching over many days.' The reason for this, says Campanella, was a very practical one.

> The reason for this is that those who are much given to speculation tend to be deficient in animal spirits and fail to bestow their intellectual powers upon their progeny because they are always thinking of other matters.[20]

In an autobiographical poem by Antonio Abbatini, we have a first-hand description of one of the academies, which in this case, he tells us, met in his home. His description confirms other reports of these gatherings of upper class and noble gentlemen for an evening with music and discussion of intellectual topics of the day.

> First, the now-lost madrigals of once upon a time
> are, at table, sung with great delight:
> the reason, for respect, I will not tell.
> There follows my address: I spread my wings
> to raise myself to the harmonious skies;
> but they are just like those of Icarus.
> Every liberty the virtuosi are allowed
> to contradict whatever I have said,
> though this role with reluctance do they play.
> Kircher has, however, always argued,
> as, too, Orlandi, general of the Carmelites,
> Dal Pane has his doubts, beloved Lelio too.
> Discussion over, as, by grace of God,
> invariably occurs without ill-will,
> due praise is then accorded he who most deserves.
> Here the unveiled truth is seen,
> since almost all are in the fore-front row
> and everything is discerned minutely.
> Then to the harpsichord the company transfers,
> and each man takes upon himself to show, with song
> and sound, his virtue, which binds the heart and soul.
> In all are set aside three hours of time,
> from nine o'clock for the remainder of the day,
> and never without wonder do those present go away.[21]

20 Campanella, *La Città del Sole*, 57.

21 Quoted in Bianconi, *Music in the Seventeenth Century*, 290ff.

On the Definition of Music

The poet, Giambattista Basile, in his *Muse napolitane* (1635) recalls the ancient concept of music as a metaphor for the divine harmony of the order of the universe.

> I remember having once heard
> From some scholars
> That this world is music,
> Music is man and everything is music,
> That heaven is upturned with music,
> That beauty is music, and the effects
> Are musical harmonies,
> And music is wholesomeness.[22]

The most interesting writer in seventeenth-century Italy on the nature of music was Athanasius Kircher (1601–1680), a German-born scholar who spent most of his adult life in Rome. His greatest work was the *Musurgia Universalis* (Rome, 1650), a virtual encyclopedia of music. While he appears to have been widely read himself, he also cites a number of scholars in Rome with whom he consulted in the preparation of his work. He also acknowledged, in his preface, his indebtedness to Mersenne's *Harmonie Universelle*, although he says the latter was more addressed to the philosopher than the practical musician.

Some critics had apparently questioned his authority to write on the subject of music, as Kircher admits in his preface.

> I hear, among other things, that this objection is made to me: 'How can the author have the audacity, since he is not a musician by profession, to undertake to correct and emend masters in the art, brought up in it almost from the cradle, and what is uppermost, to place himself as master over them, with more audacity than modesty?' To these I answer that I am certainly not and have never been a musician by profession, since it is a calling not appropriate to my religion.[23]

Kircher continues, somewhat sarcastically, saying that what his critics mean, when they say he is not a professional musician, is that he has not taught music to boys in school, conducted a church choir or been a mercenary by writing for money. On the other hand, he notes,

> From an early age I have devoted my attention not only to more distinguished arts and sciences, but also to the practice of music, with the most thorough study and steadfast labor; and let [the critics] have no doubt that I have not been concerned with musical speculation only, since various compositions printed in Germany, but under the name of others, are passed around to the greatest pleasure of listeners and held in esteem.

---

22 Quoted in Ibid., 53.

23 Athanasius Kircher, *Musurgia universalis* (1650), trans. Frederick Crane (unpublished dissertation, State University of Iowa, 1956), xix.

Kircher's *Musurgia Universalis* is divided into ten books, the first of which he entitles, 'Anatomical.' Here he deals with the nature of the production of vocal sounds, including those by animals, birds and insects, presenting in many cases their calls in musical notation. Of all the animals he discusses, he was most fascinated by the [Central] American sloth,[24] which Kircher understood sang, to the syllable 'ha,' the diatonic scale.

> It perfectly intones as learners do, the first elements of music, *do, re, me, fa, sol, la, sol, fa, me, re, do*. Ascending and descending through the common intervals of the six degrees, insomuch that the Spaniards, when they first took possession of these coasts, and perceived such a kind of vociferation in the night, thought they heard men accustomed to the rules of music.

Kircher concluded,

> If music were first invented in America, I would say that it must have begun with the amazing voice of this animal.

Book Two, 'Philological,' consists of studies of music in the ancient civilizations, in particular the Hebrew and Greek.

Book Three, 'Arithmetical,' concerns traditional music theory as it developed during the Middle Ages. Here he also presents a system of 'musical arithmetic,' through which the rules of addition, subtraction, multiplication and division of intervals are represented by special characters.

Book Four, 'Geometrical,' deals with the monochord, with geometric and algebraic systems for determining the intervals.

Book Five, 'Symphonurgic,' consists of rules for composing music in the old church style [*stile antico*].

Book Six, 'Organic music,' the medieval term for instrumental music, discusses as well geometry and acoustics. Here Kircher deals with the physical characteristics of the family of instruments, but, unfortunately, includes little information on performance practice or of aesthetic considerations. He makes the inaccurate assumption that string instruments must be the most ancient,[25] partly because of their prominence in the Old Testament, but

---

24 Kircher gives a description of this animal which he says is named from the fact that in fifteen days it does not travel as far as one can throw a spear.

> No one knows what meat it feeds on … they for the most part keep on the tops of trees … [With their feet] they have such strength, that whatsoever animal they lay hold on they keep it so fast, that it is never after able to free itself from their nails, but it is compelled to die through hunger. On the other hand, this beast so greatly affects the men that are coming towards it by its countenance, that in pure compassion they refrain from molesting it, and easily persuade themselves not to be solicitous about that which nature has subjected to so defenseless and miserable a state of body.

25 Logic would suggest instruments made of natural objects, such as flutes from bones, percussion instruments from turtle shells and trumpets from sea shells, must be older than string instruments which require a relatively advanced technology to make.

also because he assumes man always had available cords (potential musical strings) to tie things with.[26]

It is somewhat unexpected that Kircher tells us that the cornett was missing in mid-seventeenth century Rome, since it was a common instrument at the end of the sixteenth century.

> Since the cornetts attain a remarkable power in music, I certainly wonder that our Roman musicians take no interest in them, since nothing could be more suited to church music, especially if three, four, or five cornetts are accompanied by a bassoon. I certainly would think that ensembles of this sort, from time to time, would be much preferred to string ensembles for major solemnities and festivities.[27]

We like a comment by Kircher made as part of his explanation of the distribution of the natural tones of the trumpet:

> You see, therefore, how much nature abhors dissonances, so that the trumpet would rather burst than allow them.[28]

He also makes a brief reference to improvisation in the highest trumpet part, a subject relatively little discussed during the seventeenth century. This is due in part to the rather secretive nature of the trumpet guilds and their repertoire of memorized, and rarely notated, music.

> There remains an explanation of the style of music that trumpets perform … Since all instruments require different styles of compositions, it will certainly be most obvious of an ensemble of trumpets. And it is established for four trumpets that the first of them carries the top part, indulging in various *clausulae* and diminutions. Two others take the middle road; the fourth, which they also call the *bourdon*, remaining on a continuous unison, serves, as it were, in place of a bass. There are those, moreover, who use the trumpets that are called *clarinas* just the same as flutes for any kind of ensemble, and perform the soprano parts perfectly with all the diminutions displayed.[29]

Kircher mentions the peasant bagpipe which, he says, is 'the only solace of shepherds and peasants.' The new bagpipe designed for court use, the musette, he finds is 'marvelous to hear.'

> Here at Rome I have seen an instrument of this sort not without a singular delight to my soul.[30]

26 Kircher, *Musurgia universalis*, 1.

27 Ibid., 91.

28 Ibid., 94.

29 Ibid., 96ff.

30 Ibid., 99ff.

He includes in the discussion of the bagpipe the other double reeds, hautbois and dulcian.

> But among them the one that is called *fagot* in the vernacular especially stands out; nothing sweeter or more fitted for playing the bass can be imagined.[31]

Following the wind instruments, Kircher discusses the organ and he is one of few writers who describes the organ for what it really was in the Baroque: a surrogate wind band.

> The organ is like a sort of epitome and compendium of all wind instruments, and thus is deservedly the most beautiful and perfect of all.[32]

In discussing the skins used for percussion instruments, Kircher relates a charming contemporary example of folklore about sheep.

> Just one little sheep feeds us, clothes us, and entertains us with four types of musical instruments, with intestines for strings, with shinbones and horns for pipes, and finally the skin turning into a drum, so that consequently the Hebrews have declared of it not inelegantly that the live animal has one voice; dead, seven.[33]

Finally, after discussing an instrument much like the modern xylophone, Kircher is reminded of a most curious anecdote—or should we say, tale!

> Not so long ago, in order to dispel the melancholy of some great prince, a noted and ingenious actor constructed an instrument such as this. He took live cats all of different sizes, and shut them up in a kind of box especially made for this business, so that their tails, stuck through the holes, were inserted tightly into certain channels. Under these he put keys fitted with the sharpest points instead of mallets. Then he arranged the cats tonally according to their different sizes, so that each key corresponded to the tail of one cat, and he put the instrument prepared for the relaxation of the prince in a suitable place. Then when it was played, it produced such music as the voices of cats can produce. For when the keys, depressed by the fingers of the organist, pricked the tails of the cats with their points, they, driven to a rage, with miserable voices, howling now low, now high, produced such music made of the voices of cats as would move men to laughter and even arouse shrews to dance.[34]

Book Seven, 'Diacritical,' contains additional material on the ancient civilizations, the development of music during the Middle Ages and discussions of the classification of styles. Following the publication in 1643 of Marco Scacchi's *Cribrum musicum ad triticum Syferticum*, several critics adopted his classification of music in three functional divisions: church, chamber and theater. Kircher presented a much more extensive classification of

31 Ibid., 100.

32 Ibid., 102.

33 Ibid., 161.

34 Ibid., 138ff.

music, discussing first what he called 'individual styles' of music, ideas which were based on the so-called 'humors.' His second classification had to do with 'national styles.' The third classification followed Scacchi's concept of a function-based system, but Kircher's is more extended, with eight categories.

Stylus ecclesiasticus, church style with or without chant. This must be 'full of majesty, miraculously transporting the heart to contemplation of the solemn and grave, imprinting on the heart its own motion.' *Stylus motecticus* is a sub-category, with more varied and florid style.

Stylus canonicus [canon], in which the 'musical ability of a composer is shown at its most skillful.'

Stylus phantasticus [improvisation], which Kircher finds 'an extremely free and uninhibited method of composition particularly suitable for instrumental music.' He cites here the toccata, ricercar, fantasias and sonatas.

Stylus madrigalecus, 'Italian style par excellence, joyful, lively, full of sweetness and grace, lending itself easily to vocal diminutions, and eschewing slowness of movement, unless specifically required by the text.' This style, he says, is suitable for the portrayal of love, affection and pain.

Stylus melismaticus, 'particularly appropriate for measured verses and meters … sweetly sung without agitation or affected dissonance.

Stylus hyporchematicus, for feasts and festivities and *Stylus choraicus*, for dance and ballet. This style has the ability to 'excite emotions of joy, exaltation, wantonness and licentiousness.'

Stylus symphoniacus, instrumental music.

Stylus dramaticus or *Stylus recitativus*, recitative style for the representation of any of the so-called affections, or for abrupt changes of affection through sudden alternations in tonality, the so-called *Stylus metabolicus*.[35]

Book Eight, 'Miraculous Musicology,' concerns time, including the poetic meters in a number of languages and a system by which the 'unskilled in music can attain a perfect knowledge of composing in a short time.' Kircher includes in this book reproductions of a song composed by Louis XIII of France and a five-part madrigal by the emperor Ferdinand III.

Book Nine, 'The Magic of Consonance and Dissonance,' in which 'the secrets of all the science of music are brought into the light by countless experiments.' Certainly one of the most interesting parts of his work, we find here many curious and interesting things.

First, he is credited with being the person who originated the idea of playing music on drinking glasses, which was the result of his experimentation in observing the effects of the tones produced by glasses filled with wine, water, sea-water and oil, etc. This led him to acoustics in general, in the course of which he concluded that the biblical account of the fall of the walls of Jericho was not due to the sound of the trumpets, but some other physical cause.

In this book Kircher also discusses the effects of music on the mind and the use of music therapy. Here he discusses the use of music to cure the bite of the Tarantula spider, something

35 Quoted in Ibid., 50.

widely mentioned in early literature.[36] Kircher cites several histories of this phenomenon, including a girl who was bitten and was cured by the music of only a drum. In another case, however, he reports a volunteer allowed himself to be bitten by two Tarantulas, of different colors. As the bite of one responded to music and dance, but the bite of the other was made worse, the patient died. Kircher's technical explanation reads,

> The poison is sharp, gnawing, and bilious and is received and incorporated into the medullary substances of the fibers. The music has the power to rarefy the air to a certain harmonic pitch; the air thus rarefied, penetrating the pores of the patient's body, affects the muscles, arteries, and minute fibers, and incites him to dance, which begets a perspiration, in which the poison evaporates.

Kircher also devotes considerable space in Book Nine to echoes, beginning with a lovely anecdote.

> A certain friend of mine having set out on a journey, had a river to cross, and not knowing the stream, cried out *Oh*, to which an echo answered *Oh*; he imagining it to be a man, called out in Italian, *Onde devo passar*? it answered *passa*; and when he asked *qui*? it replied *qui*; but as the waters formed a deep whirlpool there, and made a great noise, he was terrified, and again asked *Devo passar qui*? The echo returns *passa qui*. He repeated the same question often, and still had the same answer. Terrified with the fear of being obliged to swim in case he attempted to pass there, and it being a dark and tempestuous night, he concluded that his respondent was some evil spirit that wanted to entice him into the torrent.

In the course of this discussion, Kircher cites a building in Pavia which would return an echo thirty times.

In this book Kircher also mentions a number of curious mechanical musical instruments,[37] including a Cymbalarian, a machine consisting of revolving bells, and a combination of a hurdy-gurdy and a harpsichord which produced the impression of a consort of viols. One device of his own invention was a wooden box, strung with gut strings, which, when placed in a window, produced sounds generated by the wind.

> The method of tuning it, which is not, as in other instruments, by thirds, fourths, fifths, or eighths, but all the chords are to be tuned by a unison, or in octaves. It is very wonderful, and nearly paradoxical, that chords thus tuned should constitute different harmony. This musical phenomenon has not as yet been observed by any one that I know of …

36 In another book, *Magnes siue De arte magnetica opus tripartitum* (Rome, 1641) Kircher also discusses 'the magnetic power and faculties of music' and 'the affections of the mind which music excites.' Here again, of particular interest is a special science which he calls 'Tarantism,' the study of the 'magnetism and amazing sympathy with music' of the tarantula.

37 Just before his death, Kircher published a book called *Phonurgia Nova* (Rome, 1673) in which he describes his invention of a Speaking Trumpet, an idea which he says he took from the new telescopes. Among other demonstrations, he adapted it to a statue in an art gallery, shocking the viewers with 'feigned and ludicrous consultations.' He also claims he constructed one version on a mountain, where the sound traveled four miles and was taken by villagers as a voice from heaven telling them to climb the mountain to celebrate the feast of Pentecost.

When it is thus disposed you will perceive a harmony in the room in proportion as the wind is weaker or stronger; for from time to time all the chords having a tremulous motion impressed upon them, produce a correspondent variety of sounds, resembling a consort of pipes or flutes, affecting the hearers with a strange pleasure.

Book Ten, 'Decachord of Nature,' focuses on the organ; the music of the spheres; the harmony of minerals, plants and animals with the heavens; political music; musical metaphysics; the music of angels and the harmony of nature.

On the Purposes of Music

In his *Adonis*, Marino includes a passage on the purposes of music. He mentions music to give courage to the lover, solace for the tormented and for the definition and enhancement of emotions in general.

Music pleases all, but more than all the rest
delights the restless souls of those in love,
nor can tormented heart find other peace
or refuge than in melody and songs.
'Tis true indeed that music has the power
sometimes to call forth doleful sighs and tears,
and thus it mingles two contrary ends;
it cheers the cheerful, saddens still the sad.[38]

The earliest Greek philosophers, indeed philosophy as we know it, began with attempts to explain the physical world. They soon fixed four basic elements (air, water, fire and earth) and four qualities (hot, cold, moist and dry). Attempts to relate man to the physical world resulted in the theory of the four 'humors,' sanguine, phlegmatic, choleric and melancholic, the balance of which determined a person's disposition, character and lifestyle. Athanasius Kircher believed the humors indigenous to a person explained his preferences in music.

Melancholy people like grave, solid, and sad harmony; sanguine persons prefer the *hyporchematic* style (dance music) because it agitates the blood; choleric people like agitated harmonies because of the vehemence of their swollen gall; martially inclined men are partial to trumpets and drums and reject all delicate and pure music; phlegmatic persons lean toward women's voices because their high pitched voice has a benevolent effect on phlegmatic humour.[39]

---

38 Marino, *L'Adone*, VII, 62.

39 Athanasius Kircher (1602–1680), *Musurgia Universalis*, quoted in Paul Henry Lang, 'Musical Thought of the Baroque. The Doctrine of Temperaments and Affections,' in William Hays, ed., *Twentieth-Century Views of Music History* (New York: Scribner's, 1972), 195.

Since it had long been assumed that these humors, and thus the person, could be affected by external influences, many philosophers also assumed that it was here that the power of music on the listener was found. Seventeenth-century philosophers attempted to explain the influence of music on the affections, but, because language can explain neither music nor the emotions, their writings were largely unheeded by practical musicians.

Kircher began by determining that there are eight basic emotions which music can affect: love, grief or pain, joy, exultancy, rage or indignation, compassion or tears, fear or distress, presumption or audacity and admiration or astonishment.[40] The philosophers in Germany tried to equate such emotions with specific elements of music, which was an effort doomed to failure since individual elements, such as intervals, for example, express little in comparison with how they are used by the composer. Very much to the dismay of those who demand more scientific sounding concepts, Kircher attempted to identify the power of music at work through descriptive, and even subjective, language. For the first emotion, love [*paradigma affectus amoris*] he finds in a madrigal by Gesualdo intervals which languish and syncopations which express 'the syncope of the languishing heart.' The second emotion, grief or pain [*paradigma affectus dolorosi*] he illustrates by describing the lament of Jephtha's daughter in an oratorio by Carissimi.

> Giacomo Carissimi, a very excellent and famous composer ... through his genius and the felicity of his compositions, surpasses all others in moving the minds of listeners to whatever affection he wishes. His compositions are truly imbued with the essence and life of the spirit. Among numerous works of great worth, he has composed the dialogue of Jephte ... After the recitative with which he ingeniously and subtly expresses the jubilant welcome accorded Jephtha by his daughter (who celebrates the victories and triumphs of her father in a joyous dance, accompanied by all sorts of musical instruments), Carissimi depicts, by means of a sudden change of mode, the dismay into which Jephtha has been plunged by this unexpected meeting with his only begotten daughter, against whom he has taken an irrevocable vow, and whom he despairs of being able to save. Joy thus gives way to the opposing affections of sorrow and grief. This is followed by the six-voice lament of the daughter's virgin companions, which Carissimi composes with such skill that you would swear you could hear their sobbings and lamentations. Having, in fact, begun with a festive dialogue, cast in the dance-like tone 8, Carissimi sets this lament in a very different mode, in this case tone 4 intermingled with tone 3. Given this tragic story to portray — a story in which joy is dispelled by the distress and intense sorrow of the heart—the composer suitably chose a mode that is as distant from tone 8 as are the extremes of the heavens from each other, that he might better express, through this opposition, the differences between the affections. And nothing is more capable than this of portraying such unhappy events, such tragic happenings interwoven with affections of a different kind.

40 *Musurgia Universalis*, I, Bk. I, iii, 6.

Antonio Abbatini, in an autobiographical poem of 1667, also refers to the ancient association of affections with the modes.

Here I go no further, since it is said:
The papacy of the *maestri* is St. Louis.
Here, indeed, I wish to live and die.
Here never does one sing in Phrygian modes,
Since nowhere is there argument and din,
But only in the Lydian, as in Paris used.
Here I draw a line and here I stop,
For I am tired and, weary as I am,
I cannot pass beyond.[41]

ENTERTAINMENT MUSIC

In Marino's *Adonis* there is a 'play within a play,' which he calls a 'Tragedy.' In reality it is a ballet, a typical court entertainment allegory with a great variety of musical and poetic styles.

Invention, Fable, and the Poem here,
with Energy, Decorum, Harmony,
plus Order firm and Wit and rare Conceit
contribute to the theme of tragedy.
The artificer prime is Eloquence,
who towers over the rest with Poesy.
And with them Meter, Numbers, Prosody
impose upon the music their control.[42]

Each one keeps step according to the time
marked by the lyre, the movement matching notes,
and with the hands and feet and the the voice,
at once strikes strings and pavement and the air.[43]

Again the scene is changed, and in a flash
the square is full of Centaurs in a dance,
one bearing a keen poignard in his hand,
one a light lance and one a heavy mace …
The trumpet blares out in a martial air:
'To war, off to the war! to arms, to arms!'

41 Quoted in Bianconi, *Music in the Seventeenth Century*, 288.

42 Marino, *L'Adone*, V, 123.

43 Ibid., V, 133.

Now one with fury seems to strike his foe;
now, now it seems that blood spills on the ground.
With art harmonic is the battle staged ...[44]

Lo, now a concert of musicians next
begins in low, in high, in blended strains,
and concords sound from various instruments,
some played by hand and others played by mouth;
in tempi bright and quick, then grave and slow,
the verses swell for those blest banqueters;
from choruses of nymphs responsive sound
the echoes of a symphony of Love.[45]

44 Ibid., V, 135–136.

45 Ibid., V, 146.

5 THE MUSICAL SCENE IN SPAIN

WITH THE DEATH OF PHILIP II IN 1598 the fortunes of Spain began to decline, due to several economic conditions.[1] The administration of the colonies had become increasingly costly and the plunder of gold and silver was no longer covering the costs of empire. The defeat of the armada made attempts to maintain sea trade more expensive. Inflation was rampant and the population base was declining due to emigration.

During the seventeenth century Spain's land holdings made it the greatest empire in the world. Unfortunately, the genetic wheel of fortune, the central problem in dynastic government, left Spain with no men capable of fulfilling the potential of this rich empire. Philip III (1598–1621) was a weak man incapable of governing, who turned the responsibility of government over to Francisco Gómez de Sandoval y Rojas, Duke of Lerma. The latter not only drained the treasury, but ruthlessly expelled 400,000 Christian Moors to Africa in order to confiscate their property.

MUSIC OF THE COURT

Spanish music in the seventeenth century suffered from the great separation between the aristocracy and the middle and lower classes. Most composers and professional musicians were forced to earn a living as servants to the court and little art music seemed to trickle down. Thus, while the publication of music was expanding enormously in Northern Europe, there was very little such activity in Spain. At the same time there appears to have been little foreign enlightenment. Although there were many foreign instrumentalists at court, their influence in bringing any of the exciting new developments from the North is difficult to document. Even the craze for Italian music which was capturing the rest of Europe only becomes a significant factor in Spain at the end of the century.

One contemporary insight into the slow development of Spanish music is offered by Domenico Cerone, who, although an Italian, wrote the first important book on music in the

1 Our purpose here is not an attempt to summarize the development of Baroque music itself in Spain, and its composers, but rather to present a brief overview of the environment in which the music was performed and its general aesthetic nature. At the same time, we take the opportunity to include important material not found in general music history texts.

Spanish language, the *El Melopeo y Maestro* (1613).[2] In Book I, Chapter LIII, he offers several reasons why he finds Spanish musical development lagging behind the Italians. He finds the Spanish 'masters' not as diligent, the teachers lacking in patience and the composers simply not writing much music. He also reports that he knew no academies for music in Spain, except for a private one sponsored by the Austrian wife of Philip II. Finally, Cerone reports that due to the strong religious roots in Spain, nearly all musical energy was devoted to the improvement of church music. Indeed, in his own book of some 1,200 pages, there is not a single illustration of instrumental music, nor any biographical information on important Spanish instrumentalists.

The music favored by the court of Philip III was entertainment music, beginning with allegorical forms in the tradition of the sixteenth century. The private entertainment of the king centered on dancing, for which the court string players devoted much of their time. Cerone notes that while the king paid his musicians unusually high salaries, few other nobles were personally active in support of music at this time.

Philip IV (1621–1665) was also little interested in government, turning over these mundane details to a cardinal, the Count of Oliveres. The cardinal involved himself in international intrigue and by 1642 had left Spain so weak that she was soon forced to give up the Netherlands and sign the Peace of the Pyrenees, which promoted the ascendancy of France. Meanwhile, the king lived a life of pleasure, which included strong support of art, poetry and the theater.

Philip was not so interested in music and between 1652 and 1655 made retrenchments in the court wind players in Madrid. No longer able to afford the importation of foreign musicians, the court ordered the leader of the court wind players, Francesco de Baldes (or, perhaps, Valdes) to organize a school for minstrels so the court would not be dependent on hiring foreign players. An extant document[3] reveals that he formed a band of twelve wind instruments, 4 soprano shawms, 2 tenor shawms, 2 'contra altos de shawm' and 4 trombones, which appears to be in imitation of the *Les Grands Hautbois* of Louis XIV in France.

Charles II (1665–1700) was a lame, epileptic, senile half-wit, whom it was impossible to educate. He presided over the final collapse of the economy of the middle and lower classes, while the aristocracy continued in blind extravagance. Following the economic decline, there was a decline in the teaching of music and by the period of Charles II sufficient competent native singers could not be found to fill the openings in the royal chapel.[4] At the urging of the pope, Charles made his heir Philip, Duke of Anjoy, and for all practical purposes gave Spain to France.

After the turn of the eighteenth century, following the marriage of Philip V to Maria Luisa of Savoy, French musicians began to play an important role in court music. Some impor-

2 Book 22 contains a number of 'enigma' canons, in the form of a cross, a key, a sword, etc., as well as one resolvable by throwing dice.

3 Edmond Vander Straeten, *La Musique aux Pays-Bas* (New York: Dover, 1969), VII, 436ff.

4 Louise K. Stein, 'The Iberian Peninsula,' in *The Late Baroque Era* (Englewood Cliffs: Prentice Hall, 1994), 413.

tant Italian musicians also began to arrive in Spain at this time, notably Domenico Scarlatti and the famous singer, Farinelli. Scarlatti followed his student, Princess María Bárbara de Braganza to Spain when she married Ferdinand and his only duty seems to have been to produce sonata after sonata.

The influence of Italian style in Spain was not without protest. In particular the Benedictine Benito Feijoo complained that the Italian music was noisy and lacking in traditional Spanish gravity. He objected that the Spanish had become slaves to a foreign taste. He particularly found the Italian use of harmony to be disturbing. 'Harmony,' he sighed, 'becomes exasperating.'[5]

CIVIC MUSIC

The relative lack of extant publications makes it difficult to judge the involvement of the middle class in secular music. Some extant collections of polyphonic songs, *cancioneros*, based on the best available poetry may have been intended more for the aristocracy than the more educated citizen class. More clearly the music of the public were the songs used in the theater.

Public Italian opera began in 1719, under the patronage of the queen. But since the queen herself was not popular with the public the opera was not a financial success and by 1735 most of the Italian singers had departed.

CHURCH MUSIC

The exclusive control of Spain by the aristocracy and the Church created a conservative atmosphere in which the sixteenth-century Church styles continued on through much of the seventeenth century. Only the arrival of the vernacular, but sacred, *villancico* offered something truly contemporary to the broad public.

None the less, some churches continued to employ large numbers of wind instruments, who were probably used primarily in the performance of large church concerti. In the cathedral in Granada during the seventeenth century one found flutes, cornetts, shawms, bassoons, horns, trumpets and trombones. In the royal chapel in Toledo, the pastoral chants were accompanied by two shawms, a small 'bassoon-serpentine' and bassoon.[6] There are also extant three Masses by Francisco Soler (1625–1688), composed for voices and wind band.[7] In

---

5 Quoted in Ibid., 426.

6 Vander Straeten, *La Musique*, VIII, 194ff.

7 Copies in E:Bc and E:G.

Portugal, during the seventeenth century, cornetts, sackbuts and bassoons regularly accompanied the singers in the Badajoz Cathedral.[8]

If anything, there seemed to be a greater enthusiasm for church music in Spanish Mexico. Torquemada, writing in 1615, found singers proficient in polyphonic music in every town of a hundred or larger and 'competent instrumentalists are also found everywhere.'[9] An Englishman in 1625 concluded the people were drawn to the churches 'more for the delight of the music than for any delight in the service of God.'[10]

In Puebla, the second largest city in seventeenth-century Mexico, the cathedral used recorders, shawms, cornetts, sackbuts and bassoons to double, or even replace the voices. Violins do not appear until the eighteenth century. Surviving documents indicate that one of the leading composers, Juan Gutiérrez de Padilla, maintained a shop in his home in which salaried workers produced 'ecclesiastical instruments,' bassoons, shawms and recorders.[11] The most important composer of this cathedral, Antonio de Salazar (1650–1715), set to music a poem by Juana Inés de la Cruz, which speaks of the typical church ensemble as being 'clarino, trumpet, cornett, trombone, bassoon, and organ.'[12]

In Portugal, through the early years of the eighteenth century, the Church music was also very conservative. John V sent his singers to study in Rome and imported music from Rome in an effort to closely follow the official style there.

8 George Grove, *The New Grove Dictionary of Music and Musicians*, ed. Stanley Sadie (London: Macmillan, 1980), IV, 817.

9 Juan de Torquemada, *Monarquía indiana*, quoted in Steven Barwick, 'Mexico,' in *The Early Baroque Era* (Englewood Cliffs: Prentice Hall, 1994), 352.

10 Ibid., 355.

11 Grove, *Dictionary*, XV, 441 and XIV, 76.

12 Ibid., XVI, 412.

6 SPANISH LITERATURE

THE YEARS 1556–1665 are often called 'The Golden Age of Spanish Literature,' but the writers most thought of under this label, Cervantes, Lope de Vega and a number of poets, lived at the end of the sixteenth century, thus we have presented them in another volume. During the seventeenth century only the playwrights continue the 'Golden Age.' The best of the remaining writers, especially some who were themselves priests, reflect an atmosphere dominated by the Inquisition and the *Index Librorum Prohibitorum*, which attempted to eliminate all literature displeasing to the Church. It is then, apart from the theater, a period of literature in decline. The literature also reflects, of course, the diminishing fortunes of Spain herself, as we are reminded in a poem of lamentations over the decline of Spain by Francisco de Quevedo.

> Excellent Sire, my lamentation
> now breaks its bounding shores:
> my song will be a flood,
>
> my cheeks are wet, my eyes
> are urns that overflow and drench
> the altars of the two Castiles;
>
> for Virtue lies in disarray
> who, though not rich, was proud;
> she sleeps, buried in vanity ...[1]

ON THE PHYSIOLOGY OF AESTHETICS

Here, as with nearly all subjects, we especially feel the long shadow of the Church, which for a thousand years had stressed the importance of Reason over all of man's faculties. An observation by Baltasar Gracián related to the Persians, but it might as well have been a reflection of the attitude of the Church.

---

1 Francisco de Quevedo (1580–1645), 'Epistola satirica y censoria,' in Angel Flores, ed., *An Anthology of Spanish Poetry* (Garden City: Doubleday, 1961), 136. Quevedo (1580–1645) was educated at a Jesuit lower school and at age sixteen entered the University of Alcalá de Henares. He took degrees in philosophy and theology, while mastering Greek, Latin, Hebrew, Arabic, French and Italian. At age fifty-nine he was accused of being the author of a poem attacking the government and was sent to prison for four years.

> It was a striking peculiarity of the Persians not to want to see their children until they were seven years old … They did not count them as their children until they were able to reason.[2]

In another place he also reflects the Church's long-held dogma that man must be ruled by Reason.

> It is an outstanding sign of wisdom to keep a cool head during fits of rage: all extremes of feeling are a falling away from reason.[3]

In spite of Gracián's close adherence to Church positions on the rule of Reason, he was much more independent in his honest recognition that some people are simply different and are motivated other than by Reason.

> In some the heart reigns, in others the head. Is there anything more foolish than to use courage to study and wit to fight?[4]
>
> ……
>
> Some people excel at quick thinking, others at quick doing. The former please, the latter astonish.[5]

Of course, we know today that Reason is only half of man, the left hemisphere of the brain. Although this was not medically understood before our era, it was frequently understood by deduction that there is another side of us, whether one calls it the 'subjective,' the 'emotional' or by any other name. And among those who had not deduced the processes, there was always the unexplainable tug of war between rational thought and feelings. A wonderful testimonial to this struggle is found in a poem by the nun known as Sor Juana Inés de la Cruz.

> This torment of love
> that is in my heart,
> I know I feel it
> and know not why.[6]

Gracián is equally at a loss for explanation and he simply evades the issue by asking,

> What does it matter if understanding rushes forward but the heart holds back?[7]

2 Baltasar Gracián, *A Pocket Mirror for Heroes*, trans. Christopher Maurer (New York: Currency Doubleday, 1996), 162. Gracián (1601–1658) was educated at Toledo and became a member of the Society of Jesus in 1619. Although he continued his works as a priest for some time, by 1640 he was well-known in literary circles.

3 Baltasar Gracián, *The Oracle*, Nr. 155, trans. L. B. Walton (London: Dent, 1953).

4 Gracián, *A Pocket Mirror for Heroes*, 29.

5 Ibid., 157.

6 Sor Juana Inés de la Cruz (1648–1695), 'Vida retirada,' in Flores, *Anthology*, 156. She was the first important poet of the New World, living and dying in Mexico.

7 Gracián, *A Pocket Mirror for Heroes*, 13.

One manifestation of this struggle between Reason and feelings, as we have often noted in these volumes, is the frequently expressed preference for the right hand. When one finds this it is the egotistical left hemisphere speaking (the only hemisphere which can speak or write) and at the same time a denial by the left hemisphere of the existence of the right hemisphere, a phenomenon which has now been thoroughly documented in clinical studies. One example in this literature of this right hand preference we find in the writings of Quevedo. In his 'The Dream of the Last Judgment,' he dreams he sees persons of various professions rising from their graves upon the sounding of the trumpet for the day of judgment. Among these, he notes,

> What alarmed me even more, however, was the sight of some two or three merchants, who, having put their souls the wrong way round, now found all five of their senses located in the fingers of their grasping right hands.[8]

As part of its emphasis on Reason, it followed that the Church also had taken the position that the eye must be the most important of the five senses. Gracián seems to be following the official line, when he observes,

> Truth is usually apprehended by the eyes; we wear it in a distorted form; it rarely reaches us in its pristine purity, and least of all when it comes from a distance; it always has some admixture of the feelings through which it is filtered; feeling tints with its own hue everything it touches.[9]
>
> ......
>
> Imagination reaches farther than sight, and deception, which usually comes in through the ear, eventually goes out through the eyes.[10]

Gracián's most charming discussion of hearing involves his explanation why we don't have *earlids*. The reader will also notice here the reference to sounds being of such brief duration, the basis of much questioning of the virtue of music in early literature.

> We have eyelids but not earlids, for the ears are the portals of learning, and Nature wanted to keep them wide open ... The ears hold court at all hours, even when the soul retires to its chambers. In fact, it is then that those sentinels ought to be most wide awake. If not, who would warn of danger? When the mind goes lazily off to sleep, who else would rouse it? This is the difference between seeing and hearing. For the eyes seek out things deliberately, when and if they want, but things come spontaneously to the ears. Visible things tend to remain: if we don't look at them now, we can do so later; but most sounds pass by quickly, and we must grab that opportunity by the forelock. Our one tongue is twice enclosed, and our two ears are twice open, so that we can hear twice as much as we speak.[11]

8 Francisco de Quevedo, *Dreams and Discourses*, trans. R.K. Britton (Warminster: Aris & Phillips, 1989), 41ff.

9 Gracián, *The Oracle*, Nr. 80.

10 Ibid., Nr. 282.

11 Gracián, *A Pocket Mirror for Heroes*, 87ff.

ON THE PSYCHOLOGY OF AESTHETICS

Gracián again reflects the teachings of the Church in his references to the emotions. The Church had long regarded emotions as the gateway to sin. Thus, as Gracián echoes, man's salvation lies in overcoming them.

> A man who is not passion's slave reveals the highest quality of soul; his superiority itself redeems him from subjection to passing, vulgar influences. There is no greater mastery than control over oneself and one's emotions; it comes to be a triumph for a man's free will.[12]

He also attempts to connect this with Art, observing,

> Art would be deficient if it merely taught you to conceal the limits of your talent. It must also teach you to disguise the impetus of your emotions …
> Discovering someone's emotions is like opening a breach in the fortress of his talent.[13]

In another place, he gives a variant of this last sentence:

> The emotions are the breaches in the defenses of the mind.[14]

Gracián also warns of the influence of the emotions with respect to judgment and taste.

> Emotion is the declared enemy of prudence and thus of wise selection. It cares nothing for what is fitting, only for its effect, and it would rather indulge its whims than hit the mark. It makes no distinction between 'best' and 'favorite.'[15]

ON THE PHILOSOPHY OF AESTHETICS

Gracián attempts no definition of Art beyond the simplistic.

> What beauty is for the eyes and harmony is for the ears, wit is for the intellect.[16]
>
> ……
>
> Self-satisfaction is the beatitude of the simple. 'Lucky you,' Michelangelo once said, 'who are content with your vile doodlings while I get no satisfaction from anything I paint.' I've always enjoyed a certain witty saying of Dante. Once, his great patron Medici, wishing to find him, in

12 Gracián, *The Oracle*, Nr. 8.

13 Gracián, *A Pocket Mirror for Heroes*, 7.

14 Gracián, *The Oracle*, Nr. 98.

15 Gracián, *A Pocket Mirror for Heroes*, 136.

16 Ibid., 63.

> disguise, in a crowd during Carnival, ordered those searching for him to ask everyone, 'Who knows what good is?' Only one answered wisely: 'He who knows what badness is.' And they knew it was Dante.[17]

He is considerably more decided when it comes to the purpose of art, however.

> Man is born a barbarian; he is saved from being a beast by acquiring culture. Culture, therefore, makes the man, and the greater his culture the greater the individual. By virtue of her culture, Greece was in a position to call the rest of the world barbarous. Ignorance is most uncouth; nothing refines so much as knowledge.[18]
>
> ......
>
> Art. She, too, is an enchantress. But whereas Circe changed men into pigs, Art changes beasts into people.[19]

In Gracián's view, one had to make a concerted personal effort to obtain the benefits which the appreciation of culture, and the development of taste, offered.

> Real talent is never easy to please. Taste must be cultivated and improved no less than the intellect. When both are outstanding, they seem born from the same womb, twins of talent, co-heirs of excellence.[20]

Interestingly, he found this was obtained not by personal experience, but by learning from a friend. In this Inquisition dominated society, one might regard this as meaning being careful what it is safe to say and believe.

> Tastes are imparted by personal intercourse and are passed on by frequenting the society of one's fellows.[21]

Finally, in the continuing decline from the Renaissance, when it was a mark of respect that a noble could perform music, Gracián says it is good to appreciate art, but not to actually practice it.

> Not all arts deserve esteem, nor all occupations. To know everything is no grounds for criticism, but *practice* everything and your good name will suffer ... Philip II of Spain chided his son for singing in his chamber.[22]

---

17 Ibid., 92ff.

18 Gracián, *The Oracle*, Nr. 87.

19 Gracián, *A Pocket Mirror for Heroes*, 60.

20 Ibid., 16ff.

21 Gracián, *The Oracle*, Nr. 65.

22 Gracián, *A Pocket Mirror for Heroes*, 20ff.

Regarding the ancient debate on whether Art should imitate Nature, Gracián avoids any philosophical stand on the issue itself and instead concentrates on Nature as something which Art can help ameliorate.

> There is no such thing as unaided beauty, and no excellence that does not degenerate into barbarism if it lacks the finishing touch of art; art redeems the bad and perfects the good. Nature usually lets us down when we least expect it: let us, then, have recourse to art. Without art, the finest of natural endowments goes unembellished, and high qualities lack half their excellence if culture be to seek. Unrefined, artless knowledge is common to all men, and every kind of endowment needs polish.[23]
>
> ......
>
> Nature breeds subtlety; art nurtures it.[24]
>
> ......
>
> Where nature is sufficient, art is unneeded.[25]

With respect to the important aesthetic question of universality, Gracián demonstrates how fine the line is between universality and popularity. When a genuine art work communicates broadly, Gracián suggests, the artist should be pleased, even if he doesn't know why.

> Do not be alone in your condemnation of something which pleases a great many people. There is something good in it because it satisfies so many, and even though there is no explanation as to why it should be so, it is a source of enjoyment.[26]

However, it is quite a different matter to aim a work at the broad public.

> Ah, how profoundly wise the man who was unhappy because his achievements pleased the many! A glut of popular applause does not satisfy sensible men ... Take no delight in the marvels of the multitude, which are no more than baubles, for general folly admires where exceptional discernment is undeceived.[27]

The early seventeenth-century Spanish writers who were Jesuits naturally followed the condemnation of actors and the theater, against which the Church had been unsuccessfully preaching since its earliest years. Quevedo, in his 'The Dream of the Last Judgment,' observes men of various professions being judged. As a lawyer was being sentenced for deforming the laws, it was noticed that there was a man crouching on all fours behind him, hoping not

23 Gracián, *The Oracle*, Nr. 12.

24 Gracián, *A Pocket Mirror for Heroes*, 13.

25 Ibid., 54.

26 Gracián, *The Oracle*, Nr. 270.

27 Ibid., Nr. 28.

to be noticed. This turned out to be an actor—who was immediately sent to hell![28] Gracián has the same opinion,

> What occupations are praiseworthy? I would exclude those that are as empty of honor as they are full of show: an actor lives rich in applause and dies poor in reputation.[29]

With one exception, poets shared the displeasure of the Church. The exception, and best Spanish poet of the seventeenth century, Luis de Góngora, returned several times in spirit to the pastoral style of the ancient lyric poets. His 'First Solitude,' for example, contains musical references that could have been written three thousand years earlier, such as,

> The pipes and psaltery of rustic Pan
> To dance and song invite ...[30]

In his poem 'Polyphemus and Galatea,' he mentions a large ensemble of these rustic pipes,

> A hundred pipes with wax and string are joined
> (A horrid din the vile contrivance makes)
> As many echoes as the pipes combined
> by string and wax the raucous music wakes.[31]

and his description of a stream,

> To the sweet concert which their skill sustains,
> Where the black pebbles' rustic harmonies
> Clash from the ivory fingers' shining keys ...[32]

In his 'Second Solitude,' Góngora again uses music as a metaphor to describe a stream, followed by a description of birds singing.

> The water, eddying round the tiny stones,
> Played on a crystalline theorbo's strings;
> Among the ivy's verdant coils there rang
> The birds' confused and yet harmonious tones;
> Many they were, and many times their choirs

---

28 Quevedo, *Dreams and Discourses*, 55. It is interesting that no musicians were among those being judged.

29 Gracián, *A Pocket Mirror for Heroes*, 28.

30 Luis de Góngora, 'First Solitude,' lines 669ff, in Gilbert Cunningham, *The Solitudes of Góngora* (Baltimore: Johns Hopkins Press, 1964). Góngora (1561–1627) was born of noble parents and educated at a Jesuit lower school and at the University of Salamanca. In 1617 he was ordained as a priest in Madrid.

31 Luis de Góngora, 'Polyphemus and Galatea,' lines 89ff, in Gilbert Cunningham, *Polyphemus and Galatea* (Austin: University of Texas Pess, 1977).

32 Góngora, 'First Solitude,' lines 345ff.

Surpassed the nine winged Muses—curving lyres
Disguised beneath their lightly feathered wings—
And sweetly, if uncertainly, they sang
Each in his diverse tongue.[33]

During the next generation the influence of the Inquisition seems to have ended such idyllic poetry. Such poetry, to the Church, had always been labeled as lies, since it dwelt with fable. Thus, it is no particular surprise to find Gracián beginning a sentence, 'A man spoke truth, though he was a poet …'[34]

Quevedo in his picaresque novel, *Buscón*,[35] which concerns the travels of Pablos, a comic anti-hero, presents an extensive satire of poets and poetry. First, on his way to Madrid, Pablos encounters an old priest riding a mule who complains that after years of submitting his poetry in 'public contests for songs and carols for Corpus Christi and Christmas' he has never been awarded the prize. As an example of one of his unappreciated sacred songs he offers the following, which, of course, consists of all the wrong emotions for the occasion.

Shepherds, is it not great fun to say
Today's Saint Corpus Christi's day?
This is a day of joyous dances
When the tiny lamb so young
Shall hear his timely mourning sung …
So sound away the gay sackbut
And lead us on our happy way.

Among the other works by this neglected poet was an epic describing 11,000 virgins, with fifty verses for each, and a comedy called *Noah's Ark*, in which the characters were cocks, rats, donkeys and wild boars. Only when he had finished the play, did he realize it could never be produced, since animals can't speak. When the poet also mentioned 900 sonnets for the 'woman I love,' Pablos asks about his personal experience in this regard and the poet responded that, as a clergyman, the sonnets were written in the spirit of prophecy.

When Pablos arrived in Madrid, reflecting on this poet as one of 'those lunatics who live off poor wretches,' he expressed his feelings by writing a proclamation against poets.

Proclamation against addle-brained, insipid and tasteless poets

Being cognizant of the fact that this species of vermin known as poets are our neighbors and Christians, though bad ones; seeing that throughout the year they worship eyebrows, teeth, ribbons, and slippers, and commit other more grievous sins, we hereby ordain that during Holy Week, all publicly known and street-corner poets be gathered together as is done with

33 Ibid., 'Second Solitude,' lines 349ff.

34 Gracián, *A Pocket Mirror for Heroes*, 30.

35 Francisco de Quevedo, *The Scavenger*, trans. Hugh Harter (New York: Las Americas Publishing Company, 1962), 66ff.

bad women, and they be informed of their erroneous ways and be converted. To this end, we do hereby set aside houses for repentant poets …

Furthermore, due to the fact that the devilish sect of men condemned to write poetry of perpetual concepts, splitters of words and perverters of reason, has infected our womenfolk with the disease of poetry, we do hereby declare ourselves revenged through the evil we have done to the latter for what the first female did to us through Adam. Because of the poverty and want that infects the globe, we order that all the couplets of the poets be burned like old trimmings, so as to extract the gold, silver and pearls, since in most verses the ladies are fashioned from all sorts of precious things, like statues with feet of clay …

Furthermore, having observed that since many poets have ceased to write Moorish ballads—although they still preserve certain remnants of them—they have turned to pastoral verse, and that, as a consequence, the cattle are thin from imbibing their tears, scorched in the flames of their loves, and so enraptured with the sound of their music that they no longer graze, we do ordain that poets shall leave that occupation, and that those who are friends of solitude shall become hermits, and the rest—since it is lively work and abounding in obscene expressions—shall devote themselves to mule tending …

Furthermore, noting the great harvest of quatrains, songs, and sonnets that have appeared during these fertile poetry years, we do ordain that all bundles of these poems which are found unsuitable for use as wrapping paper in the grocers' shops, be shipped off to the privies without further ado …

But observing in our mercy that there exist in our land three types of people so terribly wretched that they can't live without poets, that is to say, actors, blind men and the clergy, we do ordain, therefore, that a few poets shall be permitted to profess their art, provided they obtain a license from the official censor of their home town …

In conclusion, we do ordain that all poets in general stop their use of Jupiter, Venus, Apollo, and other gods, under pain of having to take these pagans for lawyers on their Judgment Day.

Later, however, Pablos himself becomes a poet. He becomes interested in writing plays, having discovered,

I was very much surprised to learn that dramatists are found among actors, for I had always thought they were intelligent and well-educated men and not people with so little culture.[36]

He wrote a play on 'the subject of Our Lady of the Rosary,' which he says was performed with 'music on the flageolets.' After this his success was assured and he was deluged with requests by 'lovesick suitors … sextons and wooers of nuns' and blind men.

36 Ibid., 135ff.

ON THE AESTHETICS OF MUSIC

There is little discussion of music in the seventeenth-century Spanish literature. An occasional interesting use of music as a metaphor reminds us that music was in fact a conversant topic in society. In his poem, the 'First Solitude,' Góngora creates a nice metaphor of 'weaving their voices in alternate song' to represent the moving of tree branches.[37] Quevedo, in his 'The Dream of Death,' used the expression 'no one sings well on an empty stomach' to mean a person should not speak if he has only something stupid to contribute to the conversation.[38]

Music is mentioned as a symbol, especially in the two ancient symbols. First, the familiar Platonic association of the well-adjusted body with harmony, a thought we find expressed now in Gracián:

> The divine philosopher was right to compare the human body to a resonant, living instrument. When it is well tuned, it makes marvelous music; and when it is not, it is all confusion and dissonance. It is composed of many, very different strings, incredibly hard to adjust to one another, and its pegs are always slipping. Some have called the tongue hardest to tune.[39]

And second, the very old Christian use of the trumpet ('the last breath') as a symbol for the Day of Judgment. In his 'The Dream of the Last Judgment,' Quevedo dreams,

> I saw a beautiful youth towering above me in the air and sounding a trumpet, though with such force that the beauty of its sound was somewhat marred.[40]

This, of course, was the trumpet announcing the day of judgment and upon hearing it Quevedo dreams that he sees rising from the grave and stirring into action all those who had, in their life, moved to action upon hearing such signals, including soldiers, hunters and miners.

> All this I could clearly read in their faces, for not one did I see who with the last trumpet echoing in his ears, was prepared to recognize it for what it was.

Of a general aesthetic nature, we find very little else about music. There is no significant discussion of the definition or even the purposes of music. We should like to mention only two observations by Gracián which might be applied to performance.

> Do not miscalculate where taste is concerned, for to do so is to turn a source of pleasure into one of irritation.[41]

......

> Nothing should be ended by breaking it off suddenly and completely.[42]

37 Góngora, 'First Solitude,' lines 540, in Cunningham, *The Solitudes of Góngora.*

38 Quevedo, *Dreams and Discourses*, 307.

39 Gracián, *A Pocket Mirror for Heroes*, 86.

40 Quevedo, *Dreams and Discourses*, 41.

41 Gracián, *The Oracle*, Nr. 233.

42 Gracián, *A Pocket Mirror for Heroes*, 144.

ART MUSIC

Apart from the dramatic literatre, there is relatively little reference to art music, although there are two interesting examples in the poetry of Góngora. In his poem, the 'First Solitude,'[43] Góngora gives the lyrics for a substantial polychoral wedding song and in his 'Second Solitude,'[44] there are lyrics for a song by a 'poor fisherman.'

In Góngora's poem, 'Polyphemus and Galatea,' we also find two references to the contemplative listener. First, a reference to 'Nor to my rustic pipe your ear refuse,' but more to the point,

> With gentle silence and attentive leisure
> At truce with strenuous sports, listen in state ...[45]

FUNCTIONAL MUSIC

Góngora also provides the only notable reference to Functional Music in this literature, a negative reflection on military music in association with the sleeping rustic shepherd.

> No trumpet shrills, no clattering drums reply,
> To interrupt his sleep with warlike sound ...[46]

ENTERTAINMENT MUSIC

Quevedo, in his 'The Vision of Hell,' discovers there the barbers who were well-known at this time as amateur players of the guitar.

> I passed along in the direction shown me, and saw—a punishment as astounding as it was just—that the barbers were all tied securely, but with their arms left free. Above their heads hung guitars and before them were boards set out with pieces for a game of draughts. When overcome by their natural inclination to strum a chord, like the typical street musicians they are, the barbers reached up for the guitars, the instrument were drawn up beyond their grasp; when they could no longer resist the temptation to take one of the pieces on the board before them, and put out a hand to do so, the boards sank down so that they could not touch them.

43 Lines 767ff.

44 Lines 112ff.

45 Góngora, 'Polyphemus and Galatea,' lines 6 and 17ff, in Cunningham, *Polyphemus and Galatea.*

46 Góngora, 'First Solitude,' lines 171ff, in Cunningham, *The Solitudes of Góngora.*

> This, then, was the punishment devised for barbers in Hell, and I could hardly leave the place where they were lodged for laughing at the spectacle.[47]

Quevedo mentions these barber-musicians again in his 'The Dream of Death.' He sees 'what seemed a group of infernal spirits, dragging with them chains of teeth, molars and incisors,' whom he recognizes as dentists. Then he observes,

> Who, I asked myself, is likely to come forward to rub shoulders with this damnable rabble? for it seemed to me that a devil from Hell would be small beer in such accursed company. Then I heard a sudden outburst of guitar music, which cheered me somewhat since it was all *passacaglias* and *vacas*. May the grave claim me if it is not barbers making their entrance!, I exclaimed. It needed little by way of wit to confirm the fact. Barbers have *passacaglias* infused into their blood and are born with guitars in their hands. What a sight it was to behold them, some plucking some strumming, and I reflected that it was a dismal outlook for the beard that is trimmed to the strains of the guitar, likewise for the arm that is bled while performing a *chaconne* or a *folia*.[48]

There is a similar passage in Quevedo's noveletta, *The Dog & the Fever*,

> When I heard a great noise of guitars approaching, I felt a little cheered. All were playing lively music, *passacalles*, and *bacanalles*. May they kill me if it be not the surgeon barbers, and they entering in. It was not difficult to tell that these people have *passacalles* infused into them, and the guitar as a natural gift. It was something to see the ones pluck and the others scrape the strings.[49]

47 Quevedo, *Dreams and Discourses*, 133ff.

48 Ibid., 235.

49 Don Francisco de Quevedo, *The Dog & the Fever*, trans. William Williams (Hamden, CT: Shoe String Press, 1954), 83ff.

7 SEVENTEENTH-CENTURY SPANISH DRAMA

The dramatic works by Calderón[1] and Molina[2] represent not only the final chapter of the 'Golden Age' of Spanish literature, but of Spain herself. The remarkable period which began with the marriage of Ferdinand of Aragón to Isabella of Castile in 1469 had included the acquisition of Granada from the Moors (1492), Navarre from the French (1515) and of course the vast new colonial empire resulting from the discovery of America. Poor management, of both economic and political resources, brought about the decline which is symbolized by the defeat of the Armada in 1588.

In general, literature followed in this decline and, indeed, one critic calls the final period of plays, from Lope de Vega to Calderón, 'unclassic ... shapeless and crude.'[3] Compared to Shakespeare's, it's true. On the other hand, these plays offer a certain realism, a glimpse of the broad society which is not otherwise available to us.

ON THE PHYSIOLOGY OF AESTHETICS

We find several references in these plays to the conflict between Reason and the emotions, caused as the natural result of our twin, but dissimilar, hemispheres of the brain. A passage in Calderón's *Life is a Dream* (II, i) reminds us of the early twentieth-century song title, 'Your eyes say Yes, but your lips say No.' In this case, Astolfo observes,

> Tell the eyes
> In their music to keep better
> Concert with the voice, because
> Any instrument whatever
> Would be out of tune that sought
> To combine and blend together
> The true feelings of the heart.
> With the false words speech expresses.

1 Don Pedro Calderón (1600–1681) was educated in the Jesuit Colegio Imperial in Madrid and at the University of Salamanca. While at the latter university he was jailed for failing to pay rent. Later he served in the army and in 1653 became a chaplain in the Chapel of the Reyes Nuevos in the cathedral at Toledo and in 1666 became head of an order of Spanish priests at St. Peter in Rome.

2 Fray Gabriel Téllez (ca. 1581–1648), who wrote under the name of Tirso de Molina was a member of the Mercedarian order and studied the Arts in Salamanca and Theology in Toledo.

3 Barrett H. Clark, *European Theories of the Drama* (New York: Crown, 1959), 81.

Calderón expresses a similar thought in his comedy, *Mornings of April and May*, which begins with a group of musicians singing on the subject of the conflict between Reason and Love.

You loved in Reason's spite,
Why hope for love again?

A familiar manifestation of the same problem is that we find words cannot express everything. Thus, Calderón's *Belshazzar's Feast* ends with Idolatry observing,

[Calderón's] faults and ours
Deign to pardon, and remember
That the poet's words but shadow
What the poet had intended.[4]

In Calderón's *The Surgeon of Honor* (Act II) we find an example of a frequent misconception in early literature, that it is the eyes, rather than the face itself,[5] which expresses emotions. Gutierre observes,

My feelings seek to break their bonds;
My poor heart dissolves in tears
And rushes to appear at
The windows of my soul, which are
My eyes.

ON THE PHILOSOPHY OF AESTHETICS

It is perhaps a reflection of the general decay in Spanish society that we find in the literature references to Beauty which are cast in a rather dark tone, even in a kind of mirror image. In Valdivielso's *The Bandit Queen*, the character Snares says,

Ah, and a haunted looking glass
Where Beauty sees her rotten skull gaze back at her;
A fearful doctor, who faints at your bedside
But then revives in time to prescribe a bitter dose;
A lawyer who wants to settle out of court,
A penitential theologian skilled in childish scruples to ruin your life ...[6]

4 The final two lines describe precisely the problem in music notation.

5 Actually, clinical research has established that it is primarily the left side of the face which expresses emotions, as the left side of the face is controlled by the right brain. It is this side of someone's face we unconsciously 'read' when seeking emotional information in another person.

6 El Maestro Josef de Valdivielso (1560–1636), *The Bandit Queen*, in R. Barnes, trans., *Three Spanish Sacramental Plays* (San Francisco: Chandler, 1969), 63.

A similar tone is found in an unusual passage in Calderón's *The Great Theater of the World*, in which we have a rare alternation of spoken dialog and sung lyrics. This, a short moral play, includes a passage dedicated to the discrediting of earthly beauty.

> Beauty. I see my beauty as in a glass before mine eyes, and it is clear and fair and lovable … The King was only master of men's flesh and bones, but I shall steal their hearts away. They shall be Beauty's slaves. Mine is the fairer realm in every part, for Beauty reigns eternal in every human heart …
>
> World. She hath forgotten Ezekiel's words: When Beauty's loveliness had been by pride assailed, its luster fled, its color paled.
>
> Voice. [*Singing*] *All human loveliness is like a little flower. It blossoms at morn and blooms its brief hour; and at the close of one swift day, its beauty withers and fades away.*
>
> Beauty. A doleful voice commandeth death to Beauty. No, no, it shall not be. Beauty may never perish, or from the world depart. And yet 'tis true, alas! The rose that bared her bosom to the sun, the rose bedecked with red and pearly white shall at night's coming be consumed quite …
>
> Voice. [*Singing*] *Eternal is thy spirit; but thy roseate beauty's fair array is but the garland of an autumn day.*
>
> Beauty. I will protest no more, nor vainly contend against all odds. From the cradle came I hither; to the sepulcher to hence.—Why played I not a better part?

Regarding the ancient aesthetic debate relative to whether Art should imitate Nature, we notice in Calderón's *The Devotion of the Cross* (III, i) a painter who takes great pride in his ability to copy Nature to a realistic degree.

> I am he who taught the art
> Of depicting fruits and trees
> After Nature; they so please
> Those who see them that they start
> Wondering at them.

On the other hand, in Calderón's *The Painter of his Dishonor* (II, lines 1137ff), the painter, Don Juan, discovers that despite his artistic imagination, he cannot surpass nature.

> I have realized
> That I cannot, for all my diligence,
> Ever have imagined them to be
> Such as you have proved them in reality.
> So then if they, in their perfection,
> Outstrip imagination's scope,
> Today my brush has not a hope
> Of following my imagination.

Finally, there is an interesting comment on the aesthetic purpose of poetry in Calderón's *The Constant Prince* (III, i). Here, a poet says his concept of aesthetics is to please everyone.

Why, what greater art can be
Than to tickle the whole town,
Please the tastes of clerk and clown,
Since your judges they must be,
Wise and foolish, saint and sinner,
Passing sentence like omniscience,
Heedless of their own deficiency.

ON THE AESTHETICS OF MUSIC

As with the plays of other countries, the frequent references to music as a metaphor, symbol or figure of speech in common conversation suggests a general musical literacy. The significance of this might be understood by recognizing the almost total absence of such figures in present day speech. Who today would describe a servant's voice as being like a trumpet, as we find in Calderón's *The Fake Astrologer* (I, lines 793ff), where Moron says,

A servant's voice is a trumpet,
It's sound will carry far and shrill.

How many ordinary people today would recognize, in Molina's *Tamar's Revenge*, the figure of speech, 'beat battle drums in time of peace,' as meaning 'an inappropriate time?'[7]

We find particularly interesting Calderón's use of musical communication as a metaphor for rational speech in *Belshazzar's Feast* (scene i), when Daniel says,

For, although the distance be
Great from wise to witless words,
Still, from two far different chords
Springs the sweetest harmony.

In Calderón's *The Mayor of Zalamea* (II, v), following the model of the ancient lyric poets, music is used as a metaphor for the sounds of nature. Crespo says,

Sit down; the gentle breeze
That murmurs through the velvet leaves of these
Old vines and bowers plays a happy host
Of tunes in rhythm with this fountain, which

7 II, 692.

Is like a zither made of silver and
Of pearls, whose pebbles are the strings upon
Which chords are played on golden frets. I hope
You will excuse the fact that we have just
This instrumental music without songs
Or voices to delight and entertain
You; our musicians are the warbling birds,
Who do not want to sing at night, nor do
I wish to force them.

A very familiar symbol is the use of the trumpet as a symbol for the day of judgment. In Calderon's *Belshazzar's Feast* (scene xiii), Death says,

Since when that dread trumpet echoes
The whole universe must tremble
To its base and die.

Finally, we are fond of a reference to the ancient Greek concept of the music of the spheres, found in Molina's *Tamar's Revenge*.[8] Amnon, contemplating the singing of Tamar, rhapsodizes,

Break forth, celestial harmony
that kindles love and voice alone,
so my reflected day may see
your sun and let me know for sure
if face be peer to melody.

On the Purposes of Music

In early literature the most commonly found purpose for music is to soothe the feelings of the listener. The relatively large number of such references in these plays may be another reflection of the general atmosphere during the decline of society in Spain at this time.

A lengthy passage dealing with the capacity of music to soothe the feelings of the listener begins with the entrance of Dina with a guitar, in Molina's Old Testament play, *Tamar's Revenge*.[9] First, Dina explains she does not need to sing for herself.

Tamar. You've brought your instrument, so sing.
In the beauty of a garden,
singing soothes the pain of love.

---

8 I, 649ff.

9 I, 320ff.

Dina. I have no pain to soothe, or need,
since I am not in love.

Soon, however, Tamar requests music.

Tamar. Oh, Dina, I am sick at heart.
Dina. It gives respite to my sadness
when I start to sing.
Tamar. In that case,
give me your instrument to play …
Music was made to soothe our care.

Tamar then sings a song which begins,

My wanton thoughts of love
like a bird of hope that sings …

In the meantime, Amnon has entered the stage and reacts as a listener to Tamar's song.

How gently, how passionately
she laments! How soft her voice!
Heavens, what bewitchment is this?
The very wind returns again
shamed by her mellifluous song—
and ashamed he might be
for being becalmed so long.
To serve as her accompaniment
he employs her voice to tune
his instruments; high pitched treble
of these leaves, bass of babbling streams …[10]
I could listen for days on end
to you, without a wink of sleep.

Finally, the reaction of Dina as a listener tells us that the music has indeed soothed.

Please go on; your music brings relief.
It cools and tames this savage heat.

10 The sound of water running over stones is a frequent suggestion in lyric poetry for the invention of music in more than one part.

In Valdivielso's *The Bandit Queen* we find a similar reference to the purpose of music to soothe.

Bandit Queen. Where are my musicians?
Musicians [within] Here we are, milady.
Bandit Queen. Play me a song to divert me a while;
When I think of treacherous Delight
I feel so melancholy.[11]

Molina's *Damned for Despair* (III, iii) offers this same purpose in the music of nature. The hermit Paulo who is walking in the woods to seek solace and addresses the birds,

Little songbirds,
innocent flatterers,
untaught musicians, idlers
among reed-beds and wild thyme,
cheer my sad spirits
with your melodies;
with your gentle voices
help me rise above my cares.

A very unusual reference of the purpose of music to sooth is found in Calderón's *The Constant Prince* (I, i) when a lady of the court of the King of Fez finds it soothing to hear the sad songs of the Christian captives.[12] The following dialog is between the captives and two attendants of the lady.

First Captive. Can Music, whose strange instrument
Was our clanking gyves and chains—
Can it be, our wail could bring
Joy into her heart? Our woe
Be to her delight?
Zara. It's so;
On this account she'll hear you; sing.
Second Captive. Ah! these sufferings exceed,
Lovely Zara, all the rest,
Since from out a captive's breast
(Save a soulless bird's indeed)
Never has a willing strain
Of music burst.
Zara. But have not you
Yourself sung many a time?

11 El Maestro Josef de Valdivielso, *The Bandit Queen*, in Barnes, *Three Spanish Sacramental Plays*, 54.

12 In II, ii, four lines of lyrics for a captive Christian song is given.

Third Captive. It's true;
But then it was no stranger's pain
To which we hoped at last to bring
Some ease. It was our own sharp grief
For which in song we sought relief.
Zara. She is listening now. Then sing.
Captives [*sing*]. *Age does not respect*
The fair or the sublime;
Nothing stands erect
Before the face of time.
Rosa. Captives, you can now retire,
And your pleasant concert end.

Twice in Calderón's *The Surgeon of Honor* reference is made to the ability of music to bring gladness. In Act II, the lady Mencía asks,

Can the music of
Your voice succeed in banishing
My sadness?
Teodora. My only wish is that
Both word and melody combined
Shall prove a source of instant gladness.

In Act III, we find the same thought.

Diego. Let's listen to the music in the street.
King. We'll hear them sing awhile. Perhaps
Their songs will help relieve my sadness.
Diego. Perhaps, your majesty. It's said
That music is a source of gladness.

Also in Act III, the shepherd, Tirso, makes a remarkable reference to the ability of music to soothe.

Well, whatever it is, by God,
we'll sing a little song for you
and drive away your sorrows.
There's nothing else that's worth a damn.

There are also some unusual instances where the listener's feelings are such that even music cannot soothe them. In Molina's *Tamar's Revenge*[13] we find,

---

13 II, 170ff.

Amnon. What's that noise? Ho, there! Who's singing?
Jonadab. The musicians that you summoned,
my good lord, to alleviate
with their harmonies the blackness
of your melancholy humor.
Amnon. Well tell them they're wasting their breath.

Later in Act II, Amnon expresses the same distrust of the ability of music to soothe, when he commands,

Sing then.
Singing is supposed to soothe me.

Similarly, in Calderón's *Life is a Dream* (II, i), shortly after a stage direction calls for 'music and song,' we find the following dialog.

First Servant. May they sing again?
Sigismund. No, no;
I don't care to hear them sing.
Second Servant. I conceived the song might bring
Some ease to your thought.
Sigismund. Not so;
Sounds that only charm the ear
Cannot soothe my sorrow's pain;
It's the soldier's martial strain
That alone I love to hear.

Another purpose for music is to offer simple delight, as we see in Calderón's *Belshazzar's Feast* (scene xvi), when Idolatry observes,

The music, too, in well-accorded note,
Not yet too near nor yet too far remote,
From many a silken string and mellow horn
Quenches the thirst with which the ear is born.

Similarly, in Calderón's *The Great Theater of the World*, after Wisdom sings a song of praise, apparently to the accompaniment of an instrument, the Author observes,

No other song hath to mine ears more sweetly sounded ever than that one bright hymn which Daniel did sing to temper Nebuchadnessar's wrath and lull the fury of the King.

The deep spiritual roots of Spanish society are evidenced in two instances in these plays where the purpose of music is for prophesy. In Calderón's *The Surgeon of Honor* (Act III) there is a group of musicians who sing songs of prophesy, and in Molina's *The Trickster of Seville* (III) songs of prophesy are sung by off-stage singers from the spirit world who accompany the 'Stone Guest.'[14]

ON THE USE OF INCIDENTAL MUSIC IN THE PLAYS

In the Spanish plays there is much less use of incidental instrumental music than in the English tradition, but a greater use of singers. In Molina's *Damned for Despair* (II, iii and III, ii) there are off-stage singers who function somewhat like the Chorus in ancient Greek tragedies, giving advice to the characters. It is undoubtedly these singers who supplied the otherwise unidentified music (III, iii) when Paulo reveals that he has heard 'Heavenly music filling the air!' Now the stage direction calls for 'music,' as two angels are seen bearing the soul of the criminal Enrico up to heaven.

In another Molina play we even find singers performing the role usually given trumpets, that of welcoming a noble. In *The Trickster of Seville* (II, lines 446ff) the marquis de la Mota enters the stage accompanied by his own musicians, who go before him singing,

For him who's waiting in anticipation,
Passing time's a source of desperation.
DON JUAN. What is that racket?
CATALINÓN. Only music, master!
DE LA MOTA. As though the muse addresses me, creating Poetry of inspiration! Who goes there?
DON JUAN. A friend! …
DE LA MOTA. Musicians, sing! My friend Don Juan's arrived!

The more expected trumpet fanfare to introduce a noble character on stage we find in Molina's *Tamar's Revenge*,[15] where a stage direction calls for 'great fanfares' for the entrance of King David.[16]

Another common role of the trumpet was to sound for a parley, as given in Calderón's *Love after Death* (III, iv),

MENDOZA. As I reached the walls of Berja
I blew a peaceful trumpet loud,
And a silent snow-white banner
Quickly answered to the trumpet;
Then I passed securely onward.

14 This play is one of the sources for Mozart's *Don Giovanni*.

15 II, 319ff.

16 See Calderón's *Belshazzar's Feast* (scene ii), for a 'Peal' of trumpets for the entrance of Belshazzar.

In the English plays, particularly those of Marston, the cornett is sometimes introduced as a kind of lesser trumpet. This seems to be intended also in Calderón's *Life is a Dream* (II, ii), where the name of a character, Clarin, is itself a play on word clarion.

Clotaldo. Because it's found
Safe, when clarions know secrets,
To lock clarions up, that so
They may not have power to sound …
It's the clarion's punishment.
Clarin. Then a horn of low degree,
Yes, a cornett, I will be,
A safe, silent instrument.

We find only one reference to horns in the stage directions of the Spanish plays, in Calderón's *The Surgeon of Honor* which begins with 'The sounds of a hunt.'

Military drums appear relatively frequently in the stage directions of Spanish plays. In Calderón's *The Mayor of Zalamea* a soldier-drummer appears several times. At the beginning of the play, another soldier who does not appreciate this instrument is thankful the instrument is not playing.

… by keeping quiet for a while
Showed mercy and stopped splitting our poor heads.

For a prison scene at the end of the play (III, xvii) a stage direction requests that the sound of 'rolling drums' off-stage accompany the dialog.

Moorish drums are called for in Calderón's *Love after Death* (II, ii). After a stage direction indicates off-stage drums playing, we read,

Malec. No Moorish tabors give that sound,
A sound that with such terror comes;
No! it's the sound of Spanish drums
That thunders through the mountains round.
Tuzani. This is a sound foreboding woe.

ART MUSIC

The Spanish plays include the lyrics for many songs. A charming example is found in Calderón's comedy, *Mornings of April and May* (I, ii), which contains an off-stage song in welcome of Spring, much in the style of the songs of the thirteenth-century troubadours.[17]

Mornings of April and May,
Fresh-scented and joyful with song,
Rouse up my maiden today:
Let her not slumber so long.

In Molina's *The Trickster of Seville* a group of shepherd musicians sing,[18]

April's sun is warm and bright,
With orange flower and lovely clover ...

To which the listener, Gaseno, makes an interesting assessment.

A fine song, lads, a joy to all our ears.
Much better than the choir we have in church!

In this same playwright's *The Trickster of Seville* (Act II, the final lines), we find an unusual cryptic reference to a wedding song.

GASEO. Begin the song!
CATALINÓN. All those who sing will soon be forced to cry.

Calderón's *The Wonder-Working Magician* (III, v) begins with a love song,

What is the glory far above
All else that life can give?
CHORUS. *Love, love.*

---

17 For other Calderón songs, see: *The Advantages & Disadvantages of a Name*, which calls for off-stage singers (Maskers) in I, iii, and a solo singer in III, ii, with some lyrics given for each; *The Painter of his Dishonor* (II, lines 1740), where the lyrics for a love song are given, in (II, lines 1820ff) the lyrics are given for a carnival song, sung by citizens in the street and in (II, 1894ff) there is an unusual scene where the lines of the song alternate with the spoken lines of Seraphine; *The Mayor of Zalamea* (II, viii), where the lyrics are given for a serenade sung by soldiers and *Belshazzar's Feast* (scene xiii) for lyrics sung by Idolatry and Vanity, and by Thought (scene xvii).

18 II, 633ff. In Molina's *Tamar's Revenge* (II); in Act III one finds lyrics for a 'shearing song' by a group of farmhands and another by a group of shepherds.

In his *The Painter of his Dishonor* there is a pretended love song. The Prince and Portia wish to be able to speak without being overheard, so Portia suggests that she play an instrument while they speak.[19]

Portia. Accompany everything we happen now to say upon
This instrument; father won't see fit this way
To come inquiring after me, listening
To how I pass the time out here;
What's more, the noise of music
Will mean he cannot hear
The sound our voices make.
Prince. It's not the first time I'll be bound
That love's expressed itself
In measured periods of sound
And improvised fantasias, for love
Makes music out of every situation.

In this same play (II, lines 1622), there is a serenade with a very rare reference to the singer accompanying himself on a harp.[20] It is also rare to find the suggestion that it would be the quality of the music which would determine the young lady's response. The Prince warns,

Listen carefully;
Depending on the tune, she'll tell me either
To approach the balcony or to retire.

In Molina's *The Trickster of Seville* a peasant girl gives a remarkable explanation for her tendency to be unmoved by the love songs of a young man.[21]

Sometimes as well he'll offer me sweet music,
The soft guitar, the shepherd's gentle flute,
Their music dedicated just to me.
Despite all this, I'm totally unmoved,
For I am ever mistress of my fate,
As far as love's concerned, it's queen and sovereign.
In fact, my greatest pleasure is his pain,
And in his suffering I find my heaven.
The other girls willingly die for him,
While I, at every opportunity,
Destroy his eager hopes with my disdain;
But isn't this the proper thing to do

19 II, 1667ff.

20 II, 1622.

21 I, 451ff.

In love's affairs? To love the man who hates
You; likewise, to despise the man who loves?
For if you favor him, you'll kill his love;
Despise him and he'll love you all the more.

FUNCTIONAL MUSIC

No extant written information can help us recreate the original effect of the music for a religious service in Calderón's *Love after Death* (II, ii). First, there is a stage direction which mentions only 'a crowd of Moors and musicians seen at a little distance.' A very short time later another stage direction reads, 'The instruments continue to play during the remainder of this scene, which is intended to be performed in a ritualistic manner.' Aside from the very rare instance at this time of music playing continuously underneath the dialog, we wish we could know what was meant by this 'ritualistic' music. One can only judge from the dialog which follows:

Maleca. What a strong and mournful feeling
This strange song awakens now!
Tuzani. At this voice terror is stealing
Through my breast, I know now how!

Religious music is also called for in Calderón's *The Great Theater of the World*, which concludes with a joyous, musical celebration of communion.

Author. The angels in heaven, and men on earth, hell's very demons, even, low kneel before this sacred Bread; now let the joyful sounds of earth, hell, heaven this Bread proclaim in sweet harmonious concord resonant. Let joyful pipes sing out their hymns.

This is followed by a stage direction reading,

Sound of hornpipes is heard.
The Tantum Ergo is sung many times.

Biblical welcome music is found in Molina's *Tamar's Revenge* where Jonadab describes the welcome of King David.[22]

Your father, my lord,
our noble king and sovereign
of Israel's twelve illustrious tribes,
who comes amidst drums and fanfares

22 II, 249ff.

in triumph to Jerusalem,
after leveling the cities
of the idolatrous Ammonite.
The courtiers are rushing out
joyfully to welcome his return,
calling down blessings on his head,
playing music, singing anthems,
dancing in the streets. Their portals
are decked with palm leaves and cedar.
In gratitude the women sing
the victory song that celebrates
the fall of great Goliath.

One finds a variety of examples of military music in these plays. Perhaps the most familiar for contemporaries was the call to battle, as in Calderón's *The Constant Prince* (I, iii).[23]

[*Trumpets resound from within*]
Fernando. But what trumpet's this, whose sound
So disturbs the air and echoes from the ground?
[*Drums from the opposite side*]
And in this direction too
Drums are heard, the music of the two
Is that of Mars.

Specific military signals for drums are found in Calderón's *Life is a Dream* (III, i), where there is a 'sound to arms' and in *The Mayor of Zalamea* (I, xviii),

Ho, drummer! Beat the call for all
The troops to go to bivouac.

In Calderón's *The Mayor of Zalamea* (I, ii) we find lyrics for a genuine soldier's marching song. Just before the song a soldier gives the purpose of this music as being to 'lighten our up-hill-and-down-dale march.' And in his *The Mayor of Zalamea* (II, xix) the title of a military popular song is given, 'A soldier's love lasts not a single hour.'

23 In Calderon's *The Constant Prince* (III, iii) the stage direction calls for military trumpet signals. In his *Life is a Dream* (II, i), Clarin observes,

For there are two things, I believe,
That are bad at keeping secrets,
A brass clarion and a lackey.

ENTERTAINMENT MUSIC

We find a reference to more sophisticated entertainment music in Molina's *The Trickster of Seville*[24] when Belisa suggests,

> Until she comes we'll entertain ourselves
> In song, and straight away begin the dance.

In Calderón's *The Painter of his Dishonor* (II, lines 1926) there is a dance scene in which there is a rare occasion when a hired occasional musician has actual lines of dialog. Seeing there are no more dancers, he tells his colleagues,

> There is no sign of other folk;
> Gentlemen, you may leave your places.

Finally, in Calderon's *Belshazzar's Feast* (scene xvii) the stage direction calls for unidentified 'music' for a banquet scene.

---

24 I, 977ff.

8 THE MUSICAL SCENE IN THE GERMAN-SPEAKING COUNTRIES

THE SEVENTEENTH CENTURY was a century of crises for the German-speaking nations.[1] Germany itself, hampered by a lack of central authority, was facing increased difficulties in trade both from across the Alps to the South and from the lack of harbors in the North. The growth of the Lutheran populations in the North and the growing of support by England, Spain and France for the Catholic South led almost inevitably to the Thirty Years' War (1618–1648).

The war began when the Emperor Ferdinand II's ambassadors to Bohemia were thrown out of a window in Prague. The fortunes of war caused troops to traverse back and forth across Germany, with Wallenstein first leading the Catholic to victory and then the Protestants under Gustavus Adolphus, King of Sweden, driving them South and defeating Wallenstein at Lützen. Before it all ended with the Peace of Westphalia, France, Spain and the Dutch were all participants. After thirty years of fighting, France and Sweden were stronger and the Dutch and Switzerland became independent. Germany was weaker, with the population in some areas having declined by thirty percent.

The impact of the Thirty Years' War on the arts was, of course, dramatic and far-reaching. With regard to music we have many testimonials to the decline in the fortunes of the musicians. In the writings of Burckhart Grossmann we can see already in the early years of the war wide ramifications in society.

> Noble music is particularly hated today, and that, too, among such as should especially cultivate it and preserve it to the glory of God. Many of these esteem it so little that they derive more pleasure, eloquence, and usefulness from the yelping of dogs, the bellowing of bulls, and the braying of asses than from the most beautiful Orphic strains, or from the well-ordered heavenly choir of our late blessed Michael Praetorius …
>
> We find Saul's spear at court and especially in the chamber of the exchequer, barring the way to music, singers, and musicians when they approach, or driving them away, so that they must flee as David fled … One cuts their bread with Saul's spear into such small bits that they almost starve to death, so that of many a one it can be said, as I often heard from the lips of an old singer, 'Music benefits well, but nourishes badly.' …
>
> In some towns and places where music formerly flourished and one praised God on Sundays and festival days with sixteen and more voices in two, three, or more choirs, one can only now

1 Our purpose here is not an attempt to summarize the technical development of Baroque music itself in the German-speaking countries, and its composers, but rather to present a brief overview of the environment in which the music was performed and its general aesthetic nature. At the same time, we take the opportunity to include important material not found in general music history texts.

> engage an old unaccompanied quartet; that cantors and organists, from whom the keys stick and the bellow freeze …
>
> No peasant familiar with the Thuringian practice … will believe me that in distinguished universities one is more ashamed of music than of Saul's spear, and that in numerous places it appears as though one wished to weed out music altogether from among its six sisters and no longer wished to acknowledge it as belonging to the liberal arts. This is indeed the actual state of affairs. Formerly honorable and art-loving students in our universities, and among them some from the aristocracy, conducted *collegia musica* at times and places of recreation … Now they are supplanted by bagpipe players and performers on the shawm, or at best by three fiddlers who play three octaves apart.[2]

In Dresden, by 1633 Heinrich Schütz was so discouraged with conditions imposed by the war that he sought to leave to work in Copenhagen.

> On account of the war conditions prevailing at present I could readily get away, because the times do not demand or allow music on a large scale, and the more so because the company of instrumentalists and singers has at present considerably diminished. Some are subject to illness and to the infirmities of age; others are occupied with the war, or have taken advantage of other opportunities, wherefore it is now impossible to perform music on a large scale or with many choirs. Furthermore, if God, as is to be hoped, improved the times, and Your Electoral Highness desired my service, a considerable readjustment and improvement of our *Collegium musicum* would have to take place.[3]

Three years later Schütz pictures a more general decline.

> Everyone can see how, as the result of the still continuing, dangerous vicissitudes of war in our dear fatherland of German nationality, the laudable art of music, among the other liberal arts, has not only greatly declined but at some places has even been completely abandoned, succumbing to the general ruination and disorder which unhappy war is wont to bring in its train.[4]

In this same year Schütz's pupil, Martin Knabe, wrote of the effects of war in the dedication of his 'Lamentation on the Protracted War: When at Last Will My Grief be Ended?'

> It is unnecessary to speak at length concerning this long-protracted, wearisome war. Suffice is to say that its destructive fire is still burning at all corners of the Roman Empire. It is enough to observe how daily, yes, hourly, so many countless sighs are emitted with broken words by many thousands of souls: Oh, if there were only peace! Oh, if only the war would come to an end! Not to mention the collapse of studies which bloodthirsty Mars occasions in all the branches of

2 Burckhart Grossmann, *116th Psalm* (Jena, 1623), quoted in Hans Moser, *Heinrich Schütz* (St. Louis: Concordia, 1936), 15ff.

3 Letter of February 9, 1633, quoted in Ibid., 145.

4 Henrich Schütz, *Kleine geistliche Concerte* (Leipzig, 1887), Preface.

> the university and among the other liberal arts, and only to recall with a few words the state of music, how this noble art, even before the other arts, has sunk to the lowest level.[5]

Toward the end of the war, the letters of Schütz take on an even more desperate character.

> Our music at present practically defunct … I cannot refrain from seeking help for our *corpori musico*, which is in desperate straits, and from petitioning that you intervene as does a *medicus* in a serious illness before that illness becomes altogether fatal.[6]

Conditions were such that even a decade after the end of the war Schütz can see no evidence of a restoration of a favorable climate for music. On 21 September 1661, he writes the elector,

> In conclusion, so far as I am personally concerned, I must protest that, after promising practically everything but the blood from my veins, actually advancing a part of my means to suffering musicians, it will be altogether impossible for me to continue here in Dresden any longer. With regard to this place I am not merely announcing but stating positively that I would prefer death to living under such harassing conditions.[7]

MUSIC OF THE COURT

When one considers the long period of war which began with the Thirty Years' War, it sometimes seems a wonder that culture developed at all in central Europe. But, while the progress rose and fell with the fortunes of individual courts, the German-speaking countries eventually made extraordinary progress in their musical life. Ironically, the driving force behind this great development in German culture came from the outside, from Italy.

The humanist movement in sixteenth-century Italy brought an end to the long held concept that music was an expression of mathematics and managed to awaken composers to the fact that music is most meaningful as an expression of feelings. Numerous Italian composers and musicians moved North to the German speaking-countries during the seventeenth and eighteenth centuries, bringing the seeds from which the German Baroque in music grew. The Germans managed to make some things their own, such as the many instrumental forms, the Intrada, Sinfonia, Concerto, Aria, Canzona, etc. These had been Church forms in sixteenth-century Italy but became secular forms in seventeenth-century Germany. Other Italian forms, opera in particular, were embraced as a kind of status symbol and would take longer to transform into something truly German.

---

5 Quoted in Hans Moser, *Heinrich Schütz*, 162.

6 Heinrich Schütz, letter to the elector of March 7, 1641, quoted in Ibid., 170.

7 Quoted in Ibid., 209.

A typical example of a great noble who wanted the status symbol of Italian musicians was Friedrich August I (1694–1733) of Dresden. Speaking of his interest in Italian opera, one contemporary wrote,

> All the arts and sciences seem to have been united in this breath of air. The extraordinary payments which the king grants the players have attracted the best and most excellent masters of this art to Dresden from Italy, the great school of music.[8]

After Ferdinand II became emperor in 1619, the strong Italian influence in the Austrian court can already be seen in the fact that such famous Italian composers as Viadana and Grillo, not to mention Victoria, dedicated works to him. Although Italian opera arrived in Vienna in 1627, in the courts of Germany it is the next decade before this form would begin to become popular. A letter by Heinrich Schütz of 1633, reflecting on his trip to Italy in 1628–1629, reveals Italian opera was yet unknown in Dresden.

> During my recent journey to Italy I engaged myself in a singular manner of composition, namely how a comedy of diverse voices can be translated into declamatory style and be brought to the stage and enacted in song—things that to the best of my knowledge … are still completely unknown in Germany.[9]

Italian opera would not appear in the court at Munich until 1653. But so pervasive would Italian opera become that the first great German opera composer, Reinhard Keiser (1674–1739), whom Mattheson called 'the greatest opera composer of the world,'[10] remained little known, then or today.

The great influx of Italian musicians during the seventeenth century did not occur without difficult adjustment. The resident German musicians must have often resented these foreign celebrities,[11] as we can see in a letter of Heinrich Schütz complaining that he was being blamed for importing them.

> More and more each day (regarding Your Highness's Italian musicians and those installed in the electoral court ensemble) not only repeatedly unpleasant judgment is passed against me by various ecclesiastics and lay persons but, furthermore, to my particular astonishment, I have learned that I am considered, and slandered as, the cause and instigator of the change.[12]

8 Gerhard Pietzsch, *Sachsen als Musikland* (Dresden, 1938), 52.

9 Quoted in Gina Spagnoli, 'Dresden at the Time of Heinrich Schütz,' in *The Early Baroque Era* (Englewood Cliffs: Prentice Hall, 1994), 176. In 1671, Bontempi and Peranda of this court produced the earliest extant German opera.

10 Johann Mattheson, *Das neu-eröffnete Orchestre* (Hamburg, 1713), 217.

11 Roger North, in England, expresses similar frustration with foreign musicians.

> Now it is set up dressed in superlatives brought from I know not where, at immense charges in profuse salary, pensions, subscriptions, and promiscuous courtship and flattery in the bargain. These far fetched and dearly bought gentlemen return home rich, buy fine houses and gardens, and live in admiration of the English wealth. [Quoted in Wilson, *Roger North on Music*, 250]

12 Quoted in Spagnoli, 'Dresden at the Time of Heinrich Schütz,' 168.

A senior chaplain in this court wondered if before long there would be any German musicians left to sing 'a German "Our Father" in church.'[13]

In addition, the resident musicians must have felt that the monies being expended on foreign musicians was money much needed for their own support. A letter of Schütz to the secretary of the Elector of Saxony makes a desperate plea on behalf of a court singer.

> But now I can no longer conceal from you that the bass singer who some time ago had to pawn his clothes again, and ever since has been living at his house like a wild beast of the woods, has informed me through his wife that he now must and wishes to leave us …
>
> It is a real pity, though, to lose such an exquisite voice in the choir. What does it matter if in other respects he is a good-for-nothing and that he must cleanse his throat daily with a keg of wine? Naturally such a wide throat needs more moistening than a narrow one.[14]

Finally, since the Italian musicians were Catholic, their desire to observe the Mass in Protestant areas caused concern. In Dresden, in 1673, they were forbidden to practice their faith. But such problems did not succeed in slowing the influence of Italian music in Germany.

In Northern Germany one finds an occasional noble who was also an active musician, such as Johann Georg II, in Dresden, who is presumed to have studied with Heinrich Schütz and was a composer of large-scale church works. Telemann, in his autobiography, relates a visit to Berlin where he secretly attended a private opera performance in which all the roles were sung by people of high rank.[15]

But, it is in the Catholic areas of the German-speaking nations that one especially finds nobles who were musicians and composers. Being Catholic, their ties with Italy were much closer than the courts of the North who regarded their Italian musicians as visiting celebrities. But the closer ties in the Catholic regions must have also made them more sympathetic to the ideals of Italian humanism and the model of the noble given by Castiglione as a man who values and can perform music.[16]

In Munich, the Elector Maximilian II Emanuel (1679–1726) listened to music every evening and was a talented performer on the viola da gamba. His son, Carl Albrecht (1726–1745), was a great patron of Italian opera composed by musicians of his household. He himself attended and directed rehearsals. He was succeeded by Maximilian III Joseph, a virtuoso on the viola da gamba and a composer of church music and concerti. He unfortunately reigned during the War of the Austrian Succession, the economic results of which forced a decline in the musical activities of this court.

---

13 Quoted in Ibid., 169.

14 Letter to Christian Reichbrodt, May 28, 1652, quoted in Gertrude Norman and Miriam Shrifte, *Letters of Composers* (New York, Knopf, 1946), 14ff.

15 The passage is quoted in Bernd Baselt, 'Brandenburg-Prussia and the Central German Courts,' in *The Late Baroque Era* (Englewood Cliffs: Prentice Hall, 1994), 234.

16 Baldassare Castiglione (1478–1529), as a diplomat for the Duke of Urbino and Popes Leo X and Clement VII, in one of the most famous books of the Renaissance, *Il Cortigiano* (The Courtier), attempts to describe the attributes of the perfect gentleman and lady from the sixteenth-century aristocratic perspective.

It is in Vienna, of course, where the association with both Italy and the influence of Italian humanism was most strongly felt. The personal involvement of the nobles in music there,[17] together with their influence on Bohemia and Hungarian musical activities, would create an environment which would in time produce a Mozart and a Beethoven.

The Emperors Ferdinand III (1637–1657) and Leopold I (1658–1705) were active composers whose music still exists. The music establishment of Leopold seems suspended between the Renaissance and the Baroque, with both a Renaissance consort of trombones and cornetts for the church and a more modern Hautboisten band for secular use. The later patronage of music by the court in Vienna can be measured by the growth of the strings in the Hofkapelle. There were approximately fifteen in 1690, twenty-nine in 1705 and forty-one in 1728. Maria Theresa, who bridges into the Classical Period, although a singer herself, was forced to reduce the musical establishment for economic reasons.

Court musicians performed for a wide variety of entertainment events, including allegorical pageants, festivals, balls, banquets and fireworks. The functional music, with new German names such as *Aufzug*, *Ritterspiel* and *Tanzspiel*, still exists in many libraries. Philipp Hainhofer, a visitor to the court in Dresden in 1629, has left us an account of how elaborate the music could be for a meal in the royal garden house.

> The space behind every portrait is hollow and set up in such a way that one can perform a certain kind of music. When one dines in this upper hall, the musicians are also positioned in the lower hall with the doors closed so that the resonance ascends delightfully through the ventilators. Above, under the ceiling, there is also an arrangement for hidden music, so that one can hear such music from thirty-two different locations, each separated.[18]

He also describes the instrument collection on the third floor of the Dresden palace. Here he lists a number of Renaissance instruments, including consorts, as well as representations of fourteen famous composers, including Andrea and Giovanni Gabrieli, de Rore, Monteverdi, de Lassus, Striggio, Willaert, Croce, Merulo, Orologgio and Sweelinck. Hainhofer adds the reflection,

> A number of these Kapellmeisters prospered; others, however, despite all their art, remained poor. Some among them indeed committed suicide.[19]

Finally, Hainhofer describes a banquet in which the music, in the Renaissance tradition, was varied in instrumentation with each composition. He reports vocal ensembles, a wide

---

17 Metastasio complains in a letter of 1734 of having to hurriedly compose a theatrical work for two archduchesses to sing. [See Burney, *Memoirs of the Life and Writings of the Abate Metastasio*, I, 156]

18 Oscar Doering, *Des Augsburger Patriciers Philipp Hainhofer Reisen nach Innsbruck und Dresden* (Vienna, 1901), 217. Charles Ogier, a French representative to a Danish wedding in Copenhagen in 1634, reports being surprised by a concert of vocal and instrumental 'invisible music.' 'It came to us through various openings and resounded now near, now far.' As the diplomats got into their carriages to leave, again 'subterranean and invisible music' was heard. See Hans Moser, *Heinrich Schütz*, 149.

19 Hans Moser, *Heinrich Schütz*, 138.

variety of string instruments and some novelty performances: a performer who fiddled with one hand and piped with the other, a trombonist who imitated figures played by cornetts and violins and music by 'several glasses blown into.'[20] Curiously, he concludes by commenting that he enjoyed everything, 'in spite of the saying "There is no song so good but that one tires of it".'[21]

On the occasion of the noble's birthday, all the components of his musical establishment would participate in the celebration. Sometimes this involved the commissioning of poets and composers to produce great allegorical productions similar to those of the Renaissance. For the birthday of the Duke of Saxony (March 5, 1621), for example, Schütz wrote 'Felicitation of Apollo and the nine Muses,' performed by 'His Electoral Grace's Collegium Musicum with twelve cornetts and as many living voices beside trumpets and timpani.'[22] When Schütz traveled to Copenhagen in 1634 for a Danish royal wedding, immediately upon his arrival, he was assigned the duty of creating music for two plays, a ballet and a masked ball![23] The ballet, based on Orpheus and other Greek gods, was given after a lavish banquet. A contemporary descriptions speaks of Orpheus singing while accompanying himself on a violin, 'in a voice that was as pleasing and charming as it was plaintive.'[24] When the devil's wives appeared, the 'noise of their cymbals and tongs' drowned out the song of Orpheus. Later, another singer, a eunuch, appeared who 'knew how to use his voice so skillfully that he was listened to with amazement by all present.' The summary by the eyewitness reads,

> Thus we find vivid and varied problems for musical treatment: soli in song form, recitatives in the new opera style, soli with obbligato instruments, different ensemble sections varied with duets, terzets, soli and choruses, and finally the introductory and closing choruses. But one sees at once that the music should be called concert music rather than dramatic music. It serves a purely decorative purpose and has no organic relationship to the content of the action.

For the birthday of Duke Christian of Weissenfels (1712–1736) a contemporary describes the performances of his trumpet choir, his wind band [*Hautboisten und Waldhornisten*] as well as the civic trombones.[25]

The great allegorical pageants of the sixteenth century become more rare during the Baroque. One noble who enjoyed this kind of extravagant display was Friedrich August I (1694–1733) of Dresden.[26] For the carnival season of 1695 he had organized a great procession of the gods, each accompanied by an ensemble of musicians. First came Jupiter and Juno

20 Ibid., 138ff.

21 Ibid., 139.

22 Ibid., 114ff.

23 Ibid., 147.

24 Ibid., 150ff.

25 Arno Werner, *Städtische und fürstliche Musikpflege in Weissenfels* (Leipzig: Breitkopf & Härtel, 1911), 55.

26 Aside from his interest in music, poetry, theater and traveling throughout Europe, he also found time to father 354 children!

with thirty-two musicians, followed by Mars and Bellona with shawms, trumpets, timpani and drums. Then Neptune with an Hautboisten band dressed as satyrs followed by Apollo with twelve musicians playing oboes, bagpipes, guitars and violins. His mistress appeared as Aurora and she had eight musicians. Interestingly, the Nine Muses were accompanied by women musicians.[27]

One of the Baroque entertainments which developed out of the Renaissance-style pageants were the so-called horse ballets,[28] which were first imported from Italy by Ferdinand III (1637–1657) for his marriage to Maria Anna, daughter to Philip III of Spain. On this occasion the names of Ferdinand and his bride were spelled out by vast numbers of cavalry on the floor of the arena. In the case of international weddings, such as this, part of the purpose was a political show of force, a symbolic demonstration of the importance of the emperor and the empire. The political aspirations were enhanced by the publication of the official programs and descriptions which were sent to courts throughout Europe.

We see the same political overtones, as well as another great horse ballet, in the entertainments—covering two years—associated with the wedding of Leopold I and Margareta Theresa of Spain. In July 1666, five months before she arrived in Vienna, her birthday was celebrated there with a grand ballet composed by the court ballet composer, Schmelzer. The following November there was another ballet, *Concorso dell' allegrezza universale*, as well as a *dramma per musica* by the Venetian composer, Ziani, given in honor of the birthday of the emperor's mother.

In January 1667, another great horse ballet was given for which rehearsals began six months earlier! For the some one thousand participants involved, a special stadium was constructed in the Burghof and the theme, 'The Contest between Air and Water,' was expressed through various gods debating on behalf of air and water. A published account of another horse ballet given by Leopold[29] tells us that the event began with the emperor leading the first dance, mounted on a richly decorated horse. Then the Duke of Lorraine entered with his party, while one heard 'a strepitosa armonia da un pianissimo *concerto* di Timpani e Trombe guerriere.' Next was an elaborate procession, centering around the allegorical figure, 'Germania,' followed by a tilting contest with the targets being sea-monsters and savages. Finally, in the horse ballet proper, to the music of a *corrente*, one saw the emperor, with Counts Dietrichstein and Preiner and the Duke of Lorraine,

> execute the first figure of the ballet in the greatest variety of curvets and volts; after which the ballet is ridden—first by four, then by six, and finally by eight knights, the figures changing as the music changes. Thereupon the riders are seen to press forward to the strains of the fiery *giga*, taking the barrier by twos—a magnificent feat never before seen at festivals of this sort. Then some gallop to the center of the field, while the rest are performing their volts and curvets. Their

27 George Buelow, 'Dresden in the Age of Absolutism,' in *The Late Baroque Era* (Englewood Cliffs: Prentice Hall, 1994), 220.

28 A form of this still exists today in Vienna in the 'Spanish Riding School.'

29 Francesco Sbarra, *La Germania esultante, Festa a Cavallo* … (Vienna, 1677).

> ballet is now carried on by threes in the four corners of the arena, while two others execute new figures in the center. Around these two the twelve entwine the round dance *treccia* (or, as it is known in Vienna, *Trezza*), which has its counterpart in another winding dance by eight riders. The two convolutions uncoil themselves, the knights reappear in the center and thence betake themselves toward the spectator's seats, making way for nine knights who execute the figures of the *sarabanda*. They form a crescent, in the center of which the emperor and the duke of Lorraine take their stand. Again we behold the knights confronting each other in pairs, executing elaborate steps, at first on the spot and then in motion. The two groups part and stride across the arena, greeted by the tumultuous applause.

The horse ballet of 1667 was followed by more ballets during Carnival. In June, Cesti's opera *La Semirami* was performed for the emperor's birthday, followed by another *balletto a cavallo* by Schmelzer in July for the birthday of the empress. More operas were given the next winter and finally in July 1668, for the wedding itself, the *Il pomo d'oro* by Cesti. This opera in five acts, to which were added six ballets, twenty-three scene changes and thirty-eight singing roles required two days for its performance.

This rapidly growing appreciation of music by the nobles in the German-speaking lands had the somewhat adverse result of making the court musicians increasingly busy. No longer merely the producers of music for meals and church, they were now, as Heinrich Schütz pointed out to his patron, involved with,

> many diverse festivities … which occurred during this time at imperial, royal, electoral, and princely gatherings, in this country and abroad, but particularly at each and every one of your own royal children's weddings, and no less at the receiving of their sacred christenings as well.[30]

And with the increasing appreciation by the nobles, higher demands followed. Before the visit of the Emperor Matthias in 1617, Schütz was instructed that his ensemble must 'acquit itself with honor and glory before the visitors.'

We may be sure that, as servants of the court, the pay of these musicians did not keep pace with the growing demands for their service. One reason for their financial difficulties was that the court musicians were often paid mostly in commodities, rather than actual money which they could save to purchase such things as clothes. A record of a court bassoonist in Weissenfels, for example, specifies as part of his yearly allowance, '20 pounds of beef, 9 portions of bread, 9 portions of wine and 18 portions of beer.'[31]

It is no wonder that the court musician often looked with envy on the life of the civic musician. Even Schütz, in the letter just mentioned, complained,

30 Memorandum of January 14, 1651 to the elector Johann Georg I, quoted in Spagnoli, 'Dresden at the Time of Heinrich Schütz,' 164.

31 Werner, *Städtische und fürstliche Musikpflege in Weissenfels*, 74.

> God knows that I would prefer with all my heart to be a cantor or an organist in a small town to remaining longer amid conditions in which my dear profession disgusts me and I am deprived of sustenance and of courage.[32]

Another court musician who served in Weissenfels, Johann Beer, also dreamed of an easier life as a civic musician.

> With the court you've got to be in one place today, tomorrow in another. Day and night, unfortunately, makes no difference. Tempest, rain, sunshine—it's all the same. Today you've got to go into church, tomorrow to the dining hall, the day after tomorrow to the theater. Compared to all this disturbance, life is somewhat more peaceful in the towns …
>
> Many princely musicians long for the city, because the service in the court is so insecure and he must be ready to move if the support for music by the noble fails or if he decides to cut back. What good are riches without stability? I say continued poverty could be called better luck than irregular riches, where one may go from a horse to an ass and from the ass even to sit in the dust …
>
> In the city one can hope for quicker advancement … this has the civic musician, but at court even if he had a doctorate in all three faculties he waits without hope. The more excellent he is, the more he will remain in his station which he once accepted, to remain used, all feathers plucked from his wings so he can not hope to soar higher.[33]

But, as they say, 'the grass is always greener on the other side of the fence.' Bach, in 1730, submitted a memorandum to the Leipzig Councilmen complaining about the difficulties of life as a German civic musician. Quite the reverse of Beer, Bach contemplates how nice it would be to be a court musician, as for example in Dresden.

> It is somewhat strange that German musicians are expected to be capable of performing at once and *ex tempore* all kinds of music, whether it comes from Italy or France, England or Poland, just as may be done, say, by those virtuosos for whom the music is written and who have studied it long beforehand, indeed, know it almost by heart, and who, *quod notandum*, receive good salaries besides, so that their work and industry thus is richly rewarded; while, on the other hand, this is not taken into consideration, but the German musicians are left to look out for their own wants, so that many a one, for worry about his bread, cannot think of improving—let alone distinguishing—himself. To illustrate this statement with an example one need only go to Dresden and see how the musicians there are paid by His Royal Majesty; it cannot fail, since the musicians are relieved of all concern for their living, free from *chagrin*, and obliged each to master but a single instrument: it must be something choice and excellent to hear.[34]

---

32 Quoted in Moser, *Heinrich Schütz*, 196ff.

33 Johann Beer, *Musicalische Diskurse* (Nürnberg, 1710), 18ff. Beer (1655–1700) was a native of Upper Austria. A further complaint which Beer could have mentioned was the dangers of accompanying the noble in his hunting. Beer, in fact, was accidentally shot and killed while on a hunt in 1700. Metastasio, in a letter of 1732, relates some details of a similar accident in which the Emperor of Austria accidently shot and killed Prince Schwaisemberg duirng a hunt. [See Burney, *Memoirs of the Life and Writings of the Abate Metastasio*, I, 87]

34 Quoted in Hans T. David and Arthur Mendel, *The Bach Reader* (New York: Norton, 1966), 123.

One observer, writing of Hamburg at the end of the Baroque, leaves the impression that the long hardships of war had permanently affected the culture. He noted that although the town had a certain pride in having Telemann in residence, 'the taste for music had totally vanished: people were more interested in educating their children to make money than to make or appreciate music.'[35]

The Hautboisten

One medium which played a prominent role in late Baroque German court music, yet which is almost never mentioned in general music history texts, was the Hautboisten band. At a time when Italian style had such a strong influence, this idea came from France and with it the modern oboe, as is reflected in the Germanized French name, 'Hautboisten.'

The influence of the court of Louis XIV on the rest of Western Europe is well documented. Frederick the Great complained in 1750,

> Everyone in Germany goes there … The French taste rules our food, our furniture, and our clothes.[36]

It should be no surprise, then, that one of the fundamental ensembles of the court of Louis XIV, the *Les Grands Hautbois*, a twelve-member oboe and bassoon band, should be imitated in the courts of Germany. It began to arrive in German courts during the final two decades of the seventeenth century, as can be documented by its appearance in Stuttgart (1680), Weissenfels (1695),[37] Dresden and Gotha (1697) and Gottorf (1699). Some German ensembles, in imitation of *Les Grands Hautbois*, even carefully had exactly twelve players. Twelve-member Hautboisten bands can be documented in Halle (1676), Jena, and Eisenberg, where the ensemble was known as the 'Apostles.'[38] A leading scholar of this field finds that by 1700 virtually every major court in Germany possessed one of the new Hautboisten bands.[39]

Furthermore, the appearance of names such as 'François Beauregard' and 'Pierre Potot' in German court records at this time suggest that the new French oboe came to Germany in the hands of French players. It is not clear if the bassoonists also came from Paris, but it is at

35 Christian Griesheim, *Die Stadt Hamburg* (Hamburg, 1760), 194ff.

36 Frederick II von Brandenburg, *Memoires pour servir à l'histoire de Brandenbourg* (1750), II, 771.

37 According to Werner, *Städtische und fürstliche Musikpflege in Weissenfels*, 95, the elector was apparently dissatisfied with the Hautboisten he engaged in this year, for two years later he replaced them by hiring an entire band [*Kammerpfeifer*] in Vienna.

38 This name gives us the best clue as to why twelve was set as the size of the ensemble. This tradition may have continued longer than we presently understand, for the great *Fireworks Music* by Handel was scored in twelve parts, the *Te Deum* by Gossec was scored for twelve and the Mozart *Gran partita* was composed for twelve winds and string bass.

39 Werner Braun, 'Entwurf für ein Typologie der "Hautboisten,"' in *Der Sozialstatus des Berufsmusikers vom 17. bis 10. Jahrhundert* (Kassel, 1971), 47.

this very time that the bassoon begins to appear in court records in Germany. It seems safe to conclude that the seventeenth-century listener considered the bassoon not so much as a contrasting instrument, as the bass of the double reed ensemble. Mattheson, for example, calls the bassoon 'the ordinary bass' of the oboe.[40]

In its second generation in Germany, by about 1715, the Hautboisten begins to include the Waldhörn. Now, with oboes, bassoons and horns, it is the same instrumentation as the first generation of aristocratic *Harmoniemusik* of the Classical Period.

On the rare occasions when modern literature mentions the Hautboisten, the author usually mistakenly associates this ensemble with the military—in part, we assume, because in the nineteenth century Hautboisten *did* mean a military band, although a large band of entirely different instruments. In the Baroque, however, it is the great quantity of both printed and manuscript extant music for Hautboisten which establishes it's indoor history, like any other ensemble.[41] These extant works are usually called 'Concerto'[42] or 'Overture,'[43] but in all cases are multi-movement compositions of substantial length and of a musical nature which entirely precludes any military use whatsoever.[44]

Aside from the evidence of the surviving music, there are also accounts of these Hautboisten bands making concert tours. One of these was the Hautboisten of the Brandenburg court in Berlin, led by an oboist-director named 'Lubuissière' (and sometimes 'Lapuisier' or 'La Bassire'), whose tours can be documented between 1693 and 1700.[45] The next leader of this Hautboisten, Gottfried Pepusch, took the band on a tour to London in 1704, where a review in the *Daily Courant* (April 4) mentions that they performed some music by his brother, 'that Eminent Master, Mr. John Christopher Pepusch' [Johann Christoph Pepusch].

Gottfried Pepusch seems to have been considered an important teacher of this new medium, for in 1703 an entire Hautboisten band came from Ansbach to study with him.[46] Six of his students were hired as an Hautboisten band in Hannover in 1705 and when Johann Mattheson visited Hannover the following year he was astonished by the 'Virtuosen,' especially the 'exquisite Bande Hoboisten.'[47]

40 Mattheson, *Das neu-eröffnete Orchestre* (Hamburg, 1713), 269.

41 All ensembles, whether string or wind, throughout the Baroque and Classical Periods had *some* functional duties. In this respect, it is fair to assume that the Hautboisten *did* sometimes appear with the duke's militia in a formal parade.

42 This is a German abbreviation of the Italian, *Concerto da camera*. Although not mentioned by standard music history texts, the concerto in Italy came in both 'da camera' and 'da chiesa' versions just like the sonata.

43 The German manuscripts are always called 'Ouverture' and never by the later musicologists' label, 'French Overture Suite.' The typical Hautboisten Overture had an extremely long first movement, in fugal style, followed by a number of short dance movements, often concluding with a minuet. A well-known example which followed this form precisely is the famous *Fireworks Music* of Handel.

44 Arthur Hutchings, *The Baroque Concerto* (New York: Scribner's, 1979), 29, observes,

> In 1730 … if a work were called concerto it was intended for 'absolute' listening, for use at a concert.

Georg Muffat, in his *Ausserlesene Instrumental-Music* of 1701, points out that concerti are not suited to dancing or the church, but are composed 'only for the express refreshment of the ear.' See Strunk, *Source Readings*, 449.

45 Braun, 'Entwurf für ein Typologie der "Hautboisten,"' 46.

46 Günther Schmidt, *Die Musik am Hofe der Markgrafen von Brandenburg-Ansbach* (Kassel, 1956), 72.

47 Johann Mattheson, *Ehren-Pforte* (Hamburg, 1740), 195.

The Aristocratic Trumpet Choir

Another ensemble which was at the center of seventeenth-century court life, yet receives only cursory mention in scholarly books on music, was the aristocratic trumpet choir. The trumpet had been associated with the noble since antiquity, as for example the high priests in the Old Testament, and this symbolism was not lost on the Baroque German noble. Many German aristocrats began expanding the size of their trumpet choir in the early years of the seventeenth century and soon twelve or more trumpets organized in a double choir, with timpani, was not unusual.[48] These choirs served as an aural coat-of-arms, announcing and identifying the noble when he traveled, serving as his ambassador, performing for his meals and entertaining his guests.

Because the trumpet is thus associated with the highest level of society, it is praised throughout seventeenth-century literature. For example, Andreas Werckmeister, to whom Bach was indebted for equal-tuning, wrote in 1691,

> God should be praised with them. Yes, the trumpet contains the correct order of all the consonances in itself and is the foremost instrument.[49]

No wonder one of these trumpeters looking back at the end of his life observed,

> A sovereign may have ever so good an orchestra, venery, royal stables, and other such ministrations, but if he does not retain at least one choir of trumpeters and timpani, there is, in my opinion, something lacking in the perfection of his household.[50]

These trumpeters formed their own guilds, in part as an attempt to maintain the standards of their profession. Thus, in a document of 1620, one Caspar Hentzschel comments on the performance of their memorized 'Toccetten, Sonaden and Serosoneten.' These, he warns his brothers, must be performed in an 'artful' manner and never in beer houses. He also recognized a 'correct musical art,' which interestingly enough he identifies as an 'ancient art which was used by the Jews and was communicated to me by an old Jew from Padua....'[51]

The trumpeter guilds were also eager to protect their domain from infringement by other musicians and during the seventeenth century they frequently called upon the aristocracy to confirm these 'rights' in legal documents. One of these, by the Emperor Ferdinand II, in 1623, states,

---

48 Detlef Altenburg, *Untersuchungen zur Geschichte der Trompete im Zeitalter der Clarinblaskunst* (Regensburg: G. Bosse, 1973), I, 24.

49 Quoted in Wilhelm Ehmann, *Tibilustrium* (Kassel: Barenreiter, 1950), 56.

50 Ernst Altenburg, *Versuch einer Anleitung zur heroischmusikalischen Trompeter- und Pauker-Kunst ...* (Halle, 1795).

51 Quoted in Johannes Reschke, *Studie zur Geschichte der brandenburgisch-preussischen Heeresmusik* (Berlin: VDI-Verlag, 1936), 5.

> No honorable trumpeter or timpanist shall allow himself to be employed with his instrument in any way other than for religious services, emperors, kings, electors and princes, counts, lords and knights and nobility, or other persons of high quality. It shall also be forbidden altogether to use a trumpet or a timpani at despicable occasions; likewise the excessive nocturnal improper carousing in the streets and alleys, in wine- and beer-houses. He who transgresses in this way shall be punished.[52]

In 1653 a new edict by the Emperor Ferdinand III was issued, due to 'various difficulties, errors and abuses' relative to the edict of 1623 by his father. The new edict deals at length with the apprentice system, after first stipulating that a prospective student must first present information relative to his 'honorable ancestry and birth.'[53] In this regard the aristocratic trumpeter is warned that if he 'behaves dishonorably toward a widow or an honest man's daughter and makes her pregnant,' even though he acknowledges the child, he may not instruct him in trumpet playing. The student must study with the noble trumpeter for two years, after which a final exam is given.

> Each master shall instruct his apprentice very diligently in his art, and shall not send him into the field until he knows his Feldstücke perfectly. In order to test this, the apprentice must present himself beforehand to the highest and oldest trumpeter and play his test piece for him. If this is not done, then as a bungler he will not be allowed to go into the field.

It is also interesting that the edict places strict limitations on how many students one trumpeter could teach, and how often, which was an attempt to guard against overcrowding the profession.

The 1653 edict again addresses the standard of behavior expected of the noble trumpeter.

> No honorable trumpeter shall let himself be heard or play the trumpet at night after the curfew hour in the alleys or cross roads, nor in public houses or wine bars, nor anywhere else, except in the houses of princely lords and noble families.

As for the trumpeters, their principal fear was that their duties might be taken over by the much more accomplished civic musicians, who, for one thing, could read music. The repeated attempts by the noble trumpeters to define the areas of performance which belonged to them suggest these efforts were not respected. Failing in this, they next attempted to restrict the instrument itself to their profession, leaving the old S-trumpet and the cornett to the civic musicians. Their concern in this regard was so paranoid that a document of 1630 suggests they wanted to prevent other musicians, especially trombonists, from even *sounding* like a trumpet.[54]

---

52 Quoted in Smithers, *The Music and History of the Baroque Trumpet*, 115.

53 Antonium Fabrum, *Europâischer Staats-Kantzley* (Leipzig, 1700), IV, 848ff.

54 Arno Werner, *Städtische und fürstliche Musikpflege in Zeitz* (Bückeburg & Leipzig, 1922), 42.

For a while the aristocratic trumpet guild was able to restrict for themselves the use of the trumpet. One finds, for example, that the city council in Leipzig had to make a formal report to the elector explaining why their music director, J. H. Schein, used trumpets in a performance in St. Thomas Church. In response, Schein was directed to use the cornett in the future![55] One famous incident in Hannover makes clear how serious this issue was perceived at the time.

> At the end of the seventeenth century in Hannover, the elector's trumpeters once broke into the house of the chief Stadtpfeifer, with whom they were at loggerheads, took his trumpet on which he was practicing and knocked out several of his front teeth with it. And what is more, these worthy Kameraden contended that they had only asserted their just right—and escaped all punishment.[56]

CIVIC MUSIC

In the lives of the ordinary citizens throughout seventeenth-century Germany, the most conspicuous and most important musical organization was the Stadtpfeifers, the civic musicians—an institution which was now at its musical peak. For nearly all of their five-hundred-year tradition these were civic wind bands. The members were specialists until the sixteenth century, when the favored consort principle required them all to be proficient on a number of instruments. Late in the sixteenth century they began to use string instruments as well, but there remained a definite hierarchy with cornetts and trombones at the top, followed by strings and then the lowly bagpipe and percussion.[57]

As with the use of consorts in the sixteenth century, instrumental variety and color was achieved by changing instruments for each composition. Thus an account of a concert by the Nürnberg Stadtpfeifers in 1643 states that they performed on strings; then on silver trumpets and clarions; a 'Greek military composition' with trumpets, drums and timpani; on bassoons and bombards in accompanying a chorus; [unnamed] winds in the instrumental performance of a motet and finally a funeral composition for male chorus and trombones.[58]

This required, of course, that each member of the Stadtpfeifers be proficient on all the basic instruments. Accordingly, when an opening occurred the applicant had to audition on many instruments. Often a local composer would be engaged to write compositions for the applicants to read at the audition. When, for example, in 1743, the Zeitz Stadtpfeifers had an

55 Gottfried Viet, *Die Blasmusik* (Innsbruck: Ed Helbling, 1972), 24.

56 Werner Menke, *History of the Trumpet of Bach and Händel* (London: W. Reeves, 1934), 26ff.

57 Ehmann, *Tibilustrium*, 23, 30.

58 Elisabeth Krückeberg, 'Ein historisches Konzert zu Nürnberg im Jahre 1643,' in *Archiv für Musikwissenschaft* (1918–1919), 590ff.

opening, they paid Johann Görner, music director of Leipzig University, twelve Thalers to compose works for trumpet, trombone, cornett, horn, and two each for strings and oboe.[59]

It should perhaps be mentioned that while the Stadtpfeifer positions were generally filled by audition, other civic positions were often obtainable by bribe. In fact, when Bach applied for an organist position in Hamburg in 1720, he was passed over in favor of a candidate named Heitmann who made a gift of 4000 marks to the town council. Perhaps more surprising than the result is the fact that the town actually advertised their openness to such a bribe.

> The question was raised whether it was desired that money should be given for the organist's post; on which point it was decided that:
>
> There were many reasons not to introduce the sale of an organist's post, because it was part of the ministry of God; accordingly the choice should be free, and the capacity of the candidates should be more considered than the money. But if, after the selection had been made, the chosen candidate of his own free will wished to give a token of his gratitude ...[60]

Bach served on one of these Stadtpfeifer audition panels in 1745 and wrote the following report to the Leipzig Town Council after the examination of the applicant, Carl Friedrich Pfaffe.

> At the command of A Most Noble and Most Worthy Council, Carl Friedrich Pfaffe, hitherto apprentice to Your Honors' Stadtpfeifers, has taken his trial examination in the presence of the other Stadtpfeifers; whereupon it was found that he performed quite well and to the applause of all those present on all the instruments that are customarily employed by the Stadtpfeifers, namely: Violin, Hautbois, Flute Travers., Trompette, Waldhorn, and the remaining bass instruments, and he was found quite suited to the post of assistant which he seeks.[61]

But, human nature being what it is, we must not assume that all Stadtpfeifers were equally fine musicians. When Bach arrived in Leipzig he found some of the Stadtpfeifers at his disposal somewhat lacking. He tactfully observed,

> Discretion forbids me to speak of their quality and musical knowledge, but it should be mentioned that some of them are *emeriti* and others are not in as good *exercitio* as they should be.[62]

But surely his predecessor at St. Thomas, Kuhnau, was exaggerating when he observed that in a hundred Stadtpfeifers there was scarcely one who could write ten words on paper, even if his life depended on it.[63]

---

59 Arnold Schering, *Musikgeschichte Leipzigs* (Leipzig: Kistner & Siegel, 1941), III, 151.

60 Quoted in David and Mendel, *The Bach Reader*, 80ff.

61 Quoted in Arnold Schering, 'The Leipziger Ratsmusik von 1650 bis 1775,' in *Archiv für Musikwissenschaft* (1921), 44.

62 Quoted in E.H. Müller von Asow, *Johann Sebastian Bach Briefe* (Regensburg, 1950), 112.

63 Kuhnau, *Musicus vexatus* (1690).

In view of these expectations, the reader might find interesting a letter of recommendation, written by a father in support of his son's application for a music position in Stettin in 1607. Particularly astonishing here is the large number of instruments the boy owned!

> My son has arrived at a point in his art where he has studied and learned diligently all the musical instruments. First, he is a good trumpeter and secondly a good cornett player and plays well the discant violin, Querpfeife, dulcian, quart-, tenor- and alto-trombone. In summary: all perfect instruments, although without proclaiming his fame—for as one says, 'Self praise stinks.' But he can prove himself where it matters, in what the ear hears and the eye sees. To cover the subject, he doesn't quarrel or criticize, and can use the instruments I have given him in praise of God: trombones, cornetts, a good quart-trombone; a dulcian consort; a large and small bombard consort; a large cornett consort; a crumhorn consort; a Querpfeiffen consort; a flute consort; and a violin consort. He can play all parts and use the fifth, sixth, or eighth voices [ie., read the various clefs], comes from a good home ... and is twenty-six years old.

The regular duties of the typical Stadtpfeifer were quite varied, as we see in a contract for one Christoph Schumann in 1726. The reader will note here in particular the participation in the well-known tower music, known as *Abblasen*; the surrogate clock duty and the regular service accompanying singers in the church.

> He should at 3:00 A.M., 9:00 A.M. and 9:00 P.M. play with diligence a spiritual Psalm, to the honor of the Almighty God and to inspire Christian prayer and to sustain the goodwill of the citizens and the entire community. Further, at night he should faithfully watch and take heed that with his assistant the horn player they mark every quarter hour with the usual horn playing. He should keep his quarters in the tower clean. He must volunteer to play in church with his instrument and assist the civic musicians with weddings, operas, and official banquets, although not permit himself, though helping, to actually take part in the ceremonies.[64]

The tower music, or Abblasen, played several times a day from a tower as indicated above, was a very important part of German civic life and deserves far greater attention by music historians. Far from performing mere chorales, the musicians played chorale canzonas, chorale fantasies, free canzonas, sonatas and suites.[65] In the quality of their performance as musicians, there was a certain 'public relations' aspect to this music, as is indicated in an ordinance from Zeitz in 1701, which speaks of the performance of Abblasen to 'better ornament the town for visitors.'[66]

More important, however, was the spiritual and psychological impact of this music, which Johann Pezel called 'a friendly and peaceful sound,'[67] on the ordinary citizen. The trombones, on which the Abblasen were most frequently performed, had themselves become symbols of God and Christian music. Thus, Kuhnau, Bach's predecessor in Leipzig, reflected,

64 Quoted in Ehmann, *Tibilustrium*, 32.

65 Ibid., 34.

66 Arno Werner, *Vier Jahrhunderte im Dienste der Kirchenmusik* (Leipzig: Merseburger, 1933), 218.

67 Ibid., 217.

> When our civic musicians at Festival time blow a spiritual song on the loud trombones, every measure stirs the image of angels singing.

No other instruments, but wind instruments, he says are played in Heaven by the angels![68]

Regarding the impact of this music on the citizen, one must first remember that there was no noise level comparable to modern towns and that the loudest sound most people would hear in their entire life was a small church organ. Therefore, it is reasonable to assume that most people in a moderate-sized town could hear this tower music. What then might be the effect of this spiritual music, floating down from on high, played by instruments which were themselves symbols of God and heard by the citizen several times a day throughout his entire life? We have heard distinguished musicians in Europe contend that this music, played continuously from the late sixteenth through the eighteenth centuries, was more responsible than any other factor for the development of the German character as we know it today.

An eloquent summary of the duties of the tower musician is given in a 1679 poem by Jacob Lottich.

> When Titan's high course is about to bring midday, the clock strikes ten;
> Then the musicians meet with all their odds and ends,
> Form a group and let us have a tune for lunch on their trombones.
> The midday music can be heard from the town hall tower,
> Almost high up in the open air; it sounds for the honor of God and to inform the people,
> So that everyone knows each day at this time it is the tenth hour.
> When Latous has departed from us with his never tiring horses
> And when we no longer see any light or any rays from him on earth,
> Then a bell is rung so that its sweet sound entices us to vespers.
> A cornettist then takes the best of his Zinken,
> Chooses a Psalm which he considers just suitable, and he pipes in an artful manner;
> He does his duty, stays on the church tower and remains awake for the rest of the night.
> In the streets guards who have been appointed for this purpose walk up and down and see
> To it that the streets are safe; they seize the trespasser against law and order;
> They prevent fire and turmoil so that everyone shall be safe while they rest.
> As often as the clock strikes, the hours are called out.
> There is no shortage of clocks: hardly anywhere would you find such ingenious clock works.
> Anyone who does not believe this should come here and see for himself that one weight alone propels two big clocks.
> As soon as Aurora gleams in gold and red hues the watchman still awake takes his trumpet, alerts and wakes up the town with a morning song.
> After that he retires and makes up for his lost sleep.[69]

68 Quoted in Ehmann, *Tibilustrium*, 55ff.

69 Quoted in Smithers, *The Music and History of the Baroque Trumpet*, 121ff.

As the above poem points out, the worker's 'noon break' came at 10:00 A.M. at a time when work had to begin with first light. It was for these concerts that the collections of sonatas by Johann Pezel[70] known as *Hora decima* ('Ten o'clock hour') was published in 1670. Among his many publications were a collection of two-part works intended for the recreational music by the musicians in the tower during their long and lonely hours on duty.[71] Yet another publication of dance movements, *Fünff-stimmigte blasende Music* may have been used for public concerts from a balcony of the city hall building.

Another important published collection associated with Leipzig is the *Vier und zwantzig Neue Quatricinia* by Gottfried Reiche. Reiche's dedication is a testimonial to the importance of these civic wind players.

> Nothing in all art can claim finer qualities than Noble Music. My pen is much too weak either to repeat here, or to say better what professional and highly-learned men have affirmed so competently. As this matchless art spreads its charms in many ways, we find in most cities the praise-worthy custom of having the so-called Abblasen sounded from churches and town halls. This is always a sign of joy and peace; because, wherever such music must be discontinued there must be national mourning, war, or other misfortune.[72]

Reiche was the senior Stadtpfeifer in Leipzig at the time of Bach and, judging by Mattheson's *Ehren-Pforte* (1740), better known than Bach. He died in service, after a parade honoring a visit by the elector of Saxony in 1734 (an occasion for which Bach contributed his 'Preise dein Glück, gesegnetes Sachsen'). One present wrote,

> On October 6th the skilled and experienced musician and Stadtpfeifer, Gottfried Reiche, … and senior member of the local musician's guild, suffered a stroke not far from his lodging in the Stadtpfeifer- gasschen, as he was on his way home, so that he collapsed and was brought dead into the house. And this is said to have occurred because on the previous day he had been greatly fatigued by playing in the royal music and had suffered severely from the smoke of the torches.[73]

Several additional collections of German Stadtpfeifer music which survive are by Daniel Speer, who served during the late seventeenth century in Breslau. Speer, who was also highly educated, has left an education treatise, *Musicalisches Kleeblatt*, which contains ensemble music with his own comments on instrumental technique. In this work, for example, he finds

70 Pezel (1639–1694) was well educated and also served as director of the collegium musicum of the University of Leipzig from 1673 to 1682. His application for cantor of St. Thomas Church in 1677 was rejected because he had been born a Catholic.

71 Johann Pezel, *Bicinia variorum instrumentorum, ut a Violinis, Cornettis, Flautis, Clarinis et Fagottis com apprendice a 2 Bombardinis vulgo Schalmeyen* (Leipzig, 1675).

72 In this dedication, Reiche makes the interesting revelation that he has composed some Sonatas for the Leipzig musicians, but has not been able to publish them due to the present state of publishing. The collection is now lost. Regarding his final comment, Kuhnau once observed, 'Nobody will pray more devoutly for the long life of his sovereign than the instrumentalists!'

73 Quoted in G. Wustmann, *Quellen zur Geschichte Leipzig* (Leipzig, 1889), I, 436.

five indispensable qualities for good trumpet playing: good health, good breath control, a fast moving tongue, willingness for constant practice and good, long trills made with the chin. He discusses the embouchure in detail, concluding with,

> Above all, an incipient shall accustom himself to draw in his cheeks, not blow them out, for this is not only unseemly, but hinders the breath from having its due outlet and causes a man pains at the temples, so that true teachers are accustomed to box the ears of their pupils to cure them of this bad habit.

The Stadtpfeifers performed for a wide variety of other civic occasions, including official civic banquets, for university functions, public and trade guild celebrations and even for courts which did not maintain their own musicians. As is more generally known, they also performed in church when needed and participated in the performances of the collegium musica.

The civic collegium musica were meetings of students and local musicians who met, sometimes in coffee houses, for the performance and enjoyment of music. The Leipzig collegium musicum had existed periodically during the seventeenth century but became more influential after 1702 when it was reorganized by Telemann. Under Telemann the group began to meet on a regular weekly basis and gave concerts for the citizens.

Bach began to become involved with the Leipzig collegium musicum after 1729, when he seems to have become more interested in secular music in general and a number of his secular cantatas and instrumental works appear to have been composed for these performances. There is extant an announcement for his public concerts in 1736 which includes several interesting details.

> Both the public musical Concerts or Assemblies that are held here weekly are still flourishing steadily. The one is conduced by Mr. Johann Sebastian Bach, Kapellmeister to the Court of Weissenfels and Music Director at the Thomas-Kirche and Nicolai-Kirche in this city, and is held, except during the Fair, once a week in Zimmerman's coffeehouse in the Cather-strasse, on Friday evenings from 8 to 10 o'clock …
>
> The participants in these musical concerts are chiefly students here, and there are always good musicians among them, so that sometimes they become, as is known, famous virtuosos. Any musician is permitted to make himself publicly heard at these musical concerts, and most often, too, there are such listeners as know how to judge the qualities of an able musician.[74]

A collegium musicum was also active in Hamburg beginning in 1660 and its emphasis was in giving concerts of new works composed in other major cities. The group, composed of local professional and amateur musicians, became widely known and after his arrival in 1721, Telemann became associated with its concerts. Expanding the scope of their repertoire, Telemann began repeating performances of works he had composed for the local church. This brought an immediate complaint from the town council.

74 Quoted in David and Mendel, *The Bach Reader*, 149.

> Because the current Kantor Telemann has thought to perform for money his music in a public inn where all manner of disorder is possible; and moreover he makes free to perform operas, comedies, and similar entertainments likely to arouse bawdiness ... and all without the consent of this most excellent Council and Citizenry; so the Oberalten of the Council seek a decree that for such music the Kantor shall be most earnestly disciplined and forbidden further such performances.[75]

In 1678 Hamburg also had the distinction of becoming the first German city to build a public opera house. It had seating for 2,000 and its more than ninety performances a year was the beginning of repertory opera in the modern sense. Although some nobles were enthusiastic over Italian opera, the climate after the period of war left many people more inclined toward religious music. It was in this context that Rector Biedermann of the Freyberg Gymnasium expressed his extreme disapproval of virtually any form of music in his school's curriculum following a performance by the students of a *Singspiel* in 1748.[76] In any case, opera was slower in developing in Germany and one must assume that this explains, at least in part, why so gifted a native composer as Reinhard Keiser (1673–1739) never received the credit he deserved.

With the arrival of Telemann in Hamburg in 1721 public concerts became a vital part of civic life. In a letter to a friend, he is enthusiastic to find strong support for concerts among the leaders of the city.

> A great advantage is added to this by the fact that, besides the presence of many persons of rank here, also the most prominent men of the city—including the entire city council—do not absent themselves from public concerts. Likewise the reasoned judgment of so many connoisseurs and intelligent people give opportunity for concerts.[77]

We imagine that such works as his concerti for Hautboisten must have been written for concerts at this time, combining as they do a direct galant style and programmatic references to Hamburg geographical features which would be familiar to that public. By the early eighteenth century there were public concerts with the public buying tickets.

During the late years of the seventeenth century another town famous for its public concerts was Lübeck. Its *Abendmusiken*, given in the Marienkirche, were even advertised by the city fathers for the purpose of attracting visitors.

In Leipzig soon after the beginning of the eighteenth century local publishers began to print music expressly intended for amateur performance by the middle class. The growing

---

75 Quoted in Josef Sittard, *Geschichte des Musik- und Concertwesens in Hamburg* (Altona and Leipzig, 1890), 61.

76 Beekman Cannon, *Johann Mattheson, Spectator in Music* (Archon Books, 1968), 96. Mattheson's book of 1750, *Matthesons bewährte Panacea ...*, was written in response and and presents his reasons why music should be part of the curriculum of every school.

77 Hans Grosse and Hans Rudolf Jung, ed., *Georg Philipp Telemann Briefwechsel* (Leipzig: VEB Deutscher verlag für Musik, 1972), 213.

appeal of this market was not lost on Bach, whose first *Clavierübung* of dance music admits in its title, 'Composed for Music Lovers, to Refresh Their Spirits.'

In his autobiography, submitted for Mattheson's *Ehrenpforte* in 1740, Telemann provides a rare first-hand account of peasant music.

> In Pless, a dominion of the Court of Promnitz in upper Silesia, where the Court used to repair for six months, as well as in Cracow, I became familiar with Polish and Hanakian music in their true, barbaric beauty. In the public taverns the band would consist of a fiddle strapped to the body, a Polish bagpipe, a bass trombone and a regal. The fiddle was tuned a third higher than usual, and could thus outscream any six ordinary violins. At places of better repute the regal was omitted, but the number of fiddles and bagpipes was augmented. Indeed, once I found thirty-six bagpipes and eight fiddles together. One can hardly believe with what inspiration bagpipers and fiddlers improvise while the dancers rest. An observant person could pick up enough ideas from them in a week to last a lifetime. In short, this music contains much valuable material, if it is properly treated.[78]

By the end of the Baroque there must have been much musical activity among the upper middle-class merchants in Germany, although this topic, with the exception of the Fugger family of Munich, has received little attention to date. The reader will recall that the great Gabrieli of Venice had dedicated his *Concerti* of 1587 to Jakob Fugger.

CHURCH MUSIC

Early seventeenth-century accounts of church music in Germany also reflect the generally unstable climate caused by the Thirty Years' War. One cantor in Dresden complains in 1619, that as a result of the daily assemblies, of drinking bouts, and of serenades, the voices were ruined, and that they changed before their time; that there were actually few good voices at hand; that the pupils spent too much time drinking toasts, and that the choir rehearsals times were often otherwise occupied.[79]

Surviving music, together with extant documents, suggest a close association between the Stadtpfeifers and the churches of Germany. It is only in the context of this ancient association between town and church that one can understand the somewhat amusing sentence in Bach's certificate of appointment in Mühlhausen, in 1707, which requires him to 'defend our common city from all harm.'[80]

---

78 Quoted in Morgenstern, *Composers on Music*, 40.

79 Moser, *Heinrich Schütz*, 156.

80 Quoted in David and Mendel, *The Bach Reader*, 55.

For most of the seventeenth century, 'Stadtpfeifer' meant mostly wind instruments.[81] Of course, the Stadtpfeifer already had their repertoire for 'Instrumentalkonzert,' some of which was suitable for performance during Communion in the Protestant Church or for the Offertory in the Catholic Church.[82] They were used sometimes to help singers hold their pitch,[83] or in the case of a Rothenburg o.T. document, just to help the rehearsal process.

> The Stadtpfeifer should appear with their instruments as early as Vesper prayer time, on Sundays and Festival days, but also during the week as the Kantor requires, to help rehearse the music to be used the following Sunday.[84]

In the Protestant churches they made possible performances of the polychoral concerti of the Italian tradition, as described by Mattheson.

> There one uses works with three or four choirs, distributed in general as follows: In one choir very good trumpets and timpani are heard; one part of timpani for six trumpets and two pair for twelve trumpets. In another choir are trombones, cornetts and other wind instruments. In a third choir are singers, of an accompanied nature called Capella … A fourth choir, yet again singers, is the main choir … all will be conducted by the director.[85]

On occasions of special celebration rich instrumental resources were employed, as we read, for example, in an account of the celebration of the Centennial of the Reformation in 1617. The eyewitness reports an interlude performed by five choirs of trumpets, in addition to works with voices and trumpets.

> The musicians of the elector of Saxony, our Gracious Lord, performed this music: eleven instrumental players, eleven singers, four organists, four lutanists, one theorbo player, three organ choir boys, five discant singers, alternating with various kinds of magnificent instruments, also with two organs, two regals, three clavicymbals, and in addition eighteen trumpeters and two timpani, all presented with appropriate solemnity under the direction of Heinrich Schütz from Weissenfels.[86]

---

81 Werner, *Vier Jahrhunderte im Dienste der Kirchenmusik*, 220, says *only* wind instruments, as the strings were still considered amateur [*burger*] instruments. An exception was the court Kapelle in Dresden, which had violins during the seventeenth century, according to George J. Buelow, 'Dresden in the Age of Absolutism,' in *The Late Baroque Era* (Englewood Cliffs: Prentice Hall, 1994), 217.

82 Arnold Schering, 'Einleitung,' *Denkmäler Deutscher Tonkunst* (Wiesbaden, 1958), XXIX-XXX, ix. Actually, original compositions for winds for Communion and Offertory exist in great numbers through the nineteenth century.

83 Josef Sittard, *Zur Geschichte der Musik … am Württembergischen hofe* (Stuttgart, 1890), I, 302,

> … und von den Instrumentisten zu [bessern] erhaltung des Toni, mit Zincken und Posannen ihr Assistenz darbei gelaistet werden.

84 Quoted in Ehmann, *Tibilustrium*, 41.

85 Quoted in Schering, 'Einleitung,' xx. Marpurg, in *Kritische Briefe über die Tonkunst* (1760), I, 17 Brief, gives a similar description of a large concerto for voices and winds he heard in a dream.

86 Matthias Hoe von Hoenegg, 'Parasceve ad solemnitatem evangelicam' [1617], quoted in MacClintock, *Readings*, 139.

Another festival, the Naumburg Princes' Day, celebrated in the spring of 1614, included a total of some ninety musicians brought by various nobles. One highpoint was a performance in the church, conducted by Michael Praetorius. He had placed one ensemble in the organ loft, another in the nave, a third by the baptismal and a boy's choir in the choir of the church. The cantor, we are told, was moved to tears.[87] So rich were the possibilities for accompanied church music because of the availability of the Stadtpfeifers, that when some choir director preferred *a cappella* music he was sometimes fired, as was the case in Wittenberg in 1628.[88]

Because the Stadtpfeifers were often required to participate in church by contract, the church was sometimes in a position to involve themselves in the affairs of the Stadtpfeifers. In Zeitz, for example, the church had a voice in the audition process for new Stadtpfeifers and in this same town the church was able to prevent the Stadtpfeifers from playing weddings and other outside jobs on Sunday.[89]

Also, since in many cases the instruments the Stadtpfeifers used belonged to the city, there must have been some fear of conflict, for there are numerous extant documents relating to churches purchasing their own instrument collections for the Stadtpfeifers to use. The St. Wenzel Church in Naumburg in 1657 owned no fewer than sixty instruments, including a consort of eight crumhorns, trumpets, trombones, a consort of Schreyerpfeife and dulcans.[90] Church records in Zeitz mention the possession of shawms until 1689 and the purchase of the new French oboe in 1691.[91]

Strings rarely appear in the church collections until the beginning of the eighteenth century. One can see the date of arrival of the violin in the St. Thomas Church collection in Leipzig in an inventory which reads,

> 1 large violin
> 1 large spinet
> 1 large Bombard and 4 smaller ones
> 1 Quart-fagott
> 6 trumpets and a small one in Eb
> 3 old trombones (alto, tenor and bass)
> 2 'new' violins, purchased in 1701.[92]

At about this time Telemann became Kapellmeister of the court at Eisenach and reports that he was ordered to hire singers who could double as violinists.[93]

87 Hans Moser, Heinrich Schütz, 76.

88 Werner, *Vier Jahrhunderte im Dienste der Kirchenmusik*, 219.

89 Werner, *Städtische und fürstliche Musikpflege in Zeitz*, 40, 43.

90 Arno Werner, 'Die alte Musikbibliothek und die Instrumentsammlung an St. Wenzel in Naumberg a. d. S.,' in *Archiv für Musikwissenschaft* (1926), VIII, 390ff.

91 Werner, *Städtische und fürstliche Musikpflege in Weissenfels*, 95.

92 Schering, *Musikgeschichte Leipzigs*, II, 114.

93 Telemann's autobiography in Mattheson, *Ehrenpforte* (1740), quoted in Morgenstern, *Composers on Music*, 41.

During the Baroque one also finds records indicating that the wind bands belonging to the aristocracy were also required to appear in their private chapels. An order of 1621, for example, by the Württemberg court of Duke Johann Friedrich (1608–1628) requires the trombone and cornett players to appear without fail for the choir rehearsals during the week.[94] It was in these private chapels, in particular, that one heard the aristocratic trumpet choirs joining in church music. This represented a problem for the choir director, for these trumpets usually did not read music and only performed memorized pieces. But since they played natural instruments, consisting of only a triad in a single key, so long as the choir director had a work in the same key, the trumpets could join in with little noticeable dissonance.[95] Another solution was to add them at the end of a composition, such was the case with the *Psalm 136* of Schütz. At the end of the Bass part of this composition, Schütz has written '*Darauff wird stracks eine Intrada zum Final geblasen*,' as a cue for just such a performance.

Monasteries also used instruments with their choirs. There is an interesting document dated ca. 1720 from the Gottweig Abbey in Austria relative to the negotiations of purchasing either a Hautbois, *Chalimou* or flute consort from the maker Jacob Denner.[96] Another document, from the monastery at Melk, deals with the purchase of two English horns and a bassoon in 1748.[97] One document from this monastery describes the performance of an ensemble of four players during the ritual of 'Bleeding' [*Phlebotomia*], a health measure practiced twice a year and attended by the public![98]

There were some anomalies within this rich practice. One was Hamburg, where toward the end of the seventeenth century the combined effects of a decline in the Stadtpfeifers [*Ratmusikanten*], together with the popularity of opera, resulted in a decline in interest in church music. Local preachers took the opportunity to attack the cantata as being too much like opera, an influence they declared to be unchristian and the work of the Devil.[99] It was also in Hamburg, as we have mentioned above, that an incompetent organist obtained a post in competition with Bach, by bribing the audition committee.

> I remember, as will still a large number of parishioners, that some years ago a certain great virtuoso [Bach], whose merits have since earned him an important cantorate [in Leipzig], presented himself as an organist in a town of no small size [Hamburg], performed on many of the finest organs, and aroused the admiration of everyone for his mastery. But there also appeared among other incompetent journeymen, the son of a wealthy artisan [named Heitmann], who

94 Sittard, *Zur Geschichte der Musik*, I, 45.

95 Praetorius discusses this performance problem at length in his *Syntagma Musicum*, III.

96 Horace Fitzpatrick, 'Jacob Denner's Woodwinds for Gottweig Abbey,' *The Galpin Society Journal* 21 (1968): 81ff, http://www.jstor.org/stable/841431.

97 Robert Freeman, 'The Practice of Music at Melk Monastery in the Eighteenth Century' (Dissertation, UCLA, 1971), 103.

98 Ibid., 151.

99 George J. Buelow, 'Hamburg and Lübeck,' in *The Late Baroque Era* (Englewood Cliffs: Prentice Hall, 1994), 201. In the early years of the eighteenth century, there were also disputes at Halle University over the use of music in the church. See Bernd Baselt, 'Brandenburg-Prussia and the Central German Courts,' in Ibid., 238.

> could execute preludes better with thalers than with his fingers. It was he (as might easily be guessed), who gained the post, although almost everyone was angered by it.[100]

Another anomaly was the Imperial court in Vienna, which continued to favor the performance of works in the sixteenth-century polyphonic style, although music of other styles was also used. This conservative and old-fashioned attitude continued quite late due to the influence of Johann Fux (1660–1741), who was also probably the last person to use the cornett in a German-speaking church. Fux, clearly, was not a man to embrace new ideas. When Mattheson wrote him for biographical details for his book on German musicians, Fux responded, 'Suffice it to say that I was considered worthy to be the first Kapellmeister to Charles VI.'

MILITARY MUSIC

During the seventeenth century, before the introduction of the new Hautboisten, the movements of the German armies were controlled by the powerful trumpet guilds which have been discussed above. These guilds were sufficiently independent that even when serving the army the trumpeters were subject to guild discipline rather than military codes.[101] Indeed, existing under imperial 'privileges,' the trumpeters expected a level of respect above that of the ordinary soldier, as Altenburg maintains.

> No colonel, cavalry captain, or commanding officer shall willfully treat a trumpeter or military timpanist badly, as was in vogue for some time. [He shall not] shame him, despise or prescribe menial labor for him without good cause, nor throw him out of the service without pay, but rather, as in the custom of old, treat him like an honorable officer.[102]

Altenburg also points out that the trumpeter was entitled to wear the ostrich feather on his hat, which was otherwise reserved to officers. But, he warns, it will be necessary for the trumpeter to augment with his own funds the clothing allowance, for it is important that a trumpeter 'shall and must live in grand style, especially when he is young and single.'

The primary duty of the trumpeter, of course, was to sound the military signals which transmitted the instructions of the officers to the troops. These signals are discussed extensively in the literature of this period and we find it particularly interesting that there was some discussion of aesthetics, even in this most functional of music. For example, Altenburg, in speaking of the *Feldstücke*, observes that such a piece,

> should be played slower for the heavy cavalry, in order to express the serious and heroic, and it should be played more briskly for the Hussars because they are the light cavalry.

100 Johann Mattheson, *Der musicalische Patriot*, 316.

101 Henry Farmer, *Military Music* (London: W. Reeves, 1912), 36.

102 Ernst Altenburg, *Versuch einer Anleitung zur heroischmusikalischen Trompeter- und Pauker-Kunst ...*, trans. Edward Tarr (Halle, 1795), 54.

In another place, he speaks of the Fanfare as something that 'makes noise enough, but contains neither art nor order.'[103] Even the military timpanist was described by Zedler, in his *Universallexikon* (1735), as one 'who knows how to strike the drum elegantly.'[104]

Beyond this duty, the trumpeter, following an ancient tradition, also served as the ambassador, carrying messages to the enemy commander and back. Altenburg provides an interesting review of the facets of this responsibility. First, he says, one must take care to put the message in a safe place, where it will not get dirty. One must not show the message, or disclose his purpose, to anyone—not even the officers of his own regiment. One must be careful to get a receipt from the enemy commander to prove the message was delivered. One must be careful not to say anything that might reveal your own army's poor circumstances, but must discreetly look around for anything that might be welcome information to one's own commander. In summary, one must 'conduct oneself soberly, moderately, and carefully, since one can otherwise easily run the risk of being shot dead!'[105]

The first true military band tradition in Germany coincides with the seventeenth century decision to create standing armies. One might point to the date of 1646, when the elector Friedrich Wilhelm (1640–1688), 'the Great Elector,' founded his *Charbrandenburgische Liebguardie*. Created at the same time was a band of four *Schalmeyer* (two discant and an alto shawm, with a dulcian) with drums which concertized [*konzertierte*] for the troops.[106]

These Renaissance shawms provided the basic German military music until 1681 when one begins to find the introduction of the modern oboe. At this time the elector in Berlin had twelve instruments, divided between 'teutschen Schalmeyern' and 'französischen hoboisten.' A chronicle of 1690 speaks of the 'French shawm, called Hautbois,' and also informs us that these musicians followed the troops into actual battle.[107]

By the period of Friedrich I (1688–1713), the true Hautboisten band, consisting of modern oboes and bassoons, can be documented throughout Germany and Austria. During the first generation of Hautboisten the players were no doubt struggling with the new French oboes. Friedrich I arranged for his Hautboisten to study for two years under Johann Theile (1646–1724)[108] and in the town of Stade a document by the local civic band complains that the nearby army Hautboisten 'have not correctly learned nor do they understand their music.'[109]

---

103 Altenburg found that, in general, by the eighteenth century the performance of military signals had become less artistic, a fact which he attributed to the introduction of notation.

104 One signal which had its origin with the drum was the *Zapfenstreich* ('to hit or close the spigot'), which informed the soldier it was time to leave the tavern and return to his quarters to sleep. The term is used as a title for a composition by Beethoven.

105 Altenburg, *Versuch einer Anleitung zur heroischmusikalischen Trompeter- und Pauker-Kunst* ..., 42ff.

106 Johannes Reschke, 'Zur Geschichte der Deutschen Militärmusik des 17. und 18. Jahrhunderts,' in *Deutsche Musik-Kultur* (1937), II, 11.

107 W. C. Printz, *Historische Beschreibung der Edelen Sing- und Klingkunst* (Dresden, 1690) and Herbert Riedel, *Musik und Musikerlebnis in der erzählenden deutschen Dichtung* (Bonn: H. Bouvier, 1959), 520..

108 Friedrich Blume, *Die Musik in Geschichte und Gegenwart* (Kassel: Bärenreiter, 1949–1968), XIII, 278.

109 O. Spreckelsen, 'Der Stader Ratsmusikanten,' in *Stader Archiv* (Stade, 1924), 32.

It was also during this period that a far-reaching development took place—the introduction of the 'Turkish Music' style. Vienna, as the Eastern most city of Western Europe, had long been subject to attacks by Turkish troops. The Turkish siege of Vienna in 1683 concerned all nations as a perceived threat against Christianity. There was a natural curiosity in Vienna about these 'heathens' and during lulls in battle citizens would run out to collect souvenirs in the battle field.[110] Reports also speak of 'duels' between the Turkish bands and the Western trumpets and timpani during these lulls.[111] This fascination continued for some time in the West and is expressed in musical works from Mozart's *Abduction from the Seraglio* to 'alla Turca' examples in Haydn and Gluck and even the Ninth Symphony of Beethoven.

Another expression of this interest in all things Turkish was the adoption of their instruments into the Western military bands. The Turkish bands themselves consisted of the wild-sounding medieval shawm, a primitive trumpet and percussion: the large bass drum, cymbals and timpani. Known as 'Mehter bands,' these instruments were doubled according to the rank of the officer to which they were attached. It was these percussion instruments which were of interest to the military officers of the West, for they added the needed volume to the relatively weak-sounding Hautboisten to enable the troops to stay in step—the fundamental essential in coordinated marching.

The introduction of the new instruments into German military use can be dated from a visit of the Turkish ambassador, Achmet Effendi, to Berlin at the beginning of the eighteenth century. The elector, as a form of welcome, had dressed up some of his musicians as a Turkish band, but the ambassador exclaimed, 'This isn't Turkish at all!' The elector, shocked by this reaction, later arranged for the ambassador to send him an entire, actual Turkish band to train his German musicians.

During the period of Frederick William I (1713–1740), an extraordinary man who worked hard to develop his nation, there are further records of concert activity by the Hautboisten military bands. Frederick himself used it to sometimes replace his usual court music.[112] One contemporary provides a few details of concerts in the field.

> In the morning, in front of the commander's quarters, the Hautboisten play a Morning Song, a newly composed march, an Intrada, and a pair of minuets, which the commander likes.[113]

---

110 The most famous artifact was a bag of beans—which led to the birth of the coffee habit in Western Europe.

111 Eugen Brixel, *Das ist Üsterreichs Militärmusik* (Graz: Edition Kaleidoskop, 1982), 21. From this siege dates the German folksong, 'Prinz-Eugen, das edlen Ritter,' used by Hindemith in his *Konzertmusik*, Op. 41.

112 Peter Panoff, *Militärmusik* (Berlin: K. Siegismund, 1944), 86.

113 Hans von Fleming, *Der vollkommene deutsche Soldat* (Leipzig, 1726), quoted in Ibid., 52. Fleming also makes an interesting comment on the new French oboes.

> During the time of the shawm there were four players: two discant, an alto and a dulcian. After the oboe took their place, one finds six oboes, as the oboes were not so strong but had a softer sound than the shawms. The *Harmonie* was now complete with two discant, two taille and two bassoons.

A rare extant example of military 'concert' music is the *lustige Feld-Music* (1704) by Johann Philipp Kreiger (1649–1725), consisting of six Suites [*Ouverture*] scored for Oboe I [three players], Oboe II [two players], Taille[114] [one player] and Bassoon [three players]. The composer states that he hopes when his music is heard in the field it will be heard 'like a ray of sun on a stormy day.'

Frederick William I also founded the first military music school in 1724. The school was housed in the Military Orphans Home in Potsdam and its original purpose seems to have been to create Hautboisten musicians from the orphans. The first director of the school was Gottfried Pepush and he appears to have been in charge of about twenty students by 1750.[115]

114 There is substantial evidence, including iconography, which identifies the taille as a tenor oboe (English horn).

115 Panoff, *Militärmusik*, 109, where there is also included a drawing of the building.

9 AESTHETIC VIEWS OF GERMAN MUSICIANS

ON THE PHYSIOLOGY OF AESTHETICS

The chief accomplishment in music by the sixteenth-century humanists was to explain that the principal virtue of music is to express feelings, as had been understood by the ancient Greeks, and to free music from the long medieval Scholastic tradition in which music was understood as a branch of mathematics. The chief accomplishment in music during the Baroque was the demonstration of this change in philosophy in actual composition. In support of the new aesthetic, some Baroque writers felt compelled to comment on the sterile aesthetics of the old Scholastic philosophy. Their challenge was essentially to find a way to explain why, as we would say today, the experience of music is of the domain of the right hemisphere of the brain, the seat of feeling and personal experience, and not the domain of the left hemisphere, the seat of concepts and rules. One musician who addressed this directly was the composer, Johann Heinichen.

> If a composer, who is more concerned with sensitivity, good taste, and brilliance in music than with paper nonsense, writes with reason one little note contrary to their antiquated, platonic rules, they want to turn him over to the Inquisition to discover whether or not he can be classed among composers. Only it is remarkable how such musical pedants, though they involve themselves so willingly in harmful, authoritative prejudices, do not notice, however, that already in our time not only native but also the most famous foreign composers have begun to neglect the unnecessary eccentricities in composition and to seek a freer way in music by refining many of the old rules …
>
> If we examine more closely the motives causing famous composers to deviate frequently from the artificial accuracies of pure theorists, then in my judgment they might be: first, they are ashamed in general of pedantry and forced school book rules … Second, they have sound practical judgment and know when and where to depart with good reason from theoretical rules. Third, they will not be slaves to the many poorly founded rules from the past, but they would rather agree with the rule, founded on reason itself, though otherwise juristic: *Cessante ratione prohibition is, cessat ipsa prohibitio*—whenever the cause for the prohibition on which a rule is based becomes null and void, the prohibition of the given rule itself becomes null and void. And this judicious practice is ten times more difficult than the frequently prescribed, dry theory. Indeed, for this very reason the unskilled theorists remain so willingly with their dull, antiquated rules, because their judgment is inadequate to allow deviation from them with reason …

> All arts and sciences have rules and must be learned through rules, if we do not wish to remain simple naturalists, ie., half-ignorant. But we must not err excessively on the side of rules; furthermore, we should not accept so crudely the equivocal word: Rule, as if we would serve as high sounding rule makers, prescribing laws even to Nature, according to which she must limit herself to *auctoritate nostra*. No! All of our useful rules must be derived from Nature; and we must investigate on all levels the will, preference, and character of this mistress and learn from her *cum submissione*.[1]

Heinichen returns to the subject of 'the old rules,' the older polyphonic style, again with even more vigor. There are some church composers, he finds, who 'have learned something besides counterpoint' and have good taste whose music delights the ear. However, those who continue to compose only in the old polyphonic style,

> those who are not endowed with good taste and who stick to a common repertory of notes are pursued by the natural punishment, resembling the original sin: their music is not liked by a single living soul. It would be better, therefore, to burn immediately their all too artificial compositions before they cool down, and to scatter the ashes into their eyes. Then at least one of the senses would gain something from it, for otherwise neither the eye nor the ear profits from such a paper art.[2]

He concludes, somewhat sarcastically, that he has known some old theater composers, who due to old age had lost all their 'creative fire and invention.' These men, he notes became for the first time good church composers.

In a more general sense, Heinichen writes that the essential abilities needed for successful composition include natural aptitude and diligence, as well, of course, as knowledge of the basic conceptual information on writing music. However, as he quotes Andreas Werkmeister, rules alone do not suffice.

> If one has no musical aptitude 1,000 rules could be illustrated with 10,000 examples and still the purpose would not be achieved.[3]

In one of Heinichen's most valuable passages, one which demonstrates brilliant deductions regarding the physiology of music aesthetics, he addresses the fundamental distinction between Baroque music and earlier music. The old music, he says, was for the eye (Reason and conceptual understanding), but modern music is for the ear.

---

1 Johann David Heinichen, *General-Bass Treatise* [1711], quoted in George Buelow, *Thorough-Bass Accompaniment according to Johann David Heinichen* (Ann Arbor: UMI Research Press, 1986), 315ff. Heinichen (1683–1729) was a prolific composer in Dresden, but is known today only because of this important treatise which deals on many aspects of performance practice.

2 Ibid., 326.

3 Andreas Werckmeister, *Nothwendigsten Anmerckungen* (Aschersleben, 1698), 40ff.

The old musicians side more with Reason, but the new with the Ear; and since both parties do not agree on the first fundamental, it is evident that the conclusions and consequences made from two contrary fundamental principles should breed just as many controversies of inferior rank and thousands of diametrically opposed hypotheses. Musicians of the past, we know, chose two judges in music: Reason and the Ear. The choice would be correct since both are indispensable to music; yet, because of the use of these two concomitants, the present cannot reconcile itself with the past, and in this the past is blamed for two errors. First, it wrongly classed the two judges and placed the Ear, the sovereign of music, below the rank of Reason or would divide its commanding authority with the latter. Whereupon the blameless Ear must immediately cede half of its monarchical domain. In addition, unfortunately, the composers of the past poorly explained the word ratio. In those innocent times (in which one knew nothing of present day good taste and brilliance in music, and every simple harmony seemed beautiful), they thought Reason could be put to no better use than the creation of supposedly learned and speculative artificialities of note writing. Therefore, they began on the one hand to measure out theoretically innocent notes according to mathematical scales and with the help of the proportioned yardstick, and on the other hand, to place these notes in musical practice on the staves (almost as if they were on a rack) and to pull and stretch them (or in the language of counterpoint, to augment them), to turn them upside down, to repeat and to change their positions, until finally from the latter resulted a practice with an overwhelming number of unnecessary instances of contrapuntal eye-music and from the former resulted a theory with amassed metaphysical contemplations of emotion and reason. Thus, one no longer had cause to ask if music sounded well or pleased the listener, but rather if it looked good on paper. In this way, the Visual perceptibly gained the most in music and used the authority of the imprudent Reason only to cover its own lust for power. Consequently, the suppressed Ear was tyrannized so long that finally it hid behind table and chairs to await from the distance the condescending, merciful glance of its *usurpatores regni* (*ratio & visus*). This grave injustice to the musical sovereign, the Ear, has been reprehended more by present-day musicians than by those of the past. They have begun vigorously to understand the many absurd and preposterous principles of the past and to form completely new ideas about the noble art of music unlike those of the learned ignoramuses. Above all, they return to the oppressed Ear the sovereignty of its realm; they displace Reason from its judicial duties and give it [Reason] to the Ear, not as Domino or co-regent, but as an intelligent minister and counselor with the absolute mandate to warn its master (the occasionally deceived Ear, if indeed 'deceived' can be spoken of) of every false step; but otherwise, Reason differs in opinion, it must serve the Ear with the complete obedience and employ all of its skill, not for the visual appearance on paper, but to give the Ear the satisfaction of an absolute ruler. Really! What has the visual to do with music? Could anything more absurd be stated? The art of painting is for the eye, music, however, for the ear. Similarly, food is for the sense of taste and flowers for the sense of smell. Would it not be ridiculous to say the dinner was especially good because it smelled good, even though it was disagreeable to the taste and stomach? It is just as absurd if one should say along with pedants: this is outstanding music because it looks so fine (I mean pedantic) on paper, even though it does not please the ear, for which music is solely made … As we must now admit unanimously that our *Finis musices* is to stir the affections and to delight the ear, the true *Objectum musices*, it follows that we must establish all our musical rules according to the Ear.[4]

4 Heinichen, *General-Bass Treatise*, 278.

However, the old Scholastic tradition of making music the child of mathematical concepts instead of feelings was slow to die. There were, and have always been, those who continued to think of music in conceptual terms. It is part of the significance of Bach that his music reached both camps. Ludwig Hudemann, in a poem of 1732, speaks of Bach's music as being for 'thinking men,' while a poem by Telemann describes Bach's music with a right-hemisphere term, 'joy.'[5] Friedrich Marpurg, in dedicating his own *Treatise on the Fugue*, Part II, to the sons of Bach in 1754, praises Bach's music for its capacity to reach, so to speak, both hemispheres of the brain. In a nice phrase, he says in Bach's music 'the heart and the understanding are set into gentle motion together with the ear.'[6] We might also add that in his biographical work, *Ehrenpforte* (Hamburg, 1740), in reference to a person who had claimed both a goal of making 'music a scientific or scholarly pursuit' and an association with Bach, Johann Mattheson adds that Bach certainly did not teach this man 'the supposed mathematical basis of composition.' 'This,' Mattheson testifies, 'I can guarantee.'[7]

ON THE PHILOSOPHY OF AESTHETICS

The aesthetic topic so often discussed by earlier philosophers, the relationship of Art to Nature, is rarely discussed by German writers on music during the Baroque. We have seen above Heinichen's comment that 'all useful rules must be derived from Nature.' In another place he seems to suggest that even the distinctions among composers are basically attributed to Nature.

> One can as little describe the differences in musical talent as one can describe the differences between all ingenuities. Generally, however, one can say that the good talents of composers differ only in degree. For Nature gives to one an animated, clear, burning spirit, but to another a tempered, modest, or even affective nature. The latter is better suited to to the devout church style, the former, however, more to the theatrical.[8]

The great German composer, Georg Telemann (1681–1767), made a similar observation which, on his behalf, we should pass on.

> Just as not everyone is born a poet, so every poet cannot write texts adaptable to music, and especially sacred music. It would be desirable for experts to explore this question.[9]

---

5 Quoted in David and Mendel, *The Bach Reader*, 226ff.

6 Ibid., 255.

7 Ibid., 440.

8 Heinichen, *General-Bass Treatise*, 285.

9 Georg Philipp Telemann, preface to T.E. Schubart, *Fortsetzung des harmonischen Gottesdienstes* (1731), quoted in Morgenstern, *Composers on Music*, 39.

Twenty years later, Johann Birnbaum discussed this relationship from a different perspective, from Art's duty to perfect Nature.

> If art imitates Nature, then indisputably the natural element must everywhere shine through the works of art. Accordingly it is impossible that art should take away the natural element from those things in which it imitates Nature—including music. If art aids Nature, then its aim is only to preserve it, and to improve its condition; certainly not to destroy it. Many things are delivered to us by Nature in the most misshapen states, which, however, acquire the most beautiful appearance when they have been formed by art. Thus art lends Nature a beauty it lacks, and increases the beauty it possesses. Now, the greater the art is—that is, the more industriously and painstakingly it works at the improvement of Nature—the more brilliantly shines the beauty thus brought into being.[10]

Another general characteristic of high art often discussed with respect to aesthetics is universality. There is, in this regard, an aesthetic question much on the mind of every composer of tonal music, for he worries over the possibility of inadvertently writing something which had been used before. It does surprise us that Heinichen found this to be a common concern already in 1711.

> Respectable and wise composers, however, shun opportunities to listen to great music shortly before they are going to compose, fearing that as it usually happens something of it will remain in their memory and that they might include it in their own work, innocently thinking it was their own thought and bringing suspicion of injudicious censors upon them.[11]

ON THE AESTHETICS OF MUSIC

The contemplation of the Baroque German musician on the definition of music no doubt began with the subject we have discussed above, the relationship of contemporary ideas with the former definitions represented by Scholastic dogma. Heinichen was thinking of this when he wrote,

> One need not even think of *Musica didactica, poetica, modulatoria* and other *Capita suprema & subalterna* common to music to realize that music has boundaries as wide as all the other sciences, arts, and advanced studies. Music is just as *theoretica & practica* as theology and jurisprudence; music is as *thetic & polemica* as other advanced disciplines, this being particularly evident in

10 Johann Birnbaum, 'Impartial Comments on … *Der Critische Musicus*,' quoted in David and Mendel, *The Bach Reader*, 244ff.

11 Heinichen, *General-Bass Treatise*, 331. Immediately upon finishing his Fourth Symphony, Mahler was astonished to notice reminiscences from one of the Brahms's symphonies and from one of the Beethoven piano concertos. [Henry-Louis de la Grange, *Gustav Mahler* (Oxford: Oxford University Press, 1995), II, 276]

> our century as one tries hard to separate oneself both in music, theory and practical music from many principles and preconceived opinions of the past.[12]

Because of the social disruption of the Thirty Years' War, Art Music developed somewhat behind that of Italy and France during the seventeenth century. It is no surprise, therefore, that discussion of the nature of German music was carried out to some degree in the context of reflections on the style found in other countries.

We have seen, in an earlier volume, that it was a goal of young men in the Northern countries to travel to Italy to 'finish' their education by absorbing the culture there. Thus it should be no surprise to find Heinrich Schütz, in requesting permission for his second trip to Italy in 1628–1629, thinking of a similar trip to improve his spirit. Indeed, years later Schütz would refer to Italy as 'the true university of music.'[13]

> … as from the first I did not come upon this idea prompted by any frivolity, as a mere pleasure jaunt or desire to travel, but through the urge for an improvement in spirit.[14]

After making this trip, Schütz documents his discovery there of a new style of church music.

> When I arrived in Venice, I cast anchor here where as a youth I had passed the novitiate of my art under the great Gabrieli—Gabrieli, immortal gods, how great a man![15]
>
> ……
>
> Staying in Venice with old friends, I found the manner of musical composition [*modulandi rationem*] somewhat changed. They have partially abandoned the old church modes while seeking to charm modern ears with new titillations.[16]

Some years later, in 1647, Schütz provided an interesting reference to the absorption of Italian style in Germany.

> Until now I have been prevented from sending [the *Symphoniae Sacrae*] to press because of the miserable conditions prevailing in our dear fatherland which adversely affect all the arts, music included; and even more importantly, because the modern Italian style of composition and performance (with which, as the sagacious Signor Claudio Monteverdi remarks in the preface to his *Eighth Book of Madrigals*, music is said finally to have reached its perfection) has remained largely unknown in this country.

---

12 Heinichen, *General-Bass Treatise*, 310ff.

13 *Geistliche Chormusik* (1648).

14 Quoted in Moser, *Heinrich Schütz*, 126. Bach's son once wrote that his father 'did not have the most brilliant good fortune, because he did not do what it requires, namely, roam the world over.' [See David and Arthur, *The Bach Reader*, 279]

15 Heinrich Schütz, *Symphoniae sacrae*, I, Op. 2, 1629, quoted in Strunk, *Source Readings*, 433.

16 Schütz, Ibid., quoted in Moser, *Heinrich Schütz*, 128.

> Experience has proved that the modern Italian manner of composition and its proper tempo, with its many black notes, does not in most cases lend itself to use by Germans who have not been trained for it. Believing one had composed really good works in this style, one has often found them so violated and corrupted in performance that they offered a sensitive ear nothing but boredom and distaste, and called down unjustified opprobrium on the composer and on the German nation, the inference being that we are entirely unskilled in the noble art of music—and certain foreigners have more than once leveled such accusations at us …
>
> As for others, above all those of us Germans who do not know how properly to perform this modern music, with its black notes and steady, prolonged bowing on the violin, and who, albeit untrained, still wish to play this way I herewith kindly request them not to be ashamed to seek instruction from experts in this style and not to shirk home practice before they undertake a public performance of any of these pieces. Otherwise they and the author—though he be innocent—may receive unexpected ridicule rather than praise.[17]

Another interesting reference to the relationship of German and Italian styles was made by Johann Scheibe, in 1737.

> Indeed, we [Germans] have finally found in music too the true good taste, which Italy never showed us in its full beauty. Hasse and Graun, who are admired also by the Italians, demonstrate by their richly inventive, natural and moving works how fine it is to possess and practice good taste.[18]

At the end of the seventeenth century, after the influence of the court of Louis XIV had begun to make itself felt throughout Europe, one begins to find interesting observations on the French style. An early example of French influence can be seen in Georg Muffat's *Florilegia* (1695), a collection of pieces which he describes as 'conforming in the main to the French ballet style.'

> In Germany the French style is gradually coming to the fore and becoming the fashion. This same style, which formerly flourished in Paris under the most celebrated Jean Baptiste Lully, I have diligently sought to master, and, returning from France to Alsace, from whence I was driven by the late war, I was perhaps the first to bring this manner, not displeasing to many professional musicians, into Austria and Bohemia and afterwards to Salzburg and Passau. Inasmuch as the ballet compositions of the aforesaid Lully and other things after his manner entirely reject, for the flowing and natural movement, all other artifices—immoderate runs as well as frequent and ill-sounding leaps—they had at first the misfortune, in these countries, to displease many of our violinist, at that time more intent on the variety of unusual conceits and artificialities than on grace; for this reason, when occasionally produced by those ignorant of the French manner or envious of foreign art, they come off badly, robbed of their proper tempo and other ornaments.[19]

17 Heinrich Schütz, *Symphoniae Sacrae*, II (1647), quoted in Morgenstern, *Composers on Music*, 29.

18 Johann Scheibe, *Critischer musicus* (1737), in Palisca, *Baroque Music*, 281.

19 Quoted in Strunk, *Source Readings*, 443.

If, Muffat suggests, composers would only notice how popular this style was with the aristocrats they might become interested in studying it. He quotes a 'discerning prince' who observed that the old-fashioned composers learned more than was necessary for the purpose of 'charming the ear.'

Another interesting discussion on the contemporary assessment of German style is found in Heinichen in 1711.

> Experience teaches that ... paper music receives more credit in one nation than in another. One nation [Germany] is industrious in all endeavors; another laughs over useless school work and tends to believe skeptically that the 'Northerners' work like a team of draft horses. One nation [Germany] believes art is only that which is difficult to compose; another nation, however, seeks a lighter style and correctly states that it is difficult to compose light music ... One nation [Germany] seeks its greatest art in nothing but intricate musical 'tiff-taff' and elaborate artificialities of note writing. The other nation applies itself more to good taste, and in this way it takes away the former's universal applause; the paper artists [Germans], on the contrary, with all their witchcraft remain in obscurity and, in addition, are proclaimed barbarians, even though they could imitate the other nations blindfolded if they applied themselves more to good taste and brilliance of music than to fruitless artificialities. An eminent foreign composer once gave his frank opinion ... regarding the differences in music of two nations.
>
> Our nation, he said, ... is more inclined to *dolcezza* in music, so much so that it must take care not to fall into a kind of indolence. Most 'Northerners,' on the other hand, are almost too inclined to liveliness in music, so that they fall too easily into barbarisms. If they would take pains over adapting our *tendresse* and would mix it together with their usual *vivacité*, then a third style would result that could not fail to please the whole world.
>
> I will not repeat the comments I made at that time, but will say only that this discourse first brought to my mind the thought that a felicitous mélange of Italian and French taste would affect the ear most forcefully and must succeed over all other tastes of the world ... Nevertheless, the Germans have the reputation abroad that if they would apply themselves industriously they could usually surpass other nations in learning. From this principle I hope that some day our composers will try in general ... to surpass other nations in matters of musical taste as well as they have succeeded long ago in artful counterpoint and theoretical accuracies.[20]

After the beginning of the eighteenth century German self-confidence was rising and occasional comments which were distinctly anti-French in character began to appear. Friedrich Niedt, for example, observed in 1700,

> The final chord must be major regardless of what goes before, except that French composers do the opposite, but everything is not good merely because it comes from France or has a French name.[21]

20 Heinichen, *General-Bass Treatise*, 281ff.

21 Friedrich Erhard Niedt, *Musicalische Handleitung* (Hamburg, 1700), quoted in Donnington, *The Interpretation of Early Music*, 141.

Telemann, in a letter of ca. 1751 to Carl Graun, makes a comment which was intended as an unfavorable reference to the theories of Rameau.

> If there is nothing new to be found in melody then we must seek novelty in harmony.[22]

By the end of the Baroque, reflection on the nature of German music had clearly produced one conclusion: Germany was stood pre-eminent in keyboard music. Martin Fuhrmann wrote in 1729,

> When I was at the Easter Fair in Leipzig recently … I had the good fortune to hear the world-famous Mr. Bach. I thought the Italian Frescobaldi had polished off the art of keyboard playing all by himself, and Carissimi was a most valued and cherished organist. But if one were to put the two Italians with their art on one side of the scales and the German Bach on the other, the latter would far outweigh them, and they would be lifted straight up into the air.[23]

Similarly, Johann Scheibe, writing in his journal, *Der critischer Musicus*, in 1737, observed,

> In some types of clavier pieces there is a clear distinction between the German style and others. In foreigners we find that neither the structure, nor the ornamentation, nor the working out of these pieces, is so perfect as in the Germans. For they know how to exploit this instrument with the greatest strength and according to its true nature better than all the other nations. The two great men among the Germans, Mr. Bach and Mr. Handel, illustrate this most strikingly.[24]

Two years later, in an article on the Italian Concerto, Scheibe adds the comment that in Bach's clavier music 'we can certainly defy foreign nations.'[25]

Perhaps the most interesting observations on the development of German style are those in which we can see the coming of the *galant* style, if not Classicism itself. One prominent characteristic of the new style was the Italian predilection for the dominance of the upper melodic voice. Georg Muffat, who was more inclined to the French style, wrote, in the Foreword to his *Florilegium Secundum* (1698), pleading for a return to balance.

> I have sought diligently to soften, by means of the sweetness of agreeable consonances, whatever seemed unusual in the upper voice, namely the violin, and also to lend distinction, by means of the artful setting of the inner voices and the bass, to whatever seemed overly vulgar [meaning, common].[26]

---

22 Quoted in Morgenstern, *Composers on Music*, 41.

23 Martin Fuhrmann, *Satans-Capelle* (Köln, 1729), quoted in David and Mendel, *The Bach Reader*, 441. Bach himself was more modest. J. F. Köhler relates he once heard Bach suggest that all you have 'to do is hit the right notes at the right time, and the instrument plays itself.' [Ibid., 291]

24 Quoted in Ibid., 230.

25 Quoted in Ibid., 234.

26 Quoted in Strunk, *Source Readings*, 446.

And, again, in the Foreword to his collection of concerti, *Auserlesene Instrumental-Music* (1701), Muffat urges the music director to assign good players as well to the middle voices, for it is no insult to play these parts,

> contrary to the deep-rooted prejudice of certain haughty persons, who faint away on the spot if one does not assign them to the violin or some other prominent part.[27]

One of the clearest harbingers of the new galant style was the appreciation of *Goût*, or taste itself. The most famous Baroque discussion of this among musicians is found in Heinichen, who contends that taste can only be acquired through personal experience.

> If experience is necessary in any art or science, it is certainly necessary in music. In this *Scientia practica*, first of all, we must gain experience … either at home, provided opportunities are sufficient, or through traveling. But what is it that one believes one must seek in the experience? I will give a single word … *Goût*. Through diligence, talent, and experience, a composer must achieve above all else an exquisite sense of good taste in music … The definition of *Goût*, *Gusto* or *guter Geschmack* is unnecessary for the experienced musician; and it is as difficult to describe in its essentials as the true essence of the soul. One could say that good taste was in itself the soul of music, which so to speak it doubly enlivens and brings pleasure to the senses. The *Proprium 4ti modi* of a composer with good taste is contained solely in the skill with which he makes his music pleasing to and beloved by the general, educated public, or which in the same way pleases our ear by experienced artifices and moves the senses … In general, this can be brought about through a good well-cultivated, and natural invention or through the beautiful expression of words. In particular, through an ever dominating *cantabile*, through suitable and affecting accompaniments, through a change of harmonies recommended for the sake of the ears, and through other methods gained from experience and frequently looking poor on paper, which in our times we only label with the obscure name of 'rules of experience …' An exceptional sense of good taste is so to say the musical *Lapis philisophorum* and the principal key to musical mysteries through which human souls are unlocked and moved and by which the senses are won over … For even the natural gift or talent endowed with most invention resembles only crude gold and silver dross that must be purified first by the fire of experience before it can be shaped into a solid mass—I mean into a finely cultivated and steadfast sense of good taste.[28]

We would like to think that it was this view of the future which Bach had in mind in a note to the Leipzig town council in 1730,

> The present *status musices* is quite different to what it used to be formerly—the art being much advanced and taste marvelously changed, so that the old-fashioned kind of music no longer sounds well in our ears.[29]

27 Quoted in Ibid., 452. We say today, 'No mother raises her child to play *second* violin!'

28 Heinichen, *General-Bass Treatise*, 285ff.

29 Quoted in Donnington, *The Interpretation of Early Music*, 99.

But some people, as always, never quite notice what is going on all around them, the foremost example in this period being, of course, Johann Fux. We also have noticed, however, this curious statement of 1752 by Friedrich Marpurg.

> Thus the manly element which should prevail in music remains quite absent from it; for it may be believed without further testimony that the composer who has made himself particularly acquainted with fugues and counterpoints—however barbaric this last word may sound to the tender ears of our time—will let something of their flavor inform all his other works, however *galant* they are meant to be, and will set himself against the spreading rubbish of womanish song.[30]

On the Purposes of Music

In the Renaissance the most frequently given purpose for music was to 'soothe' the listener's feelings. During the Baroque, as we approach the modern concept of a concert, this purpose is transformed into something with a more Aristotelian ring to it, more like the description of a catharsis, 'to refresh the spirit.' Georg Muffat, in the Foreword to his *Auserlesene Instrumental-Music* (1701) explains that in his previous collections he has sought to draw 'liveliness and grace' from the 'Lullian well.' In the present collection he now presents 'certain profound and unusual affects of the Italian manner, various capricious and artful conceits, and alternations of many sorts, interspersed with special diligence between the [ripieno] and [concertino].' The purpose of this music, as he makes very clear, is to listen to, it is concert music. It is also important to notice the variety of situations which he equates with 'concert music,' considering how limited a definition we acknowledge today (concert hall, lights off, white tie, programs, etc.).

> These concerti, suited neither to the church (because of the ballet airs and airs of other sorts which they include) nor for dancing (because of other interwoven conceits, now slow and serious, now gay and nimble, and composed only for the express refreshment of the ear), may be performed most appropriately in connection with entertainments given by great princes and lords, for receptions of distinguished guests, and at state banquets, serenades, and assemblies of musical amateurs and virtuosi.[31]

In the title pages of Bach's *Clavier Ubung*, Part III, and the 'Goldberg Variations,' he gives the purpose to 'refresh the spirits.' Similarly, when he was looking at a position in Halle, he

30 Quoted in David and Mendel, *The Bach Reader*, 268.

31 Quoted in Strunk, *Source Readings*, 449.

was sent a contract which specified that the church music should have the result that 'the members of the Congregation shall be the more inspired and refreshed in worship.'[32]

The most important purpose of music is to communicate feelings, a purpose to which Johann Scheibe paid tribute in 1739.

> Music which does not penetrate the heart nor the soul
> Does indeed consist of tones yet only is compelling to the ears,
> Which nature and art have not given sound, grace, strength,
> Is quite dead, and lacks spirit and vitality.[33]

A more typical expression of this purpose during the Baroque is given by Georg Muffat, in his *Florilegia* (1695). He writes that he has given each suite the name of 'some state of the affections which I have experienced,' namely, Piety, The Joys of the Hopeful, Gratitude, Impatience, Solicitude, Flatteries, and Constancy.

To understand what Muffat means by this we must pause to consider the influence on Baroque composers of what Bukofzer names 'the principle of the doctrine of affections and figures.'[34] Nearly every writer on Baroque music mentions this 'doctrine,' but we believe it is incorrect to suggest this 'doctrine' was something composers thought about before or while composing. The 'doctrine' was really the creation of theorists, not composers, and the epitome of it lies in the difficulty we all experience in trying to talk about emotions, or to employ the left hemisphere of the brain to describe something it knows nothing about. And it is this central irony, using intellectual concepts to explain feeling, which makes this 'doctrine' impossible, then or now, as a practical technique of composition.

Baroque theorists, who had essentially the same experiences as we, although they knew nothing of modern brain research, inherited a frame of reference which included a scholastic tradition thousands of years old beginning with the ancient writer's endless theoretical contemplation about the emotions of the soul and continuing in the medieval Scholastic concentration on 'speculative music.' Thus, after composers began to re-establish the primary purpose of the expression of feelings in their music, by the late Baroque some theorists felt compelled to explain, in the context of this long history of philosophy, and emboldened by the spirit of the oncoming Enlightenment, what they were hearing and to attempt to conceptualize it.

---

32 Quoted in David and Mendel, *The Bach Reader*, 65. J. F. Reichardt reports an occasion when Bach needed to refresh his own spirits. He had entered a room where a harpsichordist was performing. Upon seeing Bach, the performer suddenly stopped, leaving a dissonant chord hanging in the air.

> Bach, who heard it, was so offended by this musical unpleasantness that he passed right by his host ... rushed to the harpsichord, resolved the dissonant chord, and made an appropriate cadence. Only then did he approach his host and make him his bow of greeting. [Ibid., 291]

33 Poem in honor of the publication of Johann Mattheson, *Der vollkommene Capellmeister* (1739), trans. Ernest Harriss (Ann Arbor: UMI Research Press, 1981), 74.

34 Bukofzer, *Music in the Baroque Era*, 5.

The theorists who began to write treatises on this subject were mostly German and mostly very minor figures. Paul Henry Lang finds 'Manuals containing musical "figures" which corresponded to certain affections' began to appear with Mauritius Vogt's *Conclave Thesauri Magnae Artis Musicae* (Prague, 1711).[35] Bukofzer provides a more extensive list,[36] but some of the treatises he cites, such as Praetorius, only discuss feelings in music but do not construct a 'doctrine,' and others, such as Heinichen, are more than skeptical of the idea to begin with. For the most part, these attempts to create a 'doctrine' are attempts to correlate musical composition, in particular melodies, with the academic terms used in the teaching of rhetoric and oratory. In the material by Mattheson, which we quote in a separate chapter, the reader will find a generous sampling of a typical effort to do this.

The musical examples which Mattheson provides, however, are really nothing more than what we would call 'text-painting' today, and this was certainly not a new idea to the seventeenth or eighteenth century. Neither, of course, was the expression of emotions a new idea. Indeed, Emilio de' Cavalieri had already written in 1600 that the purpose of his *Rappresentazione di Anima, et di Corpo* was to 'move the listener to different emotions, as pity, joy, tears, and laughter, and other similar emotions.' Since late Renaissance music clearly had both emotion and text-painting, do we really have much left to dignify with the name, 'doctrine?' Can we really imagine that the composers of the Baroque followed the instructions of the theorists? And in the theater, where this idea was supposed to be centered, one not only had extra-musical considerations, but as Heinichen observes the composer might compose emotions not intended by the poet at all.

> I would never suggest to anyone to fill up the theatrical style with too many serious inventions ... For pathetic, melancholic, and phlegmatic music (in so far as it is based on tenderness and good taste) is effective in the church and chamber styles; but it is not well suited to the theatrical style, and one uses serious pieces simply for judicious [variety]. And if their lordships, the poets, overload us with pathetic and sorrowful arias, we [the composers] must try to sweeten these either with mixed inventions or effective accompaniments; or in those arias containing a double affection, one turns the invention more gradually to the lively element rather than the serious one. Thus, for example, with the melancholy of love, one should rather express the pleasantness of love and not the blackness of melancholy ... In summary, the theatrical style for the most part requires something moving or adroit, though I should not call it simply merry. For merry music in itself can easily degenerate into barbarism and is unpleasant to sensitive ears.[37]

35 Paul Henry Lang, 'Musical Thought of the Baroque: The Doctrine of Temperaments and Affections,' in Hays, *Twentieth-Century Views of Music History*, 201.

36 Manfred Bukofzer, 'Allegory in Baroque Music,' *Journal of the Warburg and Courtauld Institutes* 3, no. 1/2 (1939–1940): 5, http://www.jstor.org/stable/750188 (Vaduz: Kraus Reprint, 1965), cites S. Calvisius, *Exercitationes duae*, 1600; J. Nucius, *Musices poeticae*, 1613; M. Praetorius, *Syntagma musicum III*, 1619; J. Crüger, *Synopsis musica*, 1624; Volupius Decorus, *Architectonice musices universalis*, 1631; Chr. Bernard, *Tractatus compositionis augmentatus*, ca. 1650; J. C. Printz, *Phrynidis Mytilinaei*, I, 1696; Chr. Caldenbach, *Dissertatio musica*, 1664; D. Speer, *Grundrichtiger ... musikaliches Kleeblatt*, 1697; J. Heinichen, *Anweisung zum Generalbass*, 1711; M. Vogt, *Conclave thesauris magnae artis musicae*, 1719; J. Mattheson, *Critica Musica*, 1725; J. Mattheson, *Der vollkommene Capellmeister*, 1739 and J. Scheibe, *Critischer Musicus*, 1743.

37 Heinichen, *General-Bass Treatise*, 282.

Heinichen also questions whether there can be any meaningful association between emotions and tonality. This relationship, one of the most fundamental questions in early philosophy, had long been assumed to be the key to how emotions affect the listener. The long history of this idea in literature left Heinichen somewhat ambivalent. He appears to want to believe that keys have certain emotional qualities, but he immediately casts doubt on the general idea by pointing out that the real emotional meaning is found in the actual music the composer writes.

> The aria begins in E♭; for this reason, however, the invention need not be sad, serious, or plaintive, for brilliant concerti as well as joyous arias in certain cases can be composed with the greatest effect in this beautiful key. Furthermore, the previous examples … clearly show that one can express the same words and affections in various and, according to the old theory, opposing keys. For that reason, what previous theorists have written and rewritten about the properties of the modes are nothing but trifles, as if one mode could be merry, another sad, a third pious, heroic, war-like, etc.

He continues by noting that even if this were true, it would be rendered void by the conflicting tuning systems and lack of agreement on a standardized pitch. Following this, he concludes,

> In my opinion, the ancient theorists erred in their research of modal characteristics,[38] in the same way as we continue to err today in judging a musical work. If we, for example, find for this or that key … one or more beautifully tender, plaintive, or serious arias, we prefer to attribute the fine impression of the aria to the key itself and not to the excellent ideas of the composer; and we immediately establish a *proprietas modi*, as if contrary words and affections could not be expressed in this key. This, however, is worse than wrong, as can be proved to the contrary by a thousand beautiful examples. In general, one can say that one key is more suitable than another for expressing affections. Thus in the practice today using well-tempered scales, the keys indicated with two and three sharps or flats are particularly beautiful and expressive in the theatrical style … Yet, to specify this or that key especially for the affection of love, sadness, joy, etc., is not good. Should someone object at this point and say that D, A, B♭ major are much more suited to raging music than the calmer scales of A minor, E minor, and similar ones, then this actually does not prove the *proprietas modorum* even if it were so, but it depends on the inclination of the composer. For we have heard famous composers write the saddest and tenderest music in D, A, and B♭ major, etc., whereas in A minor, E minor, C minor; and in similar scales we have heard the most powerful and brilliant music.[39]

All things considered, we think there is a danger in making more out of 'the doctrine of affections' than was ever recognized by the actual composers, that is, more meets the eye than ever met the ear of the Baroque listener. Certainly we recognize that it is the glory of the Baroque that the true purpose of music, expressing feeling, had conquered the old Scho-

38 Like many early writers he did not understand the Ancient Greek modes. Unlike later Church modes they were more of the order of styles of particular groups of people.

39 Ibid., 283. The idea has never completely died.

lastic understanding of music as a branch of mathematics. Therefore we may suppose people were talking more about emotions in music than ever before. But just because people were discussing emotions, it does not necessarily follow that there was a universally understood 'doctrine.' Therefore, we believe both the sixteenth-century composer and the Classical Period composer would be surprised to be excluded, if we say, as does Palisca,

> If we want to ascertain whether we have crossed the boundary into the Baroque or out of it, there is no better test than to ask whether the expression of the affections is the dominant goal in fashioning a piece of music.[40]

Bukofzer's discussion on 'Allegory in Baroque Music' is again primarily a discussion of text-painting. However, he clearly maintains a different purpose for the Baroque composer, almost as if his emotions were not as sincere as those of the composer of the Classical Period. We can only suppose he were thinking primarily of Baroque church music in arriving at such a conclusion. Further, his conception of the 'rigidity of Baroque music, especially from the rhythmic point of view,' an idea which surely no one today believes any longer, is a conclusion which can only be reached if one only looks at the Baroque music as it appears to the eye and overlooks the entire practice of improvisation which was so fundamental to it.

> The counterblast to Baroque music took precisely the form of the discovery how to express feelings *without the intervention of the intellect*. Music no longer *meant* this or that emotion; it *was* itself the immediate expression of that emotion. This transition from the notion 'it means' to that of 'it is' marks the transition from the Baroque style to its successor, the Classical-Romantic style ...
>
> Baroque music is not, like modern music, a language of feeling, which expresses its objects directly, but a sort of indirect iconology of sound. For this reason it lacks all psychology in the modern sense. The rigidity of Baroque music, especially from the rhythmic point of view, has long since been remarked upon. But this is not a weakness of such music; on the contrary, it is its very strength. The humanization of music by means of a dynamic emotional conception of its nature appears only during the first half of the eighteenth century.[41]

Surely no one today would so describe Baroque music. If 'Baroque music is not ... a language of feeling,' then what was Corelli doing in performance when he,

> suffered his passions to hurry him away so much ..., whose eyes will sometimes turn as red as fire; his countenance will be distorted, his eyeballs roll as in an agony, and he gives in so much to what he is doing that he doth not look like the same man.[42]

40 Claude Palisca, Op. cit., 5.

41 Bukofzer, 'Allegory in Baroque Music,' III, 20ff.

42 Strunk, 'François Raguenet, *Comparison between the French and Italian Music* (1702),' 419fn.

Bukofzer was closer to the truth in his later book when he concluded,

> Since [the doctrine of affections] did not 'express' but merely 'presented' or 'signified' the affections, musically identical figures lent themselves to numerous and often highly divergent meanings. It is therefore misleading to isolate certain figures and classify them in a system of absolute meanings as joy, steps, beatitude, and so forth.[43]

We believe the conclusion by Hans T. David and Arthur Mendel more accurately describes not only Bach, but all serious Baroque composers.

> Attempts have been made to describe [the doctrine of the affections] as a kind of formula technique: a set of symbolic patterns to which Bach would recur whenever the textual situation required. But to ascribe to Bach a predominantly intellectual routine of this sort is to overestimate the importance of certain elements apparent in his music. He was neither so poorly endowed with imagination that he had to establish for himself a whole reservoir of ready-made patterns, to draw on whenever inspiration failed, nor so theoretically minded that he would heed the pedantic attempts of his contemporaries to establish music as a branch of rhetoric.[44]

The most accurate testimonial of the view of the Baroque composer may be the one inadverently expressed in 1711 by Heinichen. He means to complain that no theorist has really written the definitive work on the 'doctrine of affections.' But he was describing musicians at large, including composers, when he admits that no one is interested in this topic. For this is how it has nearly always been: composers compose and the theorists come along later, and not before.

> What a bottomless ocean we still have before us merely in the expression of words and the affections in music. And how delighted is the ear, if we perceive in a refined church composition or other music how a skilled virtuoso has attempted here and there to move the feelings of an audience through his *galanterie* and other devices that express the text, and in this way to find successfully the true purpose of music. Nevertheless, no one wants to search deeper into this beautiful musical *Rhetorica* and to invent good rules. What could one not write about musical taste, invention, accompaniment, and their nature, differences, and effects? But no one wants to investigate the matters aiming at this lofty practice or to give even the slightest introduction to it.[45]

In the end, no matter what emotions the composer was feeling and attempting to notate, a great responsibility remains to the performer to see that these emotions are to be perceived by the listener. A student of Bach relates that the latter had this foremost in mind even in the performance of the most simple music.

43 Bukofzer, *Music in the Baroque Era*, 389.

44 David and Mendel, *The Bach Reader*, 34.

45 Heinichen, *General-Bass Treatise*, 326. In a footnote, Heinichen observes that some attempts at expressing emotions in music sound mannered and make people laugh. Thus, he says, 'a mighty chasm stretches between knowledge and ability.'

> As concerns the playing of chorales, I was instructed by my teacher Kapellmeister Bach, who is still living, not to play the songs merely offhand but according to the sense [*Affect*] of the words.[46]

Heinichen concurs that the notes are not sufficient for this purpose.

> It is impossible to find the tenderness of the soul of music with mere numeric changes of dead notes.[47]

The German writer, Christoph Bernhard (1627–1692), in a treatise on singing, expresses his concern that gesture correspond with feeling.

> The question may here be raised, whether a singer's face and bearing should reflect the affects found in the text. Thus let it be known that a singer should sing modestly, without special facial expressions; for nothing is more upsetting than certain singers who are better heard than seen, who arouse the expectations of a listener with a good voice and style of singing, but who ruin everything with ugly faces and gestures.[48]

On the other hand, Bernhard's description, in 1649, of the singer's range of emotion in the Florentine style is rather remarkable.

> In the recitative style, one should take care that the voice is raised in moments of anger, and to the contrary dropped in moments of grief. Pain makes it pause; impatience hastens it. Happiness enlivens it. Desire emboldens it. Love renders it alert. Bashfulness holds it back. Hope strengthens it. Despair diminishes it. Fear keeps it down. Danger is fled with screams. If, however, a person faces up to danger, then his voice must reflect his daring and bravery.[49]

Marpurg confirms a wide variety of emotions in performance and provides an interesting discussion of the integrity of the performer.

> All musical expression has an affect or emotion for its foundation. A philosopher when expounding or demonstrating will try to enlighten our understanding, to bring it lucidity and order. The orator, the poet, the musician attempt rather to inflame than to enlighten. The philosopher deals in combustible matter capable of glowing or yielding a temperate and moderate warmth. But in music there is only the distilled essence of this matter, the most refined part of it, which throws out thousands of the most beautiful flames, always with rapidity, sometimes with violence. The musician has therefore a thousand parts to play, a thousand characters to assume at the composer's bidding. To what extraordinary undertakings our passions carry us! He who has the good fortune at all to experience the inspiration which lends greatness to poets, orators, artists, will be aware how vehemently and diversely our soul responds when it is given over to the emotions.

46 Johann Ziegler (1746), quoted in David and Mendel, *The Bach Reader*, 237.

47 Heinichen, *General-Bass Treatise*, 330.

48 Quoted in Ellen Harris, 'Voices,' in *Performance Practice: Music after 1600* (New York: Norton, 1989), 100.

49 Quoted in Ibid., 110.

> Thus to interpret rightly every composition which is put in front of him a musician needs the utmost sensibility and the most felicitous powers of intuition.[50]

Finally, from Forkel we have the interesting insight that even the instrument was a consideration for Bach in this regard.

> Bach preferred the Clavichord to the Harpsichord, which, though susceptible of great variety of tone, seemed to him lacking in soul.[51]

The most dramatic concept of the expression of emotions through music is what is generally known as 'ethos,' the ability of music to change the character of the listener. Sixteenth-century nobles, especially in Italy, felt that after a dinner party, during which there was much debating and arguing, it was important to conclude the evening by singing in order to bring everyone into 'harmony.' We find it somewhat charming, therefore, that Johann Kuhnau makes a similar argument when discussing the virtues of the collegium musicum.

> The musicians in cities commonly hold a collegium musicum every week or two. That is indeed a laudable undertaking, in part because it provides them with the opportunity to refine further their excellent art, and in part, too, because they learn from the pleasing harmonies how to speak together concordantly, even though these same people mostly disagree with one another at other times.[52]

On Performance Practice

There are some interesting comments in seventeenth-century German literature which suggest that the dynamics which appear on paper as contrasting, were in fact blended together through crescendo and diminuendo. Benedict Lechler, writing ca. 1640, says such markings 'stand, not for a series of abrupt steps, but for gradual diminuendos or crescendos.' W. M. Mylius, in 1686, makes a crescendo and diminuendo where only piano is given.

> Yet with both piano and forte it is to be noted that one does not go so suddenly from piano to forte, but one should gradually strengthen the voice and again let it decrease so that at the beginning piano is heard, forte at the middle, and once again piano as one comes to the close.[53]

50 F. W. Marpurg, *Der critische Musicus an der Spree* (Berlin), September 2, 1749.

51 Quoted in Donnington, *The Interpretation of Early Music*, 576. Bach apparently also gave active consideration to the acoustics of the room as well as in the plan for seating his musicians. See David and Mendel, *The Bach Reader*, 276, 278.

52 Johann Kuhnau, *Der musicalische Quack-Salber* (Dresden, 1700), Chapter I. Kuhnau (1660–1722), like Bach, was the music director of St. Thomas in Leipzig. Although known today as a composer, he was educated in law and mathematics and was capable in Hebrew, Greek and Latin.

53 Both are quoted in Donnington, *The Interpretation of Early Music*, 484.

On the other hand, we have quite a different, and even more subjective, concept of dynamics by Georg Muffat, in the Foreword to his collection of concerti, *Auserlesene Instrumental-Music* (1701).

> At the direction *piano* or *p* all are ordinarily to play at once so softly and tenderly that one barely hears them, at the direction *forte* or *f* with so full a tone, from the first note so marked, that the listeners are left, as it were, astounded at such vehemence.[54]

'Astounded' seems a strong expectation of the listener, but Muffat mentions this again with respect to tempo.

> In directing the measure or beat, one should for the most part follow the Italians, who are accustomed to proceed much more slowly than we do at the directions *Adagio, Grave, Largo,* etc., so slowly sometime that one can scarcely wait for them, but, at the directions *Allegro, Vivace, Presto, Più presto*, and *Prestissimo* much more rapidly and in a more lively manner. For by exactly observing this opposition or rivalry of the slow and the fast, the loud and the soft, the fullness of the [ripieno] and the delicacy of the [concertino], the ear is ravished by a singular astonishment, as is the eye by the opposition of light and shade.

Later he implies this sense of tempo continues to the very end, reminding us that the cadential ritard was probably rare before the Classical Period.

> It is earnestly requested that the listeners be maintained in continuous attention from beginning to end, until, at a given moment, all end the concerto together, forcibly and, as it were, unexpectedly.[55]

On Improvisation

That the performer was expected to finish the composition through improvisation (called 'ornamentation' by modern theorists) or by the addition of ornaments (not the same thing as ornamentation!) can be documented throughout the Baroque. Early in the seventeenth century, for example, Heinrich Schütz, in the preface to his *Resurrection History* (1623), recommends that the long sustained chords in the organ part should be performed with 'decorative and appropriate runs or passages.'[56] Again, in his *Cantiones sacrae*, Op. 4, of 1625, he writes,

54 Quoted in Strunk, *Source Readings*, 451.

55 Quoted in Ibid., 452.

56 Moser, *Heinrich Schütz*, 367.

> You organists, however, who wish to satisfy more sensitive ears I request not to spare the pains to fill in all the voices. If in customary manner you accompany only according to the *basso continuo*, I would consider this wrong and unmusical [*vanum et inconcinnum*].[57]

By 'wrong and unmusical' Schütz really meant that the composition had been left in such a manner that the details must be added by the performer.[58] Georg Muffat also mentions this in 1696, in writing of performance in the French ballet style of Lully.

> One must use with discernment certain ornaments making the pieces much more beautiful and agreeable, lighting them up, as it were, with sparkling precious stones.[59]

And this is surely what Heinichen meant as well, when he wrote of an aria,

> In this aria there is no embellishing of notes [on paper], but in a complete performance [*elaboration*] it may be so embellished with good taste, brilliance, and accompaniment that it necessarily will encounter complete success in public.[60]

We also have testimonials to the public improvisation of a number of Baroque musicians. Bach, in particular, is frequently mentioned in this regard. Marpurg, writing in 1752, recalls,

> In the minds of all those who had the good fortune to hear him, there still hovers the memory of his astonishing facility in invention and improvisation.[61]

Contemporaries recalled many fascinating occasions, such as when a famous French organist suddenly left town rather than compete in public with Bach in improvisation.

> Marchand, who had hitherto defied all organists, had to acknowledge the undoubted superiority of his antagonist on this occasion. For when Bach made bold to invite him to engage in friendly competition with him on the organ, and for this purpose gave him a theme which he jotted down with pencil on a scrap of paper, to be made the subject of improvisations, asking Marchand for a theme in return, Marchand, so far from putting in his appearance at the scene of battle, thought it better to leave Dresden by special coach.[62]

---

57 Ibid., 402. See Ibid., 294 for references to other contemporaries who disliked thorough bass technique—one called it 'cabbage chopping.' Schütz discussses the 'basso continuo' at length in the preface to his *Geistliche Chormusik* (1648) where his principal concern is that this practice not substitute for the ability to understand and write out a full score, knowledge of counterpoint, etc.

58 An extraordinary example of music as Handel left it on paper, together with how he played it can be seen in Bukofzer, *Music in the Baroque Era*, 376.

59 Quoted in Strunk, *Source Readings*, 447ff.

60 Heinichen, *General-Bass Treatise*, 372.

61 Marpurg's preface to the 1752 edition of the *Art of the Fugue*, quoted in David and Mendel, *The Bach Reader*, 267.

62 Marpurg, *Legende einiger Musikheiligen* (Köln, 1786). See also David and Mendel, Ibid., 445, 453.

And of course another famous occasion was Bach's improvisation before Frederick the Great, which resulted in the composition we know as 'The Musical Offering.'[63]

Contemporary musicians seemed most impressed in hearing Bach's improvisation while realizing a thorough bass. His son, K. P. E. Bach, recalled,

> He accompanied trios on more than one occasion on the spur of the moment and, being in a good humor and knowing that the composer would not take it amiss, and on the basis of a sparsely figured continuo part just set before him, converted them into complete quartets, astounding the composer of the trios.[64]

A similar description of Bach's improvisation was recorded by Johann Daube.

> By his exceedingly adroit accompaniment he gave it life when it had none. He knew how to imitate it so cleverly, with either the right hand or the left, and how to introduce an unexpected counter-theme against it, so that the listener would have sworn that everything had been conscientiously written out. At the same time, the regular accompaniment was very little curtailed. In general his accompanying was always like a *concertante* part most conscientiously worked out and added as a companion to the upper voice so that at the appropriate time the upper voice would shine. This right was even given at times to the bass, without slighting the upper voice. Suffice it to say that anyone who missed hearing him missed a great deal.[65]

And while Bach was still alive, Lorenz Mizler wrote,

> Whoever wishes truly to observe what delicacy in thorough bass and very good accompanying mean need only take the trouble to hear our Kapellmeister Bach here, who accompanies every thorough bass to a solo so that one thinks it is a piece of concerted music and as if the melody he plays in the right hand were written beforehand. I can give a living testimony of this since I have heard it myself.[66]

Not all listeners were so appreciative of Bach's musicianship. On at least one occasion, his superiors in the church resolved to reprove him,

> for having hitherto made many curious *variationes* in the chorale, and mingled many strange tones in it, and for the fact that the Congregation has been confused by it.[67]

63 See Ibid., 176, 179, and 260.

64 Quoted in Ibid., 277.

65 Ibid., 256.

66 Ibid., 231.

67 Ibid., 52.

In an atmosphere where literally all performers improvised on the basis of the music before them, one must imagine that such distinguished composers as Bach would have become discouraged at hearing lesser musicians transforming their music. Bach, in particular, towards the end of his life began to write out 'all the notes.' This was the beginning of the end of the tradition of the player contributing to the text of the composition, although it would take until the middle of the nineteenth century for this kind of improvisation to finally die out.[68]

This new practice brought the complaint from players that the composer was doing *their* job, that the music had become so cluttered that one could no longer see the important notes of the melody, etc. In 1737, Johann Scheibe anonymously wrote a 'Letter from an able Musikant Abroad' which attacked the new practice.

> Every ornament, every little grace, and everything that one thinks of as belonging to the method of playing, he expresses completely in notes; and this not only takes away from his pieces the beauty of harmony but completely covers the melody throughout. All the voices must work with each other and be of equal difficulty, and none of them can be recognized as the principal voice. In short, he is in music what Mr. von Lohenstein was in poetry. Turgidity has led them both from the natural to the artificial, and from the lofty to the somber; and in both one admires the onerous labor and uncommon effort—which, however, are vainly employed, since they conflict with Nature.[69]

Since this was obviously directed at Bach, a lengthy series of publications began debating this point. The first to come to the defense of Bach was written by Johann Birnbaum the following year.

> The Honorable Court Composer is neither the first nor the only man to write thus. From among a mass of composers whom I could cite in this respect, I will mention only Grigny and Du Mage, who in their *Livres d'orgue* have used this very method. If the latter, I can find no reason why it should deserve the name of fault. On the contrary, I consider it, for reasons which cannot be disregarded, as a necessary measure of prudence on the part of the composer. To begin with, it is certain that what is called the 'manner' of singing or playing is almost everywhere valued and considered desirable. It is also indisputable that this manner can please the ear only if it is applied in the right places but must on the contrary uncommonly offend the ear and spoil the principal melody if the performer employs it at the wrong spot. Now experience teaches further that usually its application is left to the free whim of singers and instrumentalists. If all such men were sufficiently instructed in that which is truly beautiful in the manner; if they always knew how to employ it where it might serve as a true ornament and particular emphasis of the main melody; in that case it would be superfluous for the composer to write down in notes once more what they already knew. But only the fewest have a sufficient knowledge, and the rest, by an inappropriate application of the manner, spoil the principal melody and indeed often introduce such passages as might easily be attributed, by those who do not know the true state of affairs,

68 Thus the touching scene of Berlioz pleading with an oboist in Frankfurt to just play what he wrote. Even today we do not aspire to play exactly what is written.

69 Quoted in David and Mendel, *The Bach Reader*, 238.

to an error of the composer. Therefore every composer, including the Hon. Court Composer, is entitled to set the wanderers back on the right path by prescribing a correct method according to his intentions, and thus to watch over the preservation of his own honor.[70]

One contemporary, Johann Gesner, has left a description of Bach conducting in 1738. In this, which must have been a rehearsal, he appears to have been as florid as his counterpoint.

If you could see him … singing with one voice and playing his own parts, but watching over everything and bringing back to the rhythm and the beat, out of thirty or even forty musicians, the one with a nod, another by tapping with his foot, the third with a warning finger, giving the right note to one from the top of his voice, to another from the bottom, and to a third from the middle of it—all alone, in the midst of the greatest din made by all the participants, and, although he is executing the most difficult parts himself, noticing at once whenever and wherever a mistake occurs, holding everyone together, taking precautions everywhere, and repairing any unsteadiness, full of rhythm in every part of his body.[71]

Finally, there is a comment about the public which is worthy of quotation. In an earlier volume, we have seen that Gesualdo complained that a noble to whom he had given some madrigals kept them closely guarded for himself, preventing any opportunity for a wider public to get to know them. Samuel Scheidt (1587–1654) curiously makes the opposite point in a letter to Duke August of Brunswick.

Since I do not desire to have these symphonies appear in print, whereby they would become common, I have made bold to dedicate them, together with some spiritual madrigals, to Your Lordship for your ducal chapel.[72]

ART MUSIC

We have seen above the appreciation by some of Bach's improvisation with a thorough bass. One who held a different view was Heinichen, who reminds the keyboard accompanist that his job is 'to second the voice and not to stifle or disfigure it.' He finds there are accompanists who add so much improvisation in showing their 'clever vanity' that they hurt the performance.

We mention this here because of a subsequent comment which offers an enlightening view of the developing attitudes toward real concerts. He suggests that the art is more important than the individual.

70 Ibid., 236.

71 Ibid., 231. His son reported that Bach conducted an orchestra with a violin as he played. See Ibid., 277.

72 Letter to duke August of Brunswick, June 19, 1642, quoted in Norman and Shrifte, *Letters of Composers*, 16.

> Whoever plays in a concert must play for the honor and perfection of the performance and not for his own particular honor. It is no longer a concert when each plays only for himself.[73]

We should also mention that the extraordinary achievements of the civic wind band in Germany during the seventeenth century, which resulted in musical repertoire still performed everywhere today, declined severely in the early years of the eighteenth century. And it was of the decline of these guilds that Johann Scheibe wrote in 1739,

> You absurd guild which loves only laziness,
> Which denominates as masters those who are yet unskilled,
> Which in fact wants much written; yet never thinks,
> Which dispatches musical foolishness into the world day and night,
> Which so frightfully tortures and torments the sensitive ear,
> Which almost rejects music's cause out of tastelessness,
> Must throw down pen and paper, reflect,
> and examine yourself.[74]

EDUCATIONAL MUSIC

In the Foreword to Georg Muffat's *Florilegium Secundum* (1698) we find a rare early reference to music intended for an educational purpose. This collection he says,

> owes its origin more to Your Reverend Highness' zealous concern for the education of the youthful higher nobility resident at your court than to my desire to tickle the ear.[75]

The most perceptive comments regarding the need for improvement in music education are found in Heinichen.

> Work of reform in composition and music would be as useful as it would be necessary (even the critics would not deny this). And it seems to me that this important, but surmountable, and certainly useful effort would not be ill-spent if a well-schooled, unprejudiced composer would take composition in hand and separate the chaff from the grain by abolishing all musical quackery, metaphysical contemplations, barbaric nomenclatures, ridiculous classifications, antiquated, abolished rules, and similar fruitless nonsense, while choosing only the useful rules truly applicable to the real practice. By bringing these rules into a correct and accurate classification, a well-founded, orderly, and useful method could finally be chosen to determine how and in what manner similar excellent principles could be given to a naturally-talented student and how

73 Heinichen, *General-Bass Treatise*, 215.

74 Poem in honor of the publication of Johann Mattheson, *Der vollkommene Capellmeister* (1739), trans. Ernest Harriss (Ann Arbor: UMI Research Press, 1981), 73.

75 Quoted in Strunk, *Source Readings*, 445.

> to put them into practice. In this way, the innocent art of composition would be cleansed of all sophistry, prejudice, and especially of the blind faith with which many rules were held for good and true up to now, only because the ancient musical Christian church had held them for true.[76]

Heinichen also makes an interesting observation on the progress of modern education in general as it finally began to abandon the old Church-dominated, theory-oriented Scholastic university traditions.

> Formerly one studied only philosophy until one was twenty-four or twenty-five before advancing to higher studies. Today they leave the university at twenty with more knowledge. Formerly it took five years to finish the law course, and even then one did not know how in practice to dispute in order to regain a stolen egg from a farmer. Today three years is sufficient to complete the entire philosophical and law courses. What is the reason for such great changes in the times? Answer: The changing of old, pedantic methods, since today one usually studies all things more completely, more briefly, and with greater vigor, for which a good order or a good, applicable method is absolutely necessary.[77]

Finally, Heinichen also includes a comment on the role of the teacher.

> Many years ago I had the opportunity to recognize by my own experience that the greatest hindrance to the ambitious student in this knowledge lies purely in the confused leadership of the teacher.[78]

We get a view of quite a different kind of music teacher in Friedrich Erhardt Niedt (d. 1717), who published a satire, *Musikalische Handleitung*, in 1700, which portrays music practice in Germany during the late seventeenth century. That this is satire, and not fiction, and thus reflects experience known to him, may be seen in his story of a musician who was invited to consider a position in the town of 'Dantzfurt,' where an organist had just died. Upon his arrival there the musician found he was expected, as part of the contract, to marry 'my lady's chambermaid.' As fictional as this may seem, such circumstances actually occurred. In one notable instance, Johann Mattheson was invited to Lübeck, in 1703, as a candidate for a position succeeding Buxtehude but found that he was expected to marry Buxtehude's daughter!

We are particularly interested in Niedt's account of the experience of a private keyboard student, for the insights it may reflect on both pedagogy and discipline. His teacher began with simple popular songs, progressing to dance music such as '*sarabandes*, a *courante simple*, and a *ballo*.'[79] The next level of difficulty was the 'dreadful long *praeludia*, *toccate*, *ciaconne*, *fughe*, and more such zoological marvels.' These his teacher demanded he learn from memory, as a prerequisite to the final goal, the study of thorough bass.

76 Heinichen, *General-Bass Treatise*, 376.

77 Ibid., 377.

78 Ibid.

79 Quoted in Strunk, *Source Readings*, 459ff.

> I worked hard, and many a time, over those splendid pieces of writing, my master roughly boxed my ears, slapped my face, rapped me on the nose, pinched my ears, and pulled my hair; at other times I was treated to live coals, the strap, and more such delicacies. Willy-nilly, he was determined to beat music into my head. But, for all his good intentions, this would not do; the more he abused me, the more stupid I became; indeed, be it said in all modesty that, though I had to work for at least half a year over a single *toccata* or *praeludium* and *fuga*, when I came to play it—just when things were going splendidly and at the best—I stuck fast all of a sudden and could recall neither beginning nor end. At this, from my master's kindly fists there rained down on my ears some three score blows; meanwhile he consoled me with words like these: 'May you be this, that, and the other, you bloodhound! Even the sparrows on the roof will learn before you do!' In this manner I had spent seven years with my master before I could play five *praeludia* and the chorale, or German psalm, in two parts.

Finally, the student was ready to be taught the art of thorough bass.

> From the first I was in terror, thinking 'Now you will really begin to catch it!' I had noticed that whenever he and the cantor tried anything over together they often came to blows over the thorough bass; I could only conclude that my own head would still more often be the target. In instructing me, my master's procedure was as follows. He showed me neither rules nor figures—even to him the numerals standing above the bass were no better than towns in Bohemia; he simply played the bass through for me once or twice, saying: 'You must play it thus and so—that's the way I learned it.'[80] But if I was not getting on, you would have been entertained to see the admirable means my master found to teach me the art after his own fashion. The *sexta* was situated behind my right ear, the *quarta* behind my left, the *septima* on my cheeks, the *nona* in my hair, the false *quinta* on my nose, the *secunda* on my back, the *tertia minor* across my knuckles, the *tertia major* and *quinta* on my shins; the *decima* and *undecima* were special sorts of boxes on the ear. Thus, from the whereabouts of the blow or kick, I was supposed to know what to play; the best part of it was that continual kicking in the shins made my feet active on the pedals, the use of which I was also beginning to learn at this time ... Once he hit upon an extraordinary measure; since with no foundation none of his teaching could drive the thorough bass through my head, he actually decided to kick it into me. Seizing my hair, he pulled me down from the organ bench on which I was sitting before the keyboard, threw me to the ground, lifted me up by the hair so that, when I fell back, my head struck sharply against the floor, and then trampled all over me, stamping on me for some time.

At length, Niedt assures us, the student was thrown down a set of stairs.

We get a view of the expectations of the more conservative teacher in the list of demands which Bach was given as part of his contract when he was hired at St. Thomas church in Leipzig. Included in his oath, were the following.

80 The present writer once had the educational experience of hearing the most famous conducting teacher in Europe play non-stop through *Figaro* on the piano, as a lesson in how to conduct it. At the final chord, the teacher stood and exclaimed, 'Das ist *Figaro*,' and left the room.

> I shall set the boys a shining example of an honest, retiring manner of life, serve the school industriously, and instruct the boys conscientiously;
>
> Not take any boys into the school who have not already laid a foundation in music, or are not at least suited to being instructed therein;
>
> [I will] faithfully instruct the boys not only in vocal but also in instrumental music;
>
> Treat the boys in a friendly manner and with caution, but, in case they do not wish to obey, chastise them with moderation or report them to the proper place.[81]

Bach's son, K. P. E Bach, confirms that in his private teaching Bach would refuse to take a student in composition until he had seen evidence of their talent.[82] The son also provides an overview of Bach's pedagogy. Bach, we are told, omitted 'all the dry species of counterpoint that are given in Fux and others,' beginning instead with studies in four-part part-writing. After this came the study of adding individual parts to the Chorale, followed by thorough bass study and finally original counterpoint.

FUNCTIONAL MUSIC

Among the more progressive composers one finds rather outspoken criticism of the old Renaissance church polyphony. Heinichen finds the Church the appropriate locale for counterpoint and, although he admits it has a value for students and that he was an 'ardent champion of it' in his own youth, he nevertheless seems cool to its musical potential.[83] German church music, he says, 'tolerates neither too much fire, inspiration, nor gay ideas.' In his warning to composers in overusing counterpoint, he reveals a general hostility to the old polyphonic style in a series of specific criticisms. Most counterpoint, he finds, is based on the 'lifeless manipulation of notes but not on the actual sound,' thus 'the more one sinks into the excesses of such stereotyped artifices, the more one necessarily must depart from the Ear.' The excessive use of counterpoint, he says, 'is the shortest path to musical pedantry, ruining many fine talents that otherwise could have been developed into something worthy.' Furthermore, he finds writing counterpoint laborious, on the order of a farmer loading manure onto wheelbarrows! From such study, one can make a dull contrapuntist out of any dumb boy, but one cannot make a composer with good taste.

Another who criticized the polyphony style was Johann Mattheson, who, in quoting the text to Bach's Cantata Nr. 21, provides a witty demonstration of the nonsense of this style.

> I, I, I, I had much grief, I had much grief, in my heart, in my heart. I had much grief, etc., in my heart, etc., etc., I had much grief, etc., in my heart, etc., I had much grief, etc., in my heart etc., etc., etc., etc., etc. I had much grief, etc., in my heart, etc., etc....[84]

81 Quoted in David and Mendel, *The Bach Reader*, 91ff.

82 Ibid., 279.

83 Heinichen, *General-Bass Treatise*, 280ff.

84 Quoted in David and Mendel, *The Bach Reader*, 299.

During the seventeenth century there were some German composers who found it much more difficult to break with the past. The gifted composer, Samuel Scheidt, at one point confessed that he heard nothing which surpassed the old style.

> I am astonished at the foolish music written in these times. It is false and wrong and no longer does anyone pay attention to what our beloved old masters wrote about composition. It certainly must be a remarkably elevated art when a pile of consonances are thrown together any which way.
>
> I remain faithful to the pure old composition and pure rules. I have often walked out of the church since I could no longer listen to that mountain yodeling. I hope this worthless modern coinage will fall into disuse and that new coins will be forged according to the fine old stamp and standard.[85]

As a matter of fact, Scheidt, in his arrangements for his own funeral, requested his former student, Christoph Bernhard of Hamburg, to compose a funeral motet in the style of Palestrina.[86]

Scheidt's own principal concern, relative to church music, seems to have been in the realm of performance. In a letter describing the church music in Halle, in 1630, where he was director of music, he observes,

> unlike the Chapel's [choir] now, whose voices are as the lowing of bullocks, sheep, and calves, their gullets filled with plums besides, so that neither [words nor music] can be understood; yea, they sing so flat that one would rather stop one's ears and flee from the church.[87]

One practice which both progressive and conservative observers could join in opposing was the introduction of popular music into the church service. Martin Geier, in his funeral sermon for Schütz, warned,

> If you will forgive me, gentlemen of the music profession, there now prevails in the church an altogether new kind of song, but one that is prolix, abrupt, fragmentary, dancelike, and not at all reverential. It is better suited to the theater and the dance hall than to the church. In seeking Art, we are losing time-honored devotion to prayer and song.[88]

Another who complained of the influence of the theater was Christian Gerber, who wrote in 1732,

> Although a moderate kind of music may remain in the church, especially since the late Dr. Dannhauer considers it an ornament of divine service (although all theologians do not agree on this point), yet it is well known that excesses often occur, and one might well say with Moses:

85 Letter to Heinrich Baryphonus, January 26, 1651, quoted in Norman and Shrifte, *Letters of Composers*, 17.

86 Moser, *Heinrich Schütz*, 221.

87 Samuel Scheidt, letter to Rector Christian Gueinzius, April 2, 1630, quoted in Weiss, *Letters of Composers*, 40ff.

88 Moser, *Heinrich Schütz*, 702.

> 'Ye take too much upon you, ye sons of Levi.'[89] For it often sounds so secular and gay, that such music better suits a dance floor or an opera than a divine service. Least suitable of all is it, in the opinion of many pious souls, to the Passion, when the latter is sung.
>
> Fifty and more years ago it was the custom for the organ to remain silent in church on Palm Sunday, and on that day, because it was the beginning of Holy Week, there was no music. But gradually the Passion story, which had formerly been sung in simple plain chant, humbly and reverently, began to be sung with many kinds of instruments in the most elaborate fashion, occasionally mixing in a little setting of a Passion Chorale which the whole congregation joined in singing, and then the mass of instruments fell to again. When in a large town this Passion music was done for the first time, with twelve violins, many oboes, bassoons, and other instruments, many people were astonished and did not know what to make of it. In the pew of a noble family in church, many Ministers and Noble Ladies were present, who sang the first Passion Chorale out of their books with great devotion. But when this theatrical music began, all these people were thrown into the greatest bewilderment, looked at each other, and said: 'What will come of this?' An old widow of the nobility said: 'God save us, my children! It's just as if one were at an Opera Comedy.' But everyone was genuinely displeased by it and voiced just complaints against it. There are, it is true, some people who take pleasure in such idle things, especially if they are of sanguine temperament and inclined to sensual pleasure.[90]

In a letter to the Leipzig town council after his appointment, Bach promised to write music of such a nature,

> that it shall not last too long, and shall be of such a nature as not to make an operatic impression, but rather incite the listeners to devotion.[91]

89 Numbers 16:7.

90 Quoted in David and Mendel, *The Bach Reader*, 442, 229ff.

91 Johann Sebastian Bach, letter to the Leipzig town council, May 5, 1723, quoted in Weiss, *Letters of Composers*, 65.

10 JOHANN MATTHESON

JOHANN MATTHESON (1681–1764) was not only a very prolific writer on a wide variety of musical subjects, but an experienced singer, performer on organ and harpsichord and respected composer. Although educated in law, he became an opera singer while young and it was this experience, no doubt, which led him to understand that melody was the primary vehicle for the communication of emotion in music. His exhaustive defense of this idea makes him an important harbinger of the Enlightenment in music.

In Mainwaring's biography of Händel, Mattheson came across a reference to himself in which he is described as a good composer, but 'no great singer, for which reason he sang only occasionally.' In his translation of this book, Mattheson added the following note which seems to us to confirm how his philosophy developed from his activity as an artist:

> To say that he sang only occasionally is simply ridiculous, when the statement is made of a man who remained on the stage for fifteen years, who nearly always played the chief role and whose natural manner of singing, whose gestures and whose action—all of which are most essential in every opera—aroused in the audience feelings of fear and terror, pity and lament, joy and pleasure.[1]

ON THE PHYSIOLOGY OF AESTHETICS

In this volume, as well as in the two preceding volumes on the sixteenth century, we have characterized the fundamental basis for development of the new style we call Baroque music as a departure from mathematics-based music in favor of music based on feeling. In the writing of Mattheson in particular we can see a careful, lengthy and constant effort to explain why mathematics cannot be the basis for music.

In his *Neu-Eröffnete Orchestre* Mattheson attacks the old notion of mathematics-based theory in music by going directly to the elements upon which the older theorists had based their reasoning, in particular the nature of the intervals. In his discussion of whether the interval of the fourth should regarded as a consonance or dissonance, Mattheson concludes it is not a matter of mathematics, but rather a matter of the ear, that is how the fourth is used. The reader should particularly notice, as a hallmark of the Baroque's movement away

1 Quoted in Cannon, *Johann Mattheson, Spectator in Music*, 27.

from music based on concepts to music based on feeling, that Mattheson specifies here that music communicates with 'the inner soul.'

> Numbers in music do not govern but merely instruct. The Hearing is the only channel through which their force is communicated to the inner soul of the attentive listener … The true aim of music is not its appeal to the eye, nor yet altogether to the so-called 'Reason,' but only to the Hearing, which communicates pleasure, as it is experienced, to the Soul and the 'Reason.' Hence, if the testimony of the ear is followed, it will be discovered that in its relation to the surrounding sounds and harmony, the fourth will be either consonant or dissonant.[2]

Such views, which will seem obvious to most modern readers, were in their time nevertheless a direct attack on the old mathematics-based theories of music created by the Church, thus there resulted in letters and books attacking Mattheson for his views. Johann Buttstedt, an organist in Erfurt, attacked Mattheson in a book, *Ut, Mi, Sol, Re, Fa, La, Tota Musica et harmonia Aeterna … entgegen gesetzt Dem neu-eröffneten Orchestre …*, in which he contends that since German music is now practiced only by craftsmen [*Spielmanns-Wesen*] the current musicians are not even educated in the older rules.

> How many musicians will one find today who have real knowledge? Most of them do not even know how many styles and modes there are and what music is suitable for ecclesiastical or motet styles. The knowledge of such styles is almost entirely lost … Why? [Modern music] is hard to understand and not well paid for. And so, instead of correct knowledge mere *Galanterie* suffices, just as the finery of ladies once consisted of pearls and golden chains but now of mere ribbons and laces.[3]

To defend himself, Mattheson published a new book, *Das Beschützte Orchestre*, in which he appealed to a number of distinguished German musicians to join in the debate over mathematics versus feelings. One who responded was the most old-fashioned of all, Fux, author of the monument to the former style, *Gradus ad Parnassum*. He was particularly angered by an attack, in this latest book by Mattheson, on the medieval theorist, Guido d'Arezzo, to whom Fux believed all subsequent music was indebted.

> I am not at all a blind worshiper of superstitious antiquity; but until something better has been invented, I shall venerate in every way what through so many centuries the noblest masters have held to be good and proper.[4]

Some distinguished musicians, however, came to the defense of Mattheson. Handel wrote Mattheson at this time, taking a very practical approach to the debate.

---

2 Johann Mattheson, *Das Neu-Eröffnete Orchestre* (Hamburg, 1713), 126ff. Mattheson also writes at length in opposition to the old dogma that mathematics is the basis of music in his book, *Das Forschende Orchestre* of 1721.

3 Quoted in Cannon, *Johann Mattheson*, 135ff.

4 Ibid., 140.

> The question seems to me to reduce itself to this: whether one should prefer an easy & most perfect Method to another that is accompanied by great difficulties capable not only of disgusting pupils with Music, but also making them waste much precious time that could better be employed in plunging deeper into this art & in the cultivation of one's genius?[5]

Johann Heinichen, in language much stronger than Mattheson's, ridiculed the old-fashioned theorists as having wasted their entire life in pursuit of *rudera antiquitatis.*

> All will be sheer Greek to those steeped in prejudices when nowadays they hear that a moving music composed for the ears requires even more subtle and skillful rules—to say nothing of lengthy practice—than the heavily oppressive music composed for the eyes which the cantors of even the tiniest towns maltreat on innocent paper according to all the venerable rules of counterpoint ... And we Germans alone are such fools as to jog on in the old groove and, absurdly and ridiculously, to make the appearance of the composition on paper, rather than the hearing of it, the aim of music.[6]

Johann Kuhnau also was strong in his support of Mattheson.

> As regards the great controversy that the gentleman of Erfurt has brought upon you, I do not believe that, save for him, anyone will disapprove of your *Orchestre.* This is especially true of your point of view in matters of the solmisation and the old ecclesiastical modes; for you wrote your *Orchestre* for a *galant-homme* who, being no professional musician, has not the least interest in amusing himself with innumerable old freaks which are usually outmoded at best and worth—virtually nothing.[7]

In his *Der vollkommene Capellmeister* of 1739 Mattheson returns to this question.[8] Here he begins with the basic point that mathematics is an aid to music, as it is to most disciplines. However, 'they are wrong who believe or want to teach others that mathematics is the heart and soul of music' or that it is responsible for changes in emotion in the music. He begins his argument with the concept of proportions in general, which he finds in natural, moral, rhetorical and mathematical relationships. For the first three of these, natural, moral and rhetorical relationships, Mattheson maintains no precise mathematical measure is possible. One cannot, for example measure the distance from the earth to the sun precisely because the flames leaping out from the sun render no fixed edge. His comment regarding precision in language is quite perceptive. Everyone would agree, he supposes, that 'life' is a positive, happy word. But if one says 'life is denied,' the meaning is changed. Thus, 'the heart's emotion no longer has its basis in mere sounds and words.'

5 George Friedrich Handel, letter to Johann Mattheson, February 24, 1719, quoted in Weiss, *Letters of Composers*, 63.

6 Quoted in Cannon, *Johann Mattheson*, 141ff.

7 Quoted in Ibid., 142.

8 Johann Mattheson, *Der vollkommene Capellmeister* (1739), trans. Ernest Harriss (Ann Arbor: UMI Research Press, 1981), Foreword, VI.

Turning to music, he proposes two rhetorical questions:

1. If someone wants to be a sound musician, must he not attain this through mathematics?
2. Cannot one become an admirable composer and musician without thorough knowledge of the arts of measuring?

Now if someone says yes to the first question, and no to the second, then he contradicts ancient and modern experience, indeed, his own eyes, ears, hands, the combined senses of all mankind, and shuts the only door through which his intelligence gives him what he has. Whereas if he answers no to the first question and yes to the second, then mathematics cannot possibly be the heart and soul of music.

From this he concludes mathematics can measure, but not determine the essence of a thing. 'Everything that goes on in music is based on mathematical relationships of intervals just about as much as seamanship is based on anchors and cables.'

However one defines the mathematical relationships of sounds and their quantities, no real connection with the passions of the soul can ever be drawn from this alone.

Mathematics is only the 'science, theory and scholarship' of music. To introduce what exists beyond this he quotes Andreas Papius.

'The mere *cognition of the ratio* of a step, a half step, a comma, the consonances, etc., will bring the name virtuoso or artistic prince to no one, but rather the minute examination *according to the laws of nature* of the various works which are produced by great artists: from this we can understand the composer's *soul*, in regard to how and to what extent, in his particular work, one thing more than another masters the *human mind and emotions*, which is the *highest pinnacle of the discipline of music*.'

Again, his point here is that mathematics can measure the elements of music, but not how these elements are used. It is the latter, not the former, which concern feelings in music.

A perfect understanding of the human emotions, which certainly are not to be measured by the mathematical yardstick, is of much greater importance to melody and its composition than the understanding of tones … This is certain: it is not so much good *proportion*, but rather the apt *usage* of the intervals and keys, which establishes the beautiful, moving and natural quality in melody and harmony. Sounds, in themselves, are neither good nor bad; but they become good and bad according to the way in which they are used. No measuring or calculating art teaches this.

How then does one describe the role mathematics plays in music, together with its other elements? Mattheson offers the following metaphor:

The human mind is the paper. Mathematics is the pen. Sounds are the ink; but Nature must be the writer. Why have a silver trumpet if a competent trumpeter is not available?

Mattheson points out that sculptors know and can measure the proportions of the human body, but 'heart and soul … and beauty is not on this account to be found in such mathematical measuring; but only in that force which God put in Nature.' Similarly, in painting, when 'mathematics ceases entirely, true beauty really first begins.' And so with music,

> A composer can succeed quite well without special mathematical skills. Many who virtually climbed to the pinnacle of music can hardly name or interpret all parts of mathematics; not to mention anything more … However, the best mathematician, as such, if he were to want to compose something, could not possibly achieve this with mere logic.
>
> Let it be said once in fact for all: Good mathematical proportions cannot constitute everything: this is an old, stubborn misconception.

The point, he says, is this: 'music draws its water from the spring of Nature; and not from the puddles of arithmetic.' The composer expresses something understood from Nature. Only then can this be mathematically expressed, but not the other way around. When Mattheson speaks here of Nature, he is also thinking of God.

> Mathematics is a human skill; nature, however, is a divine force … Now the goal of music is to praise God in the highest, with word and deed, through singing and playing. All other arts besides theology and its daughter, music, are only mute priests. They do not move hearts and minds nearly so strongly, nor in so many ways …
>
> Music is *above*, not in *opposition* to mathematics.

In conclusion, Mattheson cannot resist taking a shot at those remaining exponents of the old mathematics-based polyphony.

> I have occupied myself with music, practical as well as theoretical, with great earnestness and ardor for over half a century already: I have also met many very learned *Mathematici* in this not insubstantial time who thought they made new musical wonders out of their old, logical writings; but they have, God knows! always failed miserably. On the other hand, I have quite certainly and very often experienced that not a single famous actor, musician, nor composer, not only in my time but as far as I can remember having read or heard about, has been able to construct even a simple melody which was of any value on the feeble foundations of mathematics or geometry … What will happen in the future is yet to be seen.

In another place, Mattheson makes this point again.

> The entire art of harmonic calculating and measuring, even if we also were to include algebra, cannot alone produce a single skilled Capellmeister; whereas our very best composers have scarcely ever taken a ruler in hand for the sake of their beautiful work.[9]

9 Ibid., I, vii, 11.

It is also with respect to the older polyphonic style that Mattheson contends it is wrong to say that melody derives from harmony, as was the case in that style. Rather, harmony derives from melody (as in the case of the Baroque).[10]

A question which had been debated throughout the early Christian era by philosophers was the relationship between Reason and the emotions. Under the influence of the church, these early philosophers assigned little value to the emotions in general. It is only with the Enlightenment that the emotions began to be understood as an important part of man. Today we understand Reason and the emotions to be separate but equal, represented by their respective hemispheres of the brain. Mattheson was one of a number of early writers who attempted to begin to balance the scales.

> Science differs from Art in this, that the former comprehends and comprises a matter from its principles through reasoning only; whereas the latter requires practical application, and as an inseparable component.[11]

In his discussion of the classifications of music, Mattheson reaches back to the familiar distinction made by the medieval universities: *speculative*, or *theoretical*, 'which deals only with inner consideration and deliberation,' and *practical* music, which is performance.[12] Contrary to the medieval tradition (and that of some universities today!), Mattheson makes a determined effort to connect the two.

> That type of contemplation or theory is however to be preferred to all others which does not delve so deeply into shallow, mental considerations that action is forgotten; but turns its main aim toward actual practice and usage ... Whoever wants to make good use of both aspects must never separate them, but keep them fast together, like body and soul.

He observes that while it is an intelligent thing to ponder, contemplate and reflect on a piece of music before performing it, it sometimes works the other way around. That is, the study seems to be a 'corroboration of that which one finds to be true in practice.'

ON THE PSYCHOLOGY OF AESTHETICS

One of the most interesting, and extensive, discussions by Mattheson is found under the chapter title, 'On the Art of Gesticulation,' which is a study of emotions as expressed by gesture.[13] The proper term he gives for this art is *Hypocritica*, which Mattheson says Cas-

10 Ibid., Foreword, VII.

11 Ibid., I, i, 5.

12 Ibid., I, ii, 24ff.

13 Ibid., I, vi.

siodorus defined as 'silent music.' Quintillian defined it as 'the science of hand gesticulation,' but used the term *chironomy*.

But the word Hypocritica, for Mattheson, means more than chironomy, for *Hypo* (under) and *Crisis* (criticism) suggests the submission of one's thoughts for judgment. This should be thought of in a positive sense, as a form of stimulation, and not in the ill-meant 'hypocrisy.' The origin, and source of power, for gesture is found in its universality. First, Mattheson points out that language itself only developed as a shadow of action.[14] Second, he touches on a very important point.

> Words do not move a person who does not understand the language; discriminating words are good only for discriminating minds; but everyone understands the well-used facial expression, even young children with whom neither words nor beatings have as much effect as a glance.[15]

This observation is more important than Mattheson realized, with respect to universality, for modern research has shown that both facial expressions and the basic emotions are universal and the latter are formed before birth and are thus not learned, but genetic.

Mattheson classifies this subject under *oratorical*, which directs the movement of the body; the *histrionic*, which belongs to plays and requires much stronger gesturing than the first; and the *saltatorial*, which deals with all kinds of steps and leaps.

The oratorical is closely related to music, for, he says, music is 'an oratory in tones' and the ancient orators 'gleaned their best rules from music.' It is here, of course, that Mattheson becomes most critical. Regarding the singers in church he writes,

> It would be desirable that if no proper gestures take place out of bad habit, at least nothing of a quite inappropriate, indecent, or cold and indifferent mien would occur: of which unfortunately! we are so little lacking that often the most serious and sacred pieces are sung and played in such a shameless manner, chattering, smirking, trifling, so that devout listeners are very annoyed.
>
> I have attended many, many a Passion and Requiem which to my great chagrin evoked audible joking and laughter.[16]

Secular concert music is criticized for similar reasons.

> If we go from the church to the concert room, one likewise encounters quite marvelous and diverse unseemly poses at Concerts which sometimes do not have anything in common with what is going on … [Most players] seem to me like people who care only about filling their stomach and not about elegant taste.
>
> Can the attentive listener be moved to pleasure if he is constantly disturbed by the noise of someone beating time, be it with his feet or hands? If he sees a dozen violinists who contort their bodies as if they are ill? If the clavier player writhes his jaw, wrinkles his brow, and contorts

14 Ibid., I, vi, 5.

15 Ibid., I, vi, 6.

16 Ibid., I, vi, 11ff.

> his face to such an extent that it could frighten children? If many of the wind instrumentalists contort or inflate their facial features so that they can bring them back to their proper shape and color in half an hour only with difficulty?[17]

While on the subject of vocal music, Mattheson also considers national differences.

> If we turn from playing to singing, oh! that is when the misery really begins. Look at the fervor with which the French men and women singers present their pieces, and how they almost always seem really to feel what they are singing. Hence the reason that they strongly stir the emotions of the listeners, particularly their countrymen, and replace through gesticulation and mannerisms what they lack in thorough instruction, in strength, or in vocal ability.
>
> The Italians carry this even further than the French; indeed, sometimes they even go a little too far: As in almost all their undertakings they frequently overstep the limits and love the extremes. Meanwhile they frequently have tears in their eyes when they perform something that is melancholy; and on the other hand, their heart is overjoyed when there is something enjoyable: for they are very emotional by nature …
>
> Only the cool Germans, although they have revealed to the Italians their great musical abilities through the three great H's, namely Händel, Heinichen and Hasse, on the one hand place their greatest merit in the fact that they look just as stiff and unemotional with the sad as well as the cheerful affections with which their music deals … they sing very decently and rigidly, as if they had no interest in the content, and are not in the least concerned with the consideration of the proper expression or meaning of the words … as is demonstrated daily by teachers and students. On the other hand, it is quite a favor if they do not gossip with, trifle with or ridicule their neighbors during rests; even if the things of which they sing would be worthy of the highest attention.[18]

The true goal for both church and concert performance, Mattheson summarizes, is 'that gesture, words and music form a three-part braid, and should perfectly harmonize with each other toward the goal that the feeling of the listener be stirred.'

Turning to the theater, here, he says, is 'the real college for all sorts of gesticulations.'[19] *Hypocritica*, communication through gesture, is what an actor does. It is in pretending what he is not, notes Mattheson, that we get the origin of 'hypocrite.' Here also one finds the dance, in which *Hypocritica* 'is as indispensable as the feet themselves.' So closely related are the dancer's gestures and the music, that he finds most dancing masters prefer to write their own melodies. If the composer is to compose the dance music, then he must understand dance and in this regard Mattheson points to Lully who 'personally instructed all his actors, actresses, and male and female dancers in this art of gesticulation.'[20]

---

17 Ibid., I, vi, 15ff.

18 Ibid., I, vi, 18ff.

19 Ibid., I, vi, 23ff.

20 Ibid., I, vi, 26.

In conclusion, Mattheson points to the importance of gesture in all the arts of ancient Greece and Rome, including mime and pantomime which he says often moved the spectators to tears. The system of notation of gesture, of which he regrets precise knowledge is now lost, was called *Orchesin* in Greek and *Saltationem* in Latin. As a summary of the importance of these relationships in the ancient world, he quotes a contemporary, Charles Rollin, *Histoire ancienne* (Paris, 1730–1738).

> The art of gesticulation also belongs to music, it illustrates and teaches the steps and postures of dance as well as of the common walk, together with the postures which one uses in a public oration. In short, music comprehends all the art of composing and writing public utterances that have nothing to do with singing, through which annotations the sound of the voice is speech as well as the tempo and movement of the gestures would be ordered: which was a very useful art to the ancients but is completely unknown to us.[21]

ON THE AESTHETICS OF MUSIC

ON MUSIC IN SOCIETY

Mattheson begins his first important book, *Das Neu-Eröffnete Orchestre*, with a startling chapter entitled, 'The Fall of Music and its Cause.' Thus, his view in 1713 was that 'through misuse and ignorance the noble art of music, contrary to its very purpose, causes, alas!, more ill-humor than pleasure among many.'[22] The first reason Mattheson gives for this decline must be seen in context with his belief expressed in later writings, that the true essence of music was something very close to Nature. But, if we may paraphrase him in modern terms, left-brained man, the product of traditional education (then as now), is compelled to think that the Truth of a thing can be evident only if it can be expressed in rational thought. The experience of music is associated with the non-verbal right hemisphere of the brain, even though the academic world prefers to turn music into a rational subject because it is easier to talk about. The student, and unfortunately especially the layman, is therefore led to believe that he knows nothing of music unless he knows the conceptual form of it. Mattheson expressed it in this way:

> For they are persuaded that this beautiful and perfect creation, which a beneficent God has given us men for our pleasure, and likewise as a model of the eternal, harmonious Splendor, depends solely upon deep learning and laborious knowledge. To prove this, they dispense their

21 Ibid., I, vi, 35. Mattheson concludes this chapter with an account of the Imperial composer in Vienna in 1730, Francesco Conti, who, having 'used his art of gesticulation in a most wicked manner,' was placed on bread and water, beaten by a priest and forced to stand before the doors of St. Stefan Cathedral in a long hairy coat holding a black candle for an hour!

22 Mattheson, *Das Neu-Eröffnete Orchestre*, 1. We cite the original page numbers, but the English translation is by Cannon.

> philosophical rules and scholarly vagaries, not only with great authority, but likewise with such obscurity that one has a rightful aversion for the stuff, and would rather remain in permanent ignorance than to go through such *horrenda*.[23]

But Mattheson, having been a performer, knew that rational concepts cannot well describe the experience of music. Thus he advises the pursuit of performance, after the necessary foundation, as a means of finding a 'healthy idea of music, purified of all unnecessary school-dust.'

Mattheson himself could not entirely escape the Germanic need to conceptualize music, as can be seen in his attempt to explain melody through the rules of rhetoric. And so another reason he gives for the decline of music, not quite the reverse of the first one, was that there are too many composers who just write lots of notes without knowing what they are doing. His third cause for the decline of music is also educationally oriented: the ancient guild system, through which music was learned as a trade rather than as an art.

Two additional negative circumstances, Mattheson finds, the artist must simply accept as being the way things are. These are the ignorance and poor taste of the general public and the fact that good musicians are not well paid.

In the Foreword to his *Der vollkommene Capellmeister*,[24] Mattheson continues his somewhat pessimistic view of the relationship of music and society. He finds many noble and educated persons who know nothing about music, either because they lack the time to study it or fail to understand the 'dignity and great benefit' which derives from music. On the other hand, most of those who practice music are rarely scholarly. They merely take pleasure from music, turning it into,

> a menial trade, an item to market, a means to obtain food, indeed even into a society of flagellants, and nothing more.

At the same time, he finds some who merely collect beautiful musical instruments (and are called 'true connoisseurs') and others who think music exists merely to please and to pass the time. All of the above, he says, are on the wrong path.

In a chapter called, 'On the Use of Music in the General Public,'[25] Mattheson focuses primarily on the need for civic and church officials to be musically educated in order to oversee the use of music under their supervision. His most extensive complaint regards a custom ushered into Germany with the Reformation under which no music could be performed for an entire year as part of the observation of the required period of mourning following the death of a noble.[26]

---

23 Ibid., 2ff.

24 Mattheson, *Der vollkommene Capellmeister*, Foreword, II.

25 Ibid., I, v.

26 Ibid., I, v, 30.

In his *Das Neu-Eröffnete Orchestre*, Mattheson makes a few interesting observations on current national styles.[27] He finds in the compositions of the Italians the most beauty, due in part to 'their polished and *insinuante* artistic ideas.' There is no question, he concludes, that all nations who desire to be distinguished in music 'have borrowed nearly everything from the Italians, and have imitated them completely in all things.'

The fame of the French lies not so much in their composition as in their execution, especially in dance music where they are the masters. The English style he characterizes as a 'flat-footed imitation of the Italian style.' And as for the music of his own country,

> Among the educated Germans the esteem for music has never been really small or thoroughly prosperous either. In fact, this noble art … has come to be treated somewhat sleepily and indifferently; hence the great revolution in musical affairs has not come to my countrymen as it has to those in other lands … Our German virtuosi, who are—to speak dispassionately—altogether worthy to bear such a title with honor, are much more deserving of esteem than whole bands of foreigners … But a contemptible custom affecting these matters has come to pass; we prefer anything that is foreign, not necessarily because of its beauty and value, but merely because it is foreign to our own people, and things which are not bad or simple in themselves suffer the odium of being merely native.

On the Origin of Music

Mattheson, who was fundamentally a religious man, concludes, after considering theories advanced earlier, that music had its origin with the angels, before the creation of the earth.[28] While vocal music must be older than instrumental music with man, he finds no reason to doubt that the angels played instruments. While man might have once heard such music in Paradise, after the Fall and the expulsion from the Garden of Eden, this knowledge was lost.

27 Mattheson, *Das Neu-Eröffnete Orchestre*, 200ff.

28 Mattheson, *Der vollkommene Capellmeister*, Foreword III. He apparently finds his evidence for this in Job 38:7,

> when the morning stars sang together,
> and all the sons of God shouted for joy.

In his book, *Behauptung der Himmlischen Musik* … (1747), Mattheson elaborates on his belief in the existence of music in Heaven and the origin of music in angels worshiping God.

On the Definition of Music

Mattheson, as a composer himself, begins by observing that it is not sufficient to define music as simply playing or singing well (which was a basic definition of music in the latter Middle Ages) for 'the noblest part of music [is] composing.'[29] Indeed, he points out that in Italy a singer is called *Musico*, an instrumentalist, *Suonatore*, but the composer, 'who often has the least to say about his work,' is called *Maestro*! The correct, basic definition of music, therefore, is:

> Music is a science and an art of placing proper and pleasing sounds prudently, uniting them correctly with one another, and presenting them sweetly, to promote God's honor and all virtue through their euphony.[30]

He follows this by observing that 'nothing is accomplished by science alone; art is required as well.' By this he means you cannot speak of music without speaking of performance.

Next Mattheson turns to the classifications of music and begins with a review of the medieval classifications of 'universal music' (music of the spheres, etc.), 'human music' (having to do with the soul, etc.) and 'actual music.' Since the first two classifications cannot be actually heard, he explains he will discuss only 'actual music.'[31] The goal of actual music, he says, is that

> which would through the instrument of the ears please the sense of hearing which dwells in the soul, and would thoroughly move or stir the heart or soul.[32]

Regarding such performance, Mattheson gives the highest aesthetic value to singing.[33] Although he observes that singing is almost always done with instruments ('singing without instruments has mostly been done away with'), such music is still called *vocal* music. Indeed, he says, even if the instruments play as skillfully and charmingly as possible, as soon as the voices enter they get all the attention.

After Baroque composers generally won the victory of establishing for music the role of expressing emotions, replacing the old mathematics based concepts, a new question became the subject of debate: are the emotions expressed by melody or by harmony? While Mattheson believed that it was melody which expressed emotions, others, in particular Rameau, argued for harmony. Johann Scheibe wrote a letter praising Mattheson for understanding that melody was based in Nature, while harmony was merely the product of craft—of which he points to J. S. Bach as a tiresome example.[34]

29 Ibid., I, ii, 11ff.

30 Ibid., I, ii, 15.

31 Ibid., I, ii, 21ff.

32 Ibid., I, ii, 24.

33 Ibid., I, ii, 38ff.

34 Cannon, *Johann Mattheson*, 89.

For Mattheson, his entire understanding of the definition of music was centered on his conviction that melody was the primary element in music which communicates feeling.[35] This was, of course, a philosophy which would become even more fundamental in the following Classical Period. The growing emphasis on melody had its roots both in the abandonment of the old polyphonic style and in the new emphasis on feelings, as confirmed in the popularity and influence of opera.

Mattheson begins his lengthy discussion of the art of writing good melodies with a discussion of the *loci topici*, which represent a conceptual attempt to organize an explanation of music after the model of rhetoric. These he intends as tools for the composer in the invention of melody, as for example *causa efficiens* refers to the way a story might suggest the design or nature of a prospective melody. Another is *Materia-circa quam*, which refers to the actual thoughts a composer has while writing, and here Mattheson highly recommends thinking of a beautiful female.[36] One of the most important of these is *locus descriptionis*, for it is here that the emotions might inspire the writing of a melody. Mattheson observes that one must not think that words are the only source of the communication of emotions in music, but even,

> in purely instrumental music, always and with every melody, the purpose must be to present the governing affection so that the instruments, by means of sound, present it almost verbally and perceptibly.[37]

Other *loci* take into consideration the type of listener who will hear the melody and the acoustics of the hall in which the melody will be heard [*locus effectorum*]. When you borrow a melody from someone [*locus exemplorum*] you should develop it or do something nice with it, or as Mattheson puts it, pay back what you have borrowed with interest.

The above represent points of inspiration or starting points. A discussion of actually writing the melody, for which he uses the Greek verb *Melopöie*, together with the characteristics of a good melody come next.[38] In his introduction to these characteristics, Mattheson stresses his most basic beliefs about melody: that melody communicates the emotions; that Art is the servant of Nature (too much art obscures the beauty of Nature); and that harmony must be taken from melody and not the other way around as in earlier polyphony.

With this foundation, Mattheson now discusses at some length the four basic qualities which a good melody must have.[39] The first quality is that it be *facile*, a concept which Mat-

35 Mattheson, *Der vollkommene Capellmeister*, II, iv. Recent clinical research confirms his deduction.

36 Ibid., II, iv, 62.

37 Ibid., II, iv, 45. In another place [Ibid., II, v, 40], without explanation, he recounts hearing a French singer sing an unaccompanied song on stage which had such charm that 'it enraptured the listeners,' but when this same actor later played this melody on an alto flute the result was 'truth so plaintive and touching that it caused real sorrow among the listeners.'

38 Ibid., II, vff.

39 Ibid., II, v, 48ff.

theson associated with its ability to communicate, for he stipulates, 'we cannot have pleasure in a thing in which we do not participate.' His seven characteristics of facility are,

> 1. There must be something in all melodies with which almost everyone is familiar.

This is something which, according to Mattheson, the ear demands. We might add that modern clinical research in brain function appears to confirm this.

> 2. Everything of a forced, farfetched, and difficult nature must be avoided.

What he means by this, he says, can be seen in the works of 'mannered composers' easier than being described in words. Errors of this nature tend to result from lack of intelligence or ability in invention, whereby 'loss of natural fertility is replaced with wondrous curiosities.' In this regard, Mattheson quotes a fine composer who observed that only with the greatest diligence and practice could he achieve what those with only half his ability could.

> 3. One must follow nature for the most part, practice to some degree.

Mattheson's thought here is rather interesting. 'Practice,' here, includes tradition and academic concepts with its artificial constraints. Therefore the one least experienced in the 'science' of composition will be the one most likely to compose something natural. The experienced composer must act as a 'dilettante' if he hopes to capture the natural quality of great art. 'Nature never lacks beauty, naked beauty, only sometimes it buries it under a discreet disguise or a theatrical mask. Our gem cutters can polish the diamond; but they cannot give it any other luster or purity than that which nature has already given it.' Thus, it follows,

> 4. One should avoid great artifice, or hide it well.

Artifice, observes Mattheson, should never be confused with great art. If the composer must embellish his melody, he should imitate the fencer with his feints.

> 5. In this the French are more to be imitated than the Italians.

This, he says, because the French taste requires a cheerful, lively spirit, which is a friend of decorous pleasantry, and an enemy of all of that which reeks of trouble and toil. Also, Mattheson quotes a French treatise which suggests that the French considered their art closer to Nature than that of the Italians.

> If we find Italian music to be a rival, then we must not forthwith banish it to misery; but also must not quote it foolishly, but avoid all of the most superficial and enrich ourselves with its beauty. For although we French occasionally adopt Italian teachings on the high art, the Italians on the

> other hand, as regards grace and charm, are also frequently inclined to consult the harmony of our land in order to be so much closer to charming Nature: which is always simple, always sincere, and finds no beauty where constraint reigns, no tenderness where artifice plays the master.[40]

> 6. Melody must have certain limits which everyone can attain.

Mattheson advises that to encourage performance opportunities, the range of the melody should not exceed an octave.

> 7. Brevity is preferred to prolixity.

Here Mattheson is thinking primarily of retention by the listener.

The second basic quality which a good melody must have is *clarity*, for which Mattheson gives ten characteristics.[41]

> 1. The *caesuras* and divisions should be observed precisely: not just in vocal but also in instrumental pieces.

Mattheson observes that he is amazed that everyone thinks such phrasing points are not needed in instrumental music. But without them, he says, there can be no clarity.

> 2. One must always aim at one specific passion.

In general, he says every melody should express one primary emotion. Without this the listener can make nothing of it but 'idle singing and playing.' Here Mattheson suddenly turns to education and expresses his amazement that music composed for educational purposes emphasizes various theories but is devoid of emotion.[42] And while using this emotionless music, what do the teachers do?

> Do they not become angry, do they not perspire, do they not rejoice; do they not cry; do they not clap their hands; do they not threaten? Who wants to say that this would pertain more to mere, cold instructions, than to the vivid affections? … If one wants to enhance strong ideas and theories and wants to make a worthy contribution to them, then such cannot take place halfheartedly.

In short, he says, 'everything which happens without praiseworthy affections, is nothing, does nothing, signifies nothing: be it where, how and when it may.' The most simple child's game is never without passion, not only incidentally, but by preference: no infant can be said to be free of it.

---

40 Ibid., II, v, 63, quoting Jean Baptiste Gresset, *Discours sur l'harmonie* (Paris, 1737).

41 Ibid., II, v, 50 and 72ff.

42 Ibid., II, v, 79ff.

3. A meter must not be altered without reason, without need, nor without intermission.

Mattheson criticizes the French recitative for constant changes in meter, which results in seeming to have none at all. He says meter must be uniform, for it is 'the soul of melody.'

4. The number of beats should be proportionate.

He prefers an even number of pulses in even the slowest Adagio and states that fast movements should never have an odd number of beats in the bar.

5. No cadence should appear contrary to the usual division of the beat.
6. The accent of the words should be closely observed.

Here Mattheson's concern was that the melody be composed in such a way that the melodic accent falls on the most important word of the sung sentence.

7. One must very carefully avoid embellishment.

'Daily experience,' says Mattheson, 'shows us what kind of terrible patchworks are pasted together from neglecting this commandment of melodic beauty.' By way of illustration, he quotes an anonymous observer:

> The arias are so varied and intricate that one becomes impatient before the end comes. The composer is satisfied if he writes only nonsensical notes, which the singers, through thousands of contortions, make even more absurd. They laugh during the saddest performance, and their Italian excesses always appear at the wrong place.[43]

As for himself, Mattheson thinks,

> Such embellishment, whether produced by a composer lacking in taste or an arrogant vocalist, reminds me of nothing more than a far too opulent livery for pages or trumpeters, where all is completely covered with gold and silver lacing to such an extent that one can perceive neither the cloth nor its color.

This comparison, he sighs, is still too kind.

8. One must aim at a noble simplicity in expression.

'Sensible simplicity … must not be understood as something stupid, absurd, or vulgar; but rather as something noble, unembellished and quite singular.' This is evident, Mattheson finds, in many other areas.

43 Ibid., II, v, 101.

> Simplicity constitutes the most important point in writing and reading as well as in singing and playing, indeed in the whole of human affairs: and if ever innate characteristics were to occur, this certainly would be the right place.
>
> This much is beyond dispute, that men, some more than others, also excel in this matter according to how the physique and the orderly or disorderly mixing of the humors are fit or unfit for sensation. Noble thoughts always have a certain simplicity, something of the unaffected, and only a single aim. Whoever presents such without any constraint, according to the simple laws of nature, will be succeed.[44]

> 9. One must precisely examine and differentiate the writing style.

Here he is thinking of not confusing the appropriate styles for church, theater and chamber, as well as those styles appropriate for specific instruments ('one should not set military pieces for lutes').

> 10. One must not base the aim on words, but on their sense and meaning: not look to sparkling notes, but to expressive sounds.

Though last, Mattheson warns, this is the most important, and equally so for instrumental music.

> For the fact that not a single melody should be without meaning, without aim, or without affection—even though without words—is established by this, and through the laws of nature.

The third basic quality which a good melody must have is that it must be *flowing*. For this he provides eight rules.[45]

1. One should pay careful attention to the uniformity of the meters or rhythms.
2. Also, preserve precisely the geometrical proportion of certain similar phrases, namely the *numerum musicum*, i.e., the measurement of melody by numbers.

In the first of these Mattheson was concerned with some basic order of the rhythms at the level of the beat, although an unvarying beat would 'cause impropriety and disgust.' In the second, Mattheson is looking for a kind of sequential metric form, based on the internal rhythms within the measure.

3. The fewer formal cadences which a melody has, the more flowing it most certainly is.
4. Cadences must be selected and the voices for these managed well before one proceeds to the pauses.

---

44 Ibid., II, v, 104ff.

45 Ibid., II, v, 51 and 110ff.

Aside from the obvious concern with the interruption of the melody, Mattheson was also bored by the lack of variety he heard in cadences.

5. In the course of melody, the little intervening resting places must have a certain connection with that which follows.
6. The overly staccato style is to be avoided in singing; unless a special circumstance requires it.
7. Do not take the passages through many sharp jolts, through little chromatic steps.
8. A theme must not impede or interrupt the melody in its natural course.

The fourth quality which a good melody must have is the most important, *charm*. Here Mattheson supplied eight rules:

1. Steps and small intervals are preferred to large leaps.
2. One should cleverly vary such small steps.
3. Collect all sorts of unsingable phrases, in order to avoid them.
4. On the other hand, select and amass ones which sound good as models.

In illustrating these four rules, Mattheson provides for the most part melodic idioms of the sixteenth-century style.

5. Observe well the relationship of all parts, members and limbs.

This refers to aesthetic correspondence of the internal melodic parts of a form such as the da capo aria form.

6. Employ good repetitions, yet not too often.
7. Begin with sounds which are pure, related to the key.
8. Employ reasonable runs or colorful figures.

Following this, in Chapter Six and Ten, Mattheson discusses the rhythmic notation of melody, in particular as it relates to accompanying a text. It is here that he revisits the ancient Greek poetry rhythms. In Chapter Seven he discusses the next higher level of the organization of time, which he calls mensuration and movement. Mensuration, for Mattheson, is meter, but his descriptions have to be read in the context of their era for he says some things are impossible, metrically, which are common today. It is in connection with mensuration that he places *arsis* and *thesis*.

Movement is, he says, 'what the Italians commonly indicate only with some adjectives such as: *affettuoso*, *con discrezione*, *con spirito*.'[46] While he does not list in that sentence, *allegro*, *adagio* and *vivace*, etc., his choice reminds us that all these terms originally carried some character association and not just speed. We can also see this in the chapter of a contemporary

46 Ibid., II, vii, 7.

book he cites here, '*Les mouvements differents sont le pur espirit de la Musique*.'[47] Mattheson himself says movement is a 'spiritual thing,' not a physical thing (meter), and depends not on 'precepts and prohibitions,' but 'feeling and emotion.'

To find the correct movement, the performer must 'probe and feel his own soul' as well as 'feel the various impulses which the piece is supposed to express.'[48] The ability to correctly find the movement, Mattheson observes, is a knowledge which 'transcends all words' and 'is the highest perfection of music, and it can be attained only through considerable experience and great gifts.'

In Chapter Eight and Eleven Mattheson considers the construction of a melody to reflect the necessary emphasis required by the text (most of his examples associate the highest pitch of the melody with the point of emphasis). Chapter Nine, 'On the Sections and Caesuras of Musical Rhetoric,' treats form. These chapters contain very little which is enlightening or important beyond the obvious.

Since the previous chapters had their focus on the expression of the feelings of the text through melody, Mattheson now addresses the question of the expression of emotions in instrumental music in a chapter called 'On the Difference between Vocal and Instrumental Melodies.'[49] Before getting to the most important topic, Mattheson offers a few interesting observations, such as 'instrumental melody will always have more fire and freedom than vocal melodies'[50] and that vocal music is never concerned with key, whereas this question is a significant one in instrumental music.

Mattheson finds 'instrumental music can indeed do without the words themselves, but not the affections.'[51] That instrumental music can indeed express emotions is obvious in practice, he observes, but 'never in theory.' By this he means it is a subject difficult to write about, although he himself makes an admirable summary.

> The proper goal of all music [melody] can be nothing other than the sort of diversion of the hearing through which the passions of the soul are stirred: thus no one at all will obtain this goal who is not aiming at it, who feels no affection, indeed who scarcely thinks at all of a passion; unless it is one which is involuntarily felt deeply. But if he is stirred in a more noble way and wants to move others with harmony, then he must know how without the words to express sincerely all the emotions of the heart through selected sounds and their skillful combination in such a way that the listener might fully grasp and clearly understand therefrom, as if it were actual speech, the impetus, the sense, the meaning, and the expression, as well as all the pertaining divisions

47 Jean Rousseau, *Méthode claire, certaine et facile pour apprendre à chanter la musique* (Paris, 1678).

48 Mattheson, *Der vollkommene Capellmeister*, II, vii, 18ff.

49 Ibid., II, xii.

50 Ibid., II, xii, 21, says the French can't give up their dotted instrumental rhythms because they would be 'like chefs without salt.' He finds these to be used much less in vocal music.

51 Ibid., II, xii, 30ff.

> and caesuras. It is then a joy! Much more art and a better imagination is required if one wants to achieve this without, rather than with words.[52]

With the absence of text, the performer must take even more careful note of the Italian expressions at the beginning of the composition for clues to the emotions. Here the reader may be surprised by Mattheson's understanding of the characters associated with the familiar 'tempo' terms.

> An *Adagio* indicates distress; a *Lamento* lamentation; a *Lento* relief; an *Andante* hope; an *Affetuoso* love; an *Allegro* comfort; a *Presto* eagerness …[53]

These qualities, Mattheson finds, can appear in a composer's music, 'out of his *genius*,' even if he is unaware of it. He also finds emotional content in larger formal designs.

> If I hear the first part of a good overture, then I feel a special elevation of soul; the second expands the spirits with all joy; and if a serious ending follows, then everything is brought together to a normal restful conclusion.

And finally a wonderful observation on the listener.

> Whoever pays attention can see in the features of an attentive listener what he perceives in his heart.

On the Purposes of Music

There is no doubt that Mattheson believed the central purpose of music, after praising God, was the communication of feeling. The whole question of the 'passions,' Mattheson suggests, is perhaps more the province of the philosopher than the Kapellmeister, but on a practical level it is fundamental to composer and performer if they are to communicate with the listener.[54]

In reflecting on the emotions in general, he observes that 'most are not the best, and certainly must be curtailed or kept in check.' Love is an emotion frequently represented by music and in these cases the composer should 'consult his own experience.' Sadness is second only to love in its use by composers, no doubt, he observes, 'because almost everybody is unhappy.' It is for this reason that sacred music employs this emotion so effectively because it represents the 'penance and remorse, sorrow, contrition, lamentation and the recognition of our misery.'

---

52 Ibid., II, xii, 31.

53 Ibid., II, xii, 34ff.

54 Ibid., I, iii, 52ff.

Regarding the expression of emotions through music, Mattheson first gives several obvious illustrations which we might recognize today as simple text-painting: Joy, being an expansion of our soul, represented by large and expanded intervals; Sadness, being a 'contraction of these subtle parts of our body,' represented by small intervals and Hope and Depression through obvious melodic direction.

Mattheson then turns to more specific prescriptions for representing emotions through music.[55] Pride, Haughtiness and Arrogance are represented by a 'bold, pompous style … majestic musical figures which require a special seriousness and grandiloquent motion.' For these, the melodic line must invariably ascend. The opposite emotions of Humility, Patience, etc., are represented by humble music with descending melody.

Stubbornness 'deserves a special place among the emotions that are appropriate to musical rhetoric,' and is represented by 'so-called capricci … namely when one writes such peculiar passages in one or another voice which one is resolved not to change, cost what it may.' For Anger, Ardor, Vengeance, Rage, Fury and other such 'violent emotions' it is not enough,

> that one rumbles along strongly, makes a lot of noise and boldly rages: notes with many tails will simply not suffice, as many things; but each of these violent qualities requires its own particular characteristics, and, despite forceful expression, must still have a becoming singing quality.

Hope, 'which is a pleasant and soothing thing, consisting of a joyful longing which fills the spirit with a certain courage.' This, therefore, 'demands the loveliest use of the voice and the sweetest combination of sounds in the world.'

Mattheson assigns dissonance to the expression of the unpleasant, disagreeable, frightening and horrible, although interestingly enough 'the spirit even occasionally derives some peculiar sort of comfort from these.' Despair should be represented by 'unusual passages and strange, mad, disordered sequences of notes.' In contrast, Composure is best represented by a 'soft unison.'

In summary, Mattheson, in acknowledging the difficulty of his subject, makes some comments which reflect on the characteristics of the left and right hemispheres of the brain. First he observes that although the emotions are like a bottomless sea, one can write very little about them. And, he says, where nature and morals are shortchanged, 'reason and wisdom cannot be diverted and naked wit takes the lead.'[56]

Finally, he suspects most composers who fail to effectively express emotions in music do so because they do not know their own desires or what they actually wanted to achieve. But failure in this has significant implications for the listener.

> Is it then astonishing that with pieces thus formed, where true natural theory of sound together with the pertaining science of human affections are completely absent, merely the ears of the

55 Ibid., I, iii, 72ff.

56 Ibid., I, iii, 83, 88.

> poor, simple, and self-righteous listeners are tickled, but their hearts and minds are not aroused in proper measure.[57]

Mattheson did not attribute as much influence on the emotions to tonality as one might have expected. In his review of tonality[58] he does refer to the association of the Greek modes with the peoples for whom they were named.

> It is probably that the Dorians had a coarser, more manly, and deeper speaking voice than the Phrygians; and that on the other hand the Lydians sang finer and more effeminately than the others. For the Dorians were a modest, virtuous and peaceful people; the Phrygians however used more noise than foresight; whereas the Lydians, forefathers of the Tuscans, were everywhere described as sensual people.

He also observes that noticeable differences can still be found in the singing of the various areas of Italy during his time, not to mention in other countries. The Mixolydian mode he claims was invented by the lyric poetess, Sappho, to accommodate the fact that she could not sing low enough for the Lydian mode. The voice, Mattheson assures us,

> stemmed from quite natural causes in a young voluptuous widow, since the heat of passion in the long run dries out and contracts certain tubes so that they, especially in the throat, from a lack of sufficient humors cannot stretch adequately enough and cannot produce a low-pitched sound.[59]

Turning to the Middle Ages in his survey of tonality, Mattheson calls this long period 'the worst and most confused theory on modes that one at any time could have invented.' And he was right, it was a long struggle to explain the laws of tonality in mathematical terms, without benefit of the understanding of the laws of physics.[60]

Mattheson devotes little space to the theories of tonality of his own era, the late Baroque. He principally points out that music was now based on the triad and states, without elaboration here, that,

> the nature and character of each key, namely whether it is happy, sad, lovely, devout, etc., are actually matters of the science of melody.[61]

In his *Neu-Eröffnete Orchestre*, Mattheson discusses in more detail the natural emotions of specific scales, yielding some interesting conclusions.[62] The key of F-sharp minor, for example, he finds,

57 Ibid., I, iii, 89.

58 Ibid., I, ix.

59 Ibid., I, ix, 16ff.

60 Ibid., I, ix, 23ff.

61 Ibid., I, ix, 47.

62 Mattheson, *Das Neu-Eröffnete Orchestre*, 231ff.

> is a key characterized by sadness, but a sadness more pensive and lovelorn than tragic and gloomy; it is a key that has about it a certain loneliness, an individuality, a misanthropy.

Mattheson's discussion of style in music is also closely tied to the general topic of the emotions. He follows what seems to be the consensus for the late Baroque by beginning with the classification of music into church, theater and chamber,[63] but this too was synonymous with style, for the church style, for example, exists apart from whether the music is performed in a church building. Beyond this, Mattheson considers it more important to think of the distinctions 'high, middle and low' styles, or 'noble, moderate or trifling.' These classifications are also considered apart from those of church, theater and chamber, or location of performance. Thus, one can speak of 'high' as meaning something different in different mediums, as for example, 'what is *elevated* in the theater is very different from what is elevated in dinner music.' Or, one can speak of high, medium and low within a single medium. In the case of church music, for example, Mattheson suggests that,

> 'Divine majesty, heavenly splendor, rapture and magnificence' are naturally required for the *elevated* style; 'Devotion, contemplation, etc.,' belong to the *middle* style; while 'Repentance, supplient entreaties, etc., stand under the banner of the *low* style.'[64]

Next, Mattheson mentions some additional aesthetic qualities, beginning with 'expressiveness.' Expressiveness, he finds, must exist in all music, apart from any regard to other classifications. 'Naturalness,' he regards as somewhat different. Naturalness is required if an elevated style is to sound magnificent. A low style with artistic elaborations, on the other hand, would be unnatural.

Now Mattheson attempts to address the emotions with the purpose of establishing some correlation with style.[65] His discussion is so interesting, from the perspective of illuminating late Baroque thought on the 'affections,' we will quote it at length.

> Among those emotions which one commonly attributes to the high style are many which do not deserve to be called high at all, in the good sense. For, what can be lower than anger, fear, vengeance, despair, etc. Beating, boasting, snoring is indeed not true nobility. Arrogance is itself only an inflating of the soul, and actually requires more bombast than nobility for expression: now the most haughty are again unfailingly the most angry, in their feelings one debility after another takes the helm. For, though anger will have the *appearance* of being action of a great spirit, still it springs in *fact* from an effeminate heart: one would have to consider it then a special, holy, and just bureaucratic wrath, which nevertheless should punish and discipline, without any indignation.

---

63 Mattheson, *Der vollkommene Capellmeister*, I, x. Mattheson attributes this classification to Marco Scacchi, an Italian Kapellmeister for the kings of Poland and to his manuscript book in 'the public library of St. John in Hamburg.'

64 Ibid., I, x, 10.

65 Ibid., I, x, 22ff.

Great and valiant spirits are forbearing; but small and timid souls can endure nothing. Frivolous people are easily provoked and are as quickly moved to anger, as is the turning around of weather-cocks or weather vanes on the roofs. In short, anger is a ridiculous emotion. It sounds quite base and does not entail an elevated presentation.

Fear and fright are indeed probably the most foolish emotions in the world, and really deserve nothing so little as something of the elevated in their expression. Alas! One finds these unfortunate impulses in all creatures, even in those which seem to have no other emotion and are scorned. Nothing can however be lower than miserable human vengeance, which has so little noble in it that it finds a place only in the most depraved hearts.

If we come to despair, then that is the extreme to which fear can lead: hence one would have to set it on the highest peak of sadness if it really is to have something of nobility. The Italians therefore rightly call all malicious and dangerous people, whose spirit is dejected and lost, *Huomini tristi.*

I will meanwhile not deny that something of strength, turbulence, passion and ecstasy is required if one desires to express properly these and similar passions in music; just as the affections of impetuosity, vengeance, etc., are so constituted that they, according to the difference in station, have the appearance of a high proud quality, although they deny its strength. Here one must also admit that this presumptuous arrogance occasionally requires something of the stately in oratory and music (yet greatly different from the true type); but which is not at all of the mighty, majestic, etc.

Shrieking and grumbling is suitable in anger and quarreling; an uneven, broken, shocking, trembling style in fright; something of daring with vengeance; something frantic with despair; something turgid with arrogance; as long as it did not come out too naturally and arouse disgust: but all of this has nothing to do with the elevated style.

But whoever would want to relegate devotion, patience, diligence, desire, etc., to the middle style might be considered only as moderately devout, moral, patient, diligent and desirous. Indeed, desire corresponds in very many ways with the highest and most emphatic emotion in and outside of the world, namely love, how then can it be relegated to the middle of the road? It is true that desire is according to the nature of the desired object also small or large, high or low, and so on; yet it is the same with almost all emotions.

On the one hand diligence can have much of nobleness, on the other it can have something trifling as the goal. In the last case it would be a work in the dark so to speak (*obscura diligentia*) and would not even deserve to stand in the middle, but rather at the low end. There is nothing at all high-flown about patience, though always something noble: and everyone knows that devotion serves to lift the spirit.

Finally, common dance songs either all, or at least most of them, would indeed have to embody something of the beggarly, slavish, cowardly, disconsolate, base, boorish, stupid, and clumsy, if these qualities of the low style were to be found in them. Low and base are again very different, and if we indeed should exclude from this the most nonsensical peasant dances, though not the clever *Land-Tänze, Country Dances,* then for all of that there probably would be no one who would expect beggars in a spirited minuet, slaves in a happy rigaudon, cowards in an heroic entrée, despair in a lusty gavotte, or base spirits in a magnificent chaconne.

> Drinking songs and lullabies, amorous little pieces, etc., must not always be indiscriminately called trifling: if they are done quite naturally they are often more pleasing and have greater impact than high and mighty concerti and stately overtures. The former no less require their master in their own way than the latter. Yet, what am I to say? Our composers are all kings; or of royal descent ... They do not fret over trivialities.

Mattheson now begins to examine the church, theater and chamber styles with regard to more specific aesthetic considerations. For his readers he describes the old chant style and notation, adding an interesting observation confirmed in other sources but rarely mentioned in general history texts, that in this style there was 'ever so many embellishments and artificialities used therewith.'[66] He next turns to the motet style, in which he specifies that the accompanying instruments do *not* improvise. He mentions that he particularly appreciates the older motets by Hammerschmidt, whom he says 'has done more for the glory of God than a thousand opera composers.' In general, however, such works in the old polyphonic style he calls 'the greatest art,' however,

> art is not nature. If this could succeed in expressing the passions and the true sense of words, then there would be nothing which compares with it, and the half-educated would soon burn their fingers on it.[67]

The previous two forms Mattheson finds used only in the church, but one which is found in church, theater and the chamber is the madrigal. With regard to the reference to the church here, Mattheson has in mind the cantata, oratorios and passions which he regards as having 'the true madrigal's nature in them.' Regarding the madrigal in the chamber, Mattheson points to the great polyphonic examples of the sixteenth century, which he associates with 'concertizing' but 'seem very strange to us: since they do not conform to present-day tastes at all.'[68]

Mattheson, in his *Neu-Eröffnete Orchestre*, points out that in his time many more styles are now possible in church music, including arias and recitatives. In the case of the latter, however, more restraint, seriousness and *soliditè* is required than when these forms are used in the theater.[69]

Regarding the instrumental style, Mattheson first defines instrumental music as nothing other than 'speech in tones or oratory in sound.'[70] Instrumental music, he suggests, must be 'always based on one specific emotion.' Another very interesting observation, especially for this early period, suggests that only certain affections can be associated with certain instruments.

66 Ibid., I, x, 37.

67 Ibid., I, x, 50.

68 Ibid.,I, x, 56.

69 Mattheson, *Das Neu-Eroffnete Orchestre*, 155.

70 Mattheson, *Der vollkommene Capellmeister*, I, x, 63ff.

> Just as every instrument has its own nature, this style is divided into about as many secondary styles as there are instruments. One for example composes completely differently for violins than for flutes; not in the same way for lutes as for trumpets, etc., for which insight, labor and experience is required.

Regarding the use of the instrumental style in the church, Mattheson cautions that such music must have 'a special solemnity and a serious quality ... lest it smack of a loosely-united overture.' But he does not mean by this that instrumental church music must be dark in mood, on the contrary joyful instrumental music can contribute to the atmosphere for devotion.

> Yet one should not indiscriminately abandon all vivacity in the sacred service, especially since the style of writing under discussion often naturally requires more joyousness and cheerfulness than any other, namely according to the subject and circumstance giving occasion for it. Indeed, the instrumental style serves primarily for presenting those very things for which voices are not always appropriate or suited ... Joy does not contradict seriousness; for then all mirth would have to consist of jesting. A cheerful disposition is best disposed for devotion; where such is not to be done mechanically or simply in a trance.

One type of instrumental music in the church which Mattheson cautions the composer about is the canon. If the composer wants to bring such works 'out of the classroom, as out of its true element,' it should be done 'cautiously and seldom.'

The theatrical style, says Mattheson, requires more skill in composition than either church or chamber music because it must be 'the most natural and have nothing constrained or farfetched.'[71] Even in an instrumental overture for the theater, Mattheson contends, neither the 'opulence nor inner depth, which is characteristic of this very style in the church' is required. In fact, he continues, profundity itself is contrary to the character of stage plays,

> whose mark of distinction is always something of the playful and fictitious, which is not supposed to produce any profound, serious impression; but only a serviceable and hence more diverting, incidental presentation rather than a durable, engaging one: with which in fact emotions are touched and moved, through the perception of the vision and hearing, yet are not greatly disturbed by seriousness, and various untoward passions are not often presented. The feelings imparted by the stage are sometimes not unpleasant; but they last only a moment and produce no lasting impression: since everyone knows that the thing is artificial.[72]

But it is in opera, Mattheson finds, that the composer has the opportunity to freely express emotions in music.

> [Opera is the best medium of all for expressing] each and every *Emotion* since there the composer has the grand opportunity to give free rein to his invention. With many surprises and with as

71 Ibid., I, x, 72ff.

72 Ibid., I, x, 79.

> much grace he there can, most naturally and diversely, portray love, jealousy, hatred, gentleness, impatience, lust, indifference, fear, vengeance, fortitude, timidity, magnanimity, horror, dignity, baseness, splendor, indigence, pride, humility, joy, laughter, weeping, mirth, pain, happiness, despair, storm, tranquility, even heaven and earth, sea and hell, together with all the actions in which men participate …
>
> Through the skill of composer and singer each and every *Emotion* can be expressed beautifully and naturally better than in an Oratorio, better than in painting or sculpture, for not only are Operas expressed in words, but they are helped along by appropriate actions and above all interpreted by heart-moving music.[73]

In two different books Mattheson writes that the purpose of opera is not only pleasure, but that it has a definite didactic role. First, speaking of the general value an opera house has for a city, he notes,

> Scholars, artists, artisans come along too, and the city takes on the kind of eminence with a good opera as it has with good banks. For the latter are for service, the former give pleasure; the latter serve to give security; the former to instruct.[74]
>
> ……
>
> A good opera theater is nothing less than an advanced school of many of the fine arts, including together and simultaneously architecture, scenography, painting, mechanics, dancing, acting, moral philosophy, poetry and most especially music, united most pleasantly and always giving new demonstrations for the edification and pleasure of distinguished and sensible spectators.[75]

Dance music is associated primarily with the theater and here Mattheson recommends French music, for France 'remains the true school of dance.'[76] The style of composition for dance, Mattheson calls *hyporchematic*, the components of which he identifies as 'strict metrical division; a slow rhythm in the proper pattern; a uniform, serious yet lively movement; an appropriate length; and unity among the parts,' together, of course, with correspondence between melody and dance steps.

Regarding the chamber style, Mattheson first turns to instrumental music which he says has a completely different character than instrumental music in the church and theater style.[77] The chamber style 'requires far more diligence and perfection than elsewhere, and must have pleasant, clear interior parts,' by which he apparently meant that everything was more exposed to the listener. Instrumental music 'clearly asserts superiority in the chamber style; indeed, even if the melody should occasionally suffer a little thereby, it is still embellished, ornamented and effervescent. That is its distinctiveness.'

---

73 Mattheson, *Das Neu-Eröffnete Orchestre*, 167ff.

74 Johann Mattheson, *Der musicalische Patriot* (Hamburg, 1744), 176.

75 Johann Mattheson, *Die neueste Untersuchung der Singspiele* (Hamburg, 1744), 84.

76 Mattheson, *Der vollkommene Capellmeister*, I, x, 80ff.

77 Ibid., I, x, 104ff.

Under the subject of the chamber, Mattheson also discusses several kinds of popular songs and canons, etc., as well as dance music. Regarding the latter, he mentions in particular the Polish dance style, *à la Polonoise*, which he says is so interesting that there is no hesitation to provide 'serious words and lyrics.' This style, he says, 'often has a quite strange and pleasant effect.'

Mattheson writes that discussion of types of chamber forms could be extended considerably if one wanted to continue into the secondary branches. Among these forms which deserve study, he finds,

> especially the field or martial style would be of no small consideration. For although marches and such manly melodies belong to the hyporchematic style; still the martial music itself has, in many respects, things which are somewhat peculiar to it which might be worth investigating.

Mattheson also finds specific associations between forms and emotions.[78] He begins his discussion with vocal music and in particular *chant* which he considers the epitome of 'noble simplicity.' Mattheson does not speak much of contemporary church vocal forms here, but does make a remarkably negative reference in passing to the old motet style of the sixteenth century.

> [In the motet] there were no passions or emotions to be seen for miles; no breaks to be found in the musical rhetoric, indeed rather caesuras in the middle of a word with an adjacent pause; no true melody; no true charm, indeed no meaning: all based on a few words which often meant little or nothing, such as *Salve, Regina Misericordiae*, and the like.[79]

Mattheson adds, in case anyone should think he has been too severe, that he can show contemporary examples of famous composers who are still writing works 'with all the above defects.' How, he wonders, can intelligent composers issue such works and call them good?

The nature of the *aria* is to express a 'great affection,'[80] whereas the *cavata* (madrigals, sonnets and poems) aim rather for a 'penetrating observation.' Mattheson's discussion of the *recitative* reflects his concern that it must have as much emotion, with as clearly defined accents, as the principal song. He recognizes its greater rhythmic freedom, noting 'the recitative has a beat; but it does not use it.'[81]

---

78 Ibid., II, xiii ff.

79 Ibid., II, xiii, 72.

80 Ibid., II, xiii, 56, adds that the principal emotion of opera is 'intense love.'

> However, it invariably excites a large amount of disquiet and emotionalism with jealousy, sadness, hope, plea, vengeance, rage, fury, etc. I really would seek the most important character of an opera in *disquiet* itself, if that would not make me suspect.

81 Ibid., II, xiii, 22.

Turning to vocal music of a lighter nature, Mattheson gives one of the most detailed discussions of the *serenade* to be found in early literature.[82] First of all, he associates the form with outdoor music, and in particular evening music.

> Nowhere can a serenade better be heard than on the water in calm weather: for then one can use *in their full strength* all sorts of instruments, such as trumpets, drums and Waldhorns, which in a chamber would sound too intense and deafening.

Mattheson makes a number of interesting remarks about how the emotions of this kind of music contrast with other vocal forms.

> The principal characteristic of serenades must always be tenderness, *la tendresse*. I say the principal characteristic: for there are very many secondary qualities with this form. The cantatas, each for itself, employ all sorts of affections and passions; though only one at a time, and they use these in a historical manner, narratively. Serenades on the other hand tend to deal mainly with nothing other than with tender and strong love, without pretense, and moreover the composer as well as the poet must certainly construct everything accordingly with these, if he wants to bring out their true nature. There is not a melody so small and not a piece so large that it can forego having a certain principal characteristic prominent before others and over others, and distinguishing it clearly from the others: otherwise it signifies little or nothing.
>
> Consequently it runs against the true nature of the serenade if one makes use of it so to speak outside of its element (I mean the emotion) with felicitations, public pageants, commencements at universities, etc. Political and military affairs are foreign to it; for the night is devoted to nothing with such intimate acquaintance as love and sleep. These other affairs are served by oratorios and aubades or morning-songs of all kinds,[83] and are particularly characterized by a grandiose, pompous, rousing quality, in secular matters, which harmonizes badly with the tenderness and secret emotions of the heart. Hence oratorios need more voices; whereas a solo or only a couple of singers can be used for serenades; which is another good mark of distinction.

For two other lighter vocal forms, Mattheson identifies the principal emotions for the *balletto* as 'pleasure and amusement' and for the *pastorale* as 'a certain purity and kindheartedness.'

Among Mattheson's discussion of the major instrumental forms,[84] his comments on the Sonata are most enlightening. The Sonata, he says, is a form,

> whose aim is principally towards complaisance or kindness, since a certain Complaisance must predominate in sonatas, which is accommodating to everyone, and which serves each listener. A melancholy person will find something pitiful and compassionate, a sensuous person something pretty, an angry person something violent, and so on, in different varieties of sonatas …

82 Ibid., II, xiii, 40ff.

83 The aubade had its origin as a morning song in the medieval tradition of the watch tower musician playing special music just before dawn to warn illicit lovers that it was time to hurry back to their own beds!

84 Mattheson, *Der vollkommene Capellmeister*, II, xiii, 137ff.

> For some years rudimentary sonatas for the clavier have been composed with good success … [but] they aim more toward movement of the fingers than the heart. Yet amazement over uncommon dexterity is also a type of emotion, which often gives rise to envy; although it is said, its true mother is ignorance.

He does not find as much variety in emotions in the *Concerto grosso*, but rather a tendency toward 'sensuous pleasure.' To this he adds a fascinating reference to the concerto *style* in the sixteenth-century definition.

> Most [concerti] depend upon the full elaboration, indeed, one even overdoes it, so that it resembles a rich table which is set not for hunger but for show. Once can easily guess that in such a contest, from which all concerti get their name, there is no lack of jealousy and vengeance, or envy and hate, as well as other such passions.[85]

Mattheson also mentions a large number of other instrumental forms, each of which is identified with specific emotional qualities.[86] Among these are,

Minuet	moderate cheerfulness
Govotta	true jubilation
Bourrée	contentment and pleasantness, not so degenerate as the gavotte
Rigaudon	somewhat trifling joking
La Marche	somewhat heroic and fearless, yet not wild and running
Entrée	noble and majestic
Gigue [87]	ardent and fleeting zeal
Polonaise	frank and free
Angloise	stubbornness
Hornpipe	frivolity
Sarabanda	to express ambition
Courante	sweet hopefulness
Allemanda	a content or satisfied spirit
Chaccone	more satiating than tasteful
Intrada	to arouse longing

For all of Mattheson's pleas that the purpose of music was to move the listener, he appears to have been reluctant to go beyond this to an ancient Greek concept of ethos. He appears to want to believe that music can change character, and appears to accept the basic logic, but nevertheless he hesitates.

---

85 Ibid., II, xiii, 139.

86 Ibid., II, xiii, 81ff.

87 Mattheson associates with the Gigue the French *Loure*, which he identifies with 'a proud, arrogant nature'; the Spanish *Canarie*, 'eagerness, swiftness and simplicity'; and the Italian *Gige*, used for 'fiddling, … extreme speed and volatility.'

> Plato thought men's habits change with music, namely when it is changed; Cicero maintained however if habits were to change, then music would change. Both can serve our purpose, and neither is wrong. Music and customs should be altered together, so that the former does not damage the latter, nor the latter the former. It is the same with the political …
>
> Besides it is quite regrettable that none of us now knows what constitutes *Musica moralis*. If ethical, or moral philosophy, which concerns the inner man, were only well cultivated; then morals, or ethics which concern the extrinsic, would function better.[88]

Mattheson also quotes the author Lohenstein, in this regard, observing that this is 'a statement which can arouse to deeper insight.'[89]

> The eyesight, the sense of smell, the sense of taste and the sense of touch serve the body; but only the sense of hearing is reserved for the soul and our morals.

On the other hand, Mattheson seemed comfortable with the concept of music therapy and not only reviews many of the anecdotes of the healing powers of music found in ancient literature, but he also provides some contemporary examples.[90] He says he received a letter from the Queen of Spain in 1737 in which she testifies that her husband was completely cured of 'black melancholy' by her having organized a concert every evening before dinner. So impressed was the king, that he began to study music himself.[91] He mentions a professor at Göttingen who attributed the alleviation of pain in limbs with the effect music has on muscles. A particularly interesting report is that seventeenth-century Americans,

> use no other means than their somewhat coarse method of playing, by means of which they occasionally suppress and alleviate difficult infirmities and pains if not heal them.[92]

88 Ibid., I, v, 33ff.

89 Ibid., I, iii, 26. The source for Lohenstein he gives as *Arminio*, II, 90.

90 Ibid., I, iii, 43. Here he cites three publications: the *Quintessence des Novelles*, 1727, Nr. 18, which contains a Rondo which can be used as a cure for the bite of the tarantula; the *Observations de Medecine sur la maladie, appellée convulsions par un Medecine de la Faculté de Paris*, à Paris, 1732, xii, 32, which contains 'examples of music helping sick people to health'; and the *Leipziger Zeitungen von gelehrten Sachen*, 1733, 626, which discusses the author's father being cured of melancholy by music, all other remedies having been in vain.

91 Ibid., I, iii, 45.

92 Ibid., I, iii, 47 . He quotes François La Mothe le Vayer, *Oeuvres de François de la Mothe le Vayer* (Paris, 1656), I, 521.

On Performance Practice

On Singing

While the medieval theorists used to write that 'to sing well' meant understanding the mathematics-based theories of music, Mattheson says that the expression, 'to sing *properly*,' has to do with 'the emotions, as well as the styles, words, melody, harmony, etc.'[93] Because of these close relationships, Mattheson expresses the belief that only one who can sing himself can write well for singers. It is, he says, much better if ability, knowledge, consideration and execution stand together.

From among his many recommendations for training the voice,[94] we found particularly interesting his conviction that early in the training a certain amount of loud singing is necessary, for which he recommends singing in church 'as must necessarily be done, but also to hide the errors which occur among the multitude of fellow singers.' If one cannot thus practice in church, then,

> one could go to a lonely place in the field, dig a small yet deep hole in the ground, place his mouth over it, and shout into it as loudly and as long as can be done, yet always without forcing.

We are also interested to see a reference to what we call the 'pyramid' principle, a performance adjustment required by the fact that the brain genetically exaggerates the perception of higher pitches for the purpose of ease in understanding speech. Mattheson refers to the adjustment for this when he observes that experience for the past two hundred years teaches,

> that each singing voice, the higher it goes, should be produced increasingly temperately and lightly; however in the low notes, according to the same rule, the voice should be strengthened, filled out, and invigorated.[95]

On Improvisation

Improvisation is mentioned frequently by nearly all writers of the Renaissance and Baroque, but unfortunately with very few details other than the general rules for specific ornaments. Because it is so unusual, therefore, that Mattheson provides a broader view of the importance and the aesthetic role in performance practice in church, theater and chamber performance,

93 Ibid., I, i, 7.

94 Ibid., II, i.

95 Ibid., II, iii, 15.

we will quote him at some length.[96] Mattheson uses the term 'fantasy' for improvisation, being a reference to the spontaneous flow of thoughts.

> The name fantasy is normally detested; although we do have a style of writing with this name which is a favorite and which maintains its place *mainly* with the orchestra and on the stage, not only for instruments but also for vocalists. It actually consists not so much in the writing or composing with the pen, as in the singing and playing that occurs spontaneously, or as is said, *extempore* ... Though the so-called *Fantasie*, *Capriccie*, *Toccate*, *Ricercare*, etc., may be written down or printed, they really belong [in this classification], not to mention the *boutades* and preludes.
>
> Italian musicians very often take the opportunity to show off their ideas thus, and avail themselves of this style to the special pleasures of the connoisseur; whether or not the fantasy were actually written down and the vocalist or the instrumentalist were thus saved the trouble; or which is always better, the composer were to do nothing further than to note the appropriate place where such spontaneity could be employed as one wishes. Such commonly occurs at a cadence, be it at the end or anywhere else. But this takes clever minds which are stock full of inventions and are rich in all sorts of figures (sometimes overly so).
>
> Not to mention other artists, the famous Händel often composed accompaniments in his operas in which the clavier alone was performed, according to the player's whim and ability, without direction in its style: which requires a special person, and the few others who have tried to imitate him had a great deal of trouble with it; though they were otherwise rather firm in the saddle.
>
> We have stated above that this fanciful style has its place in the operas; though, with the qualification: *mainly*; since nothing keeps it from also being heard in churches and chambers. In this respect it is peculiar in that it is *one and the same* everywhere; whereas when the other writing styles are used in the other main types they are in many respects subject to a different arrangement. What would the organists do if they could not improvise spontaneously in their preludes and postludes? [Otherwise] this would indeed only yield something awkward, memorized, and inflexible.
>
> How often does not a skilled violinist (not to mention other instrumentalists) amuse himself and his listeners in the most agreeable way when he merely improvises and quite alone? That which occurs every day on the clavier, as the most appropriate instrument for this, on the lute, the viol da gamba, flute and so on, is familiar; if one only thinks on it and puts it in its proper class: and does it as the skilled throats of the prima donnas do it, especially the Italians. One can best perceive such among those who are endowed with similar skill at the court and on the stage. Only it is a pity that there are no rules available for such art of improvisation!
>
> For this style is the freest and least restricted style which one can devise for composing, singing, and playing, since one sometimes uses one idea and sometimes another, since one is restricted by neither words nor melody, but only by harmony, so that the singers' or players' skill can be revealed; since all sorts of otherwise unusual passages, obscure ornaments, ingenious turns and embellishments are produced, without close observation of the beat and pitch, though these do occur on paper; without a regular principal motif and melody, without theme

96 Ibid., I, x, 88ff.

> and subject which would be performed; sometimes fast sometimes slow; sometimes with one sometimes with many voice parts; also sometimes a little behind the beat; without meter; yet not without a view to pleasing, to dazzling and to astonishing. Those are the essential characteristics of the fantasy style.
>
> One is restricted in this style of writing only to the rules of harmony, to no others. Whoever can bring to bear the most artistic embellishments and the rarest inventions does the best. And if occasionally a rather fast type of beat slips in, it only lasts a moment; if no other follows, then the meter ceases. The principal motifs and subjects cannot be completely ignored just because of the improvisatory nature; they may however not be done in sequence, much less be regularly performed: hence those composers who work out formal fugues in their fantasias or toccatas do not maintain the integrity of this style, for nothing is so very contrary to it as order and constraint.

On Ornaments

Mattheson does not engage in extensive explanation of the performance of specific ornaments in his *Der vollkommene Capellmeister*, because, he says, even if he did, his comments would soon be out of date anyway. Also, he admits, this is an art in which it is much easier to point to what is bad than to teach what is good. He calls the art of adding ornaments to a melodic line, *Modulatoria*,[97] and presents a discussion of the academic terms used to represent the elements of oratory, which he wants to suggest might form the foundation for possible ornamentation.[98]

Mattheson also makes a few important observations which touch on aesthetics. First, he points out that ornamentation 'depends more on the skillfulness and sound judgment of a singer or player than on the actual prescription by the composer of the melody.'[99] He is quick to point out that ornamentation can spoil a beautiful melody, a tendency toward which 'I can never pardon the French musicians.' In his conclusion, he provides some hints regarding his sense of aesthetics in this form of improvisation.

> This does not mean we despise ornaments. Well-used embellishments are not to be despised at all, whether the composer himself designs them, if he is a skilled singer and player; or whether the performer produces them extemporaneously. We however most severely criticize the misuse, and also the insolence of the singers and players who at the wrong time and without discretion presume to use such excessive ornaments, from lack of good taste, indeed, good sense; as well as the annoying fanaticisms of some much too fantastic composers with their insane ideas, which they consider as jewels and pearls regardless of the fact that they are usually only polished and coated glass.[100]

97 Ibid., II, iii.

98 Ibid., II, xiv. These parts of speech are: introduction, report, discourse, corroboration, confutation and conclusion.

99 Ibid., II, xiv, 40.

100 Ibid., II, xiv, 43.

By this he means that if the original contribution by the composer is lacking, ornaments cannot disguise this. In another place he makes this more clear.

> To say, however, that the most miserable melodies should be beautiful to the hearing if they are performed well, is not in accord with nature and truth. Many a connoisseur of colorful notes and embellishments considers any unornamented melody as miserable; though it is so only in miserable eyes and not fundamentally. A rotten tree cannot bear fruit, no matter where one transplants it. The shrewdest ornamentation accomplishes only as much here as the skilled gardener who can improve a sound plant by diligent nursing, but if it is worth nothing he can never achieve anything proper. Some instrumentalists and singers know how to find ways to destroy quickly the most beautiful melody; but it is impossible for them, and even all of the artists of the world, to make beautiful the most wretched.[101]

On the Conductor

Finally, we find in the *Der vollkommene Capellmeister* a rather rare early description of the qualities needed in a good conductor.[102] He begins by placing the greatest emphasis on the integrity and character of the conductor and points to examples he has known of conductors who had cheated their singers out of money due them. But in general,

> He should in no way be offensive or scandalous in his living and conduct, for commonly the greatest contempt arises from that. A good reputation and esteem are such delicate things that with a single false step everything one has gained for oneself in many years through great assiduousness can be destroyed.

A central challenge for the conductor, in Mattheson's view, is the need to balance being friendly as a person with the necessary authority in rehearsal.

> A director of the choir must not be lazy with unconstrained words of praise, but must copiously employ them, even if he finds only scant cause for them among his students. But if he is to and must admonish and contradict someone, then he should do it quite seriously, yet as gently and politely as is possible. Affability is considered a most favored and rewarding virtue by people in all ranks: a director then should of course also strive for it, and should be very gregarious, sociable and obliging: especially when he is not performing his official tasks. In his official duties,

101 Ibid., I, x, 32.

102 Ibid., III, xxvi.

> becoming seriousness and precise observation of them probably does more service than too great familiarity.[103]

As for conducting itself, while some 'pound with sticks, keys and feet,' he has found 'that a little sign, not only with the hand but merely with the eyes and gestures, could accomplish most of this; if only the performers would assiduously keep their eyes on the director.'

The personal accomplishments which Mattheson believed were important for a conductor included ability to sing, to play the clavier, knowledge of tuning, knowledge of principles of seating plans and 'the greatest difficulty' of all: having the discernment required to succeed in divining the sense and meaning of another composer's thoughts.

He stresses the importance of rehearsals and points out that the conductor often needs the rehearsal as much as the players.[104] Reminding us that most Baroque performances were also premieres, Mattheson adds that one important purpose of the rehearsal is make the necessary corrections.

> It is no disgrace but rather an honor to improve that which has not turned out well. How then can one know or perceive it without rehearsal?

With regard to the rehearsal, he cannot help but add that some responsibility lies with the attitudes of the individual musicians as well.

> The director as well as the performers should set their heart and soul on nothing other than the service of God … [they] must certainly put away all other, dissolute thoughts, and must direct their mind, from reverence, only on the holy work at hand. If this occurs, then the execution will proceed well: for all mistakes which are made derive from inattentiveness and from such a disposition wherewith one is at another place with his thoughts.[105]

A final requirement for the successful conductor or composer contains some timeless advice.

> A composer and director of music must be of a vigorous, high-spirited, indefatigable, diligent, and energetic nature; yet also orderly: yet most often the most active are deficient in this last. Idleness must be hated as a devil, because it is his place of repose …
>
> Neither impatience nor a sudden flush of emotion serves any purpose here. If one does not have enough desire or deep-felt love for the thing so that he can suppress many a displeasure

103 Ibid., III, xxvi, 7. He points to the ideal example of J. S. Cousser, formerly Kapellmeister at Wolffenbüttel, who so charmed and helped his singers cordially in his home that they all loved him. However, in rehearsal, the musicians,

> almost all had fear and trembling before him, not only in the orchestra but also on the stage: for he knew how to reproach a person for his errors in such a sharp manner that often the eyes of the latter filled with tears. On the other hand, he calmed down again immediately, and diligently sought an opportunity to bind the thus-produced wounds through extraordinary politeness.

104 Ibid., III, xxvi, 23.

105 Ibid., III, xxvi, 25.

over it and so that adversity cannot alienate him from his noble plan; then he is not well suited for the exercise of this discipline and its sphere of duties.

Indeed, with music and its pursuit very few roses are strewn in the path; moreover persons of authority and in high esteem seek, though it is unfair, to suppress and disparage everything about it as much as possible … A master must have the heart in such circumstances to set a cheerful example for others, and must know how to create in himself so many pleasures from this noble pursuit that he would always be in the position, all obstacles notwithstanding, of finding his greatest peace in harmony and of reviving his spirit.[106]

EDUCATIONAL MUSIC

In his *Der vollkommene Capellmeister*, Mattheson, in passing, gives a rather impressive list of topics which must be taught if the 'essence of music' is to be understood.[107] The list includes all the elements of what we would call theory and composition today, plus organ building. Included as well are acoustics, music history,[108] a study of how music functions in society and the training of the voice as well as various instruments.[109] Interesting specific topics include,

The special qualities of a conductor.
Expression in singing.
The difference between vocal and instrumental melodies.
How to direct, produce and execute music.

In another place,[110] Mattheson focuses specifically on the education and skills needed by the Kapellmeister and composer. Without education, he says, a musician can exercise his trade, but he cannot be an artist. This education need not be found at a university, but can be gained at home under 'clever leadership.'

The specific requirements of this education begin with languages: Greek, Latin, French and Italian, the language of the theater. Without these languages, how can the Kapellmeister ever be a *galant homme*? He must also have considerable knowledge in poetry and, in an emergency, be able to write good verse himself.

106 Ibid., II, ii, 55ff.

107 Ibid., I, i, 9ff.

108 Ibid., I, iv, 6ff, divides the field of music history into Chronology, Biography and the study of instruments. He divides the history of music into three eras: the beginning of time until the sixth century AD (a total of 4,000 years!), the sixth century until 1600, and 1600 until the present (1739). This last period, he says, contains so much material that the first two periods seem only trifling by comparison.

109 Ibid., III, xxiv, discusses the need for someone to write an up-to-date treatise on instruments. He mentions the fine work by Praetorius [of 1619], but points out that 'all musical instruments have changed a great deal since then.' The topics which he recommends for such a book range from a technical description and how to actually play each instrument to discussion of their use in churches, theaters and chambers.

110 Ibid., II, iiff.

Mattheson considered music to be a 'substantial part of erudition and one of the disciplines which is closest to theology.' Perhaps this explains his following statement that 'whoever advances in music and goes backwards in morals walks like a crab and misses the proper goal.'

For the composer, in addition to the usual studies in the klavier, counterpoint and harmony, Mattheson gives the highest priority to being able to sing, which he clearly believed was an essential key to understanding the emotions in a composition.

> If the stirring of the affections and passions of the soul depends on something quite different, namely upon the skillful composition of an intelligible, clear, and expressive melody; then no one who is not well experienced in the art of singing can reach this goal.[111]

But, for composition, not everything can be learned, in particular 'a good natural ability or innate instinct and spirit.' To find if he has this, Mattheson recommends his looking into his own heart to see,

> whether he would be satisfied with mere patchwork and pieces from diverse sources, which were toilsomely collected by begging?

It is not necessary, when one composes a dirge or lamentation, to begin to cry, 'yet it is absolutely necessary that he open his mind and heart to the affection at hand.' For how, Mattheson asks, will he be able to excite a passion in other people's feelings if he has not experienced it himself?[112] Here Mattheson, remarkably, adds a precise comment on the nature of the communication of emotions in music, that they are both universal and personal at the same time.

> He must also study the affective disposition of his listeners as much as possible. For although it is true: Each head has its own mind; still a certain propensity, a certain taste, usually predominates with wise and attentive listeners.[113]

Mattheson would have probably acknowledged that composers are 'born, not made,' for he found that in some cases Nature has left the requisite qualities incomplete.

> One sometimes encounters fine minds without true desire and love for it; thus one encounters nothing more seldom than the required diligence and necessary, untiring industry, joined together with these two things, natural ability and real desire: because commonly not a little laziness and idleness, lasciviousness, comfortableness, and the like, tend to go side by side with innate gifts and inclinations.
>
> A so-called natural disposition without ambition or love is like a buried treasure … Desire and diligence without natural ability is really the worst of all.[114]

---

111 Ibid., II, ii, 40, 44.

112 Ibid., II, ii, 64ff.

113 Ibid., II, ii, 66.

114 Ibid., II, ii, 59ff.

This role which Nature plays, led Mattheson, in another place, to comment on the treatment of students.

> Natural stupidity or innate simplicity is among the failures of the intellect which no one can rightfully punish, though it can be deplored or at best ridiculed. Desiring to make youngsters intelligent with thrashing is not only futile, but godless. Many examples verify that beatings make heads ten times more dumb than they were previously. This is and remains abysmally characteristic of education in almost every guild and apprenticeship.[115]

FUNCTIONAL MUSIC

While we have seen above that Mattheson was strongly critical of the Renaissance vocal music of the church, there is an interesting passage in the *Der vollkommene Capellmeister* in which he seems to have a nostalgic fondness for the old cornett and trombone consorts which were also so much associated with church music. It is interesting here, however, that the cornett, which was so praised for its beautiful sound during the sixteenth century, he now thinks of as penetrating and harsh.

> Here this question occurs to me: why then do the good cornetts and trombones, which were formerly closely related and were highly esteemed as staples by the expert civic musicians as well as the composers, seem to be banished now so completely from the churches, at least from the ones here, as if they had been discovered to be incompetent? For the former instrument is still very penetrating, with all its harshness; whereas the other sounds very majestic, and fills a large church beautifully. Whoever wants to may answer this question.[116]

115 Ibid., II, ii, 30. Mattheson specifically was thinking, in the last statement, of Turmbläser guilds.

116 Ibid., III, xxv, 7.

FUNCTIONAL USE

11 GERMAN LITERATURE

WE PRESENT HERE A SAMPLING OF PASSAGES in seventeenth-century German literature which reflect on aesthetics in music, but we must remind the reader that the extended economic, political and religious turmoil which followed the Thirty Years' War produced a climate which was not conducive to literature which concerned itself with the arts. Grimmelshausen, describing an evening of princely entertainment which is interrupted by an announcement that war has broken out, creates figures of speech which neatly characterize this cultural environment.

> Such news spoiled all jesting, and all jollity died away like the bellows of a bagpipe when the wind is gone out. The minstrels and the guests dispersed themselves even as tobacco smoke, which leaves but a smell behind it.[1]

ON THE PHYSIOLOGY OF AESTHETICS

We have mentioned in these volumes numerous examples of early philosophers and writers who arrived by deduction at some level of awareness of the rational and experiential division of man occasioned by our separate but equal hemispheres of the brain. The poet known as Angelus Silesius recognized this distinction in the contrast which he drew between the 'intellect' and the 'heart,' as well as in his observations on the inadequacy of language.

> Now that my eye
> Has seen the essence of the mind,
> No words that could describe it
> Can I find.
>
> The longest way to God,
> The indirect,
> Lies through the intellect.

1 Hans Jacob Christoffel von Grimmelshausen, *The Adventurous Simplicissimus*, trans. A. T. Goodrick (Lincoln: University of Nebraska, 1962), II, iv. This work is considered to be one of the important early examples of the German novel and is really the only such work known today from this period. Grimmelshausen (1625–1676) was born of a humble family and at age ten was captured by Hessian troops. He seems to have experienced some foreign travel and by 1667 was working as a civic official in what is now Gernheim in Baden.

The shortest way lies through the heart.
Here is my journey's end
And here its start.

Unknowable, unnameable,
You seem the other pole.
And yet
My human heart
Contains You whole.[2]

Another passage which refers to the limitations of the left hemisphere reads,

All proofs and arguments
Cannot distort the sight
Of him who is awakened
To his own inner light.[3]

It is also a reflection of the twin hemispheres of the brain that one finds throughout early literature numerous instances in common expressions in which there is a clear preference for the right hand. This is an unconscious recognition of the facts that only the left hemisphere can read or speak, that the left hemisphere has a decided tendency not to recognize the very existence of the right hemisphere and that each hemisphere operates the opposite hand. It is in this regard that we notice that when Grimmelshausen describes a period in the adventures of Simplicissimus when he 'became so godless and wicked that no villainy was too great,' it is under the chapter title, 'How the Huntsman went too far to the left hand.'[4]

ON THE AESTHETICS OF MUSIC

We have mentioned above the fact that the cultural climate in seventeenth-century Germany was not conducive to concentration on the arts. We feel a sense of this reflected in a 1683 poem by Ernst Stockmann (1634–1712), in his dedication of a publication of madrigals to Heinrich Schütz.

As long as noble Schütz devotes
His art to song, it will be pure;
His music, with its silver notes,
Unsullied, surely will endure.

---

2 Johann Scheffler, *The Book of Angelus Silesius*, trans. Frederick Franck (New York: Knopf, 1976), 103ff. Scheffler (1624–1677) studied at the Elizabeth Gymnasium and as a medical student at the University of Strasbourg and at the University of Padua. In 1653 he became a Catholic and took the name Angelus Silesius ('God's Silesian Messenger').

3 Ibid., 110.

4 Grimmelshausen, *The Adventurous Simplicissimus*, III, 163.

The music that they write today
Goes piping on its worldly way,
And though perchance it fills the ear,
The harmony the heart would hear
Is wholly lost.[5]

On the Purpose of Music

Because in Germany the intensity of the Reformation was felt more strongly than in most other countries at this time, we find poetry which associates music with the praise of God. In a poem by Catharina Regina von Greiffenberg, music expresses the joy of the Resurrection of Christ,

Angels, blow your trumpets! Seraphines sing and ring,
Jubil-Jubil-Jubilate sing the rapturous Heavenly Choir.[6]

A similar poem by Matthäus Apelles von Löwenstern says praise Him with trumpet, and,

Great bands of angels round him soar,
Psalter and harp make His glory more.[7]

There are also some very unusual poems on religious themes. For example, the somewhat dark observation by the devout Angelus Silesius,

How out of tune
Your pious whine
With the awesome harmony
Of the divine ...[8]

C. Eltester has written an extraordinary religious poem describing a young lady singing a song to the accompaniment of a theorbo, which is almost sensual in its imagery.

---

5 Quoted in Moser, *Heinrich Schütz*, 201.

6 Catharina Regina von Grieffenberg (1633–1694), 'Auf die fröhlich- und Herrliche auferstehung Christi,' in George Schoolfield, *The German Lyric of the Baroque* (New York: AMS Press, 1966), 127. Born in a castle in Lower Austria, after the death of her husband she was reared by her uncle. She was highly educated and, after acquiring the approval of the Church, married her uncle. Her final literary works were commentaries on the life of Jesus.

7 Matthäus Apelles von Löwenstern (1594–1648), 'Alcaic Ode,' in Ibid., 215. Löwenstern began his career as a lowly teacher and then became Kapellmeister in Bernstadt. He had the good fortune to marry an aristocratic young lady, which, in time, led to his becoming an imperial counselor to Ferdinand III, who also raised him to nobility.

8 Scheffler, *The Book of Angelus Silesius*, 97.

When, fairest maid, there stirs your mouth all filled with sense,
And then there through your lips a tone inspired does sing,
Which by sweet song does bear the Lord His offering,
The heavens are themselves seduced to reverence.

A something which comes near to bearing us from hence,
A hidden current shows—our heart enamoring,
And even through secret force the spirits capturing—
That paradise within your voice has residence.

It seems the angels are descended from the sky
And make themselves through you our choir's ally,
For what men everywhere do round them hear and heed,
And what your lovely mouth in heaven's wise has sung,
That is a masterpiece poured from the angels' tongue,
Which does the very soul from out its being lead.[9]

A poem by Friedrich Spee promises God will hear these musical forms of praise.

A measure sweet you will begin,
You strings in fair dispute,
You dulcian, lute, and violin,
You cymbal, harp and flute,
Trombone, cornett, and trumpet clear,
And horns bent in a bow,
God shall indeed your praises hear.[10]

A closely related purpose of music suggested by Daniel Omeis is to help fill the listener with religious ecstasy.

If here sweet notes can bring me near to ecstasy,
How blissful I shall hear the angels' melody,
My God, when they for You Your thrice blest praises sing,
And through eternity Your grace and glory ring.

My soul turns full of soul, when it a sweet sound hears.
The sweetest song of all, oh God, from You appears.
Oh, in Your awfulness let key and tune resound,
That, where I pleasure find, Your pleasure too be found.[11]

9 C. Eltester (d. ca. 1732), 'Als sie ein Lied in die darzu gespielte Theorbe sangl,' in Schoolfield, *German Lyric of the Baroque*, 93.

10 Friedrich Spee (1591–1635), 'Anders lob auss den wercken Gottes,' in Ibid., 285. Born a noble, Spee received a Jesuit education and became a priest in 1622. Assigned as father-confessor to criminals condemned to death, he witnessed the death of more than 200 persons accused as witches which caused him to work to bring this practice to an end. He was also noted for having converted an entire town (Peine, in Hannover) to Catholicism.

11 Magnus Daniel Omeis (1646–1708), 'Wenn du etwas Liebliches hörest,' in Ibid., 239. Omeis studied law at the Universities of Altdorf and Strassburg and eventually became a professor of poetry at the former.

The purpose of music most frequently mentioned in early literature was to soothe the listener. In Grimmelshausen's *The Adventurous Simplicissimus*, Simplicissimus, while carrying out his duties as a shepherd encounters a poor religious hermit, whom he imagines to be a wolf (never having seen one). He made a 'mighty noise' on his bagpipe, which the hermit interpreted as being made by the devil. Later Simplicissimus hears the hermit sing a song which, in part, credits music with the ability to soothe the weary.

Of God his power and God his might:
Nor darkness hinders us nor night
Our praises so to bring.
Echo the wanderer makes reply
And when thou singst will still be by
And still repeat thy strain.
All weariness she drives afar
And sloth to which we prisoners are,
And mocks at slumber's chain.[12]

A more traditional reference to the ability of music to soothe the listener is found in a poem by Conrad Bayer, written for the marriage of Heinrich Schütz.

Music, sweet harmony,
Over all the elements
Rightly art thou exalted;
Nothing can be compared to thee.
To God's own praise and honor
Dost thou most rightly turn,
His fame to magnify.

The human voice and song
And sound of instrument
Are pleasing thus to God;
And in the whole wide world,
Nothing doth please man more,
Renew the heart and mind
And drive away all sadness.[13]

Another purpose of music often mentioned in early literature is simply to offer delight. Georg Harsdörffer, in a poem written to be published with an engraving which pictured musical instruments, surveys the delight music offers a broad range of society.

12 Grimmelshausen, *The Adventurous Simplicissimus*, I, vii.

13 Quoted in Moser, *Heinrich Schütz*, 104.

All men self-chosen targets may well essay;
One loves perchance the performance of art music,
Takes joy in organs and trumpets,
The slow cornetts and great flutes.

Trombones, violins, lutes and still others
Many love besides music's model.
A lesser soul loves the revelry of
the peasant and civic wind bands.

Of lyre, cither and the hunting horn's echo
In field and village bring joy.
Jew's harp and triangle and shawm
All are the roistering mob's imaum.

Each may praise his preference as he will;
Artistic and inartistic, string and senses play,
I think none of them would argue,
Listen, hear the players speak.[14]

A poem which mentions the delight of music as part of a wedding celebration says, in the first stanza, 'The night is young, cheer up, have some more food and drink.' After this we find,

The cornetts wink and the strings quake
For sweet music's splendors our ears do excite.[15]

A more negative view of musical delight is found in Daniel von Czepko's 'Life is a Play,' where he asks 'Who drums and sings for [life's play]?' The somewhat demeaning answer is, 'Base pleasure's endless sway.'[16]

Finally, there is an extraordinary poem in praise of music by Wenzel Scherffer von Scherffenstein which lists a broad range of purposes of music.

You conqueress of time, friend to festivity,
You conjuress and yoke of madness' malady,
You monitress of woe, you child Pierdine,
You mistress stern to wrath, our senses' cooling wine,
You augmentress of joy, dear banquet of the ear,
You Heaven's charity, the heart's high-treasured cheer,

14 Georg Philipp Harsdörffer (1607–1658), 'Alcaische Ode,' in Schoolfield, *German Lyric of the Baroque*, 179. Harsdörffer was a nobleman who wrote plays as well as poetry. We have made some changes, as this edition sacrifices meaning for rhyme.

15 Johann Klaj (1616–1656), 'Auf! güldenes Leben!,' in Ibid., 195. Klaj was a student of theology at Wittenberg who found greater pleasure in the artistic environment of Nürnberg.

16 Daniel von Czepko (1605–1660), 'Das Leben en Schauspiel,' in Ibid., 85. Czepko's father's family included a long line of Lutheran pastors, but his mother was of Polish nobility. Czepko studied medicine, then law, but eventually became a tutor for noble families in Silesia.

Sweet music, evermore the angels' exercise,
You serving maid of God, who then would you despise,
You most benignant queen! That open with your art
The way to emperor's and king's and princes's heart.
Though some deny to you their grace and reverence,
The recreants are those, who have not soul to sense
You noble loveliness ...
You're of that order which each sense of human kind
And its most inner soul can bring to bay and bind,
And through those might a man is moved to such extent
That vanquished at his feet lies even black lament.
You can as medicine the evil damp destroy,
And make incorporate the vital sprites of joy.
You are to every man, whatever call he be,
Most useful and most fond, and nourish commonly
The prayers of pious folk; high wisdom has increased
For wise men by your strength, nor is your part the least
Within the balm of those who lonely lives must lead.
You can for government of house or cohort breed
A proper temperance within the human breast.
You bear no little load of salutary rest
Into our failing flesh, our healthiness to raise.
You harvest merry's thanks and melancholy's praise.[17]

ART MUSIC

An important value of the seventeenth-century novels and stage plays is that they had as a goal portraying the life of the common man as it really was. It was of the late sixteenth-century plays, which introduced this aesthetic ideal, that the playwrights used the expression that the play 'should mirror life.' Thus we are interested that Grimmelshausen provides us with unusual detail regarding the performance of several kinds of art songs in his famous novel. First, we find Simplicissimus, after a period of practice, beginning to entertain ladies by singing love songs.

> About this time came Martinmas: then with us Germans begins the eating and swilling, and that feast is full conscientiously observed till Shrovetide: so was I invited to different houses, both among the officers and burghers, to help eat the Martinmas goose. So it was that on such occasions I made acquaintance with the ladies. For my lute and my songs made all to look my way, and when they so looked, then was I ready to add such charming looks and actions to my

17 Wenzel Scherffer von Scherffenstein (1603–1674), 'Der Musik Lob,' in Ibid., 263. This poet was also the court organist for the dukes of Brieg.

> new love songs (which I did myself compose) that many a fair maid was befooled, and ere she knew it was in love with me.[18]

The most interesting clues to one specific occasion for Art Music is found in a long discussion relative to Simplicissimus's invitation to participate in a stage play.[19] This invitation came while Simplicissimus was visiting the court in Paris and following his solo performance before the court. Of particular interest here are the references to the reputation of 'common' musicians. Also, the suggestion of French praise for a German singer is rarely found elsewhere.

> [The king's Master of Ceremonies] begged that I would, to honor him and to please the high personages present, let them hear a German song sung to the lute. This I did willingly, being in the mood (for commonly musicians are whimsical people), and so busied myself to play my best, and did so please the company that the Master of Ceremonies said it was a great pity I could not speak French: for so could he commend me greatly to the king and queen. But my master, fearing that I might be taken from his service, answered him, I was of noble birth and thought not to sojourn long in France, and so could hardly be used as a common musician. Thereupon the Master of the Ceremonies said he had never in his life found united in one person such rare beauty, so fine a voice, and such admirable skill upon the lute.

Simplicissimus was now invited to participate in a comedy which was to be performed before the king and he accepted, offering to learn the material in French if it were given to him in advance. In the extant repertoire of seventeenth-century stage plays in all countries one finds numerous references to songs being sung in the course of the play and frequently the lyrics for these songs are given. However, there is almost never any reference to the style of the actual music or the quality of the performance itself. Thus, the few adjectives in the following are rare reflections on what may have been typical performances of incidental singing in the plays of this period.

> The tunes of the songs I had to sing I could play at once perfectly upon the lute; for I had the notes before me: and thereafter I received the French words, to learn them by heart and likewise to pronounce them, all which were interpreted for me in German, that I might use the actions fitted to the songs. All this was easy enough to me, and I was ready before any could have expected it, and that so perfectly ... that ninety-nine out of a hundred that heard me sing would have sworn I was a born Frenchman. And when we came together for the first rehearsal, I did behave myself so plaintively with my songs, tunes, and actions that all believed I had often played the part of Orpheus, which I must then represent, and shew myself vexed for the loss of my Eurydice. And in all my life I have never had so pleasant a day as that on which our comedy was played.

18 Grimmelshausen, *The Adventurous Simplicissimus*, III, xviii.

19 Ibid., IV, 244ff.

After pausing to mention that he was given something to make his voice clearer (again something often mentioned at this time, both for singers, actors and preachers, but without useful details), he continues.

> Now was I crowned with a wreath of laurel and clad in an antique sea-green robe in which all could see my neck, the upper part of my breast, my arms above the elbow and my knees, all bare and naked. About it was wrapped a flesh-colored cloak of taffety that was more like a flag than a cloak: and in this attire I languished over my Eurydice, called on Venus for help in a pretty song, and at last led off my bride: in all which action I did play my part excellently, and gazed upon my love with sighs and speaking eyes. But when I had lost my Eurydice, then did I put on a dress of black throughout, made like the other, from out of which my white skin shone like snow. In this did I lament my lost wife, and did conjure up the case so piteously that in the midst of my sad tunes and melodies the tears would burst forth and my weeping choked the passage of my song: yet did I play my part right well till I came before Pluto and Proserpina in hell. To them I represented in a most moving song their own love that they bore to each other, and begged them to judge thereby with what great grief I and my Eurydice must have parted, and prayed with the most piteous actions (and all the time I sang to my lute) they would give her leave to to return to me: and when they had said me 'Yes,' I took my leave with a joyful song to them, and was clever enough so to change my face, my actions, and my voice to a joyful tune that all that saw me were astonished. But when I again lost my Eurydice all unexpectedly I did fancy to myself the greatest danger wherein a man could find himself, and thereupon become so pale as if I would faint away: for inasmuch as I was then alone upon the stage and all spectators looked on me, I played my part the more carefully and got therefrom the praise of having acted the best. Thereafter I set me on a rock and began to deplore the loss of my bride with piteous words and a most mournful melody, and to summon all creatures to weep with me: upon that, all manner of wild beasts and tame, mountains, trees, and the like flocked round me, so that in truth it seemed as if it were all so done in unnatural fashion by enchantment.

Following the performance, Simplicissimus tells us,

> I gave myself up to the temptations of the French women, that entertained me secretly and rewarded me with many gifts for my services, till in the end I was wearied of so vile and shameful a trade.

Finally, Angelus Silesius makes an observation on the aesthetics of the performance practice of love songs when he observes,

> The nightingale
> Does not resent
> The cuckoo's song.
> But you, if I don't sing
> like you,
> Mock me as wrong.[20]

20 Scheffler, *The Book of Angelus Silesius*, 63.

FUNCTIONAL MUSIC

In the German poetry of this period we find no descriptions of Church music, other than references to praise such as are mentioned above. The functional music which probably most came to mind for seventeenth-century Germans was military music, and this was not a pleasant topic. In a poem about Lucifer's armies, Klaj writes,

> The loud, bright field trumpet
> Drives away our fear of death.[21]

Grimmelshausen makes a passing reference to the military music of trumpets, drums and fifes as 'horrible music.'[22]

ENTERTAINMENT MUSIC

Grimmelshausen provides us with several valuable portraits of the itinerant musician, beginning with Simplicissimus before he had begun his travels and become more worldly.

> I was a fine performer on the bagpipe, whereon I could produce most dolorous strains.[23]

He employed this instrument in his profession as a shepherd.[24] Simplicissimus cites some examples of shepherds who figured famously in ancient literature, including a reference to a passage in Strabo[25] in which it is claimed the ancient Arabians used the bagpipe to encourage the sheep and lambs to eat. Simplicissimus himself was trained on the bagpipe by his father for the purpose of playing 'manfully' to frighten off the wolves.

> So I began to make such ado with my bagpipe and such noise that it was enough to poison all the toads in the garden, and so methought I was safe enough from the wolf that was ever in my mind.

Later in this story Simplicissimus was captured and here we find that in the interval he had become a lute player.

---

21 Klaj, 'Die Soldaten Luzifers singen,' in Schoolfield, *German Lyric of the Baroque*, 197.

22 Grimmelshausen, *The Adventurous Simplicissimus*, II, xxvii. He also makes passing reference to the military drummer serving as a diplomatic escort [III, xvi] and to two military drum signals, 'to picket' and 'bivouac duty' [IV, xi].

23 Ibid., I, iff.

24 Sigmund von Birken mentions in a poem, 'Bring us sweet singing to shepherd-boy's shawm.' 'Hirtengedicht,' in Schoolfield, *German Lyric of the Baroque*, 73. Birken (1626–1681), son of a Lutheran pastor, studied at Jena and became a tutor at the Wolfenbüttel court, where one of his students was Anton Ulrich.

25 This attribution to Strabo we consider to be spurious.

> So then the colonel's wife sent to another colonel's wife that could play well upon the lute, and therefore always had one by her, and begged her for the loan of it: which, when it came, she handed to me with the command that I should play. But my view was they should first give me to eat; for an empty stomach accorded not well with a fat one, such as the lute had.[26]

Still later Simplicissimus had gained the ability to play the harpsichord and sing,[27] and still later to compose.

> Among the citizens I had most friendship with the organist, for music I loved and, without bragging, had an excellent voice which I had no mind to let rust: this man taught me how to compose, and to play better upon that instrument, as also upon the harp: on the lute I was already a master; so I got me one of mine own and daily diverted myself with it.[28]

In another book, which Grimmelshausen casts in the form of a continuation of the original 'Simplicissimus' book, an itinerant fiddler, Springinsfeld, is introduced. The street fiddler is a very frequent figure in the seventeenth-century literature in all Western European countries, but almost no details are ever given other than mention of his presence. The colorful descriptions which Grimmelshausen provides are therefore all the more welcome. We first meet this wandering violinist when he enters a tavern.

> There entered the room an old beggar with a pegleg who, like me, had been driven by the cold to the stove in the room. He had hardly warmed himself a bit when he drew forth a small treble violin, tuned it, stepped up to our table, and played a tune. At the same time he so artfully hummed and squeaked with his lips that anyone who only heard him but did not see him would have perforce believed that three different stringed instruments were being played. He was a rather poorly clad for the winter, and to all appearances had not had a good summer either, for his haggard body bore witness that he had been obliged to tighten his belt, and his sparse hair that he also must have suffered through a serious illness.[29]

As we can see from this description, Springinsfeld was primarily an entertainer, not a violinist. Later, in a description of an outdoor performance, we learn more of this fiddler's skills.

> [He] whisked out his fiddle and began to put on a show and at the same time to play the fiddle. He shaped his lips into a triangle, a square, a pentagon, a hexagon, yea, into a heptagon, and while he was playing the fiddle, all the while he made music with his mouth too, as he had done earlier in the inn, but since the fiddle, which had been tuned in the warmth of the room, would not play right in the cold, he imitated all sorts of bird and animal calls [on it], from the lovely forest song of the nightingale to, and including, the frightful howl of the wolf, as a result of

26 Grimmelshausen, *The Adventurous Simplicissimus*, II, xix.

27 Ibid., II, xxix.

28 Ibid., III, xvii.

29 Hans Jacob Christoffel von Grimmelshausen, *The Singular Life Story of Heedless Hopalong* (Detroit: Wayne State University Press, 1981), 6.

> which we had attracted in less than a quarter of an hour an audience of more than six hundred people, who looked on wide-eyed and open-mouthed with astonishment, forgetful of the cold.[30]

In another place this fiddler reveals that he did rather well, observing that most of the people who gave him money did not themselves have one-tenth the money he had accumulated.[31] We are also provided with some information on the early education of this wandering entertainer.

> [My father-in-law] raised me till I reached my eleventh year and taught me all the principles of his art, such as how to blow the trumpet, beat the drum, play the fiddle and the pipes (both the shawm and the bagpipes), how to do sleight-of-hand tricks, to jump through hoops, and do other strange and clownish things …[32]

This fiddler in time married a 'hurdy-gurdy girl,' in a wedding occurring during a fair and attended by 'puppeteers, acrobats, sleight-of-hand artists, ballad singers, pin peddlers, scissors' grinders, tinkers, hurdy-gurdy girls, master beggars, rogues, and other honorable rabble.'[33] The reader will notice here the general level of society with which the popular song writer was associated. In another book, Grimmelshausen mentions the 'ballads men write in praise of harlots.'[34]

The hurdy-gurdy girl is also pictured at work for a banquet in the house of a 'great gentleman.' The sound of this instrument caused the other musicians to flee!

> Now when dessert was on the table and the dancing was supposed to begin, unexpectedly the sound of a hurdy-gurdy was also heard coming from where the musicians were sitting, to the great consternation of all who were in the hall. The first to run away were the musicians themselves, who heard the rasping sound close by, and yet did not see anyone.[35]

It is a wonder, the narrator observes, that people were not crushed to death in the doorway.

Finally, a poem by G. List mentions with contempt the low poets and musicians of the tavern.

> You discord-blowing flutes
> Of starveling verse-recruits
> Will pipe, to get a sourish beer,
> Bold jests for all the world to hear![36]

---

30 Ibid., 26.

31 Ibid., 102.

32 Ibid., 42.

33 Ibid., 86.

34 Grimmelshausen, *The Adventurous Simplicissimus*, I, xxiv.

35 Grimmelshausen, *The Singular Life Story of Heedless Hopalong*, 93.

36 G. List (d. ca. 1720), 'Auf die Liederlichen vers-verderber,' in Schoolfield, *German Lyric of the Baroque*, 215. This poet has not been precisely identified.

12 LEIBNIZ AND GERMAN PHILOSOPHY

One of the first things one notices in reading German philosophy of the Baroque is the emergence of a new and genuine self-confidence. Leibniz, for example, freely and without hesitation criticized Descartes, Spinoza, Newton and the entire English School of philosophical writers, not to mention the ancient philosophers including even Aristotle. Reflecting this self-confidence is also a new sense of nationalism, which is sometimes expressed in interesting characterizations of other nationals. We don't see this yet in Kepler, who, writing at the beginning of the seventeenth century, observed, 'Germany is just as famous for corpulence and gluttony as Spain is for genius, discernment, and temperance.'[1] By the end of the century, however, Leibniz was feeling a distinct sense of German superiority.

> One need not worry about the Italians, who are ready to receive the yoke, and who have degenerated from the virtue of their ancestors.[2]

The Frenchman, according to Leibniz,

> allows himself no repose, and leaves none to others; the grave and the serious pass for ridiculous, and measure or reason for pedantic; caprice, for something gallant, and inconstancy in one's interactions with other people, for cleverness: everyone meddles with others' affairs in private houses, and pursues people to their very homes, and picks shameful fights. Youth above all glories in its folly and in its disorders.[3]

1 Johannes Kepler's (1571–1630) *Dream*, note 61. See Edward Rosen, *Kepler's Somnium* (Madison:University of Wisconsin Press, 1967), 45. This work, written in 1609, is a curious fictional description of life on the moon.

2 Gottfried Wilhelm Leibniz, 'Mars Christianissimus' (1683), in Patrick Riley, *The Political Writings of Leibniz*, (Cambridge: Cambridge University Press, 1972), 133. Leibniz (1646–1716) was reared in a highly educated family, his father being a professor at Leipzig University. Leibniz also entered Leipzig University, receiving a bachelor's degree in philosophy at age sixteen and two doctorates by age twenty-one. Leibniz was a brilliant mathematician, having discovered the foundations of differential and integral calculus. As a philosopher his works have limited value today due to his inclusion of the soul into many of his explanations.

3 Leibniz, 'Manifesto for the Defense of the Rights of Charles III' (1703), in Ibid., 157.

ON THE PHYSIOLOGY OF AESTHETICS

Philosophers of the German Baroque remained in considerable darkness with regard to the true nature of thought process in the brain. Unlike Descartes, who had proclaimed purposes for parts of the brain, such as the pineal gland, with no evidence whatsoever in support, Leibniz was more honest. In an early treatise, he observed,

> Thought is a sensible quality either of the human intellect or of something 'I know not what' within us which we observe to be thinking. But we cannot explain what it is to think any more than what [the color] white is.[4]

Similarly, a few years later he wrote,

> Now that we are conquerors of the world, there assuredly remains an enemy within us; everything is clear to man but man, the body to the mind, and the mind to itself.[5]

It did seem obvious to Leibniz that speech itself must be an important key to the function of the thought process. For this reason he speculated rather broadly on the origin of speech and on the chronological development of the parts of language. He wondered, for example, which came first, proper or generic names.[6] After noting that monkeys have the physical components for speech, but do not speak, Leibniz adds,

> We must also consider that we could *speak*, i.e., makes ourselves understood by the sounds of the mouth without forming articulate sounds, if we availed ourselves of musical *tones* for this effect; but more art would be necessary to invent a *language of tones*, whilst that of words may have been formed and perfectly gradually by persons who found themselves in a state of natural simplicity. There are, however, people like the Chinese, who by means of tones and accents vary their words, of which they have only a small number.[7]

Several comments should be made with regard to this passage. First, all philologists today agree that some form of vocal music did in fact exist as pre-speech in early man. It is our speculation that the sung-speech of Chinese opera may be the nearest remnant extant today of this early pre-speech. Finally, we should also note that in the early nineteenth century

4 Leibniz, 'A New Method for Learning and Teaching Jurisprudence' (1667), I, xxxiv, in Leroy Loemker, *Philosophical Papers and Letters* (Dordrecht: Reidel, 1956), 89.

5 Leibniz, 'Elements of Natural Law' (1670–1671), in Ibid., 132.

6 Curiously, among his various speculations, the one obvious factor which apparently did not occur to Leibniz at all was the fact that all languages use the same five vowel sounds. This has immense implications regarding the relationships of vocal sounds and emotions in early man. In his discussion of a few vowel sounds he does refer to Johann Becan (1518–1572) a Belgian scholar who believed that Adam spoke German!

7 Leibniz, *New Essays Concerning Human Understanding* (1704), trans. Alfred Langley (La Salle: The Open Court Publishing Company, 1949), III, i, 1. Leibniz himself was inclined to believe that mathematics was the universal language and in a treatise, 'The Art of Discovery' (1685), he suggests that a way might be found for mathematics to express basic grammar, etc.

there was great interest in the idea of inventing a universal language based on music and two inventors came forth with such systems.[8]

The most important break-through in modern understanding of brain function has been the discovery of the separate, but equal, natures of the left and right hemispheres of the brain. Earlier philosophers, of course, had noticed many of the problems which modern clinical research explains. Among these, as Leibniz observes, is the difficulty the left, rational hemisphere has in describing many of the sensory impressions of the right hemisphere.

> Additional simple primitive terms are all those confused phenomena of the senses which we certainly perceive clearly, but which we cannot explain distinctly, neither define them through other concepts, nor designate them by words.[9]

The foremost problem, of course, is expressing feelings in words.

> I admit that men frequently happen to be wrong when indeed they discuss seriously and speak in accord with their feeling.[10]

This difficulty was one of the factors which contributed to the medieval Church's great suspicion of emotions in general. In one place, even Leibniz appears to fall back into this kind of thinking.

> It has often been observed that emotions in the mind lead to illness, but this is not astonishing, since pleasant motions always accompany joyful feelings, and great motions always accompany vehement feelings.[11]

The principal difficulty for early philosophers, lacking our understanding of the complete separation of language (left hemisphere) and the emotions (right hemisphere), was that they had to attempt to explain everything in terms of *one* mind. Thus whenever Leibniz mentions the emotions, we sense his struggle to explain how they function in the mind.

> First of all, by the term *idea* we understand *something which is in our mind*. Traces impressed on the brain are therefore not ideas, for I take it as certain that the mind is something other than the brain or a more subtle part of the the brain substance.
>
> There are many things in our mind, however, which we know are not ideas, though they would not occur without ideas—for example, thoughts, perceptions, and emotions.[12]

8 See David Whitwell, *La Téléphonie and the Universal Musical Language* (Austin: Whitwell Books, 2012).

9 Leibniz, 'An Analysis of the Elements of Language,' in *General Investigations Concerning the Analysis of Concepts and Truths*, trans. Walter O'Briant (Athens: University of Georgia Press, 1968), 33.

10 Leibniz, *New Essays Concerning Human Understanding*, Op. cit., III, x, 13.

11 Leibniz, 'Toward a Philosophy of What There Actually Is and Against the Revival of the Qualities of the Scholastics and Chimerical Intelligences' (ca. 1710–1716), quoted in *Philosophical Essays* [of Leibniz], trans. Roger Ariew and Daniel Garber (Indianapolis: Hackett, 1989), 313.

12 Leibniz, 'What is an Idea?' (1678), in Loemker, *Philosophical Papers and Letters*, 207.

Early philosophers were also misled by assuming that both the emotions and the senses were experienced in the body, rather than entirely in the mind as we know today. Leibniz makes this error in the following.

> Since the power proper to the mind is understanding, it follows that we will be the happier the clearer our comprehension of things and the more we act in accordance with our proper nature, namely, reason. Only to the extent that our reasonings are right are we free, and exempt from the passions which are impressed upon us by surrounding bodies. Yet it is impossible to evade these passions entirely, since the mind is affected in various ways by its body.[13]

And again following the earlier philosophers, the frustration in trying to explain the emotions in rational terms often led to simply concluding that man must let Reason rule.

> The highest perfection of man consists not merely in that he acts freely but still more in that he acts with reason. Better, these are both the same thing, for the less anyone's use of reason is disturbed by the impulsion of the emotions, the freer one is.[14]

The most interesting passages in Leibniz, with regard to characteristics we associate with left and right hemisphere function, are when he touches on one of the Arts. In the following, we might say he speaks of the right hemisphere understanding as 'clear,' and only the left hemisphere understanding as 'confused.'

> In order better to understand the nature of ideas, we must to some extent touch upon the various kinds of knowledge. When I can recognize one thing among others but cannot say in which its differences or properties consist, my knowledge is *confused*. In this way we sometimes know *clearly*, and without having a doubt of any kind, if a poem or a picture is well done or badly, because it has a certain 'something, I know not what' which either satisfies or repels us.[15]

Another interesting passage is found in a discussion of the nature of free will, where Leibniz seeks to make the point that will and thought are entirely separate. The implication in this discussion is that he seemed to correctly understand that music (right hemisphere) is not the same thing as 'thinking.'

> He who should say that the power of speaking directs the power of singing, and that the power of singing obeys or disobeys the power of speaking, would express himself in as proper and intelligent a manner, as he who says, as has been usual, that the will directs the understanding, and that the understanding obeys or disobeys the will. Nevertheless this manner of speaking has prevailed, and has caused, if I am not mistaken, much confusion, although the power of thinking operates no more upon the power of choosing and the contrary, than the power of singing upon that of dancing. I grant that this or that thought may furnish man the occasion of exercising his

13 Leibniz, 'On the Elements of Natural Science,' II, (1682–1684), in Ibid., 280.

14 Leibniz, 'Criticala Thoughts on the General Part of the Principles of Descartes' (1692), 'On Article 37,' in Ibid., 388.

15 Leibniz, 'Discourse on Metaphysics' (1686), xxiv, in Ibid., 318.

> power of choosing and that the mind's choice may be the cause of its actually thinking on this or that thing, just as actually singing a certain tune may be the occasion of dancing such a dance.[16]

Christian Wolff's discussion of the soul seems to imply a remarkable deduction of the two sides of man represented by the separate hemispheres of the brain.

> The soul has two faculties, the cognitive and the appetitive. We are certain of this by experience ... It is also clear that each of these faculties can function faultily. The cognitive faculty can stray from truth and the appetitive faculty from goodness ...[17]

He names the part of philosophy which treats the cognitive faculty, logic, and that which treats the appetitive faculty, practical philosophy.

One of the most fundamental beliefs of Leibniz, with regard to the function of the brain, was that we are born with some form of genetic information supplied by God. It was a topic which he devoted more discussion to than any other philosopher of his time.

> Everywhere there are innumerable minds. There are minds in the human egg even before conception, and they are not lost even if conception never takes place.[18]
>
> ......
>
> I believe that this disposition of our soul, insofar as it expresses some nature, for, or essence, is properly the idea of the thing, which is in us and is always in us whether we think of it or not ... Nothing can be taught us the idea of which is not already in our minds, as the matter out of which our thought is formed.[19]

Leibniz's most extensive writings on the general subject of genetic knowledge is found in his *New Essays on Human Understanding* (1704) which was written in refutation of John Locke's *Essay Concerning Human Understanding* (1690). In his preface, Leibniz associates Locke with those who believe man is born a 'blank slate,' whereas he finds a passage in the New Testament to prove this is not true.

> Our differences are upon subjects of some importance. The question is to know whether the soul in itself is entirely empty as the tablets upon which as yet nothing has been written (*tabula rasa*) according to Aristotle, and the author of the Essay [Locke], and whether all that is traced thereon comes solely from the senses and from experience; or whether the soul contains originally the principles of many ideas and doctrines which external objects merely call up on occasion, as I

---

16 Leibniz, *New Essays Concerning Human Understanding*, II, xxi, 17ff.

17 Christian Wolff, *Preliminary Discourse on Philosophy in General* (1728), trans. Richard Blackwell (Indianapolis: Bobbs-Merrill, 1963), III, lx. Wolff was an honored professor in several German universities, a professor emeritus of the Imperial Academy of St. Petersburg, and translated into English and Italian.

18 Leibniz, Notes made in Paris, February, 1676, in Loemker, *Philosophical Papers and Letters*, 160.

19 Leibniz, 'Discourse on Metaphysics' (1686), xxvi, in Ibid., 320.

> believe with Plato, and even with the schoolmen, and with all those who interpret in this way the passage of St. Paul where he states that the law of God is written in the heart.[20]

Leibniz continues by contending that the Stoics called this genetic knowledge, 'fundamental assumptions,' while contemporary mathematicians call it 'general notions.'

> Julius Scaliger in particular named them *semina aeternitatis*, also *zopyra*, ie., living fires, luminous flashes, concealed within us, but which the encounter of the senses makes appear like the sparks which the blow makes spring from the steel. And the belief is not without reason, that these glitterings indicate something divine and eternal which appears especially in the necessary truths ... The senses, although necessary for all our actual knowledge, are not sufficient to give it all to us, since the senses never give us anything but examples, ie., particular or individual truths.

In this same preface, Leibniz also points to some inconsistencies in Locke, for the purpose of suggesting that perhaps Locke believed in some form of genetic knowledge but did not recognize it as such.

> Perhaps our clever author will not wholly differ from my view. For after having employed the whole of his first book in rejecting innate intelligence, taken in a certain sense, then nevertheless, at the beginning of the second and in the sequel, admits that ideas, which do not originate in sensation, come from reflection. Now reflection is nothing else than attention to what is in us, and the senses do not give us what we already carry with us.

Six years later, Leibniz refined this idea somewhat by contending that this genetic knowledge is not actual reason, but only its components.

> I do not affirm the preexistence of rationality. Yet one may believe that in the preexisting germs there has been already prepared and preestablished by divine grace what at some future time is to issue therefrom, namely, not only the human organism, but also rationality itself, contained in a sealed blueprint to be carried out later.[21]

---

20 Leibniz, *New Essays Concerning Human Understanding*, Preface. The St. Paul reference is found in Romans 2:15,

> They show that what the law requires is written on their hearts, while their conscience also bears witness and their conflicting thoughts accuse or perhaps excuse them on that day when, according to my gospel, God judges the secrets of men by Christ Jesus.

21 Leibniz, 'A Vindication of God's Justice Reconciled with His Other Perfections and All His Actions' (1710), lxxxii, in *Monadology and Other Philosophical Essays*, trans. Paul Schrecker (Indianapolis: Bobbs-Merrill, 1965), 132.

On the Senses

The primary interest on the part of the seventeenth-century German philosophers relative to the senses was regarding their role in the formation of intelligence. We might begin by quoting a typical criticism by Leibniz.

> Descartes himself had a rather limited mind. He excelled all people in speculation, but he discovered nothing useful for the portion of life which falls under the senses, and nothing useful in the practice of the arts.[22]

In an early treatise, Leibniz says some perception of sense occurs in the mind, but some perception occurs in the bodily organs. Touch, for example, he says is perceived in the hands, etc., which we understand today is incorrect.[23] A decade later he understands the senses have a separate, distinct role in understanding, if not the cause of anything.

> There remain two ways of knowing contingent truths. The one is experience; the other, reason. We know by experience when we perceive a thing distinctly enough by our senses; by reason, however, when we use the general principle that nothing happens without a reason.[24]

Two years later he elaborates on this idea and here we see a distinct inequality between the senses and Reason.

> We can say that we receive our knowledge from without through the ministry of the senses, because certain exterior things contain or express more particularly the reasons which determine our soul to certain thoughts ... But ... it is always false to say that all of our notions come from the senses which are called external; for the notions which I have of myself and of my thoughts, and, consequently of being, of substance, of action, of identity, and of many others, come from an internal experience.[25]

By 1702 Leibniz arrives at his final understanding, which is that information derived from the senses can be clearly perceived, but understood indistinctly by Reason. This is essentially the position which all earlier philosophers took and in terms of modern medical understanding we would say that it is explained best by the fact that Reason can only discuss rational things. Accordingly, what follows is actually a description of only the left hemisphere's understanding. One could never convince a lover or a listener of music that his perception of the object was 'confused.'

---

22 Leibniz, letter to Molanus, ca. 1679, quoted in *Philosophical Essays* [of Leibniz], 241.

23 Leibniz, 'A New Method for Learning and Teaching Jurisprudence' (1667), I, xxxiv, in Loemker, *Philosophical Papers and Letters*, 89.

24 Leibniz, 'On Freedom' (ca. 1679), in Ibid., 265.

25 Leibniz, 'Discourse on Metaphysics' 1686), xxvii, in Ibid., 320ff.

> To use the analogy of an ancient writer, we use the external senses as a blind man uses his stick, and they help us to know their particular objects, which are colors, sounds, odors, tastes, and tactual qualities. But they do not help us to know what these sensible qualities are or in what they consist ... So it can be said that *sensible qualities* are in fact *occult qualities* and that there must be others *more manifest* which could render them understandable. Far from understanding sensible things only, it is just these which we understand the least. And even though we are familiar with them, we do not understand them the better for that, just as a pilot does not understand the nature of the magnetic needle, which turns to the north, better than other men, although he has it constantly before his eyes in the compass, and as a result scarcely even has any more curiosity about it.
>
> I do not deny that many discoveries have been made about the nature of these occult qualities. So, for example, we know what kind of refraction produces blue and yellow and how these two colors mixed produce green. But we still cannot understand as a result how the perception we have of these three colors follows from these causes. Also, we do not have even nominal definitions of such qualities, in order to explain the terms. The purpose of nominal definitions is to give marks sufficient to aid in recognizing things. For example, assayers have marks by which they distinguish gold from all other metals, and even if a man has never seen gold, these marks could be taught him so that he could recognize it unmistakably should he some day encounter it. But this is not the case with these sensible qualities; no mark for recognizing blue, for example, can be given to one who has never seen it. Thus blue is itself its own mark, and in order that a man may know what blue is, one must of necessity show it to him.
>
> For this reason it is usually said that the *concepts* of these qualities are *clear*, since they serve us in recognizing them, but that these same concepts are not *distinct*, because we cannot distinguish or develop the content included in them. It is an 'I know now what' which we perceive but for which we cannot account ...
>
> Since therefore our soul compares the numbers and the shapes of colors, for example, with the numbers and shapes discovered by touch, there must be an *internal sense* where the perceptions of these different external senses are found united. This is called the *imagination*, which comprises at once the *concepts of particular senses,* which are *clear* but *confused*, and the concepts of the common sense, which are clear and distinct.
>
> ......
>
> There are thus three levels of concepts: those which are sensible only, which are the objects produced by each sense in particular; those which are at once sensible and intelligible, which appertain to the common sense; and those which are intelligible only, which belong to the understanding. The first and second together are imaginable, but the third lies beyond the imagination. The second and third are intelligible and distinct, but the first are confused, although they may be clear and recognizable.[26]

In terms of music, this last idea, that objects of the senses can be clear and recognizable but confused, would suggest that Leibniz might have believed the audience member could have a clear and recognizable idea of the music but not understand it. In the case of music

26 Leibniz, 'On What is Independent of Sense and Matter' (Letter to queen Sophia Charlotte of Prussia, 1702), in Ibid., 547ff.

specifically, we reject this possibility, for music is its own form of truth, which, not dependent on understanding of 'intellectual' descriptions of it, bypasses Reason completely. This is proved everyday all over the world by people who listen to, and love, music, but 'know nothing' about it.

One of the most important German philosophers of the Baroque, with respect to his influence on German culture, was Christian von Wolff (1679–1754). Following the systematic styles of Descartes and Leibniz, he was the bridge to Kant in defining the rational process of knowledge. It is curious to us that his masterpiece, *Preliminary Discourse on Philosophy in General*, while its topics include theology, the natural sciences, ethics, politics, mathematics and philosophy, omits the arts as an independent discipline—with the exception of civic architecture. Given his influence in the German academic community, we cannot help but wonder if someone would have given Wolff flute lessons, if there might be music in the German universities today.[27]

Departing from the dogma of the medieval Church, and Scholastic university tradition, Wolff assigns genuine importance to the senses. He simply separated the senses from rational understanding and equated information derived from the senses with personal experience.

> By means of the senses we know things which are and occur in the material world ... Knowledge acquired by the senses and by attention to ourselves cannot be called into doubt.[28]

This form of knowledge, one of three basic kinds of knowledge according to Wolff, obtained by personal experience, he calls *history*.

Wolff's second kind of knowledge, that based on the reasons for things, he calls *philosophy*. This kind of knowledge he assigns a higher value to, for to know the reason for some fact is more important than to merely know the fact exists. This should be understood as a direct restatement of both the old Church and Scholastic university dogma. This was the rationale, for example, for the early universities teaching only the so-called 'speculative' music and ignoring completely the so-called 'practical' music. Wolff's third kind of knowledge, that which deals with the quantity of things, he calls *mathematics*. Of these three, he finds the lowest in merit to be historical knowledge.

> Common historical knowledge is the lowest grade of human knowledge. For historical knowledge is acquired by the senses attending to things which actually are or occur ...
>
> And thus the reason is clear why vulgar knowledge and knowledge of things which we use in life and of many other things is historical. For with vulgar knowledge we go no further than those things which we first notice by means of the senses.[29]

27 By music, we mean, of course, performance.

28 Christian Wolff, *Preliminary Discourse on Philosophy in General*, I, 1ff.

29 Ibid., I, xxiiff.

It is in this 'lowest grade of knowledge' that Wolff places the Arts. Although in the following he meant by 'Arts' primarily crafts, it seems clear he would have included painting, sculpture and, no doubt, music.

> Art often reduces secret historical knowledge to common historical knowledge. The operations of art and also experiments often bring to light facts of nature which otherwise would be hidden. Hence it makes no difference to the knower whether nature presents things to the senses or whether art provides the senses with things which otherwise would escape their notice. With the help supplied by art only attention and acumen are needed to arrive at the contents of both secret and common historical knowledge. Therefore, by means of art, secret knowledge is reduced to common knowledge.[30]

With respect to music, we might imagine him suggesting that 'secret' historical knowledge is that gained by the personal experience of the composer, while 'common' historical knowledge would be the form in which this 'secret' knowledge is given over to students.

Turning to the second of his kinds of knowledge, philosophy, he adds a new definition, 'Philosophy is the science of the possibilities insofar as they can be.'[31] We can see the influence of Descartes and Leibniz when Wolff explains that the 'science' of engaging in philosophy entails the presentation of propositions and the legitimate sequence of immutable principles. It is also interesting that he maintains, 'the principles of philosophy must be derived from experience. The principles are demonstrated by experiments and confirmed by observations.'[32]

Wolff now elaborates a number of specific disciplines within philosophy. He calls the branch of philosophy which is concerned with God, natural theology, that which is concerned with the soul, psychology, and that which treats bodies, physics. Further branches of philosophy include such diverse disciplines as ethics, politics and economics.

On Education

In Johannes Kepler we find a curious passage in which he reflects on the negative side of the liberal arts.

> Medicine gives instruction about poisons …; metaphysics absurdly exaggerates its goals …; ethics recommends loftiness, which is not beneficial to everybody; astrology supports superstitions; optics supplies illusions; music panders to the passions, geometry to unjust rule, and arithmetic to greed.[33]

30 Ibid., I, xxiv.

31 Ibid., II, xxix.

32 Ibid., II, xxxiv.

33 Kepler's note 37, in Rosen, *Kepler's Somnium*, 50ff.

Leibniz, in an early treatise on the teaching of Jurisprudence, mentions that 'beasts' are capable of certain learning, pointing by way of example to the 'recent exhibit in Vienna of horses dancing in a ring.'[34] Infants, he says, are no better than beasts until they begin to use reason, therefore teachers might adopt some of the techniques used to train animals. He also recognizes some genetic knowledge, which he calls 'infusion,' although this can be either divine or diabolical in in source.[35]

Teaching is to the soul, observes Leibniz, as medicine is to the body. The characteristics of good teaching are that it be 'sound, swift and pleasant.'[36] With regard to learning he emphasizes mnemonics (the technique of memory), and it is interesting he associates emotion with effective memory, something which has been confirmed in clinical research.[37] His mention of music here will remind the reader that music was often used in church schools as a means of helping the boys learn Latin.

> Those signs are most mnemonic which are most perceptible, so to speak, such as words which are not merely heard but are heard with joy—for example, songs.[38]

ON THE PSYCHOLOGY OF AESTHETICS

In view of the fact that we so often find Leibniz reflecting earlier Church philosophy, it is somewhat surprising to read his rather pragmatic comments on Pleasure and Pain. In an early treatise he writes,

> There is no one who deliberately does anything except for the sake of his own good, for we seek the good also of those whom we love for the sake of pleasure which we ourselves get from their happiness. To love is to find pleasure in the happiness of another …
>
> For everything pleasant is sought for its own sake, and whatever is sought for its own sake is pleasant.[39]

Twenty years later, he offers these definitions,

> *Happiness* is a state of permanent joy … *Joy* is a pleasure which the soul feels in itself. *Pleasure* is the feeling of a perfection or an excellence.[40]

34 Leibniz, 'A New Method for Learning and Teaching Jurisprudence' (1667), I, iv, in Loemker, *Philosophical Papers and Letters*, 85. This still exists, of course, in the form of the famous 'Spanish Riding School' in Vienna.

35 Ibid., I, ix.

36 Ibid., I, xvii.

37 Modern research suggests that *all* distant memories have strong emotional components.

38 Ibid., I, xxiii.

39 Leibniz, 'Elements of Natural Law' (1670–1671), in Ibid., 134, 136.

40 Leibniz, 'On Wisdom' (ca. 1690–1698), in Ibid., 425.

By the first years of the eighteenth century, Leibniz was struggling with, as we would say, problems associated with our separate brain hemispheres. He wonders about the relationship of emotions and Reason to happiness.

> We know that it is the reason and the will which lead us towards happiness, but that feeling and appetite carry us only towards pleasure. Now although pleasure cannot receive a nominal definition, any more than light or color, it can nevertheless receive like them a casual, and I believe that at bottom, pleasure is a feeling of perfection and pain a feeling of imperfection, provided it be marked enough to make us capable of perceiving it.[41]

And he is fully aware of the problem that language does not serve well to describe many forms of pleasure.

> As the sensations of the body, like the thoughts of the mind, are either indifferent or followed by pleasure or pain, the ideas of them cannot be described any more than all other simple ideas, nor can the words which serve to designate them be defined.[42]

Leibniz goes on to contend that all the passions have their basis in Pleasure and Pain. He also observes here that 'languages lack words sufficiently suitable to distinguish' these passions. He also points to the mixture of the passions, employing the illustration of listening to music.

> It appears to me to signify a state in which pleasure predominates in us, for during the profoundest sorrow and in the midst of the most poignant grief one may take some pleasure as in drinking or hearing music, but the unpleasant feeling predominates and so in the midst of the most acute pain the mind can be joyful.

ON THE PHILOSOPHY OF AESTHETICS

Leibniz seemed to understand the Arts as being primarily experiential, rather than as a product of Reason. The only rational process, in his view of aesthetics, was simply in following good examples.

> It is true that the art of thinking must first be sought in examples of good thinking about things used as models. But after it has been found in these, we may attend directly to the art, so that it may itself become good and serve as a model, though without abandoning the practice and study of good thinking. A painter, sculptor, or architect studies ancient models and formulates

41 Leibniz, *New Essays Concerning Human Understanding*, II, xxi, 41ff.

42 Leibniz, Ibid., II, xx.

> an ideal from them. But these matters have also been reduced to rules which can be followed. Yet no one stops viewing beautiful works of art [as art].[43]

Wolff was also aware that Art had its own 'rules' and since he had defined philosophy as the knowledge of the reason for things, he found it curious that he knew of no philosophy of law, medicine or the arts. He argued that each of the arts should have a [published] philosophy, adding,

> Insofar … that art assists philosophy, we do not hesitate to add that many useful things would redound to the arts from the philosophy of the arts, if the latter were available for public use.[44]

Later, he expands on this idea as follows,

> A philosophy of the arts is also possible, although it has up to now been neglected. One could call it technics or technology … Or if you prefer, it is the science of the things which man produces by using the organs of the body, especially the hands.
>
> Technology should not explain how the structure of the body makes possible the motion of the hands and the other organs which are required to produce a work of art. This discussion belongs to physics. Rather it should give the reason for the rules of art and of the works produced by art … It is clear that a philosophy of art is possible, although it presupposes the rest of philosophy. For there are rules of art which contain the reasons of things, just as there are inferences between philosophical theorems. If these rules had not been discovered by inventors, they would be unknown by the artisans who put them to use. What is even more amazing is that artisans often lack a distinct notion of the rules by which they work.[45]

On Beauty

Since Leibniz apparently did not reflect on the independent inherent aesthetic qualities of beauty in art, and since he seemed unaware of the importance of the non-rational side of the personality, for him Beauty was simply a virtue as a form of pleasure.

> We seek beautiful things because they are pleasant, for I define beauty as that, the contemplation of which is pleasant.[46]
>
> ……
>
> Since the contemplation of the beautiful is pleasant in itself, and a painting of Raphael affects a sensitive person who understands it, although it brings him no [material] gain, so that he keeps

43 Leibniz, Letter to Gabriel Wagner (1696), in Loemker, *Philosophical Papers and Letters*, 469.

44 Christian Wolff, *Preliminary Discourse on Philosophy in General* (1728), II, xxxix.

45 Ibid., III, lxxi.

46 Leibniz, 'Elements of Natural Law' (1670–1671), in Loemker, *Philosophical Papers and Letters*, 137.

> it in his [mind's] eye, as the image of a thing which is loved; when the beautiful thing is itself capable of happiness, this affection passes over into pure love.[47]

Leibniz also considered elegance in art to be an element which contributes to pleasure. In his preface to the publication of a sixteenth-century work by Nizolius, Leibniz suggests that the three most praiseworthy marks of speech are 'clarity, truth and elegance.'[48] 'Elegance,' he defines as that which is *pleasant* to hear or read. He goes on to suggest that elegance/pleasure 'can be of great service in securing attention, in moving minds, and in impressing things more deeply on the memory.'

> There are two things which make us take notice—eloquence and demonstration. The former moves the emotions and brings the blood to boil, so to speak. The latter creates a clear comprehension in the mind. Hence the former vanishes unless it takes on demonstrative form and is only the senseless ecstasy of a mob agitated by frantic emotions.[49]

On Art and Nature

Medieval literature, and medieval Church philosophy, gave little consideration to Nature, other than as a synonym for God. Sixteenth-century philosophers, and musicians, began to think about man, and his emotions, as a part of Nature and separated from theology. During the Baroque, Nature becomes an increasingly prominent topic, central to the Enlightenment and initiates a movement which, of course, climaxes in Romanticism.

The German mathematician-philosophers, on the other hand, thought of Nature primarily as a series of natural laws. Thus, Johannes Kepler, in one of his notes to *The Dream*, defines the true philosopher as one who 'never stops asking questions, acquiring information … thinking about them repeatedly, and applying them to the laws of Nature.'[50] Leibniz added that the laws of Nature were the artwork of God.

> Universal nature is, so to speak, the *artifice of God*, and such a work, indeed, that any natural machine whatever consists further of infinite organs (this is the true, but little noted, distinction between *nature* and *art*) and so entails an infinite wisdom and power on the part of its author and governor.[51]

---

47 Leibniz, 'Codex Iuris Gentium' (1693), in Riley, *The Political Writings of Leibniz*, 171.

48 Leibniz, 'Preface to an Edition of Nizolius' (1670), in Loemker, *Philosophical Papers and Letters*, 121.

49 Leibniz, 'Elements of Natural Law' (1670–1671), in Ibid., 132.

50 Kepler's note 22, in Rosen, *Kepler's Somnium*, 45.

51 Leibniz, 'On Nature itself, or on the Inherent Force and Actions of Created Things' (1698), in Loemker, *Philosophical Papers and Letters*, 499.

The question of whether art should imitate nature, and the concept of art as a 'mirror' of nature, are topics discussed throughout Western literature. The early seventeenth-century German philosopher, Jacob Böhme, incorporates these ideas into his theological explanations. For example,

> Thus we recognize the eternal Unground out of Nature to be like a mirror. For it is like an eye which sees, and yet conducts nothing in the seeing wherewith it sees; for seeing is without essence, although it is generated from essence, viz., from the essential life.
>
> We are able then to recognize that the eternal Unground out of Nature is a will, like an eye where in Nature is hidden; like a hidden fire that burns not, which exists and also exists not. It is not a spirit, but a form of spirit, like the reflection in the mirror. For all the form of a spirit is seen in the reflection or in the mirror, and yet there is nothing which the eye or mirror sees; but its seeing is in itself, for there is nothing before it that were deeper there. It is like a mirror which is a container of the aspect of Nature, and yet comprehends not Nature, as Nature comprehends not the form of the image in the mirror.
>
> And thus one is free from the other, and yet the mirror is truly the container of the image. It embraces the image, and yet is powerless in respect of the form, for it cannot retain it. For if the image departs from the mirror, the mirror is a clear brightness, and its brightness is a nothing; and yet all the form of Nature is hidden therein as a nothing; and yet veritably is, but not in essence.[52]

Böhme also finds Nature to be a fundamental contributor to the concept of Pleasure and Pain. Also evident here is a return to the medieval Church connection between any form of desire and pleasure and sin.

> We now consider Desire, and find that it is a stern attraction, like an eternal elevation or motion. For it draws itself into itself, and makes itself pregnant, so that from the thin freedom where there is nothing a darkness is produced. For the desiring will becomes by the drawing-in thick and full, although there is nothing but darkness …
>
> And here we are to recognize two forms of Nature, viz., sour (astringent), that is, Desire, and then the sting, which makes in the desire a breaking and piercing, whence feeling arises, that is, bitter, and is the second form of Nature, a cause and origin of the essences in Nature …
>
> It is now clear what the first will to fire operates and effects, viz., stern, hard, bitter, and great anguish, which is the third form of Nature; for anguish is as the center where life and will eternally take their rise. For the will would be free from the great anguish, and yet cannot …
>
> Seeing then the great and strong mind of the form of anguish goes thus in itself as a wheel, and continually breaks the stern attraction, and by the sting brings into plurality of essences; but in anguish, the wheel disposes again into a one, as into a mind: therefore now the anguishful

52 Jacob Böhme, *Six Theosophic Points* (1620), trans. John Earle (Ann Arbor: University of Michigan Press, 1958), I, viff. Böhme (1575–1624) coins the term 'Unground' to represent the dark and irrational abyss that precedes being, but the concept is also inseparable from his discussions of Good and Evil.

> life is born, viz., Nature, where there is a moving, driving, fleeing and holding, as also a feeling, tasting and hearing. And yet it is not a right life, but only a Nature-life without a principle.[53]

In addition, Böhme uses Nature to develop his strong interest in the mystery of God and the creation. 'Magic,' he says, 'is the mother of eternity … It is the original state of Nature.'[54] It is in this context that he writes of the senses.

> For the senses are the flash from the fire-spirit, and bring with them in the light the flames of Majesty; and in the darkness they bring with them the flash of terror, as a fierce flash of fire.
>
> The senses are such a subtle spirit that they enter into all beings, and take up all beings into themselves. But the understanding tries all in its own fire; it rejects the evil and retains the good. Then Magic, its mother, takes this and brings it into a being.
>
> Magic is the mother from which Nature comes, and the understanding is the mother coming from Nature.[55]

Finally, we should note an interesting observation by Wolff on the purpose of poetry.

> The philosopher writes in order to communicate, and not to persuade, as does the orator, nor to please, as does the poet.[56]

ON THE AESTHETICS OF MUSIC

ON THE DEFINITION OF MUSIC

Leibniz, in an early comment on the nature of music, first seems to reflect only the old medieval definition of music as a branch of mathematics.

> Music is subordinate to Arithmetic and when we know a few fundamental experiments with harmonies and dissonances, all the remaining general precepts depend on numbers; I recall once drawing a harmonic line divided in such a fashion that one could determine with the compass the different compositions and properties of all musical intervals. Besides, we can show a man who does not know anything about music, the way to compose without mistakes.[57]

But, he apparently realized this was too narrow and calculated. This definition omits the artistic aspect entirely and fails to account for the artist who appears to write without regard

53 Ibid., I, xxxviiiff.

54 Ibid., V, iff.

55 Ibid., V, xvff.

56 Christian Wolff, *Preliminary Discourse on Philosophy in General* (1728), V, cxlix.

57 Leibniz, untitled manuscript, known as 'Precepts for Advancing the Sciences and Arts' (1680), in Philip Wiener, *Leibniz Selections* (New York: Scribner's, 1951), 42ff.

to 'the rules' as well as the performer, who requires practice, not just knowledge of the rules of the art. Therefore he expands his scope considerably, beginning with the aspects of the beautiful and the eloquent. As a speaker should model his orations after Cicero,

> so in music what a man needs in order to compose successfully are practice as well as a genius and vivid imagination in things of the ear. And as the making of beautiful verses requires a prior reading of good poets, noticing turns and expressions which gradually tinge one's own style, 'as they who walk in the sun take on another tint,' in the same way a Musician, after noticing in the compositions of talented men a thousand and one beautiful cadences and, so to speak, phrases of Music, will be able to give flight to his own imagination furnished with these fine materials. There are even those who are naturally musicians and who compose beautiful melodies just as there are natural poets who with a little aid and reading perform wonders, for there are things, especially those dependent on the senses, in which we do better by letting ourselves go automatically by imitation and practice than by sticking to dry precepts. And as playing the clavichord requires a habit which the fingers themselves have to acquire, so imagining a beautiful melody, making a good poem, promptly sketching architectural ornaments or the plan of a creative painting require that our imagination itself acquire a habit after which it can be given the freedom to go its own way without consulting reason, in the manner of an inspired Enthusiasm ... But reason must afterwards examine and correct and polish the work of imagination; that is where the precepts of art are needed to produce something finished and excellent.

Leibniz now turns his attention to the amateur, and as he addresses education and the art process at this level he returns to a more rational perspective.

> As the common man is eternally befogged by a badly understood distinction between practice and theory, it is still appropriate to explain in a few words what is solid in that distinction and how it should be understood. I have already explained that there are things which depend rather on the play of imagination and on spontaneous impressions than on reason and that in such things we need to form a habit, as in bodily exercises and even in some mental exercises. That is where we need practice in order to succeed.
>
> There are other matters in which we can succeed through reason alone, aided by a few experiments or observations. We can even learn these at some other person's expense. We see excellent geniuses succeeding in their first attempt within the profession they apply themselves to, and by virtue of their natural judgment put old practitioners to shame. But that is not a usual occurrence, and this is how we must regard it.
>
> In all matters where it is possible for judgment aided by a few precepts to avoid application and experiment, we can always reduce all of a science with its subordinate parts to a few fundamentals or principles of discovery sufficient to determine all the questions which can arise in the circumstances by combining with the principles the exact method of the true Logic or art of discovery.
>
> But to succeed actually with this precept in practice we must distinguish among the things encountered; we must know whether decisions must be made immediately or if we have the leisure time to reflect with exactness. In the first case, the precepts combined with the method

> will not suffice, at least in the present state of the art of discovery, for I believe that if it were perfected as it should, and as it could be, that we might penetrate with ease a vein of thought which now takes too much time and explanation. Therefore, in order to obtain good decisions quickly in an embarrassing situation we have to have an extraordinary power of genius or long enough practice to make us think automatically and habitually what otherwise would require investigation by reason. But when we have the leisure time to reflect, I find that theory can forestall practice in all matters capable of precepts and reasons even if the latter are based on the foundation of experience provided that after the foundation is laid we can give a rational account of everything done. But this holds only if we know how to reflect methodically in order not to let anything escape of the circumstances to be accounted for.
>
> And even theory without practice will incomparably be superior to blind practice without theory, when the practitioner is obliged to face some situation quite different from those he has practiced, because not knowing the reasons for what he is doing, he will be stopped short, whereas he who possesses the reasons discovers the exceptions and the remedies.

An important element of the definition of music is that it is a form of Truth, a direct form of Truth between composer and listener. Indeed, it should be noted that the experiential nature of music, whose fundamental characteristic is the communication of feelings, is located in the right hemisphere of the brain, and it is one of the realities of the right hemisphere that it cannot lie. It is Truth personified, and Leibniz seemed to be aware of this. First, however, he addresses Truth in other forms of communication.

> Wit and imagination is better received than truth wholly dry. It goes well in discourse where you only seek to please; but at bottom, order and clearness excepted, all the art of rhetoric, all these artificial and figurative applications of words, serve only to insinuate false ideas, to excite the passions and seduce the judgment, so that they are nothing but pure frauds. Nevertheless this fallacious art is given the first rank and rewards. It is evident that men care but little for truth and much prefer to deceive and to be deceived. This is so true that I doubt not that what I have just said against this art is regarded as the result of an extreme audacity. For eloquence, like the fair sex, has charms too powerful to allow itself to be opposed.[58]

Later in this discussion, Leibniz makes a passing reference to this aspect of Truth in painting and in music. Painting, he says, makes the Truth vividly clear. Music makes it believable.

> It is as in painting and music, which are [also] abused, one of which often represents grotesque and even hurtful imaginations, and the other softens the heart, and the two amuse in vain; but they can be usefully employed, the one to render the truth clear, the other [music] to make it effective, and this last result must be also that of poetry which contains rhetoric and music.

58 Leibniz, *New Essays Concerning Human Understanding*, III, x, 34.

On the Perception of Music

The aspect of the perception of music which Leibniz seemed most aware of was its expression of Pleasure and Pain by means of consonance and dissonance. He first mentioned this in 1671, in a letter to Magnus Wedderkopf. Leibniz several times uses the word 'harmony' in the Platonic idiom meaning God's perfect organization of the world. Then, in suggesting that some evil must always accompany good, he observes that dissonance was a necessary part of pleasing music.

> Sins are good, that is, harmonious, taken along with their punishment or expiation. For there is no harmony except through contraries.[59]

In a record of a conversation with Baron Dobrzensky, in 1695, Leibniz mentions this again.

> I believe that God did create things in ultimate perfection, though it does not seem so to us considering the parts of the universe. It's a bit like what happens in music and painting, for shadows and dissonances truly enhance the other parts, and the wise author of such works derives such a great benefit for the total perfection of the work from these particular imperfections that it is much better to make a place for them than to attempt to do without them.[60]

In the following, Leibniz's first analogy would seem to us to suggest that one cannot judge the whole by a single part. When he continues with the subject of music, the analogy is not the same, but rather an analogy of the mixing of pleasure and pain in life.

> If we look at a very beautiful picture but cover up all of it but a tiny spot, what more will appear in it, no matter how closely we study it, indeed, all the more, the more closely we examine it, than a confused mixture of colors without beauty and without art. Yet when the covering is removed and the whole painting is viewed from a position that suits it, we come to understand that what seemed to be a thoughtless smear on the canvas has really been done with the highest artistry by the creator of the work. And what the eyes experience in painting is experienced by the ears in music. Great composers very often mix dissonances with harmonious chords to stimulate the hearer and to sting him, as it were, so that he becomes concerned about the outcome and is all the more pleased when everything is restored to order. Similarly we may enjoy trivial dangers or the experience of evils from the very sense they give us of our own power or our own happiness or our fondness for display … By the same principle it is insipid always to eat sweets; sharp, sour, and even bitter things should be mixed with them to excite the taste. He who has not tasted the bitter does not deserve the sweet; indeed, he will not appreciate it. This is the very law of enjoyment, that pleasure does not run an even course, for this produces aversion and makes us dull, not joyful.[61]

---

59 Leibniz, Letter to Magnus Wedderkopf (May, 1671), in Loemker, *Philosophical Papers and Letters*, 147.

60 Leibniz, *Philosophical Essays* [of Leibniz], 115.

61 Leibniz, 'On the Ultimate Origination of Things' (1697), in Loemker, *Philosophical Papers and Letters*, 489ff.

But one comment of 1704 is quite different. Here he seems to credit the production of Pleasure and Pain in music [*sound*] not to the composer and his materials, but to God.

> [When] the body produces pleasure or pain or the idea of a color or sound, we seem compelled to abandon our reason, to go beyond our own ideas, and to attribute this production solely to the *good pleasure* of our Creator.[62]

A very important aspect of the perception of music which must be mentioned is the genetic musical information which is carried into birth, a fact which modern clinical research has convincingly demonstrated. Since Leibniz was a great believer of genetic knowledge in general, we notice two passages which seem to suggest that perhaps he was thinking of this with respect to music as well. In the first passage he speaks of the unconscious memory of music, in the context of a discussion of genetic knowledge.

> It seems that our clever author claims that there is nothing *virtual* in us, and indeed nothing of which we are not always actually conscious; but he cannot take this rigorously, otherwise his opinion would be too paradoxical; since, moreover, acquired habits and the stores of our memory are not always perceived and do not even always come to our aid at need, although we often easily recall them to the mind upon some slight occasion which makes us remember them, just as we need only the beginning of a song to remember it.[63]

Some philosophers have suggested that genetic information contributes to our dreams.[64] We were thinking of this when we read a passage in Leibniz, who believed that the average man often dreamed of music, although if he were awake he would find it difficult to recreate this music.

> Noteworthy, too, is what Colomesius tells in his lesser works about a song which Gaulminus dreamed about the immortality of the soul. I do not believe that there is a mortal man who would not confess to me that there have often occurred to him while he dreamed, spontaneously and as if made in a moment, elegant visions and skillfully fashioned songs, verses, books, melodies, houses, gardens, depending upon his interests—visions which he could not have formed without effort while awake. Even such unnatural things as flying men and innumerable other monstrosities can be pictured more skillfully than a waking person can do, except with much thought. They are sought by the waker; they offer themselves to the sleeper.[65]

---

62 Leibniz, *New Essays Concerning Human Understanding*, IV, iii, 7.

63 Leibniz, Ibid., preface.

64 As for example, Carl Sagen who believed that the monsters which occur in the dreams of children, who have never seen monsters, represent genetic memory of the dinosaur period.

65 Leibniz, 'A Fragment on Dreams' (ca. 1666–1676), in Loemker, *Philosophical Papers and Letters*, 115.

On the Purposes of Music

Leibniz clearly believed the primary purpose of music was to provide pleasure. We can see interesting evidence of this in a passage where he is expressing the thought that a physician should not just concentrate on our pain, but should also study the source of our pleasures. 'To this end he should make use of such aids as characteristics, optics, *music*, perfumes, cooking ...'[66]

In a treatise of ca. 1695, our mathematician-philosopher finds pleasure in music in the rules of harmony. He must have regarded it as a paradox, that when one follows *these* rules too consistently the result may not be so good.

> The pleasures of sense which most closely approach pleasures of the mind, and are the most pure and the most certain, are that of music and that of symmetry, the former [being pleasure] of the ears, the latter of the eyes; for it is easy to understand the principles [*raisons*] of harmony, this perfection which gives us pleasure. The sole thing to be feared in this respect is to use it too often.[67]

In 1714, he returns to his thesis that, as we would say today, things of the right hemisphere are understood in a 'confused' manner in the left hemisphere. This seems to be the only problem for him in otherwise finding his pleasure in music in 'the numbers.'

> Even the pleasures of sense are reducible to intellectual pleasures, known confusedly. Music charms us, although its beauty consists only in the agreement of numbers and in the counting, which we do not perceive but which the soul nevertheless continues to carry out, of the beats or vibrations of sounding bodies which coincide at certain intervals. The pleasures which the eye finds in proportions are of the same nature, and those caused by other senses amount to something similar, although we may not be able to explain them so distinctly.[68]

Finally, there is only one place where Leibniz touches on the most important purpose of music, to move the feelings of the listener. In addition to his observation that music 'moves the mind,' perhaps we might regard it as another of his suggestions of genetic understanding of music, when Leibniz says the performance 'creates a sympathetic echo in us.' His comments on the relationship of rhythm and the emotions here are also interesting. This passage follows a discussion of happiness, joy, and pleasure which begins 'Wisdom is merely the science of happiness or that science which teaches us to achieve happiness.'

> We do not always observe wherein the perfection of pleasing things consists, or what kind of perfection within ourselves they serve, yet our feelings [*Gemüth*] perceive it, even though our

66 Leibniz, 'Elements of Natural Law' (1670–1671), in Ibid., 132.

67 Leibniz, 'On Felicity' (ca. 1694–1698), in Riley, *The Political Writings of Leibniz*, 83.

68 Leibniz, 'The Principles of Nature and of Grace, Based on Reason' (1714), in Loemker, *Philosophical Papers and Letters*, 641.

> understanding does not. We commonly say, 'There is something, I know not what, that pleases me in the matter.' This we call 'sympathy.' But those who seek the causes of things will usually find a ground for this and understand that there is something at the bottom of the matter which, though unnoticed, really appeals to us.
>
> Music is a beautiful example of this. Everything that emits a sound contains a vibration or a transverse motion such as we see in strings; thus everything that emits sounds gives off invisible impulses. When these are not confused, but proceed together in order but with a certain variation, they are pleasing; in the same way, we also notice certain changes from long to short syllables, and a coincidence of rhymes in poetry, which contain a silent music, as it were, and when correctly constructed are pleasant even without being sung. Drum beats, the beat and cadence of the dance, and other motions of this kind in measure and rule derive their pleasurableness from their order, for all order is an aid to the emotions. And a regular though invisible order is found also in the artfully created beats and motions of vibrating strings, pipes, bells, and indeed, even of the air itself, which these bring into uniform motion. Through our hearing, this creates a sympathetic echo in us, to which our animal spirits respond. This is why music is so well adapted to move our minds, even though this main purpose is not usually sufficiently noticed or sought after.[69]

On Opera

One of the interesting aspects of Baroque philosophy is the varying national responses to opera. While France enjoyed a vigorous philosophical debate, one finds almost no important literature by the Italians. The Germans, lacking the literary heritage of France and Italy, drew on their greater concern for moral principles. One early reference to opera, in 1624, during the tragic years of the Thirty Years' War, understandably finds its purpose as bringing joy and recollection of the more pleasant things of life to the viewer.

> Lyric poetry, a genre highly suited to music, requires in the first place a free and happy mind; unlike the other genres, it must be adorned with many beautiful maxims and precepts … Concerning its themes: it is capable of describing anything that can be contained in a brief composition — gallantries, dances, ballets, beautiful women, gardens, vineyards, eulogies of modesty, the vanities of life, etc., but above all exhortation to joy.[70]

One of the most valuable German contributions on the subject of opera is by the Hamburg librettist, Barthold Feind (1678–1721).

Reflecting the strict Lutheran environment, Feind disapproves of all attempts to portray religious subjects in opera. Likewise he finds in Hamburg no interest in the ancient Greek subjects.

69 Leibniz, 'On Wisdom' (ca. 1690–1698), in Ibid., 425ff.

70 Barthold Fend, *Gedanken von der Opera* (1708), quoted in Bianconi, *Music in the Seventeenth Century*, 225f.

> In Hamburg, the public is characterized by a notable aversion to the fabulous myths of the pagan deities; I would, indeed, be unable to cite a single example of this kind which had met success—convinced, however, as I am that Hamburg can boast not twenty persons with the ability to pass adequate judgment on the delicacy or virtue of an opera, and that frequently, of these twenty persons, not one can be seen at performances.[71]

Feind also believed that any form of low humor, especially clowns, mimes and Harlequins, was inappropriate for the operatic stage. Much to his disgust, however, these were not only popular but demanded by the Hamburg audience.

> Here, whatever seems vulgar and ridiculous to refined tastes now finds maximum approval—as occurred only last year on the occasion of *Le carnaval de Venise*, an opera of such absurdity and so full of nauseating and scornful gestures as to look like buffoonery. Yet this subject met with such applause as can hardly be believed.

With regard to what opera should be, Feind begins by defining opera as 'a splendid deception in which poetry and music (both sung and played) combine to the highest perfection.' He wishes to stress 'deception' for if one takes what occurs on the stage as *real*, then opera makes no sense. This, he finds, is a mistake made by some French philosophers, as for example Saint-Evremond whom he quotes.

> One feature of opera is so contrary to nature as to offend my imagination: that is, that the drama is sung from beginning to end, as though the characters represented therein had for some ridiculous reason agreed to discuss the various questions of their lives—the greatest and most trivial alike—in music.[72]

But opera is *not* real, Feind points out, 'one simply tries to *imitate* nature.' The value of having everything sung in opera, is because of the power of music to define, far beyond speech, the emotions.

> Nor do I believe that anyone can reasonably doubt the assertion that song is capable of imbuing a discourse with ten times more energy than any declamation or simple speech. What, indeed, is song if not a means of sustaining the discourse and voice with maximum energy and force?

In the communication of these emotions to the audience, the first responsibility falls to the poet, the librettist. In acknowledging the endless variety of emotions, Feind touches on the very reason why any 'doctrine of the affections,' equating specific emotions to specific musical figures, becomes impossible in practice.

> A philosopher, a noble and high-minded person, a man in love, in despair, in frenzy, a suspicious, jealous, faltering or irresolute man, etc.; each must be presented in accordance with his

71 Ibid., 312ff.

72 This entire passage is given under the chapter on French philosophy in Volume Seven of this series.

> own particular temperament and manner of speech. This, however, requires enormous ability and skill, in so far as hundreds—indeed thousands—of possibilities exist, variable in accordance with epoch, nations and traditions …

Regarding the duties of the poet, he continues,

> The words must interpret the heart of whoever is speaking and allow his temperament to shine through, the temperament of a character must correspond to his 'nature' and reflect the influence of the passion by which he is moved. The haughty will be boastful and arrogant, the magnanimous generous, a lover tender and charming, an old hand of the world sober and temperate, the historical tale of a messenger extended, etc. These are the essential elements; two or three scenes are sufficient to form an impression of the spirit and taste of a good poet. And since various characters appear in an opera, each different in passion and nature; since, moreover, each character must express his own will and actions in accordance with his nature and the laws of decorum: this is the principal reason why the opera has come to be seen as the highest yet also the most difficult of all poetic genres.

Beyond this, Feind stresses that the poet must write with the qualities of the specific singers intended in mind, for it will be through them that the emotions are communicated to the audience. The portrayal of an emotion improves in relation to its naturalness in presentation and if effectively done will provoke 'wrath, terror, hope, fury or pity in the beholder.' He cites, in this regard, English audiences crying bitterly during Shakespeare plays and French ladies crying during the plays of Racine and Corneille.

On Music for a World's Fair

Finally, in a treatise of 1675, called 'An Odd Thought Concerning a New Sort of Exhibition,'[73] Leibniz outlines an interesting proposal for a world's fair. Although nothing on this scale would be held until the nineteenth century, it is interesting to read his long list of curiosities which he recommends be exhibited. In addition to Magic Lanterns, artificial meteors, unusual and rare animals, races between artificial horses and 'the man from England who eats fire, if he is still alive,' he lists 'Rare instruments of Music' and 'Instruments that play by themselves.' In addition he recommends there be concerts, galleries of paintings, conferences and lectures for the public, with the entire exposition concluding with an opera. As for the public who would attend, Leibniz observes,

> All respectable people would want to see these curiosities in order to be able to talk about them; and even ladies of fashion would want to be taken there, and more than once.

73 This treatise can be found in Wiener, *Leibniz Selections*, 585ff.

Finally, he makes an appeal for the private support which would be necessary to make this great exhibition a reality.

> Perhaps some curious Princes and distinguished persons would contribute some of their wealth for the public satisfaction and the growth of the sciences. In short, everybody would be aroused and, so to speak, awakened; and the enterprise might have consequences as fine and as important as could be imagined, which would some day perhaps be admired by posterity.

13 JOHANNES KEPLER AND THE 'MUSIC OF THE SPHERES'

THE HEAVENLY BODIES are not only man's most ancient objects of wonder, but wonders which connect distant generations. The halos we see in even recent religious paintings are nothing more than remnants of the worship of the sun by our most remote ancestors. In the most ancient Western literature, the early Greeks have peopled the sky with the musicians of their even more remote myths. Their discovery of the lower relationships of the overtone series suggested a key to the organization of the nearest heavenly objects and, consequently, the possibility of music of the spheres.

For the next twenty centuries philosophers would discuss the music of the spheres, and offer theories why we can't hear this music. Two important discoveries in the seventeenth century seemed to dampen enthusiasm for this idea. First, when Copernicus proved the Earth was in orbit, then the ideal place to hear this music became the Sun. Second, the development of the modern telescope, which also occurred at this time, revealed such an incomprehensibly larger number of heavenly bodies that all earlier theories of cosmic organization had to be abandoned. Nevertheless seventeenth-century writers, including brilliant intellectuals, still mentioned the 'music of the spheres.' Among them, Kepler, one of the most extraordinary mathematicians of all time, has left the most extended account.

Johannes Kepler (1571–1630) began his career as a teacher of Latin and mathematics in Graz. Soon after marrying, he lost his position when all Protestant teachers were ordered out of Styria by the new archduke, Ferdinand. He was saved by an invitation to become an assistant to the astronomer, Tycho Brahe, in Prague. Thereafter he made important contributions, including the discovery that planetary orbits are elliptical and a theory of the cause of planetary motion which gave birth to Newton's theory of gravitation.

Kepler's interest in astronomy first expressed itself in a small book, *Cosmographic Mystery* (1596) which attempted to argue that Copernican theory was not inconsistent with Scripture. As first and foremost a mathematician, Kepler's basic attraction to the writings of Copernicus were due to his mathematical explanations for what had previously been rather arbitrary characteristics of planetary movement. But Kepler, like Albert Einstein centuries later, instinctively wanted to also believe in some cosmic harmony (in the Platonic sense of order) by which all things could be explained. His attempts to discover this through pure mathematics, as for example in the arithmetical relations of the radii of the planetary orbits and in the trigonometrical relation between a planet's relationship to the Sun and the power needed to propel it, were frustrating. He became convinced that the answer lay in geometry and it was a belief he could never give up. He imagined that the five solids of Greek geometry, the cube, tetrahedron, octahedron, dodecahedron and icosahedron[1] were somehow fundamental to God's design of the planetary system.

In his *New Astronomy* (1609) Kepler established the precise shape of the orbits, but these findings expressed only individual movements and brought him no closer in his search for a unified harmony. A turning point for Kepler came when he realized that in his purely geometrical and mathematical explanations he had given no consideration to *time*. It was the realization that time must be a factor in planetary design which caused him to turn his attention to *musical* harmony (which also moves through time), eventually resulting in his *Harmony of the Universe* (1619). He now began to feel that music might illustrate the logic of planetary geometry, as for example in a correspondence he saw between the overtones of a vibrating string and the division of a circle into equal arcs.

In the *Harmony of the Universe*, Book One discusses the ordering of polygons with various kinds of quantities, based on the tenth book of Euclid's *Elements*. In Book Two he attempts to illustrate how regular polygons might be fitted together to cover an area with no overlapping and no gaps. Book Three is devoted to the elements of music and the relationship of music to man.[2] The pleasure of music, says Kepler, is not merely a stimulation of one of our senses.

> The souls of men rejoice in those very proportions that God employed in the Creation, wherever they find them, whether by pure reflection, or by the intervention of the senses in matters subject to the senses, or (without the exercise of reason) by an occult, innate instinct.[3]

Music, Kepler contends, reveals to us an order which is the principle also of our own being. The task of the astronomer is to correlate the harmony within with the harmony without. In the same way, he believed mathematical insights are only discovered, not invented. It follows that God, when making man, implanted in him consciousness of the fundamental harmonies which served as a pattern in the creation of the world. In Book Four, Kepler writes,

> Geometry, co-eternal with the Divine thought before all things began (indeed, it *is* God Himself, for what is in God that is not God?), furnished God with models for fashioning the world and passed over into man with the Divine image: he did not receive it through the eyes.[4]

---

1 The tetrahedron is bounded by four equilateral triangles, the octahedron is bounded by eight equilateral triangles, the dodecahedron is bounded by twelve regular pentagons and the icosahedron is bounded by twenty equilateral triangles.

2 John Hawkins, in his *General History of Music* (1776), summarizes Book Three under his article on Kepler. Here, in Kepler's discussion of forms of government, he equates Democracy with arithmetic, Aristocracy with geometry and Monarchy with music [harmony].

3 Quoted in Angus Armitage, *John Kepler* (New York: Roy Publishers, 1966), 147ff.

4 Ibid., 148. Kepler was one of several important seventeenth-century philosophers who speculated about some form of genetic knowledge.

It is in Book Five that Kepler summarizes his theories of the 'Music of the Sphere' and the relationship of this music to planetary mechanics. He begins by reflecting on the many years of study which have brought him to this understanding, not failing to pay due tribute to those past and present who deserved recognition. It is important to remember that Kepler was about to set forth in considerable mathematical detail theories which were most unorthodox, and at a time when the idea that the Earth moved, and was not the center of the universe, was as yet by no means commonly believed. It was for this reason that Kepler concludes his introductory remarks by saying that he had decided to get up his courage and publish the book anyway. It's OK, he says, if it goes neglected for another hundred years—after all, God waited six thousand years[5] for someone [Kepler] to come along to discover the musical relationships of the cosmos.

> As regards that which I prophesied two and twenty years ago (especially that the five regular solids are found between the celestial spheres), as regards that of which I was firmly persuaded in my own mind before I had seen Ptolemy's *Harmonies*, as regards that which I promised my friends in the title of this fifth book before I was sure of the thing itself, that which, sixteen years ago, in a published statement, I insisted must be investigated, for the sake of which I spent the best part of my life in astronomical speculations, visited Tycho Brahe, and took up resident at Prague: finally, as God the Best and Greatest, Who had inspired my mind and aroused my great desire, prolonged my life and strength of mind and furnished the other means through the liberality of the two Emperors and the nobles of this province of Austria-on-the-Anisana: after I had discharged my astronomical duties as much as sufficed, finally, I say, I brought it to light and found it to be truer than I had even hoped, and I discovered among the celestial movements the full nature of harmony, in its due measure, together with all its parts unfolded in Book III—not in that mode wherein I had conceived it in my mind (this is not least in my joy) but in a very different mode which is also very excellent and very perfect. There took place in this intervening time, wherein the very laborious reconstruction of the movements held me in suspense, an extraordinary augmentation of my desire and incentive for the job, a reading of the *Harmonies* of Ptolemy, which had been sent to me in manuscript by John George Herwald, Chancellor of Bavaria, a very distinguished man and of a nature to advance philosophy and every type of learning. There, beyond my expectations and with the greatest wonder, I found approximately the whole third book given over to the same consideration of celestial harmony, fifteen hundred years ago. But indeed astronomy was far from being of age as yet; and Ptolemy, in an unfortunate attempt, could make others subject to despair, as being one who, like Scipio in Cicero, seemed to have recited a pleasant Pythagorean dream rather than to have aided philosophy. But both the crudeness of the ancient philosophy and this exact agreement in our meditations, down to the last hair, over an interval of fifteen centuries, greatly strengthened me in getting on with the job. For what need is there of many men? The very nature of things, in order to reveal herself to mankind, was at work in the different interpreters of different ages, and was the finger of God—to use the Hebrew expression; and here, in the minds of two men, who had wholly given themselves up to the contemplation of nature, there was the same conception

5 Until the nineteenth century many believed that God created the Earth in 4004 BC.

as to the configuration of the world, although neither had been the other's guide in taking this route. But now since the first light eight months ago, since broad day[light] three months ago, and since the sun of my wonderful speculation has shone fully a very few days ago: nothing holds me back. I am free to give myself up to the sacred madness, I am free to taunt mortals with the frank confession that I am stealing the golden vessels of the Egyptians, in order to build of them a temple for my God, far from the territory of Egypt. If you pardon me, I shall rejoice; if you are enraged, I shall bear up. The die is cast, and I am writing the book—whether to be read by my contemporaries or by posterity matters not. Let it await its reader for a hundred years, if God Himself has been ready for His contemplator for six thousand years.[6]

In the first three chapters, Kepler introduces and defines the terms and concepts which are fundamental to his theories which follow. Among these he finds it necessary to point out that he is working from the premise of Copernicus that it is the Earth which moves, and not the Sun. He admits this is a proposition still not generally accepted.

But because the thing is still new among the mass of the intelligentsia [*apud vulgus studiosortum*], and the doctrine that the Earth is one of the planets and moves among the stars around a motionless sun sounds very absurd to the ears of most of them …[7]

He reminds the reader of his study of the relationship of the five basic geometric figures and the planetary system and admits that he could not quite make them fit.

Let the reader recall from my *Cosmographic Mystery* which I published twenty-two years ago, that the number of the planets or circular routes around the sun was taken by the very wise Founder from the five regular solids, concerning which Euclid, so many ages ago, wrote his book which is called the *Elements* in that it is built up out of a series of propositions. But it has been made clear in the second book of this work that there cannot be more regular bodies, i.e., that regular plane figures cannot fit together in a solid more than five times.

As regards the ratio of the planetary orbits, the ratio between two neighboring planetary orbits is always of such a magnitude that it is easily apparent that each and every one of them approaches the single ratio of the spheres of one of the five regular solids, namely, that of the sphere circumscribing to the sphere inscribed in the figure. Nevertheless it is not wholly equal, as I once dared to promise concerning the final perfection of astronomy.[8]

Since Kepler admits the concept of geometric figures is not sufficient to explain the planetary organization, it follows there must be other principles at work. This, of course, will turn out to be music.

6 Johannes Kepler, *Harmonies of the World*, V, trans. Charles Glenn Wallis, in *Great Books* (Chicago: Encyclopaedia Britannica, 1939), XVI, 1009ff.

7 Ibid., 1015.

8 Ibid., 1016ff.

> Wherefore it is clear that the very ratios of the planetary intervals from the sun have not been taken from the regular solids alone. For the Creator, who is the very source of geometry and, as Plato wrote, 'practices eternal geometry,' does not stray from his own archetype. And indeed that very thing could be inferred from the fact that all the planets change their intervals throughout fixed periods of time, in such fashion that each has two marked intervals from the sun, a greatest and a least [formed by the elliptical nature of the orbits]; and a fourfold comparison of the intervals from the sun is possible between two planets: the comparison can be made between either the greatest, or the least, or the contrary intervals most remote from one another, or the contrary intervals nearest together. In this way the comparisons made two by two between neighboring planets are twenty in number, although on the contrary there are only five regular solids. But it is consonant that if the Creator had any concern for the ratio of the spheres in general, He would also have had concern for the ratio which exists between the varying intervals of the single planets specifically and that the concern is the same in both cases and the one is bound up with the other. If we ponder that, we will comprehend that for setting up the diameters and eccentricities conjointly, there is need of more principles, outside the five regular solids.[9]

In Chapter Four, 'In What Things Having to do with the Planetary Movements have the Harmonic Consonances been Expressed by the Creator?,' Kepler first studies the distances from the sun, the periodic times, the diurnal eccentric arcs, the diurnal delays in those arcs, the angles at the sun and the diurnal arcs apparent to those as if one's point of view were from the sun. From this study, and in particular the aphelion and perihelion of each planet, he arrives at some preliminary, if not quite satisfactory, relationships with music.

> Therefore the extreme intervals of no one planet come near consonances except those of Mars and Mercury.
>
> But if you compare the extreme intervals of different planets with one another, some harmonic light begins to shine. For the extreme diverging intervals of Saturn and Jupiter make slightly more than the octave; and the converging, a mean between the major and minor sixths. So the diverging extremes of Jupiter and Mars embrace approximately the double octave; and the converging, approximately the fifth and the octave. But the diverging extremes of the Earth and Mars embrace somewhat more than the major sixth; the converging, an augmented fourth. In the next couple, the Earth and Venus, there is again the same augmented fourth between the converging extremes; but we lack any harmonic ratio between the diverging extremes: for it is less than the semi-octave (so to speak), i.e., less than the square root of the ratio 2:1. Finally, between the diverging extremes of Venus and Mercury there is a ratio slightly less than the octave compounded with the minor third; between the converging there is a slightly augmented fifth.
>
> Accordingly, although one interval was somewhat removed from harmonic ratios, this success was an invitation to advance further. Now my reasonings were as follows: First, in so far as these intervals are lengths without movement, they are not fittingly examined for harmonic ratios, because movement is more properly the subject of consonances, by reason of speed and slowness. Second, inasmuch as these same intervals are the diameters of the spheres, it is believable that the ratio of the five regular solids applied proportionally is more dominant in them, because

9 Ibid., 1017ff.

> the ratio of the geometrical solid bodies to the celestial spheres … is the same as the ratio of the plane figures which may be inscribed in a circle (these figures engender the consonances) to the celestial circles of movements and the other regions wherein the movements take place. Therefore, if we are looking for consonances, we should look for them not in these intervals in so far as they are the semidiameters of spheres but in them in so far as they are the measures of the movements, that is in the movements themselves.[10]

Before going farther, Kepler pauses to consider the fundamental problem which had engaged so many earlier philosophers who had written on the subject of the 'Music of the Spheres,' that is, if there are musical pitches produced by the planets, why can't we hear them? Of all the explanations offered by earlier philosophers, Kepler is unique in transferring the experience to another sense.

> But whose good will it be to have harmonies between the journeys, or who will perceive these harmonies? For there are two things which disclose to us harmonies in natural things: either light or sound: light apprehended through the eyes or hidden senses proportioned to the eyes, and sound through the ears. The mind seizes upon these forms and, whether by instinct (on which Book Four speaks profusely) or by astronomical or harmonic ratiocination, discerns the concordant from the discordant. Now there are no sounds in the heavens, nor is the movement so turbulent that any noise is made by the rubbing against the ether. Light remains. If light has to teach these things about planetary journeys, it will teach either the eyes or a sensorium analogous to the eyes and situated in a definite place; and it seems that sense-perception must be present there in order that light of itself may immediately teach. Therefore there will be sense-perception in the total world, namely in order that the movements of all the planets may be presented to sense-perceptions at the same time. For that former route—from observations through the longest detours of geometry and arithmetic, through the ratios of the spheres and the other things which must be learned first, down to the journeys which have been exhibited—is too long for any natural instinct, for the sake of moving which it seems reasonable that the harmonies have been introduced.[11]

While in this formal work, written for posterity, Kepler seems to avoid admitting any possibility of hearing these pitches, in a private letter to Mästlin, in 1599, he adds, 'but fill the heavens with air and in very truth music will sound forth.'[12]

Kepler now changes his approach.

> I concluded rightly that the true journeys of the planets through the ether should be dismissed, and that we should turn our eyes to the apparent diurnal arcs, according as they are all apparent from one definite and marked place in the world—namely, from the solar body itself.

10 Ibid., 1026ff.

11 Ibid., 1030.

12 Quoted in Armitage, *John Kepler*, 150.

He now determines the pitch by the angle that the planet would appear to describe in one day as estimated by an observer located on the Sun. These angular velocities were severally divided by arbitrary powers of two so as to reduce them to the same order of magnitude and to bring the corresponding notes all within the compass of a single octave. The ratio between any two of these angular velocities, so reduced, determined the musical interval between the corresponding notes and indicated whether that interval represented one of the seven accepted concords.[13] Now he begins to achieve more satisfactory results (if we are willing to overlook some minor problems!).

> Accordingly, perfect consonances are found: between the converging movements of Saturn and Jupiter, the octave; between the converging movements of Jupiter and Mars, the octave and minor third approximately; between the converging movements of Mars and the Earth, the fifth; between their perihelial, the minor sixth; between the diverging or even between the perihelial, the double octave: whence … it seems that the residual very slight discrepancy can be discounted, especially in the movements of Venus and Mercury.
>
> But you will note that where there is no perfect major consonance, as between Jupiter and Mars, there alone have I found the placing of the solid figure to be approximately perfect, since the perihelial distance of Jupiter is approximately three times the aphelial distance of Mars, in such fashion that this pair of planets strives after the perfect consonance in the intervals which it does not have in the movements.
>
> You will note, furthermore, that the major planetary ratio of Saturn and Jupiter exceeds the harmonic, viz., the triple, by approximately the same quantity as belongs to Venus; and the common major ratio of the converging and diverging movements of Mars and the Earth are diminished by approximately the same. You will note thirdly that, roughly speaking, in the upper [most distant] planets the consonances are established between the converging movements, but in the lower planets, between movements in the same field. And note fourthly that between the aphelial movements of Saturn and the Earth there are approximately five octaves; for one thirty-second of 57'3' is 1'47', although the aphelial movement of Saturn is 1'46'.
>
> Furthermore, a great distinction exists between the consonances of the single planets which have been unfolded and the consonances of the planets in pairs. For the former cannot exist at the same moment of time, while the latter absolutely can; because the same planet, moving at its aphelion, cannot be at the same time at the opposite perihelion too, but of two planets one can be at its aphelion and the other at its perihelion at the same moment of time. And so the ratio of plain-song or monody, which we call choral music and which alone was known to the ancients, to polyphony—called figured song, the invention of the latest generations—is the same as the ratio of the consonances which the single planets designate to the consonances of the planes taken together … In the following chapters, the planets taken together and the figured modern music will be shown to do similar things.[14]

13 This summary is given in Ibid.

14 Kepler, *Harmonies of the World*, 1033ff

Now satisfied that he had discovered a natural correspondence between planetary movement and the relationship of pitches in the overtone series, in Chapter Five Kepler turns his attention to the search for a natural cosmic scale.

> So now, after the discovery of the consonances [*harmoniis*] which God Himself has embodied in the world, we must consequently see whether those single consonances stand so separate that they have no kinship with the rest, or whether all are in concord with one another. Notwithstanding it is easy to conclude, without any further inquiry, that those consonances were fitted together by the highest prudence in such fashion that they move one another about within one frame, so to speak, and do not jolt one another out of it; since indeed we see that in such a manifold comparison of the same terms there is no place where consonances do not occur.[15]

Before beginning to attempt to construct scale-like patterns, Kepler first makes two qualifications: he will make necessary adjustments to bring all notes into a single octave and he will ignore (for now) all pitch discrepancies less than a half-step. Working with the orbits at perihelion and aphelion, and turning a blind eye to some minor problems, he begins his first effort at scale building as follows:

> Now the aphelial movement of Saturn at its slowest, i.e., the slowest movement, marks G, the lowest pitch in the system with the number 1'46'. Therefore the aphelial movement of the Earth will make the same pitch, but five octaves higher, because its number is 1'47', and who wants to quarrel about one second in the aphelial movement of Saturn? But let us take it into account, nevertheless; the difference will not be greater than 106:107, which is less than a comma. If you add 27', one quarter of this 1'47', the sum will be 2'14', although the perihelial movement of Saturn has 2'15'; similarly the aphelial movement of Jupiter, but one octave higher …
>
> ……
>
> Accordingly all the notes of the major scale … are marked by all the extreme movements of the planets, except the perihelial movements of Venus and the Earth and the aphelial movement of Mercury, whose number, 2'23', approaches the note *c* sharp. For subtract from the 2'41' of *d* one sixteenth or 10', and 2'30' remains for the note *c* sharp. Thus only the perihelial movement of Venus and the Earth are missing from this scale.

Kepler notates the above as the pitches for a G major scale, with both a C and C-sharp. In a following effort, beginning with G at 2'15', the aphelial movement of Saturn, he arrives at a scale based on G, but with two flats. From these two efforts he concludes,

> Accordingly you won't wonder any more that a very excellent order of sounds or pitches in a musical system or scale has been set up by men, since you see that they are doing nothing else in this business except to play the apes of God the Creator and to act out, as it were, a certain drama of the ordination of the celestial movements.[16]

15 Ibid., 1035.

16 Ibid., 1038.

Following a third attempt at scale construction, Kepler constructs scale fragments for each planet, based on the eccentricity of the orbit. He finds Saturn produces G, A, B, A, G; Jupiter, G, A, B♭, A, G; Mars, F, G, A, B♭, C, B♭, A, G, F; Earth, G, A♭, G; Mercury, a C major scale; the Moon, G, A, B, C, B, A, G; and Venus, which produces only E's. From this it was evident to Kepler that the Church modes must have had their origin in the heavens.

> The signature of two accidentals in a common staff and the formation of the skeletal outline of the octave by the inclusion of a definite concordant interval are a certain first beginning of the distinction of Tones or Modes. Therefore the musical Modes have been distributed among the planets. But I know that for the formation and determination of distinct Modes many things are requisite, which belong to human song, as containing a distinct [order of] intervals …
>
> But the harmonist will be free to choose his opinion as to which Mode each planet expresses as its own, since the extremes have been assigned to it here. From among the familiar Modes, I should give to Saturn the Seventh or Eighth, because if you place its key-note at *G*, the perihelial movement ascends to *b*; to Jupiter, the First or Second Mode, because its aphelial movement has been fitted to *G* and its perihelial movement arrives at *b* flat; to Mars, the Fifth or Sixth Mode, not only because Mars comprehends approximately the perfect fifth, which interval is common to all the Modes, but principally because when it is reduced with the others to a common system, it attains *c* with its perihelial movement and touches *f* with its aphelial, which is the key-note of the Fifth or Sixth Mode; I should give the Third or Fourth Mode to the Earth, because its movement revolves within a semitone, while the first interval of those Modes is a semitone; but to Mercury will belong indifferently all the Modes or Tones on account of the greatness of its range; to Venus, clearly none on account of the smallness of its range; but on account of the common system the Third and Fourth Mode, because with reference to the other planets it occupies *e*. (The Earth sings MI, FA, MI so that you may infer even from the syllables that in this our domicile MIsery and FAmine obtain).[17]

Kepler appears to have been thinking of his deductions at about this level of complexity, when he mentions the Music of the Spheres in a letter to Wackher von Wackenfels.

> We and the entire choir of planets revolve around the Sun, subservient to him, as it were, as his own family and possession … As for the heavenly tones, they are to be reproduced in the usual manner of notation. The lowest note is always the aphelion, the highest the perihelion … Indeed, the tones of the individual [planets] are thus distinct, of course, with respect to the pitches, varying in height, of the musical scale.[18]

If the orbits of the planets produce pitches, scale patterns and implications of mode, then, Kepler suggests, it must follow that in the interaction of these orbits, harmony is produced. But some of the harmonies can only rarely be heard, as in the case of that produced by the coincidence of the apsides of Saturn and Jupiter, which occurs only once each eight hundred

17 Ibid., 1040.

18 Quoted in Eric Werner, 'The Last Pythagorean Musician: Johannes Kepler,' in *Aspects of Medieval and Renaissance Music*, ed. Jan LaRue (New York: Norton, 1966), 869.

years. Indeed, perhaps the entire harmony was heard only at the moment of the creation of the universe. If that were the case, and one could analyze harmonically and mathematically back to this sound, one could discover the precise date of the creation.

> But now, Urania, there is need for louder sound while I climb along the harmonic scale of the celestial movements to higher things where the true archetype of the fabric of the world is kept hidden. Follow after, ye modern musicians, and judge the thing according to your arts, which were unknown to antiquity. Nature, which is never not lavish of herself, after a lying-in of two thousand years, has finally brought you forth in these last generations, the first true images of the universe. By means of your concords of various voices, and through your ears, she has whispered to the human mind, the favorite daughter of God the Creator, how she exists in the innermost bosom.
>
> (Shall I have committed a crime if I ask the single composers of this generation for some artistic motet instead of this epigraph? The Royal Psalter and the other Holy Books can supply a text suited for this. But alas for you! No more than six are in concord in the heavens. For the moon sings here monody separately, like a dog sitting on the Earth. Compose the melody; I, in order that the book may progress, promise that I will watch carefully over the six parts. To him who more properly expresses the celestial music described in this work, Clio will give a garland, and Urania will betroth Venus his bride.)
>
> It has been unfolded above what harmonic ratios two neighboring planets would embrace in their extreme movements. But it happens very rarely that two, especially the slowest, arrive at their extreme intervals at the same time. For example, the apsides of Saturn and Jupiter are about 81 degrees apart. Accordingly, while this distance between them measures out the whole zodiac by definite twenty-year leaps, eight hundred years pass by, and nonetheless the leap which concludes the eighth century, does not carry precisely to the very apsides; and if it digresses much further, another eight hundred years must be awaited, that a more fortunate leap than that one may be sought; and the whole route must be repeated as many times as the measure of digression is contained in the length of one leap. Moreover, the other single pairs of planets have periods like that, although not so long. But meanwhile there occur also other consonances of two planets, between movements whereof not both are extremes but one or both are intermediate; and those consonances exist as it were in different tunings [*tensionibus*]. For, because Saturn tends from *G* to *b*, and slightly further, and Jupiter from *b* to *d* and further; therefore between Jupiter and Saturn there can exist the following consonances, over and above the octave: the major and minor third and the perfect fourth, either one of the thirds through the tuning which maintains the amplitude of the remaining one, but the perfect fourth through the amplitude of a major whole tone. For there will be a perfect fourth not merely from *G* of Saturn to *cc* of Jupiter but also from *A* of Saturn to *dd* of Jupiter and through all the intermediates between the *G* and *A* of Saturn and the *cc* and *dd* of Jupiter. But the octave and the perfect fifth exist solely at the points of the apsides. But Mars, which got a greater interval as its own, received it in order that it should also make an octave with the upper planets through some amplitude of tuning. Mercury received an interval great enough for it to set up almost all the consonances with all the planets within one of its periods, which is not longer than the space of three months. On the other hand, the Earth, and Venus much more so, on account of the smallness of their inter-

> vals, limit the consonances, which they form not merely with the others but with one another especially, to visible fewness. But if three planets are to concord in one harmony, many periodic returns are to be awaited; nevertheless there are many consonances, so that they may so much the more easily take place, while each nearest consonance follows after its neighbor, and very often threefold consonances are seen to exist between Mars, the Earth, and Mercury. But the consonances of four planets now begin to be scattered throughout centuries, and those of five planets throughout thousands of years.
>
> But that all six should be in concord has been fenced about by the longest intervals of time; and I do not know whether it is absolutely impossible for this to occur twice by precise evolving or whether that points to a certain beginning of time, from which every age of the world has flowed.[19]

For Kepler it followed logically that in this cosmic harmony, even if it were only an intellectual reality and not actually heard, could be found the origin of polyphony.

> Accordingly the movements of the heavens are nothing except a certain everlasting polyphony (intelligible, not audible) with dissonant tunings, like certain syncopations or cadences (wherewith men imitate these natural dissonances), which tends towards fixed and prescribed clauses—the single clauses having six terms (like voices)—and which marks out and distinguishes the immensity of time with those notes. Hence it is no longer a surprise that man, the ape of his Creator, should finally have discovered the art of singing polyphonically, which was unknown to the ancients, namely in order that he might play the everlastingness of all created time in some short part of an hour by means of an artistic concord of many voices and that he might to some extent taste the satisfaction of God the Workman with His own works, in that very sweet sense of delight elicited from this music which imitates God.[20]

Given this hypothesis of the origin of polyphony, it was natural for Kepler to next think of the planets in terms of the four traditional vocal ranges.

> I do not know why but nevertheless this wonderful congruence with human song has such a strong effect upon me that I am compelled to pursue this part of the comparison, also, even without any solid natural cause. For those same properties which … custom ascribed to the bass, and nature gave legal grounds for so doing, are somehow possessed by Saturn and Jupiter in the heavens; and we find those of the tenor in Mars, those of the alto are present in the Earth and Venus, and those of the soprano are possessed by Mercury, if not with equality of intervals, at least proportionately.[21]

Now, in Chapter Nine which is entitled, 'The Genesis of the Eccentricities in the Single Planets from the Procurement of the Consonances between their Movements,' Kepler sum-

19 Kepler, *Harmonies of the World*, 1040ff.

20 Ibid., 1048.

21 Ibid., 1049.

marizes his contentions and assigns them a meaning within a theological context, which is obviously intended, in part, to protect himself. And for further protection, he offers a prayer.

> Accordingly, since we see that the universal harmonies of all six planets cannot take place by chance, especially in the case of the extreme movements, all of which we see concur in the universal harmonies—except two, which concur in harmonies closest to the universal—and since much less can it happen by chance that all the pitches of the system of the octave by means of harmonic divisions are designated by the extreme planetary movements, but least of all that the very subtle business of the distinction of the celestial consonances into two modes, the major and minor, should be the outcome of chance, without the special attention of the Artisan: accordingly it follows that the Creator, the source of all wisdom, the everlasting approver of order, the eternal and superexistent geyser of geometry and harmony, it follows, I say, that He, the Artisan of the celestial movements Himself, should have conjoined to the five regular solids the harmonic ratios arising from the regular plane figures, and out of both classes should have formed one most perfect archetype of the heavens: in order that in this archetype, as through the five regular solids the shapes of the spheres shine through on which the six planets are carried, so too through the consonances, which are generated from the plane figures, and deduced from them in Book III, the measures of the eccentricities in the single planets might be determined so as to proportion the movements of the planetary bodies; and in order that there should be one tempering together of the ratios and the consonances, and that the greater ratios of the spheres should yield somewhat to the lesser ratios of the eccentricities necessary for procuring the consonances, and conversely those in especial of the harmonic ratios which had a greater kinship with each solid figure should be adjusted to the planets—in so far as that could be effected by means of consonances. And in order that, finally, in that way both the ratios of the spheres and the eccentricities of the single planets might be born of the archetype simultaneously, while from the amplitude of the spheres and the bulk of the bodies the periodic times of the single planets might result.
>
> While I struggle to bring forth this process into the light of human intellect by means of the elementary form customary with geometers, may the Author of the heavens be favorable, the Father of intellects, the Bestower of mortal senses, Himself immortal and superblessed, and may He prevent the darkness of our mind from bringing forth in this work anything unworthy of His Majesty, and may He effect that we, the imitators of God by the help of the Holy Ghost, should rival the perfection of His works in sanctity of life, for which He choose His church throughout the Earth and, by the blood of His Son, cleansed it from sins, and that we should keep at a distance all the discords of enmity, all contentions, rivalries, anger, quarrels, dissensions, sects, envy, provocations, and irritations arising through mocking speech and the other works of the flesh; and that along with myself, all who possess the spirit of Christ will not only desire but will also strive by deeds to express and make sure their calling, by spurning all crooked morals of all kinds which have been veiled and painted over with the cloak of zeal or of the love of truth or of singular erudition or modesty over against contentious teachers, or with any other showy garment. Holy Father, keep us safe in the concord of our love for one another, that we may be one, just as Thou art one with Thy Son, Our Lord, and with the Holy Ghost, and just as through the sweetest bonds of harmonies Thou hast made all Thy works one; and that from the bringing of Thy people into concord the body of Thy Church may be built up in the Earth, as Thou didst erect the heavens themselves out of harmonies.

Now Kepler provides a step-by-step summary of his logic and his contentions.

Prior Reasons

I. Axiom. *It is reasonable that, wherever in general it could have been done, all possible harmonies were due to have been set up between the extreme movements of the planets taken singly and by twos, in order that that variety should adorn the world.*

II. Axiom. *The five intervals between the six spheres of some extent were due to correspond to the ratio of the geometrical spheres which inscribe and circumscribe the five regular solids, and in the same order which is natural to the figures.*

III. Proposition. *The intervals between the Earth and Mars, and between the Earth and Venus, were due to be least, in proportion to their spheres, and thereby approximately equal; middling and approximately equal between Saturn and Jupiter, and between Venus and Mercury; but greatest between Jupiter and Mars.*

IV. Axiom. *All the planets ought to have their eccentricities diverse, no less than a movement in latitude, and in proportion to those eccentricities also their distances from the sun, the source of movement, diverse.*

V. Proposition. *Two diverse consonances were to have been attributed to each pair of neighboring planets.*

VI. Proposition. *The two least consonances, 4:5 and 5:6, do not have a place between two planets.*

VII. Proposition. *The consonance of the perfect fourth can have no place between the converging movements of two planets, unless the ratios of the extreme movements proper to them are, if compounded, more than a perfect fifth.*

VIII. Proposition. *The consonances 1:2 and 1:3, ie., the octave and the octave plus a fifth were due to Saturn and Jupiter.*

IX. Proposition. *The private ratios of the extreme movements of Saturn and Jupiter compounded were due to be approximately 2:3, a perfect fifth.*

X. Axiom. *When choice is free in other respects, the private ratio of movements, which is prior in nature or of a more excellent mode or even which is greater, is due to the higher planet.*

XI. Proposition. *The ratio of the aphelial movement of Saturn to the perihelial was due to be 4:5, a major third, but that of Jupiter's movements 5:6, a minor third.*

XII. Proposition. *The great consonance of 1:4, the double octave, was due to Venus and Mercury.*

XIII. Proposition. *The greater consonance of approximately 1:8, the triple octave, and the smaller consonance of 5:24, the minor third and double octave, were due to the extreme movements of Jupiter and Mars.*

XIV. Proposition. *The private ratio of the extreme movements of Mars was due to be greater than 3:4, the perfect fourth, and approximately 18:25.*

XV. Proposition. *The consonances 2:3, the fifth; 5:8, the minor sixth; and 3:5, the major sixth were to have been distributed among the converging movements of Mars and the Earth, the Earth and Venus, Venus and Mercury, and in that order.*

XVI. Proposition. *The private ratios of movements of Venus and Mercury, if compounded together, were due to make approximately 5:12.*

XVII. Proposition. *The consonance between the diverging movements of Venus and the Earth could not be less than 5:12.*

Posterior Reasons

XVIII. Axiom. *The universal consonances of movements were to be constituted by a tempering of the six movements, especially in the case of the extreme movements.*

XIX. Axiom. *The universal consonances had to come out the same within a certain latitude of movements, namely, in order that they should occur the more frequently.*

XX. Axiom. *As the most natural division of the kinds of consonances is into major and minor ... so the universal consonances of both kinds had to be procured between the extreme movements of the planets.*

XXI. Axiom. *Diverse species of both kinds of consonances had to be instituted, so that the beauty of the world might well be composed out of all possible forms of variety—and by means of the extreme movements, at least by means of some extreme movements.*

XXII. Proposition. *The extreme movements of the planets had to designate pitches or strings of the octave system, or notes of the musical scale.*

XXIII. Proposition. *It was necessary for there to be one pair of planets, between the movements of which no consonances could exist except the major sixth 3:5 and the minor sixth 5:8.*

XXIV. Proposition. *The two planets which shift the kind of harmony, which is the difference between the private ratios of the extreme movements, ought to make a diesis, and the private ratio of one ought to be greater than a diesis, and they ought to make one of the sixths with their aphelial movements and the other with their perihelial.*

XXV. Proposition. *The higher of the planets which shift the kind of harmony ought to have the ratio of its private movements less than a minor whole tone 9:10; while the lower, less than a semitone 15:16.*

XXVI. Proposition. *On the planets which shift the kind of harmony, the upper was due to have either a diesis squared, 576:625, ie., approximately 12:13, as the interval made by its extreme movements, or the semitone 15:16, or something intermediate differing by the comma 80:81 either from the former or the latter; while the lower planet, either the simple diesis 24:25, or the difference between a semitone and a diesis, which is 125:128, i.e., approximately 42:43; or, finally and similarly, something intermediate differing either from the former or from the latter by the comma 80:81, viz., the upper planet ought to make the diesis squared diminished by a comma, and the lower, the simple diesis diminished by a comma.*

......

It is asked whether the Highest Creative Wisdom has been occupied in making these tenuous little reckonings. I answer that it is possible that many reasons are hidden from me, but if the nature of harmony has not allowed weightier reasons—since we are dealing with ratios which descend below the magnitude of all concords—it is not absurd that God has followed even those reasons, wherever they appear tenuous, since He has ordained nothing without cause. It would be far more absurd to assert that God has taken at random these magnitudes below the limits prescribed for them, the minor whole tone; and it is not sufficient to say: He took them of that magnitude because He chose to do so. For in geometrical things, which are subject to free choice, God chose nothing without a geometrical cause of some sort, as is apparent in the edges of leaves, in the scales of fishes, in the skins of beasts and their spots and the order of the spots, and similar things.

XXVII. Proposition. *The ratio of movements of the Earth and Venus ought to have been greater than a major sixth between the aphelial movements; less than a minor sixth between the perihelial movements.*

XXVIII. Proposition. *The private ratio of movements fitting the Earth was approximately 14:15, Venus, approximately 35:36.*

XXIX. Proposition. *The greater consonance of the movements of Mars and the Earth, viz., that of the diverging movements, could not be from among the consonances greater than 5:12.*

XXX. Proposition. *The private ratio of movements of Mercury was due to be greater than all the other private ratios.*

XXXI. Proposition. *The aphelial movement of the Earth had to harmonize with the aphelial movement of Saturn, through some certain number of octaves.*

XXXII. Proposition. *In the universal consonances of planets of the minor scale the exact aphelial movement of Saturn could not harmonize precisely with the other planets.*

XXXIII. Proposition. *The major kind of consonances and musical scale is akin to the aphelial movements; the minor to the perihelial.*

XXXIV. Proposition. *The major scale is more akin to the upper of the two planets, the minor, to the lower.*

XXXV. Proposition. *Saturn and the Earth embrace the major scale more closely Jupiter and Venus, the minor.*

XXXVI. Proposition. *The perihelial movement of Jupiter had to concord with the perihelial movement of Venus in one scale but not also in the same consonance; and all the less so, with the perihelial movement of the Earth.*

XXXVII. Proposition. *It was necessary for an interval equal to the interval of Venus to accede to the 2:3 of the compounded private consonances of Saturn and Jupiter and to 1:3 the great consonance common to them.*

XXXVIII. Proposition. *The increment 243:250 to 2:3, the compound of the private ratios of Saturn and Jupiter, which was up to now being established by the prior reasons, was to be distributed among the planets in such fashion that of it the comma 80:81 should accede to Saturn and the remainder, 19,683:20,000 or approximately 62:63, to Jupiter.*

XXXIX. Proposition. *Saturn could not harmonize with its exact perihelial movement in the universal consonances of the planets of the major scale, nor Jupiter with its exact aphelial movement.*

XL. Proposition. *It was necessary to add the lemma of Plato to 1:8, or the triple octave, the joint consonance of the diverging movements of Jupiter and Mars established by the prior reasons.*

XLI. Proposition. *The private ratio of the movements of Mars has necessarily been made the square of the harmonic ratio 5:6, viz., 25:36.*

XLII. Proposition. *The great ratio of Mars and the Earth, or the common ratio of the diverging movements, has been necessarily made to be 54:125, smaller than the consonance 5:12 established by the prior reasons.*

XLIII. Proposition. *The aphelial movement of Mars could not harmonize in some universal consonance; nevertheless it was necessary for it to be in concord to some extent in the scale of the minor mode.*

Now, although he is near the end of his book, Kepler once more devotes several pages to his determination to find some logical proof that the polygons of geometry played some role in God's plan for the cosmos. In the end, as he explains in the following summary, geometry gave way to music.

Since I had fallen into this speculation twenty-four years ago, I first inquired whether the single planetary spheres are equal distances apart from one another (for the spheres are apart in Copernicus, and do not touch one another), that is to say, I recognized nothing more beautiful than the ratio of equality. But this ratio is without head or tail: for this material equality furnished no definite number of mobile bodies, no definite magnitude for the intervals. Accordingly, I meditated upon the similarity of the intervals to the spheres, i.e., upon the proportionality. But the same complaint followed. For although to be sure, intervals which were altogether unequal were produced between the spheres, yet they were not unequally equal, as Copernicus wishes, and neither the magnitude of the ratio nor the number of the spheres was given. I passed on to the regular plane figures: intervals were formed from them by the ascription of circles. I came to the five regular solids: here both the number of the bodies and approximately the true magnitude of the intervals was disclosed, in such fashion that I summoned to the perfection of astronomy the discrepancies remaining over and above. Astronomy was perfect these twenty years; and behold! there was still a discrepancy between the intervals and the regular solids, and the reasons for the distribution of unequal eccentricities among the planets were not disclosed. That is to say, in this house the world, I was asking not only why stones of a more elegant form but also what form would fit the stones, in my ignorance that the Sculptor had fashioned them in the very articulate image of an animated body. So, gradually, especially during these last three years, I came to the consonances and abandoned the regular solids in respect to minima, both because the consonances stood on the side of the form which the finishing touch would give, and the regular solids, on that of the material—which in the world is the number of bodies

> and the rough-hewn amplitude of the intervals—and also because the consonances gave the eccentricities, which the regular solids did not even promise—that is to say, the consonances made the nose, eyes, and remaining limbs a part of the statue, for which the regular solids had prescribed merely the outward magnitude of the rough-hewn mass.[22]

Finally, Kepler's concept of the 'Music of the Spheres' was based on a mathematical presumption of an observer based on the Sun. Because contemporary telescopes had not ruled out life even on the moon, much less the rest of the galaxy, he could not categorically rule out the possibility that some form of life existed there capable of hearing this cosmic music. And if not, then there is still the possibility that God has merely prepared the 'seats' for future listeners, for even the Earth was created and existed before it was inhabited and thus for a time *its* 'seats were empty.'

> From the celestial music to the hearer, from the Muses to Apollo the leader of the Dance, from the six planets revolving and making consonances to the Sun at the center of all the circuits, immovable in place but rotating into itself. For although the harmony is most absolute between the extreme planetary movements, not with respect to the true speeds through the ether but with respect to the angles which are formed by joining with the center of the sun and termini of the diurnal arcs of the planetary orbits; while the harmony does not adorn the termini, i.e., the single movements, in so far as they are considered in themselves but only in so far as by being taken together and compared with one another, they become the object of some mind; and although no object is ordained in vain, without the existence of some thing which may be moved by it, while those angles seem to presuppose some action similar to our eyesight or at least to the that sense-perception whereby … the sublunary nature perceived the angles of rays formed by the planets on the Earth: still it is not easy for dwellers on the Earth to conjecture what sort of sight is present in the sun, what eyes are there, or what other instinct there is for perceiving those angles even without eyes and for evaluating the harmonies of the movements entering into the antechamber of the mind by whatever doorway, and finally what mind there is in the sun. None the less, however those things may be, this composition of the six primary spheres around the sun, cherishing it with their perpetual revolutions and as it were adoring it (just as, separately, four moons accompany the globe of Jupiter, two Saturn, but a single moon by its circuit encompasses, cherishes, fosters the Earth and us its inhabitants, and ministers to us) and this special business of the harmonies, which is a most clear footprint of the highest providence over solar affairs, now being added to that consideration, wrings from me the following confession: not only does light go out from the sun into the whole world, as from the focus or eye of the world, as life and heat from the heart, as every movement from the King and mover, but conversely also by royal law these returns, so to speak, of every lovely harmony are collected in the sun from every province in the world, nay, the forms of movements by twos flow together and are bound into one harmony by the work of some mind, and are as it were coined money from silver and gold bullion; finally, the curia, palace, and praetorium or throne-room of the whole realm of nature are in the sun, whatsoever chancellors, palatines, prefects the Creator has given to nature: for them, whether created immediately from the beginning or

22 Ibid., 1078ff.

to be transported hither at some time, has He made ready those seats. For even this terrestrial adornment, with respect to its principal part, for quite a long while lacked the contemplators and enjoyers, for whom however it had been appointed; and those seats were empty. Accordingly the reflection struck my mind, what did the ancient Pythagoreans in Aristotle mean, who used to call the center of the world (which the referred to as the 'fire' but understood by that the sun) 'the watchtower of Jupiter'; what, likewise, was the ancient interpreter pondering in his mind when he rendered the verse of the Psalm as: 'He has placed His tabernacle in the sun.'[23]

23 Ibid., 1080.

14 THE MUSICAL SCENE IN THE LOW COUNTRIES

THE PEOPLES OF THE LOW COUNTRIES,[1] part Flemish and part Dutch, part Catholic and part Calvin and heir to the cultural influences of Spain and Austria, had in spite of all evolved into a disciplined society of order. Discipline in commerce created prosperity and Amsterdam became the financial center of the Western nations. Discipline of the mind produced more freedom than could be found almost anywhere in Europe, not to mention the foundation of new universities and an expanded book trade.

A policy of tolerance welcomed immigrants, including Jews, who contributed to the economic prosperity. Among the benefits of this unusual society was an environment which allowed women to develop as rarely known before. Among these ladies were Maria Tesselschade (1594–1649), a poet, painter, sculptor and musician, and Maria Schuurman (1607–1678), who was known as the 'Minerva of Holland.' The latter was active in art, mathematics, philosophy and especially languages. Reading eleven and speaking seven, one of her contemporaries observed, 'If all the languages of the earth should cease to exist, she herself would give them birth anew.'

Early in the seventeenth century there were amateur literary societies, known as *Rederijkersmakers* [Chambers of Rhetoric], which became popular in Amsterdam. One who frequented these was the important Dutch poet, Joost van den Vondel,[2] who wrote serious tragedies filled with poetry that recalls the lyric poets of antiquity. In his *Lucifer*, for example, we find actual metaphors used by the ancient Greek poets, such as the 'sonorous and unslaking harmony'[3] made by babbling brooks, as well as joyous hymns of marriage.

O choristers of love,
Whose choral hymns and harmony
Amid the flow of radiant ray
Make heaven's hall with music gay,

1 Our purpose here is not an attempt to summarize the technical development of Baroque music itself in the Low Countries, and its composers, but rather to present a brief overview of the environment in which the music was performed and its general aesthetic nature. At the same time, we take the opportunity to include important material not found in general music history texts.

2 Joost van den Vondel (1587–1679), after inheriting a hosiery shop from his father, engaged in a program of self-education through which he studied Latin, Greek, Italian, French and German. Considered one of the most important Dutch poets of this period, he wrote some twenty-eight plays. He entered into a close relationship with Maria Tesselschade after his wife, and her husband, died.

3 Joost van den Vondel, *Lucifer* (Schiedam, 1875), I, lines 121ff.

And fill our hearts with melody,
And steep our hearts in bliss untold.[4]

The high achievement in painting, which this rare environment produced, is known to all.

CIVIC MUSIC

During the second half of the sixteenth century the Low Countries separated into two states, the Northern, Protestant Dutch Republic and the Southern, Catholic Netherlands. Without the traditional patronage of an aristocratic government or the Church, music making became centered in the civic upper and middle classes.

An interesting reference to this kind of musical activity is found in the writings of the Englishman, Roger North.

> The practice of the voice, by way of *sol-fa*, [should be] greatly encouraged in the use of private music; for what can be more delightful to a society (as I have heard it is used in Holland) than to meet, and make consorts of 3 and 4 voices, for which purpose many have been composed by the best masters and printed in Italy; but more with Latin and Italian words and in my judgment very sublime.[5]

A similar tribute to the civic interest in Antwerp can be seen in a letter by the important English composer, John Bull, to the mayor and aldermen of that city. After explaining he was forced to leave London for reasons of religious persecution, he says he came to Antwerp, 'as being the most famous in Europe for holding all the arts in higher esteem than elsewhere.' If offered a position, Bull promises to 'gladly serve Your Worships not only in whatever church services it shall please you to command, but also to play during banquets and feasts at which the city may desire to uphold its renown by means of music.'[6]

During the seventeenth century many towns began to form amateur singing societies called *collegia musica*. Participants tended to be upper middle class professionals and with their equal emphasis on the social and musical activities, these societies may be said to be the harbingers of civic music in Europe today. The concerts by these groups, as well as private recitals, were encouraged by the town governments. Indeed, one civic document from Leiden points to the values of having the citizens enjoying the 'edifying activity of listening to music' rather than time spent in drinking.[7] The organist of the town church was an obvious person the town could call on for public recitals and this function was often part of his

4 Ibid., II, lines 500ff.

5 Quoted in Wilson, *Roger North on Music*, 285.

6 John Bull, letter to the Mayor and Aldermen of Antwerp, Fall, 1614, quoted in Weiss, *Letters of Composers*, 35ff.

7 Martin Medforth, 'The Low Countries,' in *The Early Baroque Era* (Englewood Cliffs: Printice Hall, 1994), 210.

contract. Even the famous Sweelinck, organist of the Oude Kerk, in Amsterdam, was required to perform for an hour each day, either before or after the service.

In terms of iconography, some of the most documented civic music in the Low Countries during the seventeenth century was associated with the *ommegang*, the special processions joined by civic, religious and military organizations. Such an *ommegang* was organized for the visit of the archduchess Isabella to Brussels in May 1615. In fact, to capture all the celebrations given her, Isabella commissioned the painter, Anthonis Sallaert, to paint a record of her visit. In the painting of the opening event, we see the Brussels civic band of six members playing a cornett, trombone, curtal, and three shawms. The trombonist appears to be holding a piece of music in his hand, which has led to the suggestion that perhaps he played a cantus firmus above which the others improvised.[8] For the *ommegang* itself, Isabella commissioned the court painter, Dennis van Alsloot, to paint six canvases of the procession.

Descriptions of the *ommegang* during the early years of the eighteenth century are quite different. Now, instead of the Renaissance instruments, we find the Hautboisten band of modern oboes and bassoons, as for example in an account of this procession in Grammont in 1718.[9]

During the seventeenth century these civic wind bands continued to perform concerts for the citizens. A civic edict from Mechlin in 1606 orders these concerts to occur every Sunday and feast day, for one half-hour beginning at eleven o'clock in the morning. The musicians were to play the concert 'for the honor of the city,' on 'schalmayen, trompettes et autres instruments.' Finally, to prepare for the concert the band was ordered to rehearse at least twice per week.[10] Such civic documents after 1700 again refer to the new band of oboes and bassoons. Vander Straeten documents such a concert in Audenarde in 1700.[11]

The movement of the Italian styles north, and the musicians which brought them, created considerable pressure on the civic institutions as they attempted to restrict performances to themselves. Thus in Brussels, for example, civic edits appear in 1606, 1651, 1662, 1665, 1682, 1685, 1699, and 1721, all intended to support the civic musicians—but nothing could stop the Italian tide.

As these ancient civic bands began to decline, at the beginning of the eighteenth century, other civic activity began to blossom. Collegia musica became more proficient and some evolved into semi-professional concert organizations. It is in this period that performance of opera, both French and Italian, begins to occur in the Low Countries. Performances of Lully's large-scale theater works were especially popular at the beginning of the eighteenth century. Beginning just before mid-century public concerts in the modern sense began to occur.[12]

8 Richard Leppert, 'Musical Instruments and Performing Ensembles in Flemish Paintings of the Seventeenth Century' (Dissertation, Indiana University, 1973), 165ff.

9 Edmond Vander Straeten, *La Musique aux Pays-Bas* (Brussels, 1867), IV, 74.

10 Raymond Van Aerde, *Ménéstrels communaux ... à Malines, de 1311 à 1790* (Malines: Godenne, 1911), 40ff.

11 Vander Straeten, *La Musique*, IV, 74.

12 Rudolf Rasch, in 'The Dutch Republic,' in *The Late Baroque Era* (Englewood Cliffs: Printice Hall, 1994), 399.

CHURCH MUSIC

The Dutch Reformed Church attempted to restrict music to congregational singing, with the organ as the only officially permitted instrument. Nevertheless during the seventeenth century there is sufficient evidence to suggest a continuing tradition of instrumentalists, especially wind instrumentalists, accompanying the singers in church. One finds this evidence both in the extant music[13] and in the church and civic documents which describe the services—and we are not even thinking of the bassoonist who seems always to appear in Low Countries church records as a colleague of the continuo.

Not everyone appreciated the addition of these instruments however. One still heard in some quarters the old medieval objection to instrumental music, based on its exclusion in the New Testament. Other complaints sound very much like those of Puritan England, but there is an additional anti-monarchical accent. Libert Froidmont (d. 1653), a doctor of theology at the famous University of Louvain, for example, wrote a treatise entitled, 'Is it necessary to hear the music of the Princes?' He complains that in church one hears 'luths, lyres frémissantes, des clairons, des flutes, des cornets, des trompettes,' in addition to the organ, all of which 'gargle' the praises of the noble and tend to obscure the voices.[14]

It is interesting to find, among all the contemporary debate on the nature and role of church music, that the most important composer of church music, Jan Pieters Sweelinck (1562–1621), held an aesthetic of music still firmly rooted in Plato. In a letter to the Burgomasters and Aldermen of Amsterdam of 1603, Sweelinck reflects,

> So great is the correspondence between music and the soul that many, seeking out the essence of the latter, have thought it to be full of harmonious accords, to be, indeed, a pure harmony. All nature itself, to speak the truth, is nothing but a perfect music that the Creator causes to resound in the ears of man, to give him pleasure and to draw him gently to Himself. This we recognize at a glance in the excellent arrangement, the splendid proportions, and the orderly movements and revolutions of the celestial bodies. Therefore some have declared that the Firmament is the original Patron of Music and a true image of the elemental region, as can be observed in the number of elements and their four primary qualities and in the wondrous manner in which their opposites are reconciled.
>
> This is the reason why the sages of ancient times, considering that each thing has the property of turning, moving, and inclining toward and in accordance with its like, made use of music not only to bring pleasure to the ear, but principally to move and moderate the emotions of the soul. They appropriated it for their oracles in order to gently instill yet firmly incorporate their doctrine into our minds, and thus, having awakened them, could raise them more easily to the contemplation and admiration of the divine.[15]

13 As for example the 'Pieces d'orgue,' by Lambert Chaumont (ca. 1630–1712), which includes movements with titles such as 'récits de cornet, tierces en taille, basses de trompettes, et basses de cromorne.' Civic documents referring to accompanied church music can be found in Vander Straeten, *La Musique*, IV 135, fn. 3, 272ff and 289.

14 Ibid., I, 186.

15 Quoted in Norman and Shrifte, *Letters of Composers*, 3.

Sweelinck, in this same letter, also speaks of his setting of the Psalms of David (1604) and justifies his effort with the following.

> It is true that others before me have labored at this, but as with human faces, there being no two that resemble each other in all respects, so is it with the conceptions and creations of the spirit.

Finally, it is also interesting to find in the Low Countries a continuation of the medieval church dramas. A prototype opera given by the College of Jesuits in Liège in 1695 includes instrumental interludes called 'Symphonie des Hautbois' and 'Symphonie de Flûte douces.'[16] In Brussels, in the same year, there was given a 'biblical tragedy,' during which the Brussels civic wind band [*Joueurs de hautbois de Bruxelles*] performed.[17]

MILITARY MUSIC

Little research has been done in the area of military music in the Low Countries, however, we can see representatives of such music in two interesting paintings, both dating before the period of the introduction of the Hautboisten bands. The *Procession of the Military Guilds*, by Denis van Alsloot pictures a total of twenty-eight fife and drum players, organized with one fife for each two drums. In the *Triumph of Isabella*, by the same artist, one sees at the head of a group of 'Turkish' cavalrymen, a single trumpeter accompanied by a mounted (black) timpanist.

16 Vander Straeten, *La Musique*, III, 52ff.

17 Ibid., IV, 184.

MILITARY MUSIC

15 SPINOZA AND HUYGENS

WILL DURANT, IN HIS SURVEY OF WESTERN PHILOSOPHY, *The Story of Philosophy*, calls Spinoza's *Ethics*, 'the most precious production in modern philosophy.' But during the years since Durant wrote that in 1926, medical research in brain and body function has established facts that render some of Spinoza's most fundamental propositions to be based on assumptions which are physiologically invalid. The brilliance of Spinoza's logic remains, but his conclusions lack relevance.

Like all early philosophers, including Durant, Spinoza did not have the advantage of modern clinical research in brain function. Principally, we know today that we physically have two brains, and not one. We know we have a right brain which processes and stores kinds of understanding which are utterly unlike those processed and stored in the left brain, yet both are *equally real and valid*. Earlier philosophers, oblivious to this information, were forced to try to explain everything in terms of *one* brain, which of course was the rational (left) one. Thus Spinoza, who was undoubtedly aware of his difficulty in describing the emotions in the language of the left brain, was forced to more or less write off emotions as being 'confused' ideas. And that is exactly what they are from the left brain's perspective, as anyone knows who has ever tried to describe love or music in ordinary language.

Spinoza is rare among philosophers in the fact that he scarcely mentioned the word 'music.' The fact that he apparently was unaware of the central purpose of music, being an expression of feeling, is no surprise to the reader of Spinoza's lengthy discussion of the emotions. Emotion, to Spinoza, meant primarily the instinctive urges necessary to survival, such as hunger and love/sex, and the urges which had always been a concern to churchmen, such as greed, etc. Nowhere in his discussions of the emotions do we find an awareness of the genetic and universal aspects of emotions, the need to express feelings or their role in the sensitive aspects of the personality. It is as if a part of him were closed off, which moves us to reflect on the events of his life.

Benedict (originally Baruch) de Spinoza (1632–1677) is generally called the greatest Jewish philosopher of the modern era, but that only reflects his point of origin. The great Jewish history, the Old Testament, Spinoza found to be deliberately metaphorical and allegorical. Perhaps discovering that precision is the death of faith, Spinoza would conclude,

> For my own part, as I confess plainly, and without circumlocution, that I do not understand the Scriptures, though I have spent some years upon them.[1]

Soon, his reading extended much beyond the realm of the Jewish literature, to the investigation of theology at large and, after he mastered Latin and the philosophical works of all the ancient writers. He began to think in terms of an all-encompassing God, who was inseparable from everything in Nature, including the mind of man. He was much attracted, therefore, by Descartes, not only for his 'scientific' style of discussion, but for his famous statement, *Cogito, ergo sum*,[2] that the mind is the only thing one can really know. Spinoza, in a sense, attempted to extend Descartes beyond the mind.

His wide-ranging ideas soon got him in trouble with the Jewish authorities, who had hoped he would become the great spokesman of their faith. The Jewish leaders attempted to bribe him (an amount equal to about $1,000.00) to recant some of his statements, but his refusal led to his excommunication. The excommunication order forbade the Jewish faithful to speak to him, write to him, live under the same roof with him or approach him closer than 'four cubits.'

Now his father sent him away, his sister would attempt to cheat him out of his small inheritance and old friends ignored him. He found refuge in an attic room[3] in a house owned by Mennonite Christians near Amsterdam. Living there, seeing few people and supporting himself grinding optical lenses, should we be surprised that his right hemisphere, feeling and experiential world slipped away from view?

ON THE PHYSIOLOGY OF AESTHETICS

We will attempt to summarize the philosophy of Spinoza with respect to those ideas which might be related to aesthetics in general or which might have influenced future thinking with respect to aesthetics. Preliminary to this, however, there are two problems in language which must be mentioned.

First, because Spinoza was attempting to account for all human activity within the confines of one rational mind, he has found it necessary to use some common words in ways that can be quite confusing to the reader. The most troublesome of these is his use of 'subjective' to mean what we understand today by 'objective.' For example, Spinoza states that an actual physical circle is obviously something literally different from our idea of a circle. Today we would say our idea of a circle, as it pertains to physical *description* is a left brain concept. Our idea of a circle in so far as it is our mental imagining a circle, or recognizing one visually,

1 Benedict de Spinoza, Letter to William de Bylenbergh, quoted in R. Ellwes, *Philosophy of Benedict de Spinoza*, (New York: Tudor Publishing, 1936), 342. Unless otherwise indicated, all English translations are taken from this edition.

2 'I think, therefore I am.' Oddly enough, it never occurred to Descartes, who doubted everything else, to doubt this!

3 Prompting Anatole France's wry comment that if Napoleon had been more brilliant he would have 'lived in a garret and written four books.'

is best described as a right brain function. Spinoza, having no clue of the separate natures of understanding of our two hemispheres, calls the rational idea of the circle a 'subjective essence.' He finds no further truth than this necessary and when we search for the truth, it is the 'subjective essences of things, or ideas, for all these expressions are synonymous.'[4] In both cases, of course, we would use 'objective' today.[5]

Second, because for Spinoza there was a 'union' among God, Nature and much of man, these terms are sometimes used as a metaphor, one for the other. Certainly, as a theologian, the concept of God was ever present.

> Every idea of everybody, or of every particular thing actually existing, necessarily involves the eternal and infinite essence of God.[6]

Actions as well, and 'all things which come to pass, come to pass according to the eternal order and fixed laws of nature.'[7]

But if man is synonymous with God, this is not to suggest that God enjoys any attributes of man.

> God is without passions, neither is he affected by any emotion of pleasure or pain.[8]

Why, he says, 'there are men lunatic enough to believe that even God himself takes pleasure in [hearing] harmony.'[9]

In his 'On the Nature and Origin of the Mind,' Spinoza offers this definition:

> By Idea, I mean the mental conception which is formed by the mind as a thinking thing.[10]

It is a perfectly acceptable and concise definition of the rational left hemisphere of the brain. He distinguishes certain kinds of 'thinking,' such as knowing information on the basis of having been told, knowing on the basis of experience, knowing on the basis of deduction and knowing on the basis of direct immediate observation. But, he was wrong about some things. His understanding of there being only one mind, a rational mind, caused him to give this proposition:

> The order and connection of ideas is the same as the order and connection of things.[11]

4 Spinoza, 'On the Improvement of the Understanding,' in Ibid., 10ff.

5 In addition, Spinoza uses substance, for reality or essence; perfect, for complete; ideal, for object; and formally, for objectively.

6 Spinoza, *The Ethics*, 'Of the Nature and Origin of the Mind,' Proposition XLV.

7 Spinoza, 'On the Improvement of the Understanding,' in *Philosophy of Benedict de Spinoza*, 4.

8 Spinoza, *The Ethics*, 'Of the Power of the Understanding, or of Human Freedom,' Proposition XVII.

9 Ibid., 'Concerning God,' Appendix .

10 Ibid., 'Of the Nature and Origin of the Mind,' Definition III.

11 Ibid., Proposition VII.

But this is true only of the left hemisphere. It has no meaning for the right hemisphere, as for example in looking at a spatial object, such as a painting.

The lack of accurate contemporary medical knowledge left him conspicuously in error with regard to all aspects of how the brain works the body as a machine. Cases of 'phantom limb' (where a person experiences feeling in a limb no longer present) if nothing else demonstrate the following propositions to be wrong.

> The human mind has no knowledge of the body, and does not know it to exist, save through the ideas of the modifications whereby the body is affected.[12]
>
> ......
>
> The human mind does not involve an adequate knowledge of the parts composing the human body.[13]

In his 'On the Origin and Nature of the Emotions,' Spinoza returns to this idea. The modern reader can hardly believe he means this.

> Body cannot determine mind to think, neither can mind determine body to motion or rest or any state different from these, if such there be.[14]

In his following explanation, however, we can see not only that he believed this, but the surprising extent of his ignorance of real brain function.

> No one knows how or by what means the mind moves the body, nor how many various degrees of motion it can import to the body, nor how quickly it can move it. Thus, when men say that this or that physical action has its origin in the mind, which latter has dominion over the body, they are using words without meaning, or are confessing in specious phraseology that they are ignorant of the cause of the said action, and do not wonder at it.[15]

The principal proof that the mind cannot be proven to operate the body, in so far as Spinoza was concerned, came from the observation of sleep-walkers, the assumption being that sleep-walkers do not engage in 'rational' thinking. Similar 'evidence' in support for the presumed inability of the mind to control the body, Spinoza saw in the fact that men are not as prone to keep silence, as they are to speak, and in the non-rational infant who cries for milk.

With this concept of the single rational mind, it follows that one becomes more effective as a person the more one fills up this mind with rational ideas. It may be the beginning of modern education's incorrect, but long-held, premise that the child is born with a 'blank blackboard' mind, when Spinoza states,

12 Ibid., Proposition XIX.

13 Ibid., Proposition XXIV.

14 Ibid., Proposition II.

15 Spinoza, *The Ethics*, 'Of the Origin and Nature of the Emotions,' Proposition II.

> The more things the mind knows, the better does it understand its own strength and the order of nature.[16]

And from the same perspective, Spinoza equates 'error' only with this kind of left brain information.

> Falsity consists in the privation of knowledge, which inadequate, fragmentary, or confused ideas involve.[17]

As we will see below, 'confused ideas' refers to the emotions! It is worth pointing out that false information *is* much more likely to occur in the left hemisphere, where all knowledge is second-hand, something which we have been told or we have read, than in the right hemisphere, where direct personal experience is involved. Furthermore, lying occurs *only* in the left hemisphere. The right hemisphere never lies.

On the Emotions

Before considering Spinoza's writings on the emotions, it is important to point out that again his entire philosophy is constructed upon a premise which is lacking a vitally important piece of information, again due to his lack of access to modern medical and psychological findings. He failed to know, and failed to understand by observation and deduction, that the basic emotions are universal and genetically in place before birth. Consequently, aside from conclusions which are simply wrong, instead of understanding emotions as an innate part of the *species*, he tends to build his philosophy on the old Church foundations that the emotions are animal instincts against which the *individual* man must strive to overcome.

But we find it curious that a man of such deliberate thought did not arrive by deduction at the understanding that some form of emotions are genetic. He obviously understood they were in place in early man, before man could reason.

> We must admit that the first man did not have it in his power to use reason correctly, but was subject to passions like ourselves.[18]

Because he failed to understand emotions are genetic, we can see that he is on the wrong track even with children, in assuming their emotions are entirely learned.

16 Spinoza, 'On the Improvement of the Understanding,' in Ellwes, *Philosophy of Benedict de Spinoza*, 12. It is the reverse: the child is born with all the genetic information of 500 million years, of every species, which he discards mostly as unneeded as he becomes 'educated.'

17 Spinoza, *The Ethics*, 'Of the Nature and Origin of the Mind,' Proposition XXXV.

18 Spinoza, *Tractatus Politicus*, II.

> We find that children, whose body is continually, as it were, in equilibrium laugh and cry simply because they see others laughing and crying; moreover, they desire forthwith to imitate what ever they see others doing.[19]

But this is wrong. Children do not learn to display basic emotions only by observation. All the basic emotions and facial expressions are already displayed by the fetus.

Again, we can see him thinking emotions are like rational, left hemisphere learning when he states the following as an Axiom.

> Modes of thinking, such as love, desire, or any other of the passions, do not take place, unless there be in the same individual an idea of the thing loved, desired, etc.[20]

His lack of understanding that the basic emotions are universal and genetic blinded him to another important characteristic of the emotions. It is correct to say that the basic emotions are universal, but that they become personalized by individual experience. In other words, it is due to genetics that everyone has a general understanding of the word 'pain,' but each person also has an individual understanding of pain reflecting the sum of his experience with pain.[21] In one proposition, Spinoza appears, at first sight, to understand this.

> Any emotion of a given individual differs from the emotion of another individual, only in so far as the essence of the one individual differs from the essence of the other.[22]

But in fact he has missed the point, failing to see that it is the varying experience which produces the varying understanding of the emotion. By 'essence' he means something quite different from experience, as is made clear in what follows.

> Hence it follows, that the emotions of the animals which are called irrational ... differ only from man's emotions, to the extent that brute nature differs from human nature. Horse and man are alike carried away by the desire of procreation; but the desire of the former is equine, the desire of the latter is human. So also the lusts and appetites of insects, fishes, and birds must vary according to the several natures.

And again, it is his failure to understand the true innate character of the emotions that cause Spinoza to concentrate more on the object than the experience.

19 Spinoza, *The Ethics*, 'Of the Origin and Nature of the Emotions,' Proposition XXXII.

20 Spinoza, *The Ethics*, 'Of the Nature and Origin of the Mind,' Axiom III.

21 It is the same with other right hemisphere characteristics, such as spatial objects and individual personal experiences. Everyone knows what 'cat' means, but upon hearing the word, each person 'pictures' an individual and different cat based on one's experience.

22 Spinoza, *The Ethics*, 'Of the Origin and Nature of the Emotions,' Proposition LVII.

> There are as many kinds of pleasure, of pain, of desire, and of every emotion compounded of these, such as vacillations of spirit, or derived from these, such as love, hatred, hope fear, etc., as there are kinds of objects whereby we are affected.[23]

But this is wrong. The significance is not that the objects of pleasure vary, but that the *experience* of the individual with pleasure varies. He continues along this same misunderstanding:

> Different men may be differently affected by the same object, and the same man may be differently affected at different times by the same object.[24]

From this premise of emotions based on objects, Spinoza concludes that men fear, love and hate different things. And from this it is but a short step to the Church's position that man's emotions vary as much as their judgments and that it is the individual who must conqueror his emotions. It would be more accurate to say that right hemisphere understanding, including the emotions, is largely genetic, universal, and differs through *experience*, while left hemisphere understanding is entirely learned and varies according to the individual's *learning*. We might add, in passing, that Spinoza in his major work, *The Ethics*, does not discuss the significance of experience at all. For him, personal 'experience' seemed to be something apart from the necessities of Reason, as he explains in a letter to Simon de Vries.

> You ask me if we have need of experience, in order to know whether the definition of a given attribute is true. To this I answer that we never need experience, except in cases when the existence of the thing cannot be inferred from its definition.[25]

With these precautions, we now turn to Spinoza's basic philosophy of the emotions. In his *Ethics*, Part III, 'On the Origin and Nature of the Emotions,' Spinoza tells us immediately that he will treat the emotions (of the right hemisphere) as a left hemisphere property and that his analytical approach will be in the language of the left hemisphere.

> [I wish] to set forth with rigid reasonings those matters which they cry out against as repugnant to reason, frivolous, absurd, and dreadful ... I shall consider human actions and desires in exactly the same manner, as though I were concerned with lines, planes, and solids.[26]

He begins his discussion with this definition.

> By Emotion I mean the modifications of the body, whereby the active power of the said body is increased or diminished, aided or constrained, and also the ideas of such modifications.

---

23 Ibid., Proposition LVI.

24 Ibid., Proposition LI.

25 Spinoza, Letter to Simon de Vries, quoted in Ellwes, *Philosophy of Benedict de Spinoza*, 320.

26 Spinoza, *The Ethics*, 'Of the Origin and Nature of the Emotions,' Introduction.

> If we can be the adequate cause of any of these modifications, I then call the emotion an activity, otherwise I call it a passion, or state wherein the mind is passive.[27]

Spinoza means by an 'active' emotion one such as when we say, 'I love you.' A passive emotion is one which works by itself against us, such as the 'animal instincts' like hunger or the moral instincts such as greed. It is significant, we mention again, that he displays no recognition of any of the emotions being an actual part of the personality, as they are in the right hemisphere of the brain.

In his first proposition he defines two states of the mind.

> Our mind is in certain cases active, and in certain cases passive. In so far as it has adequate ideas it is necessarily active, and in so far as it has inadequate ideas, it is necessarily passive.[28]

Later he will explain that the emotions are among the 'inadequate ideas.'

> Emotion, which is called a passivity of the soul, is a confused idea.[29]

In the Corollary which follows, we can also see a hint of what is to follow, namely that it is the 'adequate ideas' which are man's defense against the emotions.

> Hence it follows that the mind is more or less liable to be acted upon, in proportion as it possesses inadequate ideas, and contrariwise, is more or less active in proportion as it possesses adequate ideas.[30]

He continues by offering his contention that every 'adequate' idea is 'in God.' However, since, as we have noted above, Spinoza has said that God cannot have emotions, it is necessary for him to avoid attempting to explain how God can have 'inadequate' ideas.

Next he explains that it is these adequate and inadequate ideas which control the mind.

> The activities of the mind arise solely from adequate ideas; the passive states of the mind depend solely on inadequate ideas.[31]

In the commentary which follows we can see him moving toward the conclusion of most branches of theology, that the emotions are morally bad.

---

27 Ibid., Definition III .

28 Ibid., Proposition I.

29 Ibid., 'General Definition of the Emotions.'

30 Ibid., Proposition I, Corollary.

31 Ibid., Proposition III.

> Passive states are not attributed to the mind, except in so far as it contains something involving negation, or in so far as it is regarded as a part of nature which cannot be clearly and distinctly perceived through itself without other parts.[32]

It is the natural state of man's mind, as he explains later, that it desires the 'adequate' ideas.

> The mind endeavors to conceive only such things as assert its power of activity.[33]

But the mind is also capable of conceiving its own passive state with its 'confused ideas' of emotions.

> The mind, both in so far as it has clear and distinct ideas, and also in so far as it has confused ideas, endeavors to persist in its being for an indefinite period, and of this endeavor it is conscious.[34]

Given this, he forms the definition, 'Desire is Appetite with Consciousness.' From this point on, Spinoza offers a large number of definitions of specific emotions, but the focus is entirely on those emotions which can be related to man's moral state. A sampling follows.

> Love is nothing else but Pleasure accompanied by the idea of an external cause. Hate is nothing else but Pain accompanied by the idea of an external cause.[35]
>
> ……
>
> Hope is inconstant Pleasure, arising from the image of something future or past, whereof we do not yet know the issue. Fear is an inconstant Pain …
>
> If doubt is removed, Hope becomes Confidence and Fear become Despair …
>
> Joy is Pleasure arising from the image of something past whereof we doubted the issue. Disappointment is the Pain opposed to Joy.[36]

Spinoza continues in this fashion with such emotions as Indignation, Envy, Over-Esteem, Disdain and Benevolence.

Although it was the last thing on Spinoza's mind, there are a few of his propositions which might be applied in musical circumstances. We mention a few of these in case they might be ideas which the reader might wish to explore further in Spinoza's commentary.

We think of the following proposition with respect to the particular vividness of emotions for the listener when experiencing 'live' music.

32 Ibid., Proposition III, Note.

33 Ibid., Proposition LIV.

34 Ibid., Proposition IX.

35 Ibid., Proposition XIII.

36 Ibid., Proposition XVIII, Note II.

> An emotion whereof we conceive the cause to be with us at the present time, is stronger than if we did not conceive the cause to be with us.[37]

We would recommend the following proposition be associated with the clinical research which demonstrates a genetic preference for certain melodic patterns (even in infants), in contrast to those composer's choices which might be called rational or academic.

> An emotion toward that which we conceive as necessary is, when other conditions are equal, more intense than an emotion toward that which is possible or contingent, or non-necessary.[38]

The same clinical research is also relevant to the following proposition, which we associate with Schönberg's metaphor of a 'musical square,' advanced to represent the listener's ability to predict music to be heard, on the basis of that which has been heard.

> A man is as much affected pleasurably or painfully by the image of a thing past or future as by the image of a thing present.[39]

Spinoza continues with the following commentary:

> Wherefore the image of a thing, regarded in itself alone, is identical, whether it be referred to time past, time future, or time present … Thus the emotion of pleasure or pain is the same, whether the image be of a thing past or future.[40]

Curiously, he did not seem to notice that this is not true with respect to Time itself.

ON THE MORAL IMPLICATIONS OF EMOTIONS

As a spiritual man who had investigated thoroughly the major religions, past and present, Spinoza can be forgiven for seeing the emotions almost exclusively in their relationship to man's moral condition. Although Spinoza did not apparently realize the significance of the genetic, universal emotions which man brings to birth, he did observe that all individual men seemed to be ruled by their emotions in their daily life.

> Experience teaches us no less clearly than reason, that men believe themselves to be free, simply because they are conscious of their action, and unconscious of the causes whereby those actions are determined; and, further, it is plain that the dictates of the mind are but another name for the appetites … Every one shapes his actions according to his emotion, those who are assailed

37 Spinoza, *The Ethics*, 'Of Human Bondage, or the Strength of the Emotions,' Proposition IX.

38 Ibid., Proposition XI.

39 Spinoza, *The Ethics*, 'Of the Origin and Nature of the Emotions,' Proposition XVIII.

40 Ibid., Proposition XVIII.

> by conflicting emotions know not what they wish; those who are not attacked by any emotion are readily swayed this way or that.[41]

Spinoza mentions this in two other books.

> But for everyone always to be guided by reason alone is far from easy; for each is seduced by his own pleasure, and it is very common for greed, pride, envy, anger, etc. to take such a hold upon the mind that no place is left for reason.[42]
>
> ......
>
> Men are led more by blind desire than by reason; and so their natural power, or natural right, must not be defined in terms of reason, but must be held to cover every possible appetite by which they are determined to act, and by which they try to preserve themselves. Admittedly, the desires which are not based on reason are instances of human passivity rather than of human activity.[43]

It is therefore no surprise to find, in his major discussion of the emotions in the *Ethics*, a discussion which he entitles, 'Of Human Bondage, or the Strength of the Emotions.' In his prefatory remarks he observes,

> Human infirmity in moderating and checking the emotions I name bondage; for, when a man is a prey to his emotions, he is not his own master, but lies at the mercy of fortune: so much so, that he is often compelled, while seeing that which is better for him, to follow that which is worse. Why this is so, and what is good or evil in the emotions, I propose to show in this part of my treatise.[44]

Spinoza's view of man's predicament did not include the dire spiritual warnings of the medieval Catholic Church. Instead, he was more compassionate, finding that men are conscious of their actions and appetites, but ignorant of the causes, which he attributed entirely to Nature. In a series of propositions, he seems almost apologetic for the burden Nature has placed on man.

> The reason or cause why God or nature exists, and the reason why he acts, are one and the same. Therefore, as he does not exist for the sake of an end, so neither does he act for the sake of an end.[45]
>
> ......

41 Ibid., Proposition II.

42 Spinoza, *Tractatus Theologico-Politicus*, XVI.

43 Spinoza, *Tractatus Politicus*, II.

44 Spinoza, *The Ethics*, 'Of Human Bondage, or the Strength of the Emotions,' Preface.

45 Ibid.

> We are only passive, in so far as we are a part of Nature, which cannot be conceived by itself without other parts.[46]
>
> ……
>
> It is impossible, that man should not be a part of Nature, or that he should be capable of undergoing no changes, save such as can be understood through his nature only as their adequate cause …[47]
>
> Corollary. Hence it follows, that man is necessarily always a prey to his passions, that he follows and obeys the general order of nature, and that he accommodates himself thereto, as much as the nature of things demands.
>
> ……
>
> The force of any passion or emotion can overcome the rest of a man's activities or power, so that the emotion becomes obstinately fixed to him.[48]

At the same time, there are some propositions by Spinoza which are clearly questionable in light of modern understanding. The following one seems almost Platonic in its emphasis on the importance of bringing man's nature into harmony.

> In so far as a thing is in harmony with our nature, it is necessarily good.[49]

In the following proposition, however, it is clear that he was not thinking of the emotions as being 'part of our nature.'

> In so far as men are a prey to passion, they cannot, in that respect, be said to be naturally in harmony.[50]

But, the emotions are clearly part of our nature, and Spinoza cannot have it both ways. The next proposition we also find open to question.

> Men can differ in nature, in so far as they are assailed by those emotions, which are passions, or passive states; and to this extent one and the same man is variable and inconstant.[51]

We believe it is more accurate to suppose that men are born identical with respect to the basic emotions, but their expression, and perhaps their understanding of them, begin to vary in the course of life due to their experiences. To accept that men carry different genetic emotional

46 Ibid., Proposition II.

47 Ibid., Proposition IV.

48 Ibid., Proposition VI.

49 Ibid., Proposition XXXI.

50 Ibid., Proposition XXXII.

51 Ibid., Proposition XXXIII.

information to birth would necessitate the belief that genes from another species is carried in some men to the degree that noticeable behavior characteristics emerge.

We disagree with another proposition to the extent that we do not regard that which is 'in nature' about man as having anything to do with Reason.

> In so far only as men live in obedience to reason, do they always necessarily agree in nature.[52]

It would be more accurate to say that in the depository of the left hemisphere of the brain all men are potentially equal. No one has a personal answer to the question, 'What is two plus two?' It is in the right hemisphere, the experiential us, where we are truly unique and different from all others.

Finally, we wish to make two observations with regard to the following proposition.

> In the state of nature, no one is by common consent master of anything, nor is there anything in nature, which can be said to belong to one man rather than another: all things are common to all.[53]

First, in arriving at the comment 'all things are common to all,' how could he fail to notice the universality of emotions. Didn't he notice all smiles are the same? In another respect, however inadvertently, he was correct. Much of the understanding of the *right* hemisphere *is* held in common by all men. This is true for emotions in their basic, universal quality and it is also true with regard to the expression of feeling in music. No one owns Mozart.

On How Reason Can Overcome the Emotions

In the final part of Spinoza's discussion of the emotions, which he entitles 'Of the Power of the Understanding or of Human Freedom,' he promises to show 'how far reason can control the emotions.' The first, and most important, step he contends is in bringing Reason into play in the identification of the emotion.

> An emotion, which is a passion, ceases to be a passion, as soon as we form a clear and distinct idea thereof.
>
> Proof. An emotion, which is a passion, is a confused idea. If, therefore, we form a clear and distinct idea of a given emotion, in so far as it is referred to the mind only, by reason; therefore the emotion will cease to be a passion.
>
> Corollary. An emotion therefore becomes more under our control, and the mind is less passive in respect to it, in proportion as it is more known to us.[54]

---

52 Ibid., Proposition XXXV.

53 Ibid., Proposition XXXVII.

54 Spinoza, *The Ethics*, 'Of the Power of the Understanding, or of Human Freedom,' Proposition III.

In his commentary which follows, Spinoza emphasizes that everyone has the power to clearly and distinctly understand himself and his emotions and in order to attain this he must chiefly direct his efforts toward acquiring a clear and distinct knowledge of every emotion. He concludes,

> The mind has greater power over the emotions and is less subject thereto, in so far as it understands all things as necessary.[55]

He begins to sound like one of the medieval Church philosophers when he warns that the emotions which are contrary to our nature are bad, 'in so far as they impede the mind from learning.'[56] Curiously, in another place he observes,

> Desire which springs from reason cannot be excessive.[57]

Finally, he returns to his concept of the unity of all things in God:

> The mind can bring it about, that all bodily modifications or images of things may be referred to the idea of God.[58]

And it is here that we find Spinoza's purpose, for in the triumph of Reason over the emotions we find God.

> He who clearly and distinctly understands himself and his emotions loves God, and so much the more in proportion as he more understands himself and his emotions.[59]

This is his thesis, that given the unity of God, man and the emotions, in knowing his emotions man learns to know God. It is curiously out-of-step in a century in which the musicians were discovering that to know the emotions is to know *man*. With regard to the emotions, the musicians were the harbingers of the Enlightenment to come; Spinoza lived too late for the ideas he held.

---

55 Ibid., Proposition VI.

56 Ibid., commentary under Proposition X.

57 Spinoza, *The Ethics*, 'Of Human Bondage, or the Strength of the Emotions,' Proposition LXI.

58 Spinoza, *The Ethics*, 'Of the Power of the Understanding, or of Human Freedom,' Proposition XIV.

59 Ibid., Proposition XV.

ON THE PSYCHOLOGY OF AESTHETICS

An additional topic which Spinoza discusses in the context of the emotions is the relationship they bear to Pleasure and Pain, states of mind which also have inseparable psychological relationships with all art. In Spinoza's view, Pleasure and Pain were at the very core of man. His reasoning, in this regard, begins with his contention that,

> In the mind there is no absolute or free will; but the mind is determined to wish this or that by a cause.[60]

Next he finds that the 'dictates of the mind are but another name for the appetites.'[61] Still later he concludes, 'Pleasure and Pain are identical with desire or appetite.'[62] And finally,

> Among all the emotions attributable to the mind as active, there are none which cannot be referred to pleasure or pain.[63]

From this, Spinoza offers such obvious propositions as, 'Pleasure is good, Pain is bad' and 'Mirth is always good, Melancholy is always bad.'[64] A following proposition must be classified as 'weird science,' for we know today that all feeling is found in the brain, not in the body.

> Desire arising from a pleasure or pain, that is not attributable to the whole body, but only to one or certain parts thereof, is without utility in respect to a man as a whole.[65]

Spinoza's comments on Pleasure which appear to have a more personal character seem to be lacking in a sense of joy. In a list of 'certain rules of life as provisionally good,' Spinoza states that man should indulge in Pleasure only in so far as it is necessary for preserving health.[66] Certainly a dismal passage concerning the sensual pleasures has a personal ring to it.

> When such pleasure has been gratified it is followed by extreme melancholy, whereby the mind, though not enthralled, is disturbed and dulled ... When our hopes happen to be frustrated we are plunged into the deepest sadness.[67]

60 Spinoza, *The Ethics*, 'Of the Nature and Origin of the Mind,' Proposition XLVIII.

61 Spinoza, *The Ethics*, 'Of the Origin and Nature of the Emotions,' Proposition II, Note.

62 Ibid., Proposition LVII.

63 Ibid., Proposition LIX.

64 Spinoza, *The Ethics*, 'Of Human Bondage, or the Strength of the Emotions,' Propositions XLI and XLII.

65 Ibid., Proposition LX. Also the rose has no odor, it is we who provide it when we smell it.

66 Spinoza, 'On the Improvement of the Understanding,' in Ellwes, *Philosophy of Benedict de Spinoza*, 5.

67 Ibid., 2.

In some references to Pleasure and Pain we find Spinoza returning to what seems to be primarily moral considerations.

> As love is pleasure accompanied by the idea of an external cause, and hatred is pain accompanied by the idea of an external cause; the pleasure and pain in question will be a species of love and hatred.[68]

An even stronger moral tone is conspicuous in the proposition,

> The knowledge of good and evil is nothing else but the emotions of pleasure or pain, in so far as we are conscious thereof.[69]

ON THE PHILOSOPHY OF AESTHETICS

The last mentioned proposition, which contends that good and evil are synonymous with pleasure and pain, brings us to one of only two references to music in all the major works of Spinoza. Here he contends good and bad do not exist in Art, they are merely the opinions of the observer.

> The terms Good and Bad have no positive quality in things regarded in themselves, but are merely modes of thinking, or notions which we form from the comparison of things one with another. Thus one and the same thing can be at the same time good, bad, and indifferent. For instance, music is good for him that is melancholy, bad for him that mourns; for him that is deaf, it is neither good nor bad.[70]

The only other comment in Spinoza which could at all be associated with the Good or the Beautiful in Art is, like one comment about Pleasure above, tied to health.

> If the motion whose objects we see communicate to our nerves be conducive to health, the objects causing it are styled Beautiful; if a contrary motion be excited, they are styled Ugly.[71]

Among the few observations on art in general which are to be found in the writings of Spinoza, we find a reference to the ancient question: Is art in the artist or the art object? For Spinoza, the art is clearly in the mind of the artist, and it exists even if the work is not created.

---

68 Spinoza, *The Ethics*, 'Of the Origin and Nature of the Emotions,' Proposition XXX.

69 Spinoza, *The Ethics*, 'Of Human Bondage, or the Strength of the Emotions,' Proposition VIII.

70 Ibid., Preface.

71 Spinoza, *The Ethics*, 'Concerning God,' Appendix.

> If an architect conceives a building properly constructed, though such a building may never have existed, and may never exist, nevertheless the idea is true; and the idea remains the same, whether it be put into execution or not.[72]

When the architect makes something perfectly according to his plan, he has brought it to perfection in his opinion. But, in accordance with his statement above, that Good and Bad are only 'modes of thinking,' Spinoza points out again that other viewers will differ in their assessment.

> But, after men began to form general ideas, to think out types of houses, buildings, towers, etc., and to prefer certain types to others, it came about, that each man called perfect that which he saw agree with the general idea he had formed of the thing in question, and called imperfect that which he saw agree less with his own preconceived type, even though it had evidently been completed in accordance with the idea of its artificer.[73]

Since Spinoza regarded Art to be in the mind of the artist, he appears to have concluded that the essential education in art lay in the passing on of personal experience.

> Academies, that are founded at the public expense, are instituted not so much to cultivate men's natural abilities as to restrain them. But in a free commonwealth arts and sciences will be best cultivated to the full, if everyone that asks [permission] is allowed to teach publicly, and that at his own cost and risk.[74]

Spinoza promised to expand on this idea, but at nearly this point he left this treatise unfinished. We would add that it is, above all, only the expression of the artist which varies. The basic emotions behind the Art remain universal.

The only other reference which Spinoza makes to any specific Art, in his major books, is to the stage actor, whom he equates with prostitutes and a sovereign running drunk or naked through the streets![75]

ON THE AESTHETICS OF MUSIC

We have quoted above Spinoza's reference to music in which he seems to suggest that music has no universally understood purpose. All is left to the judgment of the listener, which is in agreement with the original meaning of aesthetics when this separate field of philosophy was invented by Aristotle.

72 Spinoza, 'On the Improvement of the Understanding,' in Ellwes, *Philosophy of Benedict de Spinoza*, 23.

73 Spinoza, *The Ethics*, 'Of Human Bondage, or the Strength of the Emotions,' Preface.

74 Spinoza, *A Political Treatise*, VIII, 49.

75 Ibid., IV.

Spinoza makes the same point in the only other reference to music to be found in his major works, one we have quoted a portion of above.

> Whatsoever affects our ears is said to give rise to noise, sound, or harmony. In this last case, there are men lunatic enough to believe that even God himself takes pleasure in harmony; and philosophers are not lacking who have persuaded themselves, that the motion of the heavenly bodies gives rise to harmony—all of which instances sufficiently show that everyone judges of things according to the state of his brain, or rather mistakes for things the forms of his imagination.[76]

The reader will notice in this passage a reference to the concept advanced by the ancient Greeks known as the 'Music of the Spheres.' While Spinoza clearly rejects the existence of such music, there were still other important philosophers as late as the seventeenth century who were not so quick to reject the notion. Among these was the greatest continental scientist in the age of Newton, Christian Huygens,[77] who left a charming speculation of the music of the spheres in his *The Celestial Worlds Discovered: or, Conjectures Concerning the Inhabitants, Plants and Productions of the Worlds in the Planets* (1698).

Huygens begins his book by stating his belief that it is not unreasonable to assume the other planets are also inhabited.

> A man that is of Copernicus's opinion, that this Earth of ours is a planet, carried round and enlightened by the Sun, like the rest of them, cannot but sometimes have a fancy, that it's not improbable that the rest of the planets have their dress and furniture, nay and their inhabitants too, as well as this Earth of ours.[78]

The possibility that there was similar life on the other planets appeared to be supported, as far as Huygens was concerned, by the fairly recent discoveries of life forms in America.[79] Huygens observes that the same animals are found in America, with only small variations, as are found in Europe. Obviously, he says, God could have made entirely different animals in America, if He had wanted to. That He elected to make the same animals with only small differences, suggested to Huygens that it was reasonable to suppose that life on other planets was also similar to that on Earth, but with small differences.

Whatever the form of life on the other planets, Huygens reasons they must also be supplied with the five senses, for without them 'neither will life be any pleasure to them, nor Reason of any use.'[80] He then comments at length on the various senses, including the following observations on hearing.

---

76 Spinoza, *The Ethics*, 'Concerning God,' Appendix.

77 Christian Huygens (1629–1695) was a Dutch mathematician, physicist and astronomer.

78 Christian Huygens, *Conjectures Concerning the Planetary Worlds*, 1ff. We quote, with modernization of spelling, the edition printed in London in 1698.

79 Ibid., 23.

80 Ibid., 43.

> [Hearing] is of great consequence in defending us from sudden accidents; and, especially when seeing is of no use to us, it supplies its place, and gives us seasonable warning of any imminent danger. Besides, we see many animals call their fellows to them with their voice, which language may have more in it than we are aware of, though we don't understand it. But if we do but consider the vast uses and necessary occasions of speaking on the one side, and hearing on the other, among those creatures that make use of their Reason, it will scarce seem credible that two such useful, such excellent things were designed only for us. For how is it possible but that they that are without these, must be without many other necessities and conveniences of life? Or what can they have to recompense this want? Then, if we go still farther, and do but meditate upon the neat and frugal contrivance of Nature in making this same air, by the drawing in of which we live, by whose motion we fail, and by whose means birds fly, for a conveyance of sound to our ears; and this sound for the conveyance of another man's thoughts to our minds: can we ever imagine that she has left those other worlds destitute of so vast advantages? That they don't lack the means of them is certain, for their having clouds in *Jupiter* puts it past doubt that they have air too; that being mostly formed of the particles of water flying about, as the clouds are of them gathered into small drops. And another proof of it is, the necessity of breathing for the preservation of life, a thing that seems to be as universal a dictate of Nature as feeding upon the fruits of the Earth.[81]

In his summary of the importance of the senses, Huygens especially mentions music.

> The eye was made to discern near and remote objects, the ear to give us notice of what our eyes could not, either in the dark or behind our back. Then what neither the eye nor the ear could, the nose was made (which in dogs is wonderfully nice) to warn us of. And what escapes the notice of the other four senses, we have feeling to inform us of the too near approaches of, before it can do us any mischief. Thus has Nature so plentifully, so perfectly provided for the necessary preservation of her creatures here, that I think she can give nothing more to those there, but what will be needless and superfluous. Yet the senses were not wholly designed for use: but men from all, and all other animals from some of them, reap pleasure as well as profit, as from the taste in delicious meats; from the smell in flowers and perfumes; from the sight in the contemplation of beauteous shapes and colors and from the hearing in the sweetness and harmony of sounds ... Since it is thus, I think it is but reasonable to allow the inhabitants of the planets these same advantages that we have from them.[82]

After having thus argued for the logic of inhabitants of other planets having hearing, and having made the assumption that certain scientific principles, such as geometry, must be the same, he concludes the residents of the other planets must also have music. In the course of his discussion, Huygens provides interesting comments on the aesthetics of music, as well as on contemporary theory and performance practice.

81 Ibid., 48ff.

82 Ibid., 51ff.

For all harmony consists in concord, and concord is all the world over fixed according to the same invariable measure and proportion. So that in all nations the difference and distance of notes is the same, whether they be in a continued gradual progression, or the voice makes skips over one to the next. Nay, very credible authors report, that there's a sort of bird in *America*,[83] that can plainly sing in order six musical notes: whence it follows that the laws of music are unchangeably fixed by Nature, and therefore the same reason holds valid for their music, as we even now proposed for their geometry. For why, supposing other nations and creatures, endued with Reason and sense as well as we, should not they reap the pleasures arising from these senses as well as we too? I don't know what effect this argument, from the immutable nature of these Arts, may have upon the minds of others; I think it no inconsiderable or contemptible one, but of as great strength as that which I made use of above to prove that the Planetarians had the sense of seeing.

But if they take delight in harmony, it is twenty to one but that they have invented musical instruments. For, if nothing else, they could scarce help lighting upon some or other by chance; the sound of a tight string, the noise of the winds, or the whistling of reeds, might have given them the hint. From these small beginnings they perhaps, as well as we, have advanced by degrees to the use of the lute, harp, flute, and many stringed instruments. But although the tones are certain and determinate, yet we find among different nations a quite different manner and rule for singing; as formerly among the Dorians, Phrygians, and Lydians, and in our time among the French, Italians, and Persians. In like manner it may so happen, that the music of the inhabitants of the planets may widely differ from all these, and yet be very good. But why we should look upon their music to be worse than ours, there is no reason can be given; neither can we well presume that they lack the use of half-notes and quarter-notes, seeing the invention of half-notes is so obvious, and the use of them so agreeable to Nature. Nay, to go a step farther, what if they should excel us in the theory and practice part of music, and outdo us in consorts of vocal and instrumental music, so artificially composed, that they show their skill by the mixtures of discords and concords? and of this last sort it is very likely the *fifth* and *third* are in use with them.

This is a very bold assertion, but it may be true for ought we know, and the inhabitants of the planets may possibly have a greater insight into the theory of music than has yet been discovered among us. For if you ask any of our musicians, why two or more perfect fifths cannot be used regularly in composition; some say it is to avoid that sweetness and lusciousness which arises from the repetition of this pleasing chord. Others say, this must be avoided for the sake of the variety of chords that are requisite to make a good composition; and these reasons are brought by Descartes and others. But an inhabitant of *Jupiter* or *Venus* will perhaps give you a better reason for this, *viz.*, because when you pass from one perfect fifth to another, there is such a change made as immediately alters your key, you are got into a new key before the ear is prepared for it, and the more perfect chords you use of the same kind in consecution, by so much the more you offend the ear by these abrupt changes.

Again, one of these inhabitants will tell you how it comes about, that in a song of one or more parts, the key cannot be kept so well in the same agreeable Tenor, unless the intermediate cadences and intervals be so tempered, as to vary from their usual proportions, and thereby to bear a little this way or that, in order to regulate the scale. And why this temperament is best

83 This, a sloth rather than a bird, was reported on at length by Athanasius Kircher in his *Musurgia universalis* (1650). We have quoted some of this description in the chapter on Italian literature.

in the system of the strings, when out of the fifth the fourth part of a Comma is usually cut off; this same thing I have formerly shown at large.

But for the regulating of the tone of the voice (as I before hinted) that may admit of a more easy proof, and we shall give you an Essay on it, being unwilling still to put you off with my own whims: I say therefore, if any persons strike those sounds which the musicians distinguish by these letters, C, F, D, G, C, by these agreeable intervals, altogether perfect, interchangeable, ascending and descending with the voice: Now this latter sound C will be one Comma, or very small portion lower than the first sounding of C. Because of these perfect intervals, which are as 4:3, 5:6, 4:3, 2:3, an account is made in such a proportion, as 160:162, that is as 80:81, which is what they call a Comma. So that if the same sound should be repeated nine times, the voice would fall near the matter a greater tone, whose proportion is as 8:9. But this the sense of the ears by no means endures, but remembers the first tone, and returns to it again. Therefore we are compelled to use an occult temperament, and to sing these imperfect intervals, from doing which less offense arises. And for the most part, all singing wants this temperament, as may be collected by the aforesaid computations. And these things we have offered to those that have some knowledge of geometry.[84]

84 Ibid., 86ff.

BIBLIOGRAPHY

Addison, Joseph. *Remarks on Several Parts of Italy in 1701*. London: J. Tonson, 1705.

Altenburg, Detlef. *Untersuchungen zur Geschichte der Trompete im Zeitalter der Clarinblaskunst*. Regensburg: G. Bosse, 1973.

Altenburg, Ernst. *Versuch einer Anleitung zur heroischmusikalischen Trompeter- und Pauker-Kunst ....* Translated by Edward Tarr. Halle, 1795.

Armitage, Angus. *John Kepler*. New York: Roy Publishers, 1966.

Arnold, Denis. 'Music at the Scuola di San Rocco.' *Music and Letters* 40, no. 3 (July, 1959): 229–241, http://www.jstor.org/stable/729389.

Asow, E. H. Müller von. *Johann Sebastian Bach Briefe*. Regensburg, 1950.

Bargagli, Scipione. *Delle lodi dell'academie. Oratione di Scipion Bargagli da lui recitata nell'Academia degli Accessi in Siena ...* Florence: L. Bonetti, 1569.

Barnes, R. *Three Spanish Sacramental Plays*. San Francisco: Chandler, 1969.

Bartholomew, Leland, ed. *Canzoni Collection by Rauerij* [Venice, 1608]. Fort Hays: Fort Hays State College.

Barwick, Steven. 'Mexico,' in *The Early Baroque Era*. Englewood Cliffs: Prentice Hall, 1994.

Baselt, Bernd. 'Brandenburg-Prussia and the Central German Courts,' in *The Late Baroque Era*. Englewood Cliffs: Prentice Hall, 1994.

Beer, Johann. *Musicalische Diskurse*. Nürnberg, 1710. Reprinted in Roloff Hans G., ed. *Musikalische Schriften: Ursus murmurat—Ursus vulpinatur—Bellum Musicum—Musicalische Diskurse*. Bern: Lang, 2004.

Berardi, Angelo. *Ragionamenti Musicali*. Bologna: Giacomo Monti, 1681.

Bianconi, Lorenzo. *Music in the Seventeenth Century*. Translated by David Bryant. Cambridge: Cambridge University Press, 1987.

Blume, Friedrich. *Die Musik in Geschichte und Gegenwart*. Kassel: Bärenreiter, 1949–1968.

Böhme, Jacob. *Six Theosophic Points* [1620]. Translated by John Earle. Ann Arbor: University of Michigan Press, 1958.

Bonachelli, Giovanni. *Corona di sacri gigli a una, due, tre, quattro, e cinque voci*, preface. Venice, 1642.

Bottrigari, Hercole. *Il Desiderio*. Translated by Carol MacClintock. Rome: American Institute of Musicology, 1963.

Boyd, Malcolm. 'Rome: the Power of Patronage,' in *The Late Baroque Era*. Englewood Cliffs: Prentice Hall, 1994.

Braun, Werner. 'Entwurf für ein Typologie der 'Hautboisten',' in *Der Sozialstatus des Berufsmusikers vom 17. bis 10. Jahrhundert*. Kassel, 1971.

Brett, Ursula. *Music and Ideas in Seventeenth Century Italy*. New York: Garland Publishing, 1989.

Brixel, Eugen. *Das ist Österreichs Militärmusik*. Graz: Edition Kaleidoskop, 1982.

Buelow, George. 'Dresden in the Age of Absolutism,' in *The Late Baroque Era*. Englewood Cliffs: Prentice Hall, 1994.

———. 'Hamburg and Lübeck,' in *The Late Baroque Era*. Englewood Cliffs: Prentice Hall, 1994.

———. *Thorough-Bass Accompaniment according to Johann David Heinichen*. Ann Arbor: UMI Research Press, 1986.

Bukofzer, Manfred F. *Music in the Baroque Era*. New York: Norton, 1947.

———. 'Allegory in Baroque Music.' *Journal of the Warburg and Courtauld Institutes* 3, no. 1 (1939–1940): 1–21. Reprint, Vaduz: Kraus Reprint, 1965. http://www.jstor.org/stable/750188.

Burney, Charles. *Memoirs of the Life and Writings of the Abate Metastasio*. New York: Da Capo Press, 1971.

Butler, Charles. *The Principles of Musik in Singing and Setting* [1636]. New York: Da Capo Press, 1970.

Caccini, Giulio. *Le Nuove Musiche*. Edited by H. Wiley Hitchcock. Madison: A-R Editions, 1970.

———. *Nuove Musiche e Nuova Maniera di Scriverle*. Edited by H. Wiley Hitchcock. Madison: A-R Editions, 1978.

Campanella, Tommaso. *La Città del Sole*. Translated by Daniel Donno. Berkeley: University of California Press, 1981.

Cannon, Beekman. *Johann Mattheson, Spectator in Music*. [New Haven:] Archon Books, 1968.

Carter, Tim. 'The North Italian Courts,' in *The Early Baroque Era*. Englewood Cliffs: Prentice Hall, 1994.

Castiglione, Baldassare. *The Book of the Courtier*. Translated by Charles Singleton. New York: Norton, 1959.

Cavicchi, A. 'Inediti nell' episolario Vivaldi-Bentivoglio.' *Nuova Rivista Musicale Italiana* (May/June, 1967).

Clark, Barrett H. *European Theories of the Drama*. New York: Crown, 1959.

Cunningham, Gilbert. *Polyphemus and Galatea*. Austin: University of Texas Press, 1977.

———. *The Solitudes of Góngora*. Baltimore: Johns Hopkins Press, 1964.

David, Hans T. and Arthur Mendel. *The Bach Reader*. New York: Norton, 1966.

de Brosses, Charles. 'Lettres familières écrites en Italie en 1739,' in Carol MacClintock, *Readings in the History of Music in Performance*. Bloomington: Indiana University Press, 1979.

———. *Lettres familières sur l'Italie*. Paris: Firmin-Didot et Cie, 1931.

Di Marzo, Gioacchino. *Diario della città di Palermo*. 1971

Doering, Oscar. *Des Augsburger Patriciers Philipp Hainhofer Reisen nach Innsbruck und Dresden*. Vienna: C. Graeser, 1901.

Doni, Giovanni Battisti. *Trattati di musica* [1635]. Edited by A. F. Gori. Florence, 1763.

Donnington, Robert. *The Interpretation of Early Music*. New York: Faber, 1964.

Durant, Will. *The Age of Louis XIV*. New York: Simon and Schuster, 1963.

Ehamnn, Wilhelm. *Tibilustrium*. Kassel: Barenreiter, 1950.

Ellwes, R. *Philosophy of Benedict de Spinoza*. New York: Tudor Publishing, 1936.

Evelyn, John. *The Diary of John Evelyn*. Oxford: Clarendon Press, 1955.

Fabrum, Antonium. *Europâischer Staats-Kantzley*. Leipzig, 1700.

Farmer, Henry. *Military Music*. London: William Reeves, 1912.

Ferguson, Donald N. *A History of Musical thought*. New York: Appleton-Century-Crofts, 1948.

Fitzpatrick, Horace. 'Jacob Denner's Woodwinds for Gottweig Abbey.' *The Galpin Society Journal* 21 (1968): 81–87, http://www.jstor.org/stable/841431.

Fleming, Hans von. *Der volkommene deutsche Soldat*. Leipzig: Johann Christian Martini, 1726.

Flores, Angel, ed. *An Anthology of Spanish Poetry*. Garden City: Doubleday, 1961.

Frederick II von Brandenburg. *Memoires pour server à l'histoire de Brandenbourg*. S.l. sn., 1750. Reprinted, Berlin: Haude u. Spener, 1761.

Freeman, Robert. 'The Practice of Music at Melk Monastery in the Eighteenth Century.' Los Angeles: UCLA, Dissertation, 1971.

Freschot, Casimir. *Nouvelle relation de Venise*. Utrecht: Chez Guillaume van Poolsum, 1709.

Gasparini, Francesco. *The Practical Harmonist at the Harpsichord* [1708]. Edited by Frank S. Stillings. New Haven: Yale School of Music, 1963.

Geminiani, Francesco. *A Treatise of Good Taste in the Art of Musik* [1749]. New York: Da Capo Press, 1969.

Giazotto, Remo. *Antonio Vivaldi*. Turin: Edizioni Rai Radiotelevisione Italiana, 1973.

Giustiniani, Vicenzo. *Discorso sopra la Musica* [1628]. Translated by Carol MacClintock. Rome: American Institute of Musicology, 1962.

Gracián, Baltasar. *A Pocket Mirror for Heroes*. Transcribed by Christopher Maurer. New York: Currency Doubleday, 1996.

———. *The Oracle*, nr. 155. Translated by L. B. Walton. London: Dent, 1953.

Grange, Henry-Louis de la. *Gustav Mahler*. Oxford: Oxford University Press, 1995.

Griesheim, Christian Ludewig von. *Die Stadt Hamburg*. Hamburg: Wilhelm Drese, 1760.

Grimmelshausen, Hans Jacob Christoffel von. *The Adventurous Simplicissimus*. Translated by A. T. Goodrick. Lincoln: University of Nebraska, 1962.

———. *The Singular Life Story of Heedless Hopalong*. Detroit: Wayne State University Press, 1981.

Grosse, Hans and Hans Rudolf Jung, eds. *Georg Phililpp Telemann Briefwechsel*. Leipzig: VEB Deutscher Verlag füir Mu̇sik, 1972.

Grove, George. *The New Grove Dictionary of Music and Musicians*. Edited by Stanley Sadie. London: Macmillan, 1980.

Harris, Ellen. 'Voices,' in *Performance Practice: Music after 1600*. New York: Norton, 1989.

Hawkins, John. *General History of Music* [1776]. New York, Dover Publications, 1963.

Hays, William, ed. 'Musical Thought of the Baroque: The Doctrine of Temperaments and Affections.' *Twentieth-Century Views of Music History*. New York: Scribner's, 1972.

Heartz, Daniel. 'The Chanson in the Humanist Era,' in *Current Thought in Musicology*. Austin: University of Texas Press, 1976.

Hiller, J. A. *Lebensbeschreibungen berümter Musikgelehrten und Tonkünstler*. Leipzig: Im Verlage der Dykischen Buchhandlung, 1784.

Hutchings, Arthur. *The Baroque Concerto*. New York: Scribner's, 1979.

Huygens, Christian. *Conjectures Concerning the Planetary Worlds*. London, 1698.

Imbert, Gaetano. *La vita fiorentina nel Seicento*. Firenze: Bemporad, 1906.

Kendall, Alan. *Vivaldi*. London: Panther, 1979.

Kenton, Egon. *Life and Works of Giovanni Gabrieli*. Rome: American Institute of Musicology, 1967.

Kepler, Johannes. *Harmonies of the World*. Translated by Charles Glenn Wallis, in *Great Books* (XVI). Chicago: Encyclopaedia Britannica, 1939.

Keysler, J. G. *Travels through Germany, Bohemia, Hungary, Switzerland...* . London: A. Linde, 1756.

Kircher, Athanasius. *Musurgia universalis* [1650]. Translated by Frederick Crane. University of Iowa, dissertation, 1956.

Krückeberg, Elisabeth. 'Ein historisches Konzert zu Nürnberg im Jahre 1643.' *Archiv für Musikwissenschaft* (1918–1919).

Kolneder, Walter. *Antonio Vivaldi, his life and work*. London, 1756.

Kuhnau, Johann. *Der musicalische Quack-Salber*. Dresden, 1700.

La Mothe le Vayer, François. *Oeuvres de François de la Mothe le Vayer*. Dresden: Groell, 1656.

Leibniz, Gottfried Wilhelm. 'A Vindication of God's Justice Reconciled with His Other Perfections and All His Actions [1710]. Translated by Paul Schrecker, in *Monadology and Other Philosophical Essays*. Indianapolis: Bobs-Merrill, 1965.

Leibniz, Gottfried Wilhelm. 'An Analysis of the Elements of Language,' in *General Investigations Concerning the Analysis of Concepts and Truths.* Translated by Walter O'Briant. Athens: University of Georgia Press, 1968.

———. 'Toward a Philosophy of What There Actually is and Against the Revival of the Qualities of the Scholastics and Chimerical Intelligences,' in *Philosophical Essays.* Translated by Roger Ariew and Daniel Garber. Indianapolis: Hackett, 1989.

———. *New Essays concerning Human Understanding* [1704]. Translated by Alfred Langley. La Salle: The Open Court Publishing Company, 1949.

Leppert, Richard. 'Musical Instruments and Performing Ensembles in Flemish Paintings of the Seventeenth Century.' Bloomington: Indiana University, Dissertation, 1973.

Lesure, François. *Musicians and Poets of the French Renaissance.* Translated by Elio Gianturco. New York: Merlin Press, 1955.

Loemker, Leroy. *Philosophical Papers and Letters.* Dordrecht: Reidel, 1956.

Lumsden, Alan. 'Woodwind and Brass,' in *Performance Practice: Music after 1600.* New York: Norton, 1989.

MacClintock, Carol. *Readings in the History of Music in Performance.* Bloomington: Indiana University Press, 1979.

Maffei, Scipione. 'Nuova Invenzione d'un Gravecembalo.' *Giomale dei Letterati d'Italia.* Venice, 1711.

Marino, Giambattista. *L'Adone* [1623]. Translated by Harold Priest. Ithaca: Cornell University Press, 1967.

Marpurg, F. W. *Der critische Musicus an der Spree* (September 2, 1749). Berlin: Haude und Spener, 1749.

Marpurg, Friedrich Wilhelm. *Kritische Briefe über die Tonkunst [1760].* Hildesheim; New York : Olms, 1974.

Mattheson, Johann. *Behauptung der Himmlischen Musik…* Hamburg : Christian Herold , 1747.

———. *Das Neu-Eröffnete Orchestre.* Hamburg: Schiller, 1713.

———. *Der musicalische Patriot..* Hamburg : [s.n.], 1728.

———. *Der vollkommene Capellmeister* [1739]. Translated by Ernest Harriss. Ann Arbor: UMI Research Press, 1981.

———. *Die neueste Untersuchung der Singspiele.* Hamburg, 1744.

———. *Ehren-Pforte.* Hamburg: In verlegang des verfassers, 1740.

Maugars, André. 'Response faite à un curieux sur le Sentiment de la Musique d'Italie, Ecrite à Rome le premier Octobre, 1639,' in Carol MacClintock, *Readings in the History of Music in Performance.* Bloomington: Indiana University Press, 1979.

Medforth, Martin. 'The Low Countries,' in *The Early Baroque Era.* Englewood Cliffs: Prentice Hall, 1994.

Menke, Werner. *History of the Trumpet of Bach and Händel.* London: W. Reeves, 1934.

Miller, Clement. *Hieronymous Cardanus, Writings on Music.* American Institute of Musicology, 1973.

Misson, François Maximilien. *A New Voyage to Italy.* London: R. Bently, 1695.

Molmenti, Pompeo. *Venice.* London: Murray, 1908.

Monteverdi, Claudio. *The Letters of Claudio Monteverdi.* Translated by Denis Stevens. Cambridge: Cambridge university Press, 1980.

Morgenstern, Sam. *Composers on Music.* New York: Pantheon, 1956.

Moser, Hans. *Heinrich Schütz.* St. Louis: Concordia, 1936.

Nettl, Paul. 'Equestrian Ballets of the Baroque Period.' *The Musical Quarterly* 19, no. 1 (1933): 74–83, http://www.jstor.org/stable/738825.

Norman, Gertrude and Miriam Shrifte. *Letters of Composers.* New York: Knopf, 1946.

Northbrooke, John. *A Treatise Against Dicing, Dancing, Plays and Interludes*. London: The Shakespeare Society, 1843.
Palisca, Claude V. *Baroque Music*. Englewood Cliffs: Prentice-Hall, Second Edition, 1981.
———. *The Florentine Camerata*. New Haven: Yale University Press, 1989.
———. 'Girolamo Mei: Mentor to the Florentine Camerata.' *The Musical Quarterly* (XL).
———. *Humanism in Italian Renaissance Musical Thought*. New Haven: Yale University Press, 1985.
Panoff, Peter. *Militärmusik*. Berlin: K. Siegismund , 1944.
Pezel, Johann. *Bicinia variorum instrumentorum….* Leipzig: Impensis Authoris, 1675.
Pietzsch, Gerhard. *Sachsen als Musikland*. Dresden: Heimatwerk Sachsen, v. Baensch Stiftung, 1938.
Pincherle, Marc. 'Vivaldi and the *Ospitali* of Venice.' *The Musical Quarterly* 24, no. 3 (July, 1938): 300–312, doi: 10.1093/mq/XXIV.3.300
Pirrotta, Nino. *Music and Culture in Italy from the Middle Ages to the Baroque*. Cambridge: Harvard University Press, 1984.
———. 'Temperaments and Tendencies in the Florentine Camerata.' *The Musical Quarterly* 40, no. 2 (April, 1954): 169–189, http://www.jstor.org/stable/739669.
Pirrotta, Nino and Elena Povoledo. *Music and Theatre from Poliziano to Monteverdi*. Cambridge: Cambridge University Press, 1982.
Plato. *Georgias*.
Plato. *Ion*.
Plato. *Republic*. Translated by Paul Shorey. Cambridge: Harvard University Press, 1969.
Plato. *Symposium*.
Playford, John. *An Introduction to the Skill of Music* [1674]. Ridgewood: Gregg Press, 1966.
Poelinitz, K. L. von. *Memoirs*. London, 1737.
Portnoy, Julius. *The Philosopher and Music*. New York: The Humanities Press, 1954.
Printz, Wolfgang Caspar. *Historische Beschreibung der Edelen Sing- und Klingkunst*. Dresden: Mieth, 1690.
———. *Musicus vexatus*. Freyberg: Miethen, 1690.
Quevedo, Francisco de. *The Dog & the Fever*. Translated by William Williams. Hamden, CT: Shoe String Press, 1954.
———. *The Scavenger*. Translated by Hugh Harter. New York: Las Americas Publishing Company, 1962.
———. *Dreams and Discourses*. Translated by R. K. Britton. Warminster: Aris & Phillips, 1989.
Rasch, Rudolf. 'The Dutch Republic,' in *The Late Baroque Era*. Englewood Cliffs: Prentice Hall, 1994.
Reschke, Johannes. 'Zur Geschichte der Deutschen Militärmusik des 17. und 18. Jahrhunderts.' *Deutsche Musik-Kultur* (1937).
———. *Studie zur Geschichte der brandenburgisch-preussichen Heersmusik*. Berlin: VDI-Verlag G.M.B.H., 1936.
Riedel, Herbert. *Musik und Musikerlebnis in der erzählenden deutschen Dichtung*. Bonn: H. Bouvier, 1959.
Riley, Patrick. *The Political Writings of Leibniz*. Cambridge: Cambridge University Press, 1972.
Rosand, Ellen. 'Venice, 1580–1680,' in *The Early Baroque Era*. Englewood Cliffs: Prentice Hall, 1994.
Rosen, Edward. *Kepler's Somnium*. Madison: University of Wisconsin Press, 1967.
Rousseau, Jean. *Méthode Claire, certaine et facile pour apprendre à chanter la musique*. Paris, 1678. Reprint, Genève: Minkoff Reprint, 1976.
Rousseau, Jean-Jacques. *Confessions*, II, vii.
Sachs, Curt. *Our Musical Heritage*. Englewood Cliffs: Prentice Hall, 1947.

Sainsbury, John. *Dictionary of Musicians*. London: Sainsbury and Company, 1825.
Saredo, Luisa. 'Il Matrimonio di Vittorio Emanuele II su documenti inediti.' *Nuova Antologia* (1885).
Sbarra, Francesco. *La Germania esultante Festa a Cavallo, Rappresentata nell' Imperial Giardino Della Favorita Nel Giorno Natalitio Della Sacra Cesarea Real Maesta Dell' Imperatrice Margherita*. Vienna: Cosmerovio, 1667.
Scheffler, Johann. *The Book of Angelus Silesius*. Translated by Frederick Franck. New York: Knopf, 1976.
Schering, Arnold. 'The Leipziger Ratsmusik von 1650 bis 1775.' *Archiv für Musikwissenschaft* (1921).
———. 'Einleitung,' in *Denkmäler Deutscher Tonkunst* (XXIX-XXX). Wiesbaden: Breitkkopf und Härtel, 1958.
———. *Musikgeschichte Leipzigs*. Leipzig: Kistner & Siegel, 1941.
Schmidt, Günther. *Die Musik am Hofe der Markgrafen von Brandenburg-Ansbach*. Kassel, 1956.
Schoolfield, George. *The German Lyric of the Baroque*. New York: AMS Press, 1966.
Schütz, Heinrich. *Kleine geistliche Concerte*, preface. Leipzig : Breitkopf & Härtel, 1887.
Sittard, Josef. *Geschichte des Musik- und Concertwesens in Hamburg*. Altona: Reher, 1890.
———. *Zur Geschichte der Musik…am Württembergischen Hofe*. Stuttgart: Kohlhammer, 1890.
Smithers, Don. *The Music and History of the Baroque Trumpet*. London: Dent, 1973.
Spasgnoli, Gina. 'Dresden at the Time of Heinrich Schütz,' in *The Early Baroque Era*. Englewood Cliffs: Prentice Hall, 1994.
Spreckelsen, O. 'Der Stader Ratsmusikanten.' *Stader Archiv* (Stade, 1924).
St. Augustine. *The Confessions*.
Stein, Louise K. 'The Iberian Peninsula,' in *The Late Baroque Era*. Englewood Cliffs: Prentice Hall, 1994.
Strunk, Oliver. 'François Raguenet, *Comparison between the French and Italian Music* [1702]. *The Musical Quarterly* 32, no. 3 (1946): doi: 10.1093/mq/XXXII.3.411
———. *Source Readings in Music History*. New York: Norton, 1950.
Tosi, P. F. *Observations on the Florid Song*. London: Wilcox, 1743.
Trawick, Buckner. *World Literature*. New York: Barnes & Noble, 1955.
Tyard, Pontus de. *Les Discours philosophiques*. Paris, 1587.
Van Aerde, Raymond. *Ménéstrels communaux…à Malines, de 1311 à 1790*. Malines: L. & A. Godenne, 1911.
Van den Vondel, Joost. *Lucifer*. Schiedam : H.A.M. Roelants, 1875.
Vander Straeten, Edmond. *La Musique aux Pays-Bas*. New York: Dover, 1969.
Venice, Archivio di Stato. *Ospitali, busta 692, Noratorio Q, fol. 113r.*
Vessella, Alessandro. La Banda. Milan: Istituto editoriale nazionale, 1935.
Viet, Gottfried. *Die Blasmusik*. Innsbruck: Ed. Helbling, 1872.
Weiss, Piero. *Letters of Composers Through Six Centuries*. Philadelphia: Chilton, 1967.
Werckmeister, Andreas. *Nothwendigsten Anmerckungen*. Aschersleben : G.E. Struntze, 1698.
Werner, Arno. 'Die alte Musikbibliothek und die Instrumentsammlung an St. Wenzel in Naumberg a. d. S.' *Archiv für Musikwissenschaft* (1926).
———. *Städtische und fürstliche Musikpflege in Weissenfels*. Leipzig: Breitkopf & Härtel, 1911.
———. *Städtische und fürstliche Musikpflege in Zeitz*. Bückeburg & Leipzig, 1922.
———. *Vier Jahrhunderte im Dienste der Kirchenmusik*. Leipzig: Merseburger, 1933.
Werner, Eric. 'The Last Pythagorean Musician: Johannes Kepler,' in *Aspects of Medieval and Renaissance Music*. New York: Norton, 1966.
Whitwell, David. *La Téléphonie and the Universal Musical Language*. Austin: Whitwell Books, 2012.

Wiener, Philip. *Leibniz Selections*. New York: Scribner's, 1951.
Wilson, John. *Roger North on Music*. London: Novello, 1959.
Wolff, Christian. *Preliminary Discourse on Philosophy in General* [1728]. Translated by Richard Blackwell. Indianapolis: Bobbs-Merrill, 1963.
Wustmann, G. *Quellen zur Geschichte Leipzig*. Leipzig: Duncker & Humblot, 1889.
Yates, Frances. *The French Academies of the Sixteenth Century*. London: University of London, 1947; Nendeln: Krass Reprint, 1968.
Zarlino, Gioseffo. *On the Modes*. Translated by Vered Cohen. new haven: Yale University Press, 1983.

INDEX

D

E

F

O

P

Q

R

S

ABOUT THE AUTHOR

Dr. David Whitwell is a graduate ('with distinction') of the University of Michigan and the Catholic University of America, Washington DC (PhD, Musicology, Distinguished Alumni Award, 2000) and has studied conducting with Eugene Ormandy and at the Akademie fur Musik, Vienna. Prior to coming to Northridge, Dr. Whitwell participated in concerts throughout the United States and Asia as Associate First Horn in the USAF Band and Orchestra in Washington DC, and in recitals throughout South America in cooperation with the United States State Department.

At the California State University, Northridge, which is in Los Angeles, Dr. Whitwell developed the CSUN Wind Ensemble into an ensemble of international reputation, with international tours to Europe in 1981 and 1989 and to Japan in 1984. The CSUN Wind Ensemble has made professional studio recordings for BBC (London), the Koln Westdeutscher Rundfunk (Germany), NOS National Radio (The Netherlands), Zurich Radio (Switzerland), the Television Broadcasting System (Japan) as well as for the United States State Department for broadcast on its 'Voice of America' program. The CSUN Wind Ensemble's recording with the Mirecourt Trio in 1982 was named the 'Record of the Year' by The Village Voice. Composers who have guest conducted Whitwell's ensembles include Aaron Copland, Ernest Krenek, Alan Hovhaness, Morton Gould, Karel Husa, Frank Erickson and Vaclav Nelhybel.

Dr. Whitwell has been a guest professor in 100 different universities and conservatories throughout the United States and in 23 foreign countries (most recently in China, in an elite school housed in the Forbidden City). Guest conducting experiences have included the Philadelphia Orchestra, Seattle Symphony Orchestra, the Czech Radio Orchestras of Brno and Bratislava, The National Youth Orchestra of Israel, as well as resident wind ensembles in Russia, Israel, Austria, Switzerland, Germany, England, Wales, The Netherlands, Portugal, Peru, Korea, Japan, Taiwan, Canada and the United States.

He is a past president of the College Band Directors National Association, a member of the Prasidium of the International Society for the Promotion of Band Music, and was a member of the founding board of directors of the World Association for Symphonic Bands and Ensembles (WASBE). In 1964 he was made an honorary life member of Kappa Kappa Psi, a national professional music fraternity. In September, 2001, he was a delegate to the UNESCO Conference on Global Music in Tokyo. He has been knighted by sovereign organizations in France, Portugal and Scotland and has been awarded the gold medal of Kerkrade, The Netherlands, and the silver medal of Wangen, Germany, the highest honor given wind conductors in the United States, the medal of the Academy of Wind and Percussion Arts (National Band Association) and the highest honor given wind conductors in Austria, the gold medal of the Austrian Band Association. He is a member of the Hall of Fame of the California Music Educators Association.

Dr. Whitwell's publications include more than 127 articles on wind literature including publications in Music and Letters (London), the London Musical Times, the Mozart-Jahrbuch (Salzburg), and 39 books, among which is his 13-volume *History and Literature of the Wind Band and Wind Ensemble* and an 8-volume series on *Aesthetics in Music*. In addition to numerous modern editions of early wind band music his original compositions include 5 symphonies.

David Whitwell was named as one of six men who have determined the course of American bands during the second half of the 20th century, in the definitive history, *The Twentieth Century American Wind Band* (Meredith Music).

A doctoral dissertation by German Gonzales (2007, Arizona State University) is dedicated to the life and conducting career of David Whitwell through the year 1977. David Whitwell is one of nine men described by Paula A. Crider in *The Conductor's Legacy* (Chicago: GIA, 2010) as 'the legendary conductors' of the 20th century.

> 'I can't imagine the 2nd half of the 20th century—without David Whitwell and what he has given to all of the rest of us.' Frederick Fennell (1993)

ABOUT THE EDITOR

Craig Dabelstein began studying the piano at age seven and took up the saxophone at age twelve. Mr Dabelstein has Bachelor of Arts (Music) and Bachelor of Music degrees from the Queensland Conservatorium of Music, where he majored in the performance of classical saxophone repertoire. He also has a Graduate Diploma of Learning and Teaching and a Graduate Certificate in Editing and Publishing from the University of Southern Queensland.

He has held the principal alto and tenor saxophone chairs in the Australian Wind Orchestra and has been an augmenting member of the Queensland Philharmonic Orchestra, the Queensland Symphony Orchestra, and the Queensland Pops Orchestra. For many years he was also a member of the Queensland Saxophone Quartet.

He has been a casual conductor of the Young Conservatorium Symphonic Winds, and has previously been a saxophone teacher at the Queensland Conservatorium of Music. He is a regular conductor of the Queensland Wind Orchestra, having served as their artistic director and chief conductor from 2004 to 2009.

Craig Dabelstein is a research associate for the *Teaching Music Through Performance in Band* series of books, contributing analyses to volumes 7, 8, 1 (rev. edn), and the *Solos with Wind Band Accompaniment* volume. He served as the copyeditor and layout designer of the *Australian Clarinet and Saxophone Magazine* from 2007 to 2009 and he has written many CD and book reviews for *Music Forum* magazine. He is the editor of the second editions of the books by Dr. David Whitwell including *A Concise History of the Wind Band*, *Foundations of Music Education*, *Music Education of the Future*, *The Sousa Oral History Project*, *Wagner on Bands*, *Berlioz on Bands*, *The Art of* Musical *Conducting*, and the *Aesthetics of Music* series (8 volumes) and *The History and Literature of the Wind Band and Wind Ensemble* series (13 volumes). From 1994 to 2012 he was a staff member at Brisbane Girls Grammar School. He now teaches woodwinds and conducts bands at St. Joseph's College, Gregory Terrace, Brisbane, Australia.

www.ingramcontent.com/pod-product-compliance
Lightning Source LLC
LaVergne TN
LVHW080309110826
845155LV00023B/97
* 9 7 8 1 9 3 6 5 1 2 6 2 1 *